HOW THE JESTER BECAME KING

DAVE PORTNOY
& the Unauthorized Real Story of Barstool Sports

CHARLIE STANTON

Post Hill
PRESS

A POST HILL PRESS BOOK
ISBN: 979-8-88845-964-5
ISBN (eBook): 979-8-88845-965-2

How the Jester Became King:
Dave Portnoy and the Unauthorized Real Story of Barstool Sports
© 2024 by Charlie Stanton
All Rights Reserved

Cover Photo: Michael Hickey
Cover Design: Karolina Matsiuk
Editorial Advisor: Richie McGinniss

This book, as well as any other Post Hill Press publications, may be purchased in bulk quantities at a special discounted rate. Contact orders@posthillpress.com for more information.

This book is not associated with or endorsed by Dave Portnoy or Barstool Sports.

All people, locations, events, and situations are portrayed to the best of the author's memory. While all of the events described are true, a few names and identifying details have been changed to protect the privacy of the people involved.

Post Hill Press
New York • Nashville
posthillpress.com

Published in the United States of America
1 2 3 4 5 6 7 8 9 10

TABLE OF CONTENTS

Author's Note

I've always been interested in how popular figures and companies came to be, and before I did any research for this book, I had a basic understanding of Dave Portnoy and Barstool's story. From a creative standpoint, I knew their journey had the chance to be a compelling read. (Portnoy has been called a lot of things, but he's never been called boring). After a bit more exploration, I realized it would indeed be compelling, and in January 2021, I started writing.

I communicated directly with Portnoy, letting him know that I was working on a book about him. After sending him multiple chapters, an outline, and a detailed 78-page timeline of events related to my research, he responded by saying he did not want to participate.

While I talked to people who have worked for him about the project, I fully leaned on hundreds of blog posts, podcasts, videos, news articles, newspaper articles, Tweets, and interviews Portnoy and others have given to tell his story. These sources document his unpredictable and unvarnished rise to fame and fortune: Barstool, as you'll learn, is unique in the sense that it is almost completely transparent about what is happening at the company. This has always been one of the most captivating forms of entertainment for their fans, the other being Portnoy's life.

In this book, I refer to Portnoy by a few different titles: Dave, Portnoy, El Presidente, the Barstool founder, and others. I did this because he is known for having multiple identities and because I think it's more refreshing to readers. I do the same for Dan Katz—"Big Cat" and Kevin Clancy—"KFC." I also refer to former Barstool CEO Erika Ayers Badan by her former name, Erika Nardini, because that's the name she went by when she worked at the company. And lastly, I refer to X as Twitter, because that's what it was known as during the time this story takes place.

This author's note is a long-winded way of saying this is an unauthorized biography, and I want to be clear that Portnoy chose not to speak to me for this book. All of the quotes from Portnoy, Nardini, Clancy, Katz, Mike Kerns, Peter Chernin, Jay Snowden and others come from the public record. Each individual quote in the following chapters is listed at the back of this book, along with its corresponding source.

PROLOGUE

JANUARY 2020

"I can't fucking hear you through all that fucking baby fat you haven't fucking outgrown, you fat fuck!"

Mike Kerns held the phone away from his ear. The man on the other end of the line was firing off insults he didn't know existed. As a key dealmaker for media powerhouse The Chernin Group, Kerns was used to working with difficult personalities. And then there was working with Dave Portnoy: "Imagine the worst dress-down anyone's ever had at Barstool times a million," Kerns said of his phone call with the Barstool founder.

Several months earlier, Portnoy and Kerns had begun discussing a possible sale of Barstool Sports to Penn National Gaming—a large, publicly listed casino and gaming organization.[1] Portnoy had sold a majority stake of his wildly popular and divisive digital media company to The Chernin Group in 2016, which meant Chernin was leading negotiations with Penn.

Portnoy wasn't just along for the ride, however. He remained the face of Barstool Sports, officially listed as its Chief of Content. And while Portnoy was the star of the online reality show Barstool offered its fans, Dan Katz aka "Big Cat" had become the most popular figure at the company after Dave. Now, just as the deal with Penn reached the one-yard line, there was a holdup: Dave felt Katz wasn't being properly rewarded in the sale.

Portnoy knew Barstool would not be in this position without Katz. More important, Portnoy wanted Katz excited about the deal

---

1   Now called PENN Entertainment.

before they went all-in on sports gambling, as Katz was a key player in the industry.

But the Chernin guys had been hesitant to change Katz's compensation package. To Portnoy, Kerns was being greedy: he was acting like an agent—Kerns began his career as one—instead of a business partner, and after dealing with a few prolonged contract disputes involving different Barstool employees, Portnoy despised agents.

"This is fucking bullshit, Mike, if this doesn't happen, I'm fucking OUT!"

Dave Portnoy was going to turn down a $450M deal? An acquisition of Barstool by Penn would vault Dave's net worth past the $200M mark—way, *way* up from the several million dollars he had received in Chernin's first investment. And way, way, *way* up from the $100 he used to have to win playing online poker if he wanted to take his wife out to dinner.

What made Portnoy's ultimatum all the more baffling was that he and Kerns, along with Barstool's CEO Erika Nardini, had been exploring a sale of the company for some time, with little success. Established corporations did not feel comfortable doing business with "The Bad Boys of the Internet." According to the investment bank hired to find a deal, Moelis & Co., Portnoy's reported past indiscretions made him "too toxic" to every buyer they spoke with.

Now they finally had someone at the table. Portnoy didn't care. "We're about to have the greatest thing that's ever happened to me as an investor," Kerns explained, "and definitely ever happened to him professionally and he's like 'I'm gonna walk away from the whole fucking thing,' and I know he will. I definitely know he will."

1

"I don't understand what this money is for."

Mike Portnoy was confused. His son Dave, who at first glance looked like Mark Zuckerberg with a goatee, just told him he wanted to start...a newspaper? It was an idea the lawyer couldn't wrap his balding head around. What did that even mean? And of course, the younger Portnoy needed cash to get the venture off the ground, which is why his father was about to hand over the nest egg he and his wife Linda had saved for Dave to put towards grad school.

They sat at the four-seat table in the kitchen of their home in Swampscott, Massachusetts. Apart from the white ceiling, the space was composed entirely of stained wood, with modest square windows lining the walls. The room appeared more like the cabin of a small boat, which helped to remind them that they were never too far from the water. Swampscott, once a prominent fishing town, belonged to Boston's North Shore. It was an apt location for Dave, the eventual (self-proclaimed) captain of the Barstool Sports pirate ship, to launch.

Dave's father wore large round spectacles, was slight of stature, and ran his own legal practice out of his house. The patriarch of the Portnoy family dealt with the complexities of the law and the bullshit he heard from dubious clients. This idea felt as if it belonged in the latter category. Dave explained this endeavor was going to be a kind of newspaper focused on two of his favorite pastimes, gambling and sports; and he was going to write all the articles. The problem was Dave wasn't a writer. And Mike Portnoy's confidence in the editorial prowess of a 26-year-old software salesman was escaping him at the moment, not to mention that sports betting was illegal everywhere outside Nevada.

Although it required both money and expertise—neither of which Dave Portnoy had at the moment—starting a newspaper in the early 2000s wasn't actually *that* crazy of an idea. The internet had yet to eviscerate the print medium: only about 60% of U.S. adults were online. Despite a decline in total circulation numbers, the newspaper industry at that time was still big business. Boston in particular was a well-read market, ranking in the top five nationally in total newspaper readership among adults.

The Boston Globe and *The Boston Herald* comprised the duopoly that ruled the city's print media. They were the big boys. Both began in the mid-1800s, which meant they had a small head start on Portnoy. And when it came to sports coverage, an area to which Dave would devote the majority of his new venture, they dominated.

Sports writers from *The Globe* and *The Herald* who covered the city's famous athletes at the time were celebrities in their own right: Ron Borges, Bob Ryan, Jackie MacMullan, Michael Holley, Nick Cafardo, Dan Shaughnessy, Dave Wedge. They were granted access to the town deities—I don't think I have to explain how passionate the citizens of Boston are about their Red Sox, Patriots, Celtics, and Bruins—and this made these writers household names.

Unfortunately for Boston fans at the time, all of their teams stunk, and they had for a while. For almost two decades, there was a citywide championship drought that prefaced the early 2000s. The Celtics hadn't won a title since 1986, the Bruins since 1972, 1918 for the Red Sox, and well, the Patriots had never won anything up until that point. The endless slog of losing had turned the influential *Globe* and *Herald* sports writers against the city's teams, and that pissed off Portnoy.

"Before we started Barstool Sports, my buddies and I would sit around in our cubes and email each other all day long about sports. And while we had our fair share of arguments, one thing that we always agreed upon was just how bad the Boston sports media is these days…Why does the media, in so many cases, seem to take so much pleasure in vilifying all of the local teams?"

Then in 2002, a year before Portnoy started his paper, something peculiar happened in the world of Boston sports. They started winning. A scrawny looking 24-year-old from the University of Michigan named Tom Brady led the Patriots to an improbable Super Bowl victory, and the floodgates opened. By 2004, the Pats had won their second championship in two years; the Red Sox broke Babe Ruth's curse with a World Series title, and in the following decade, both the Bruins and Celtics would win it all. Jerry Thornton, a future writer for Portnoy and elder sidekick, reflected on this changing of the guard:

"The traditional media fed off the carcass of local failure for so long and fattened themselves so much that they couldn't adapt to a world where the Patriots were a young Dynasty and the Red Sox were ending an 86-year drought. They still acted like the scene was an upside-down pyramid with them at the top and didn't realize it had been flipped over on them by the likes of Bill Belichick and Theo Epstein…. It was into that strange dichotomy of negative coverage of a great sports scene that we stepped."

Sitting at the kitchen table, as his father held a $25,000 check firmly in his right hand, Dave sold his dad on why his operation would be unlike anything else written in the city. Dave was going to write as a fan: not some pompous and jaded columnist. He thought this was a voice that was painfully underrepresented at both *The Globe* and *The*

Herald. "Dave is hellbent on proving everything in the mainstream is wrong," Kevin Clancy, another eventual Barstool writer says. "And he won't stop until he proves he's right. It's his crusade."

But Portnoy wasn't going to be directly competing with the two heavyweights of Boston journalism, at least not yet. Dave's competition would be Boston's free alternative weekly newspapers. *The Phoenix* was the oldest, most established, and "written for hippies," Dave said. *The Improper Bostonian* was a glossy mag that was marketed to the high-end crowd. And while he sometimes actually enjoyed *The Weekly Dig*, it, like the previous two, didn't appeal to guys like him: the sports fan who "liked to get a little banged up on a Saturday and lose some money betting on basketball." *The Metro*, the largest in daily circulation, did have a real sports section. Dave thought it sucked. It was owned by a European conglomerate; what did a bunch of faceless executives in Sweden know about what it meant to be a Boston sports fan? As it turned out, Portnoy had a problem with pretty much every publication in the city, large or small.

Mike was still perplexed: Dave was just going to give away the newspaper? Dave explained that the free alternative weekly model would also allow him to advertise with offshore gambling companies. Under federal law, only free newspapers were able to take advantage of those advertisers, but the ones that existed weren't tailor-made for them. Portnoy's paper would jump on this loophole.

It was an interesting idea, and by now Mike knew Dave had always wanted to be his own boss, mostly because he had an unprecedented disdain for authority. Dave's father summed up his son's attitude in a single tweet:

> "My son did pretty well on the SAT without any test prep. Got him some test prep for a second test; he didn't want to do it. He did worse, probably out of spite."
>
> —@TheCousinMike

And as Dave explains, "I really started Barstool just so I could do my own thing. I really had a hard time working for other people."

"Yeah, that's for sure," Mike says.

After telling his father he'd already sold a year's worth of advertising to an online gambling site called PartyPoker just on his idea alone—Portnoy did have some sales experience—the money was his. Probably never to be seen again. *But at least he would get this sort of move out of his system*, Mike thought. And who knows, maybe writing a few newspaper articles was actually the perfect outlet for his son's disposition. As his former high school baseball coach put it:

"Dave always had something to say."

2

David Scott Portnoy was born to Michael and Linda Portnoy on March 22, 1977. The family moved into the Swampscott, Massachusetts home a few days before Dave entered the world, and a few years after his older sister was born.

The Portnoys were four of 14,000 residents that occupied the marginally affluent, quiet Boston suburb during the 1980s. Aside from being long-known as a fishing locale, Swampscott is considered one of the first summer destinations for the Northeastern elite, as the town sits comfortably alongside the Atlantic, with most of the main strip just feet from the water. It's the kind of close-knit place where residents gather on the 4th of July, to lounge in folding chairs and on towels laid across their Town Hall's ocean-front lawn.

Mike Portnoy was a self-employed small-claims lawyer. It was the perfect profession for a man who waxed poetically about minor inconveniences, a trait he undoubtedly passed along to Dave. During his downtime, Mike helped coach his son's little league baseball team (Dave would later blame him for his poor throwing mechanics). Linda, a slender woman with light brown hair, taught math at the local high school. Both Portnoy parents were involved in the community, and the couple owned a conventionally square, four-bedroom/two-bath yellow house which sat at the beginning of a cul-de-sac, not far from the street and their neighbors.

Inside the Portnoy home, Dave enjoyed a comical but close relationship with his parents. His father in particular, whom fans of Barstool would come to love and view as a Larry David-like figure with his frequent complaints, enjoyed the brunt of Portnoy's precociousness. Dave would make fun of his dad for being clueless about anything remotely tangential to pop culture, for being unintentionally funny, and for being, essentially, himself. It was a dynamic that would play out later as entertainment for Portnoy's followers.

> "'My dad's an idiot, but in a good way.' Thanks, Dave, for the love."
>
> —@TheCousinMike

Despite watching Dave continually belittle his father for trying and failing to set up a Zoom call, or for pronouncing Uber "Uba," along with all the other slings he endured from his overly critical son, Barstool fans would come to see that Mike Portnoy loved his son, and vice versa.

> "Congratulations to my son!! Proud of my son just as [I'm] proud of the rest of my family who are not well known but obviously so dear and important to me in every way."
>
> —@TheCousinMike

So if you're looking for that classic tale of childhood adversity, you won't find it in Portnoy's story. When describing what life was like growing up in Swampscott, Dave, in a near deadpan shrug, says he lived in a "typical middle-class town." Sports and school were the two pillars of his life during that time. He excelled in one of them.[1]

At the age of 13, Dave helped his little league team win a state championship, and a few years later in 1993, as a sophomore, he propelled the Swampscott High School baseball team to do the same. He may have thrown the ball funny, but Portnoy could hit. The following year, as a junior, Portnoy won the batting triple-crown.

---

1   Portnoy was actually a decent student in high school. He was a member of the National Honors Society and Vice President of his class. But he was a better athlete than scholar, and received interest from schools at the Division III level for baseball. According to a bio written by Barstool employee Francis Ellis, a shoulder injury prevented him from playing college baseball.

He was also that one kid on the team who made the coach laugh. During a game, Dave was known to take two steps toward the mound, ready to charge the pitcher anytime a ball came too close to him, and then quickly turn around to retreat once he realized backup wasn't coming. That's because Portnoy wasn't exactly a physical presence (Portnoy claims to be over 5'10", others have doubted this). But what he lacked in size he made up for in humor, which wasn't delivered in the typical stand-up comedian kind of way. Instead, it was more of a tear-you-down, laugh-at-your-expense brand of comedy. One could say Portnoy was a Masshole.

While his high school friends remember him as "funny and loyal," others in his class said that he didn't particularly stand out—even though Portnoy, a huge Jimmy Buffett fan, used to fully decorate his car as a shark—not sure how they don't remember that. But one thing they did remember Portnoy for was speaking his mind. "The big thing about him is he's very truthful," Elio Imbornone, Portnoy's longtime friend and Barstool fan favorite says. "You might not want to hear exactly what he wants to say, but he says what he believes and you've got to respect that." It was a surprise to none of them when this particular dynamic would come to influence his writing later on.

In 1994, Dave attempted to follow in his sister's footsteps at the University of Michigan and was deferred. Instead of giving up, he flashed the relentless attitude required of any entrepreneur. Portnoy applied to the college's nursing school after his sister told him it was easier to get into, and he could transfer over once he was accepted. It worked, and Michigan never realized that it had previously deferred him. Portnoy transferred again while he was there, this time to the school of education because it didn't have a language requirement to graduate. But Portnoy had no plans of ever becoming a teacher. "Waking up early to teach high schoolers as part of my classwork was something I hated doing," he confesses, which was a tough part of the curriculum to hate if you're going to be a teacher.

After graduating in 1999, the diehard Red Sox fan took a sales job at The Yankee Group, an IT research firm headquartered in downtown Boston. Sitting in his windowless office alone, with nothing but a computer and a black phone on his desk, he sold analysis from the 100+ analysts who covered the technology sector for the company. Dave joined the firm at the height of the dot-com hysteria. Money was flowing into tech and he took full advantage, with the recent grad bringing home nearly six figures in each of his first two years there.

While working at Yankee Group, Dave lived with five of his buddies in Boston. And it was during this stretch that Dave leaned into a vice that had always existed on the periphery of his life: sports gambling.

Mike Portnoy enjoyed horse racing, and he sometimes brought young Dave with him to the track outside Boston. After winning a few bucks on a horse, Dave was hooked. "I've been a degenerate gambler my whole life," Portnoy admits in Barstool's documentary series. Gambling became Dave's second, much-less-paying job; Portnoy met Elio after his friend and famous sports analyst Todd McShay introduced the pair solely because he knew both were addicted to sports betting (McShay set them up for a day of watching and wagering on games together—it was a gambling-fueled blind man-date). But eventually, as Portnoy explained, he crossed the Rubicon. In his mid-20s, Portnoy lost $30,000 in one year.[2]

By 2002, the internet bubble had burst. Tech stocks tanked. Portnoy sat in his office one Friday morning, bathing in the glow of the soulless fluorescent lights above him. He peered out around his door and watched as his boss walked in, only to turn around five minutes later and walk right out. Portnoy's boss was fired, along with several other senior members of the company. "I was in my [early] 20s, these were 40- or 50-year-old guys with families, and just poof…it's gone. And I just never wanted to be in the position where I could walk in and somebody could tell me that one day." Dave sat

---

2   There are conflicting accounts on how Dave and Elio met. Dave at one point would claim that he had to get Elio's number from someone else besides McShay.

in his dinky leather swivel chair and began to think that maybe it was finally time to start something on his own; he just wasn't sure yet what that something would be.

In the spring of 2003, while still working his sales job, Dave boarded a plane to Vegas. The 26-year-old wasn't yet committed to starting his own venture, but his motivation for that trip was simple: tech money had dried up, and Portnoy needed to find something else to do. "I knew I wanted to be in that field," Dave says of gambling. Portnoy figured he'd land some sort of marketing role with one of the larger casinos out there. He'd lost enough money to know that it was a lucrative business.[3]

When he sat down with the house executives, in their surprisingly ordinary offices—he was expecting something out of *Ocean's Eleven*—they bluntly informed him that he would need to spend a few years as a table dealer before moving into the corporate side of work. *Well, that wasn't happening*, Dave thought. He wasn't going from a six-figure salary to shuffling cards in a uniform. He left the meetings empty-handed.

Portnoy was still in Vegas, though, and the infamous town was abuzz more than usual. In fact, it was a critical time for the gaming industry. Chris Moneymaker became the first World Series of Poker Champion to have entered via an amateur online tournament victory, and the poker craze was on. ESPN's coverage of the WSOP tournament helped destigmatize the historically taboo hobby, which boosted the exposure of poker and gambling in general. Kids who were used to watching Kobe Bryant were now tuning in to see Phil Ivey.

Following the round of unsuccessful interviews, Portnoy met up with the guys who ran a popular online gambling site called

---

3   Portnoy also worked at Veritas Medicine for a short while after Yankee Group.

PartyPoker, whom he had met previously (he gambled *a lot*). Sitting at the hotel bar, he opined to the PartyPoker guys about the fruitless meetings with casino execs.

Sensing his audience, Dave then pitched them on a project he experimented with in college: a website he operated called www.the-gamblingman.com. "What a great URL," Portnoy says, reflecting on this early venture. As for what the site was, "I'd give out my [sports betting] picks on a daily basis," he explains. It was never meant to be more than a hobby at Michigan, something he did to procrastinate. It was still the very early days of the internet and not too many people read the site—if any. Now, given the current climate, the idea seemed like something worth revisiting. And Portnoy was convinced he could sell advertising to offshore gambling organizations like PartyPoker, whose business was booming.

Well, the PartyPoker guys put the kibosh on this fairly quickly; instead, they left the 26-year-old with a somewhat retro idea. "They said, 'don't do a website, because they're all cluttered with gambling ads," Portnoy explains, "but if you had a physical handout, we'd be interested."

3

OCTOBER 2003

Dave was sweaty and beyond exhausted as he bent down to drop off a stack of newspapers next to his bin at the Alewife T-Station in Cambridge. Sporting his questionable goatee and a beat-up Red Sox hat, his skin reeked of the cigar he had smoked inside his maroon 1992 Plymouth minivan while he trudged from station to station. His breath was a mix of tobacco and the hot Italian beef sandwich he'd ordered in between stops. Portnoy needed a shower. As he leaned over to fill the bin, he paused. The sound of fabric ripping echoed across the brown quarry tiles that lined the floors and walls of the subway entrance. Commuters turned their heads at the noise, and their eyes fixated on Portnoy. He knew immediately what had happened:

> "It might as well have been like a gunshot went off in Alewife Station. Everybody in Alewife and maybe all of Cambridge just froze. And I was reduced to doing the 'oh my god did I just split my pants?' maneuver. This, of course, is when you have a glazed expression over your face as you feel your ass to see what the damage is. Honestly, it was like time froze for a couple minutes."[1]

It was an unseasonably warm fall afternoon, just a few months after Mike Portnoy had given his son his $25,000 blessing. Dave,

---

[1]   Portnoy actually ripped his pants handing out newspapers a few years later: this writing is from June 2007. But I mention it here to give you an idea of what it was like during those early days handing out papers, and also because it's hilarious.

who had quit his sales job and moved back home with his parents to save money, was now spending it hand-delivering his newspapers to more than 100 *Barstool Sports* bins he had placed around Boston—a job that made grad school look like Margaritaville.

After all of his bins were filled, Portnoy would begin handing out his newspapers to the public, aggressively. The streets of Boston weren't for the faint of heart. "When we upgraded from black and white to color copies, I would be just screaming things like 'We got color now! We're so much better than these other (papers)!' Whatever the hook was." Like a vendor peddling overpriced beer at nearby Fenway Park, Portnoy would yell at—borderline berate—commuters to take a copy.

Portnoy was on his own when it came to distribution following *Barstool*'s first issue on August 27, 2003, when the temp company Labor Ready he hired to help him sent him mostly drifters, half of whom didn't show up. "Let's just say they weren't the most dedicated workers to ever come down the pike," Portnoy explained. And according to Portnoy, the outfit in Atlanta where he bought newspaper bins, Go Plastics, wasn't able to deliver the bins on time for the day of the launch, which only compounded this calamity. Most commuters were unable to find Portnoy's newspapers, as *Barstool Sports* sat inconspicuously inside plastic bags next to other competitors' fully marked bins.

Of the 40 train stations where workers were supposed to hand out copies of Dave's paper that day, only about 15 operated as planned. Portnoy would eventually hire local models to hand out his papers, which, to no surprise, worked better but were too expensive to continue with. "Chaotic and nearly disastrous," is how Dave described his paper's first days in existence. Unbeknownst to Portnoy, it was a phrase that would become the narrative of Barstool's entire operation for the next 20 years.

At the start of Portnoy's maiden voyage, he was able to produce several thousand copies of his weekly newspaper. This was dwarfed by the daily circulation of the 450,000 newspapers *The Boston Globe* printed, and the 300,000 distributed by both *The Boston Herald* and *Metro Boston*, the city's largest free paper. But eventually *Barstool* would reach a peak of 40,000 issues every other week, which was on par with most other alt-weekly publications such as *The Phoenix* or *The Improper Bostonian*. Reaching this number was an unlikely development to everyone around Dave in those early days, including his production manager Erin Boyce.

Boyce worked at *The Daily Item of Lynn*, a neighboring town's paper; she had extensive experience inside the publishing industry and agreed to help Portnoy after connecting through a friend of a friend. "I really only thought it would last six, maybe 12 issues. I've been in the newspaper industry for many years, and to start a publication in a dying industry is kind of unheard of. Little did I know 200 issues later, it would become part of my life for almost nine years."

Boyce's help was invaluable, but there was no doubt the 26-year-old was doing the work of five people just to produce the meager eight-page publication. Originally, Portnoy published his newspaper once a week. Mondays were the busiest in terms of writing, and Dave often stayed up past 2 a.m. finishing the last articles for that week's issue. Tuesdays, Portnoy took his work over to the nearby graphic designer, who worked with Boyce to lay out the paper. Later that day, the layout was taken to Boyce's printer, and once the thousands of copies were printed, Portnoy filled up his beaten-down minivan to the brim. "When I pick up *Barstool Sports* from our printer company, I swear I can hear her scream. I actually think the bottom of the car scrapes against the cement when it is fully loaded."

Wednesdays started at 4:30 a.m. Portnoy made the 45-minute drive south down Route 1A to Boston, dropping his publication off at the bins he had placed inside various T-stations. "I had bins at T-stops I didn't know existed before that," Portnoy said of his paper route. He also stopped at select stores, bars, and restaurants he somehow convinced to take his newspapers, like the Grand Canal bar near The Boston Garden or Bayview Liquors in Southie.

After emptying his van around 9:00 a.m., Dave headed to a T station and handed out copies of *Barstool Sports* to commuters. Around noon, he drove back to Swampscott to write; call potential advertisers (the paper had fake ones, like DirecTV, and real ones, such as the Kitty Linx Sex Toy Shop)[2]; or fix whatever part of the business was melting down that day. Around 4:00 p.m., he drove back into Boston to hand out papers again until returning home, well after dinner.

As for the rest of the week, Thursday was a repeat of Wednesday, while Friday, Saturday, and Sunday were reserved for writing. And Portnoy would spend each Monday just like the previous one, cramming in last-minute changes until the candle was burned at both ends. Unsurprisingly, this routine began taking a toll on his health, but as 2004 approached, people slowly began to read Portnoy's paper. "It was always a good reception and when I judged it, it would be 10 people who took the paper and said they enjoyed it the first time I did it. The next issue would be 20 people, and the next issue would be 40, and the next 80. So, it always was slowly growing and there was something in my gut that was like I'm on to something here."

"Welcome to the world of *Barstool Sports,* the only newspaper in Boston written by the common man, for the common man."

Those commuters who were nice enough to grab a copy of *Barstool Sports* from Portnoy read articles derived from the mission statement that introduced his first issue:

---

2   Portnoy has said several times he had fake ads in his paper, though he has never said if the DirecTV one was fake. I'm making an assumption based on how early on this was.

"Quite simply, the people at *Barstool Sports* are a bunch of average Joes, who like most guys, love sports, gambling, golfing, and chasing short skirts. We spend our NFL Sundays worrying about our fantasy football teams, and our summers worrying about the Sox. Our writers are the type of guys you'll bump into at a sports bar skipping work on the first and second days of March Madness."

Underneath the front-page manifesto, on the inaugural cover sat a giant half-page ad for Hooters, with an attractive girl, albeit in grayscale (Portnoy didn't switch to color for a while), wearing the restaurant's iconic uniform. Along with the declaration for what Barstool represented, the ad below it set the tone for what the paper would be about: sports, gambling, and most important—something he didn't mention to his father—hot women.

And for those first few months of writing, Portnoy grumbled about his gambling losses, who the most attractive contestant on MTV's *Love Island* was, and former Red-Sox-pitcher-turned-New-York-Yankee Roger Clemens:

"I haven't slept since Sunday after being forced to watch the Sunday family crowd at Fenway give Roger Clemens a standing ovation as he walked off the mound."

In a calculated yet poorly executed maneuver, Portnoy published articles under fake bylines, with names like Joe Houston and Blue Velvet (yes, Blue Velvet). Dave wanted to make his operation seem larger and more successful (hence, the fake ads as well); he didn't want people pulling back the curtain and seeing that the Wizard of Oz was in fact just a 26-year-old in his parents' basement. This produced some interesting results, as the newspaper eventually morphed into an anything-goes publication.

Here's Portnoy writing as Elle Murphy, in her (Portnoy's) weekly love advice column called "Time Out"[3]:

"The holiday season tends to bring out the inner child in all of us…tap into that playfulness, add some romance and make some special holiday memories…get a little closer with your crush during the holidays! Stop worrying about Q4 Sales goals or that you don't have enough money to get the perfect gift. The best presents come from the heart and can't be bought on Christmas Eve at the mall."

Portnoy's personality shined through in his writing, particularly his humor. He immediately understood the power of self-deprecation, a device that certainly wasn't going to be found in any column written at *The Globe*.

Here's an excerpt from his article "*The Seven Faces of No*," where he assigned a personality trait to each type of person who rejected him as he attempted to hand them his paper:

"1. Excuse Guy: Excuse Guy is the guy who just can't say no to you without explaining his actions. He wants you to understand why he isn't taking a paper. Excuses can range from 'I don't have time to grab a copy,' to a confused hand gesture, which implies he'd take a paper if he could just figure out how to do it.

"2. Joke Guy: Joke Guy thinks it's just the funniest freakin' thing in the world that you're busting ass trying to get rid of these papers. He just can't stop smiling and laughing as he says no to you."

---

3   Portnoy has openly talked about having fake bylines in his newspaper. Though he has never admitted to writing as Elle Murphy, I came across other writing where he talks about how it would be a good idea for a male publisher to write as a female, and he's only spoken about Jenna Marbles and another woman named Kati Cawley as former female contributors in the earlier days of Barstool.

Portnoy had plenty of material to work with; handing out newspapers alone in a dirty subway station was a continuously humbling task—and a far cry from the cushy, six-figure job he had held just a few months ago. It was an experience Dave noted in an early issue of *Barstool Sports*:

> "A few weeks ago, I mentioned how I was confused for a Spare Change guy while handing out papers. Well, the humiliation tour continued this past week at Back Bay T Station. I ran into a guy I used to work with in my previous life. This guy is a typical middle management suit, who honestly thinks that he is way more important than he really is. The look of surprise and disgust on his face when he saw me hawking newspapers was priceless. Then he hits me with this line, 'well, since it's you, I'll buy a paper,' and he takes out his wallet and gives me the second dollar that I have received in two weeks. I didn't bother to explain what I was doing, but instead just pocketed his dollar, gave him a paper, and sent him on his merry way."

As Portnoy continued to print his paper, one surprising development was the number of people in Boston who wanted to be writers. Like Dave, it seemed there were many other 20-somethings who loathed being buried in Excel all day as much as he did. And Portnoy began soliciting help; the founder understood he couldn't keep operating alone forever. "Want to write for *Barstool Sports*? We don't pay, but we make up for it by offering no benefits!" was a giant text box found in almost every issue during those first months.

While the number of submissions per week he received quickly reached double digits, Portnoy advised those sending him applications that he wasn't looking for another recap of the last Red Sox game, which could be read in just about every other Boston newspaper. Dave was looking for writers who took a clever and more comedic approach to stories. The goal of the paper, by now, was to entertain and make people laugh, and the writer's voice needed to fit alongside Portnoy's.

Jamie Chisholm was the first to answer the call, and Portnoy took him on in October 2003. From Malden MA, Chisholm was in his mid-20s and worked for the Massachusetts House of Representatives as the Chief of Staff for Timothy J. Toomey. A few issues later, Portnoy added Pete Manzo to his two-man crew. Manzo was similar in age to Chisholm and Portnoy, but unlike them, and pretty much everyone else in Boston, he was a Yankees fan. Surprisingly, this wasn't a deal breaker for Dave. Although Manzo worked in finance, Portnoy to this day claims he was the best writer to ever write for *Barstool*, which is probably why Dave put up with his allegiance to New York sports. And following Manzo, Portnoy's "Core Four" Barstool writers would be complete when a married dad in his 40s named Jerry Thornton, who worked for the town court in Hingham MA, applied to join Portnoy's publication.

As the group started writing for *Barstool*—all three would work without pay until 2007—they received little advice or management from Portnoy, mostly because he didn't have much experience himself. In fact, Thornton would say he could write 'Barstool sucks' 10 times in an article and Dave would not have noticed. As a result, their misspelled words and freedom to write about anything—such as how long you had to wait to *really* use the bathroom at your new girlfriend's apartment—worked to endear the crew to their readers. The Core Four of *Barstool* amplified Portnoy's common-man approach, and this began to pay off.

> "I know I'm biased and I may be crazy, but I honestly think we have the most loyal readers in town. Obviously, we don't have the most readers, but we have built a community of average guys who all can relate with what we are trying to do and have similar tastes and senses of humor."

To Portnoy's surprise—and to his production manager's—a small group of fans began to form around the *Barstool* team, which by now was three guys in their mid-twenties who weren't writers and a 40-year-old who worked at the courthouse.

4

MARCH 2004

"The bottom-line is that the paper doesn't make enough money for me to live on…. every penny I make either goes to macaroni and cheese or back into the paper…The fact that I'm dead broke is probably the hardest thing to deal with on a day-to-day basis. I'm rapidly approaching 30 years old and have more debt than you can imagine…spending all my time working on something that still may not work. The problem is that I just can't tell."[1]

While both the size of his team and his readership was growing, Portnoy was in fact very broke. After leaving his last job, Dave had somehow schemed his way into receiving unemployment, and the supplemental government income was one of the main reasons he was able to survive during that time. It cost Portnoy around $2,500 a month to produce *Barstool Sports* ($2,000 to print, $200 for graphic designer, $200-300 for gas money). Advertising was bringing in around $1,500 per month, and Portnoy bolstered this revenue by selling ugly t-shirts with the red Barstool cartoon-lettering to his readers, a strategy that would become central to Barstool's continued unlikely existence.

After some complex calculations, Portnoy determined the paper was losing around $1,000 per month, which didn't give him much runway. After incurring the costs of starting the business—Portnoy

---

1   This blurb is from March 2005, I placed it there to show how dire those early days were for Portnoy, and how he often wrote about this external crisis to his fans.

spent $10,000 on his newspaper bins alone—the $25,000 check his father had given him 6 months earlier was evaporating at a rapid pace. Sports analyst Todd McShay reflected on the precarious situation Portnoy found himself in:

> "I legitimately thought he was going to go bankrupt. And I was worried about him. And he just kept grinding. I would hear him…calling credit cards, and [saying] 'all right, if I transfer all of this money to this credit card, what kind of rate can I get?' and…maneuvering money around just to try to stay alive."

In addition to other business expenses Portnoy accrued, his affection for betting on sports was not doing anything to help his bank account. Portnoy owed tens of thousands of dollars to credit card companies: American Express, Discover Card, and First USA Bank, to name a few. Mike Portnoy reflected on this dilemma: "Anybody who thinks my son is exaggerating his gambling issues, I wish he was. Believe me, he is a legitimate degenerate."

In January 2004, Portnoy decided to switch to a bi-weekly model, a much-needed move that cut his printing costs and workload in half. And in an attempt to boost readership that month, Portnoy added a new feature that shifted the tone of his paper in a crasser direction. He would call this column "the Ms. Barstool Contest." It was an analogue knock-off of his doppelganger's FaceMash, which was exploding in popularity just down the road at Harvard. Portnoy solicited applications and nominations for girls from his readers, then matched two against each other each week side by side, with a picture of the respective contestants. A short bio sat underneath each photo, where the women answered several questions about themselves. In a shocking twist, the female deemed more attractive received more votes every time.

It was a successful addition to the paper that guys who picked it up certainly enjoyed. But it coincided with the first public airing of pushback from a female critic and the first accusation of sexism, a condemnation that would follow Dave and Barstool until the present day. A woman named Bridgette emailed Portnoy in response to paragraphs written by him like the one below:

"Well, I guess that explains why all girls hate each other, huh? It's just one giant competition to lock down some dick. Every hobag for herself. It also explains why feminists are always ugly. They know they can't beat hot chicks for dudes, so rather than face the facts, it's easier to pretend they hate men or are lesbians. In other words, science is finally backing up what I've been saying for the past decade."

Bridgette's response:

"Why do most male sports writers have to write columns where they completely alienate women? Is this the norm for a successful sports columnist? Short-sightedness + Blatant misogyny + Ignorant sexist comments = success? Have you really run out of other things to write about?"

Portnoy published her email in his next issue along with his response:

"This email hurts more every time we read it. However, I maintain that a lot of what we write truly reflects how guys think when they meet new girls."

As it turns out, Bridgette was the first of many to begin criticizing Barstool's newspaper during those early years. Portnoy's unabashed aim towards men wasn't received kindly at *The Phoenix*, one of *Barstool*'s main competitors, who would call *Barstool* "a publication with no discernible reason for existing." And Portnoy would document a run-in he had with an *Improper Bostonian* employee:

"[I] received maybe the biggest compliment I've ever received yesterday from a former sales chick at the *Improper Bostonian*… Apparently, I called them gold diggers and a bunch of other things. I have no idea the context of why I said these things, but I'm sure I said them and I stand by them…. Anyway, this Improper girl said that somebody at the *Improper* told her the only reason that the Stool existed is because my family is ultra rich and gave me a ton of money to start the thing. HA! HA! HA! Yeah, that's why I was standing there with ink all over my body doing a 48-hour-straight paper route. More importantly, if I were rich, I wouldn't be working; I'd be golfing. Anyway, the moral of the story is that *Barstool Sports* is the only paper that has the guts to rip people in print. We say the same thing about people in public as we do behind closed doors."

Ripping people was an understatement. Almost therapeutically, Portnoy lambasted the Boston establishment for not taking him seriously, a sentiment that was hurting his bottom line:

"Speaking of hounding people, a couple of groups that have refused to talk to us is the Glynn Hospitality Group and the Briar Group. If you're not familiar with these guys, they own a bunch of bars in Metro Boston like Hurricane O'Reilly's, Joe Mac's, Ned Devine's, MJ O'Connor's, and The Harp. While it seems like these places would be a perfect fit to advertise with us, they don't seem to be remotely interested in anything we have to say. If I had to guess, I'd say that I've left over 50 messages for each in the past month without so much as a return phone call. It's okay, though. I'm real persistent like that and I'll just keep calling. If I still don't hear from them by March, it may be time to start sharpening my pencil. We've developed a motto here that is 'if you won't play ball, [then] prepare to get bashed.'"

For Portnoy, this was perplexing. Those bars advertised in the *Phoenix* and *The Improper*, but the type of Bostonians patronizing their establishments weren't reading those more cerebral newspapers; they were reading Dave's. When he finally got on the phone with them, the Briar Group told him they "weren't interested in marketing that way," while the Glynn Group informed him they were looking to market to "middle-of-the-road" people. This drove Portnoy up the wall because his slogan was quite literally "by the common man, for the common man." While they may not have wanted to be associated with his profanity or spelling errors, *at least come up with a better excuse*, Portnoy thought.

Dave also reached out to Bill Simmons, a famous ESPN writer from Boston who made a name for himself after successfully launching BostonSportsGuy.com in 1998. Simmons was a talented, quick-witted writer—sort of a PG-version of Portnoy. He liked to push boundaries, just not as far as Dave did. And Dave, who looked up to Simmons at the time, thought someone from the same town who had achieved success would want to pay it forward and help another local guy. He was wrong:

> "Bill Simmons, a.k.a. Boston Sports Guy from ESPN, has slowly become a target of *Barstool Sports*. I've got to tell you that it hurts taking consistent pot shots at him. As a reminder, he denied our request for an interview. So, the mature professionals that we are, we started throwing some borderline cheap shots at him. Unfortunately, I feel like it is when you have a bad break-up with a girlfriend that you really cared about. I know that deep down I like this guy. I know he's hilarious and that I enjoy reading his stuff. Yet he

hurt me, so now I'm going to mask the pain by badmouthing him for no good reason."

Dave even went after the government, ripping on Boston Mayor Thomas Menino, or "Mayor Mumbles," as he called him. Portnoy chastised Menino for being incompetent but more important, for confiscating his newspaper bins and citing them for "infractions" Dave believed were fraudulent. Eventually, Portnoy began taking matters into his own hands, breaking into the lot where they were stored and stealing them back. As he explained to his readers:

"Yup, for the 2nd time this month Menino decided he was going to capture and hold hostage all of the Barstool News Racks. Luckily we were able to break into the city dump and free them in a scene vaguely reminiscent to the ending scene in Clear And Present Danger. Except instead of having to fight Columbian Drug Lords, we had to fight the wild kittens that live in the dump."

There was also some not-as-serious opposition from readers who were unimpressed with Dave's on-air talent. As Portnoy began to build some momentum during *Barstool*'s first year in operation, he was able to secure a radio spot on *1510 The Zone* with McShay and Elio. Dave had to pay the Zone for the airtime, but it certainly was an improvement from six months earlier when the station wouldn't even take his money. Not all listeners were fans, however, like this one:

"Tonight's show was just tedious. Your "Rant" or dialogue about your summer vacation house is fascinating. It would be cool if it was funny. I am sure this conversation is very important to the three of you. But the few of us that enjoy sports talk are tuning out. I WANT THE LAST 20 MINUTES OF MY LIFE BACK! Don't get me wrong, I think you guys are talented writers and I enjoy the newspaper. It makes for terrible radio. TALK SPORTS or at least be funny."

—Danny in East Bridgewater

Dave's response:

"Congratulations, Danny. That is easily the meanest thing anybody has ever written, said, or thought about us...I wish I could argue and say we are great, but who am I to say? We may in fact suck."

As Portnoy made his foray into radio, he also took a stab at the internet. "I figured I should have a website, because that's what everyone was doing," he said. Portnoy set up the domain a few months after the launch of the newspaper. With the *Barstool Sports* funky lettering on the front, it did feature functional links to PDFs of his articles, but that early website was essentially just pictures of his newspaper on a webpage.

A more significant development at the time, and one that would allow him (along with the website) to take full advantage of the paradigm shift that was coming, was the addition of Portnoy's *Random Thoughts* section in his paper, which was exactly what it sounds like. Unbeknownst to him, Portnoy was blogging inside a newspaper, and unsurprisingly, *Random Thoughts* became *Barstool's* most read feature.

On March 10, 2004, in one of those *Random Thoughts*, Portnoy placed a large ad for a bar in Boston's Brighton neighborhood, reminding readers that *Barstool Sports* was hosting its first-ever March Madness party at the sports bar:

"Join *Barstool Sports* Friday March 19th at Cityside Tavern.

"...It's never too early to get ready for the Tourney. *Barstool Sports* will be running its own March Madness pool...In a nutshell, we're throwing a March Madness party where only people who have entered the pool will be invited to the bar, where it will be an open bar. Chicks get in free regardless. (As always!) Hopefully, we'll get a ton of people to enter and have a blast."

The 26-year-old Portnoy sensed momentum. The number of reader emails he received was increasing, which was pretty much the only measure Portnoy could use at that time to gauge how many people were actually reading his paper (that and how many were left in the bins, but who knows what some people did with them). Dave often shared his excitement with his readers:

"We know that the concept for *Barstool Sports* is a good one...we're happy (satisfied) with the product that we're putting out on the street every Wednesday. We've developed a cult-like following of loyal readers who think like us and probably act like us...[and] As I mentioned earlier, the paper is way ahead of schedule and continues to grow at a steady rate. People seem to love the thing..."

Portnoy wanted to capitalize on the progress he had made and the sense of community he built with his readers like Danny in East Bridgewater. To get his audience out in the real world for a physical meet-and-greet would be a sizable leap in that direction, but it was doable.

♣

On a windy, 40-degree day in March 2004, Portnoy stepped out of a yellow cab. The Barstool event he advertised in his paper started at noon, but Dave decided he would show up fashionably late; he could technically arrive whenever he wanted to: it was his party.

Wearing a red Barstool ugly t-shirt under his coat, Portnoy walked toward Cityside Tavern. His eyes went up and down the restaurant's exterior: its triangular shape reminded him of the historic Flatiron building in downtown Manhattan. It was a fitting impression: Portnoy was preparing to make Cityside a Barstool landmark.

After a few seconds outside, Dave opened the door and walked in. He looked around: it was completely empty, save for one middle-aged man sitting at a table alone towards the far end of the bar. Dave quickly zipped up his jacket to hide the Stool logo underneath. For the next three hours, to his horror, not a single other person showed up to Barstool's March Madness party.

"It was the darkest day of my life."

5

"I don't know who the fuck you are, but I guess you're hitting on my daughter."

Popular Boston sports radio host John Dennis fumed audibly into his phone as he left his now-infamous voicemail for a young upstart and local competitor named Ryen Russillo. Dennis was a no-nonsense guy. The only broadcaster at WEEI who strictly wore button-down shirts and slacks in all of his promos, at 53, he could have easily been cast as one of Don Draper's rivals in the second season of *Mad Men*. His old-school, tough demeanor lent itself well to the combative nature of sports talk radio. This, along with his experience covering Boston for more than 28 years, helped Dennis win more arguments than he lost against the endless supply of local callers.

After joining the station in 1997, by 2005 his morning drive show *Dennis and Callahan* had risen to become a ratings smash. Both Dennis and WEEI sat comfortably ahead of the competition; neither were to be messed with. Which made it all the more shocking to listeners of Boston radio when they learned that during a night on the town in late August of that year, Russillo, who had allegedly said some not-so-flattering things about Dennis to others in the industry, supposedly made a pass at his daughter. Dennis's voicemail continued:

> "You're going around telling people, including my producer, that I shit on you and I don't know what [I'm] talking about. But I guess you're hitting on my daughter, and telling her

stuff like…'I want to be with you and create a scandal,' you wanna create a scandal? I'll tell you what, why don't you, at half my age, what are you, late 20s, I'm early 50s, you want to create a scandal? Why don't you come and find me, and I'll rip your fucking ears off, and your nose off, and I'll shove them up your ass, and kick your balls up around your head!"

Dennis got what he wanted. A scandal emerged from this voice-mail that Boston sports fans couldn't get enough of. Russillo was fired from his pregame and postgame coverage of the New England Patriots on WBCN Radio, a station Dennis had connections at, and major outlets picked up the story, including *The Herald*'s well-read gossip column "*Inside Track*." But Bostonians flocked in droves to the only outfit in town that had the actual audio message on file where they could click and hear Dennis's bullying tone as he stumbled and sometimes slurred through what sounded like a late-night phone call one regrets the next morning. On a little-known website called www.barstoolsports.com.

Portnoy survived his first two years running Barstool, but barely. Following the disaster that was his first attempt at bringing his "fans" together for a party, in April 2004, Portnoy did what many successful entrepreneurs before him have done: he filed for bankruptcy. It wasn't an ideal move, but his gambling debt wasn't going away, and his paper was losing money on a weekly basis. Thanks to his father Mike Portnoy, Esq., Dave was able to massage the legal system and protect his company and the remainder of his assets, which totaled around $22,000. Barstool Sports was still in operation. For now.

Still basically broke—they weren't liquid assets—Portnoy was so desperate for cash, he attempted to sell his mom's famous sour-cream cakes on the back pages of *Barstool*:

"'Simply the best cake on the planet'

—A friend of mine.
$14.00 per cake.'"

To his surprise, no one was interested in buying a homemade cake from the editor of the newspaper they were reading. (Portnoy still claims they are the best cakes on the planet.) Aside from trying to sell his readers home-baked goods, he also implored them to call his advertisers:

> "Our best shot to convince advertisers to take a chance on us is by convincing them that we have loyal readers who will support the ads that appear in our paper. That is why we always make a stink about calling our advertisers. We want them to get value out of the fact that people actually read and identify with the paper unlike a lot of the other free publications in the city...If you want to see us go toe to toe with the *Metro*'s subpar sports section, please don't be bashful about calling the crap out of [our advertisers], as that's how we try to break even. (Notice I didn't say make money because that's not even on our radar screen yet.)"

But a few months later, in October 2004, Portnoy made a change to his publication that would allow him to make it to *Barstool*'s two-year anniversary. Thanks to the recommendation and expertise of photographer Eric Levin, *Barstool Sports* began publishing pictures of local models on the cover of the newspaper. It was a move that immediately caught on. The *Barstool* issues sitting in the news stands now had barely dressed attractive women splashed across the front page, with each issue featuring a new model. Next to the buttoned-up covers of *The Metro, The Phoenix,* or *The Improper,* Portnoy's paper stood out to blue-blooded Boston men who were looking to kill some time on their commute. Unsurprisingly, guys began to pick up the paper at a faster rate. But more important, advertisers began to notice, as Portnoy describes here:

> "Once we did that, advertising opened up. Basically, companies thought we had access to these pretty girls, and that's how you get people in bars, if you have access to pretty girls, so that kind of started the advertising... Not the gambling, which I kind of thought it would [be], it was the girls."

Local bars and restaurants such as The Place, An Tua Nua, and Phoenix Landing began paying Portnoy to advertise in his paper. While none were owned by any of the major hospitality groups, it was finally a step in the right direction.

Apart from landing advertisers, the new covers turned Portnoy's lowbrow publication into somewhat of a *Playboy*-esque tabloid that high schoolers stole copies of and train-riders hid underneath copies of *The Herald*. *Barstool* even began getting noticed by the female crowd: "I honestly can't believe how many girls want to be on the cover of *Barstool Sports*. It's freaking awesome. I feel like girls in Boston think we're *Maxim* and who am I to tell them any differently? I'm just going to ride this wave until it breaks," Dave said at the time. The momentum snowballed from there. Soon Portnoy would be able to lock down ad deals with the major beer companies—Budweiser, Coors, and Miller Lite—and those deals were just large enough for Portnoy to move out of his parents' house and into a cramped month-by-month studio apartment in the South End neighborhood of Boston.

And while he was busy painstakingly completing his 48-hour paper route, Portnoy had been slowly increasing the amount of attention he paid to running the online arm of *Barstool*. That was thanks to a young Stoolie named Ian White, whom Dave had formerly handed the paper to at one of the T-stations downtown. White emailed Portnoy one day out of the blue at the beginning of 2005:

To: feedback@barstoolsports.com
Subject: Making The Website Better

"I used to read you guys all the time over the summer when I was at home in Boston, but now that I'm in Providence I barely ever read you because all your articles are in PDF format. You could really take off on the web if you had your articles in HTML instead of PDF, I can see sites like SoSH or bostonsportsmedia.com linking to you.

"Meanwhile I'm a web programmer trying to build up my resume before I move to NYC next spring and start looking for freelance work. I think we might be able to help each other out.

"Here's the deal. I could write you a web publishing setup with PHP/SQL. Nothing fancy, we can talk about what you want, but basically I'm thinking of a setup where you can copy and paste the text of your articles into a form, press a button, and voila, they're up and they look semi decent.

"I can't do any fancy-looking web design. I'm not a graphic artist. I can set you up with something that's clean-looking, simple and loads fast. That'll be a big improvement over the PDFs.

"I won't charge you because I know you can't pay, I'm just doing this for resume purposes, and anyway I like you guys and want to be able to read your stuff without my computer crashing. Maybe you could give me a subscription or a T-shirt or something.

"Let me know.

—Ian"

Portnoy immediately responded.

From: feedback@barstoolsports.com
Subject: RE: Making The Website Better
To: Ian White <ibwhite@gmail.com>

Hey Ian,

"I've been waiting for an email like this for a long time. I would love to take you up on your offer. Let me know what I need to do or get you. You can put whatever you want on your resume and we'll back it up. I'm psyched."

Originally just a placeholder where Portnoy parked the PDFs of his newspaper articles, the website became more dynamic after Ian White's upgrade (though it still just looked like links on a webpage). And underneath that same red cartoonish *Barstool Sports* title used in his newspaper, Portnoy began posting daily random thoughts that his users could click into and read at the beginning of the day. The best went into next week's paper.

While this change allowed Portnoy to provide more content for his readers, buzz generated by the John Dennis voicemail in September 2005 was Portnoy's first glimpse into the power of the internet. It was a different phenomenon; unlike anything he had experienced in his two years running *Barstool*. Different even from the new addition of the cover models. That payoff was gradual, months long. This was sudden. A Stoolie sent Dave the audio, he posted it on his webpage, and people sent around the link to Barstoolsports.com like they were Oprah giving away cars.

As waves of readers began to visit Portnoy's website following the John Dennis scandal, Portnoy realized there was another tool he could take advantage of in his effort to make Barstool a household name: his ability to manufacture controversy. Coincidently, Russillo worked at the same radio station Portnoy was able to secure his hourly spot at *1510 The Zone,* and the brass there demanded that Portnoy take the voicemail off his website. Dave refused:

> "Another outcome of us breaking the John Dennis voice-mail is that *1510 the Zone* pulled the plug on the Barstool Sports Radio Hour, which had to be the best 60 minutes of radio on the dial. Our termination resulted when I refused their request to remove the voicemail from our website... The good news is that we have gotten a ton of press from that. The Inside Track did a full-blown story on it and we've been mentioned in a billion other places. There is nothing better than being in the middle of a full-blown controversy. I feel like I'm in the WWE and that is exactly where the Stool wants to be."

The Dennis voicemail was the first time mainstream outlets mentioned Dave's scrappy enterprise, because as Portnoy realized, internet and controversy combined to make the perfect cocktail of attention (it was also evident early on that Portnoy was going to stand up for what he believed in, stubbornly and defiantly, a trait his fans would come to revere him for).

Following the voicemail saga and the traffic his site was generating as a result, Portnoy made a final change to his website that proved to be monumental. On March 27, 2006, he made this announcement:

> "Let's start this week with the big announcement in the world of random thoughts. Starting today, we are going to be posting random thoughts in a blog style on our website. What does this mean? It means that from now on people won't have to wait 24 hours in between each batch of random thoughts. Thank the freaking lord, right! The website will be updated continually through as we think of new crap to write about. I'll still send out an email each morning like I always do, but the people who don't want to wait won't have

to anymore. It's just another step towards us taking over ESPN.com as the world's most popular website."

Portnoy was now a full-time blogger.

♣

Blogging began unofficially in January 1994, when Swarthmore College undergrad Justin Hall created a site called www.linkes.net. It was simply a commentary on different sites he found from other URLs, which he posted links to, as well as some of his own original writing. Hall was later appointed by *The New York Times Magazine* as the "founding father of personal bloggers." And while it took a few years for the medium to catch on, by 2006, there were anywhere from 35-50 million blogs in operation, up from a whopping 23 total blogs in 1999.

Relative to the competition Portnoy faced while running his website, he was one of the earliest players to open shop on the fast-growing internet. BroBible and The Chive came along a few years after Barstool in 2008, Total Frat Move in 2010, Elite Daily in 2012. Others followed; out of the more well-known digital media sites, only Deadspin, which was founded in September 2005, started as early as Portnoy's. And whether coincidence or not, eventually Deadspin would become *Barstool*'s most outspoken critic.

Blogs allowed anyone with an internet dialup to become their own *New York Times*. Writers could now reach a massive audience, for free, instantaneously, and people didn't have to pay to read or watch; it was a death-sentence for newspapers, as these upstarts began to tear into their classified-ad revenues.

Media giants began to understand this, and these companies' first reactions were to partner with blogs, instead of producing their own. Time Warner eventually joined forces with popular tech blog TechCrunch, and Mashable's bloggers teamed up with CNN. But operating under the purview of a large corporation, there were obvious restrictions on what these blogs could publish, which meant they were never going to replicate the kind of entertainment Portnoy was now providing. Still, the local bigwigs in Boston joined the movement, and *The Globe* and *The Herald* hopped online. But their content suffered a similar fate: it was pretty much just a copy-paste from their paper, similar to Portnoy's early online PDFs.

Portnoy's constant updating of his blog was a much more original and nimble endeavor, and the authentic voice that he honed through the early days of the paper translated perfectly to this new medium. It fit Portnoy like a glove:

> "The thing that makes El Pres, El Pres is my ability to talk just as easily about the NBA draft as I can about *The Hills* on MTV."[1]

Portnoy provided commentary on whatever the internet had to offer that day. He posted about random online stories like a family of four dying in their dairy farm's manure pit:

> "As a professional blogger there is always a fine line we walk when discussing tragedy…But I wouldn't be doing my job if I didn't post this story because clearly suffocating to death on toxic manure fumes has to be in the discussion for worst ways to die…I'm not going to crack any jokes."

He commented on photos of the rival-town's star girlfriend:

> "Is Jessica Biel too jacked? Jeter has probably been feeding her protein shakes or something."

---

1   Dave adopted the pseudonym "El Presidente" because he drank only Presidente pilsner beer at the time. He also thought about going by "Devilfish Dave" at one point before he officially started Barstool Sports, but scrapped that idea.

And of course, he wrote about the hometown star's love life:

"It looks like Bridget Moynahan's plan to spoil Tom Brady's romantic vacation with Gisele isn't quite going to plan. And you just know that he's getting a hand job under the table too because that's how Tom Brady rolls."

This was commentary that readers wouldn't find anywhere else on the web. Some of it was off-putting, and old media dismissed bloggers like Portnoy as crude, even problematic. During a 2008 HBO panel about sports writing on the internet, Bob Costas asked Deadspin founder Will Leitch what he thought about blogging, and Leitch replied, "This is a different voice, this is a new thing." Famous author Buzz Bissinger (*Friday Night Lights*) followed by stating, "It's a disgusting voice." But traditional industry players like Bissinger piled on bloggers because deep down, they were afraid of them. Portnoy explained:

"Is there anything more hilarious than the mainstream media's fear of the blogging industry? I've never seen anything quite like it. They must feel like France did before Germany invaded them in WWII. Just a total sense of helplessness. It's like their entire universe has been turned upside down. For years and years and years sports journalists have had a virtual monopoly on how people got their information. There was no alternative. As a result, guys like Shaughnessy and Borges came to have this elitist attitude that it was their birthright to cover the local sports teams and that their opinions were the only ones that mattered. That everybody else was somehow beneath them. It's this type of attitude and total disconnect from reality which has doomed these guys. Not to mention the fact that it's hard for [a] 50-year-old guy to relate to a 25-year-old."

Portnoy continued:

"Bottom line is that people were desperate to get their info from somewhere else and blogs have filled that vacuum. So these idiots can talk all they want about morals and ethics blah, blah, blah. But the bottom line is that the reason they hate blogs so much is because they know they can't compete with them. And the gap is only going to widen in the future as they continue to get older and the demographic they need to reach gets younger. So spare me the indignation about how blogs are inherently evil. The only people who complain about this type of stuff are guys who aren't good enough writers to keep their audience."

The traditional media's use of "morals and ethics blah, blah, blah," as a defense mechanism was also hypocritical, as Portnoy would expose with the profanity-laced Dennis voicemail. *That's* how they really spoke. But even if the establishment believed people like Portnoy were juvenile wannabees, the dollars that poured into the industry began to say otherwise. Thanks to Google AdSense launching in 2003, which matched online ads to blog content, those bloggers began to make (some) money. By 2005, an estimated $100M worth of blog ads were sold. It was a rapidly growing industry, and perfect timing for Barstool to be at the forefront of this rise. Though he continued to print the biweekly newspaper, as he updated his blog at a near 24/7 clip, Portnoy began to see firsthand the long-term potential of blogging:

"The head honchos at *Barstool Sports* are convinced that our website is a potential goldmine waiting to happen. Personally I think it's the best thing we do at the Stool. Don't get me wrong I love the newspaper, but it's just so much easier to be funny with all the random pictures …and other weird crap…that you can post on a blog. In other words, if you have a set of balls and you're not visiting our website yet then it's hard for me to respect you as a man. However having said all that, I think rule #1 to having a big-time website is that it needs to work. And to be honest, I'm not sure we've mastered that concept yet. Over the past few months our website has crashed like five times."

The core four writers worked through 2005 and 2006 to keep the website afloat, though some more than others. Portnoy posted about three quarters of the blogs, with Chisholm, Thornton, and Manzo filling the remaining quota. It was a stat that was not lost on Portnoy, who publicly called out his crew and particularly Manzo (remember they weren't being paid):

"It's that time of the week folks. Yup [I'm] minutes away from climbing into the Astrovan fresh off 700 bucks' worth of repairs ready for another paper route. I won't emerge from my cocoon of horror until tomorrow night…So here is the question I am left to ponder as I get ready for my bi-weekly pilgrimage across Metro Boston. Will Pete Manzo step up and fill the blog gap that my absence will leave? Or will he let all the pressure fall on the broad shoulders of Jamie Chisholm and Jerry Thornton? It's truly a question for the ages and I guess only time will tell. As a side note, Jamie and I kicked around the idea of guest bloggers. We would rotate different people in every week to help contribute to the blog that is destined to rule the world one day. And if Manzo continues with his one blog every three days routine, the need for more quality bloggers will only intensify."

For Dave, the internet was a double-edged sword. While there seemed to be a never-ending supply of stories to write about, keeping up was all-encompassing. "Five seconds after something happened," he explained, "I was there. Whatever it was." Portnoy became obsessed with being near his laptop; he didn't break news, but he wanted his take on that news to be read first.

As for what that looked like on a daily basis, Dave usually posted his first blog between 8 and 9 a.m. and continued writing until about 9 p.m., posting around 15 blogs a day; all while continuing to write, edit, print, and deliver his newspaper. (Portnoy used the writing from the blog in his paper, which reduced a large amount of time spent on that end.) But his hard work translated to a steady increase in the number of Bostonians visiting the Barstool Sports URL. "Our website has been growing nicely lately and we need to continue to build the momentum," Portnoy stated at the time.

One aspect of the website that Portnoy took advantage of was the Barstool Message Board. It was a feature that brought life to Barstool Sports in a way that the newspaper couldn't. Users would log on and discuss the recent posts made by Portnoy, while Dave himself would respond to questions from readers, giving his thoughts on recent moves by Patriots Head Coach Bill Belichick (whom he supported so blindly that CBS News eventually posted a headline that read "Boston Blogger Asks Belichick If He Needs Anyone Murdered") or letting them know what his plans were that weekend. And celebrities emerged on the message board: Ed from Easton, Big Remy, and Dana Bible were mainstays who frequently posted and interacted with Portnoy. Dave often referenced the characters from the message board in his blogs:

"Did Dana Bible or Don Jeans from our message board make this kid cry or something?"

The message board put the sense of community Portnoy fostered into action. (In fact, two members ended up meeting and getting married.) So did the parties Portnoy began to throw in downtown Boston. Although his first one had been an abject failure, Dave didn't give up on the idea of having Barstool followers meet together in person. And in November 2005, following the buzz generated from the Dennis voicemail, Portnoy finally broke into the sacred Lyons Hospitality Group:

> "This next random thought is serving as a Barstool Sports announcement and a very important one at that. Starting next Wednesday we are starting a Trivia Night at Game On! This is huge for us. We've been trying to get in with the Lyons Group for ages and we want to impress the hell out of them…So please grab a couple of your buddies and head on down next Wednesday…Right now this is the #1 way to support the Stool."

To Portnoy's delight and relief, a solid number of Stoolies showed up for Trivia Night. A few months later, he threw another March Madness party, which this time was relatively well attended. Following these two get-togethers, an increasing number of fans began appearing at different Barstool events: The Cover Model of the Year party, Barstool Holiday parties, March Madness, Trivia, and others.[2]

Email #1 from *Random Thoughts* section

El Presidente-

"First off congrats on a fantastic March Madness Party at The Place. I was part of the 5 o'clock crowd, so I missed most of the afternoon crowd, but hanging out and watching the evening and night games there was great. Now I am pretty sure that is my first time in The Place and I could not help but notice the quality of female bartenders and waitresses there.

---

2   Dave threw a second March Madness party in 2005 and told himself if fewer than 10 people showed up again, he would quit Barstool. People showed up this time, but it was mostly friends and family. Trivia Night would become a staple of Barstool events, with groups like the Red Sox front office attending.

Which brings me to my question: What is the etiquette for a Stoolie in hitting on the staff there? ...It is wicked hard to tell if [the girls] are just trying to get tips or really interested.

Thanks Buddy
B"

Portnoy:

"Yeah.... I'm thinking [they're] working for tips as opposed to really into you. Just a guess though."

Portnoy's rallying of his base to the Boston streets was unusual for a media company; no one was meeting in chatrooms to talk about what the writers at *The Globe* or Deadspin were eating for breakfast, let alone taking the time out of their weekend to go meet them in person. And as the summer of '06 came to a close, the leader of this grassroots movement made another important announcement on his website:

"In case you've been living in a cave, I'm here to announce that Barstool Sports biggest party in the history of the universe and possibly the biggest party in the history of organized civilization is less than two weeks away. I'm obviously talking about our Ultimate White Party...As a reminder this is a private party! What that means is that you need to be on the list and if you plan on showing up with a bunch of ugly dudes think again...We want lots of hot girls there so feel free to kidnap them and bring them along.... And oh yeah, if you don't wear white you're not getting in and I'm sick of answering this question."

♣

On August 24, 2006, Portnoy once again stepped slowly out of his yellow cab. Unlike that dreary day in March two years earlier when the big Barstool bash turned out to be a depressing party of one, not only was he not bundled up in a winter jacket—he was wearing a white sleeveless shirt and tight white pants—this time Portnoy was greeted by a colossal number of Stoolies, all mirroring his attire, eager to get into his event.

The White Party would go down in Barstool lore: several thousand people attended. Thornton, in his mid-40s with a wife and kids, got kicked out of the event for being party to two girls climbing on top of the bar and making out. "They handed me their phones and my job was to take pictures of them," Thornton explained. "My proximity to them was enough to get the bouncers to say 'Ok, you're out of here.' Dave eventually came out and said, 'I heard you got kicked out,' and I'm telling him the circumstances and he just said, 'Huh. It's always the last guy you figure.'"

But before being removed from the event, Thornton was able to have a brief moment of reflection. "I will never forget talking to Chisholm and Manzo, looking out over the scene at this massive White Party and saying to each other, 'Look at what this has become.'"

The occasion proved Portnoy's digital approach was working. Barstoolsports.com boasted 100,000 monthly unique visitors by the time 2006 was over.

"The Stool was profitable this year. In fact, 2006 was a banner year for us, but you wouldn't know it by my bank account."

And as Portnoy explained years later, "From that point on, it became clear that [the website] was going to be the history of Barstool."

6

A large, bearded, middle-aged man wearing a plaid button down and khakis stood outside the front steps of the Satterthwaite home in the suburb of Abington, MA. Before knocking, his eyes wandered around the property at 58 Highland Road. It was actually a relatively nice place, with a spacious-looking barn attached to a decently wide one-story grey house. The Satterthwaites lived towards the back of a quiet, dead-end street. *They paid a premium for privacy*, the man thought. *Too bad.*

"Where the fuck is Dave Portnoy!?!?!?" he boomed in a thick Boston accent as he banged loudly on the front door. Barbara Satterthwaite, a tall, regal 52-year-old woman, was sitting in her kitchen perusing the latest issue of *Town & Country* when she heard the screaming from outside. Frightened, she hustled to answer the door, only to come face to face with what looked like a lumberjack ready to remove her head with both hands.

Upon seeing her, the man calmed down slightly, and explained to Barbara that racy photos of his 19-year-old daughter had appeared on a website whose headquarters were listed at this address. And he was there, he told her in no uncertain terms, to make sure they got taken down.

Barbara, mortified, apologized to the man profusely. She let him know that Portnoy wasn't there, but "He's my daughter's boyfriend, and I will make sure they are deleted, today."[1]

---

1   The quotes on this page (and the previous one) are based on Portnoy's explanation of what happened. And the Satterthwaite home is based on its current listing, so it is possible the house looked different when Portnoy was there.

The father didn't thank her, but instead informed her that if they weren't off the site by sundown, well, that was going to be a big problem for everyone involved. He wasn't planning on going to the police, he said. And that wasn't meant to reassure her.

Dave Portnoy poured himself a brimming glass of chocolate milk. The 30-year-old blogger was dressed in his usual workday attire, baggy sweatpants and a Patriots t-shirt. His gut hanging out beneath the grey chin of the Pats logo, Portnoy spun the top back onto the jug and placed it back into his fridge. Technically, it was his girlfriend Renee's parents' fridge.

Renee Satterthwaite first met Portnoy when she was working for a modeling agency in Boston. It was the same company Dave had hired to hand out his papers for less than two weeks, and after McShay had the brilliant idea of telling Dave he should hang out with the models he was employing, Renee and Dave hit it off.

Satterthwaite wasn't anything remotely like the man she was dating, who was six years her senior; she was an attractive brunette with a wide smile who also happened to be a skilled equestrian rider. She was *classy*. But there was something about the bawdy entrepreneur that Renee was drawn to: "I always thought he was really funny, he was like no one I had ever met before, [but] I was a little bit confused (as to) what he was doing, what this business plan was all about."

After Portnoy moved out of his studio apartment in South End (and ditched the goatee), Renee offered her parents' house as a refuge. Dave was able to live rent-free with some semblance of privacy, thanks to the Satterthwaites' barn, which basically split the house into two separate living units. Keeping his expenses down was a critical requirement at this point in Dave's venture, because although Barstool's website was growing nicely, he still wasn't making enough money to survive comfortably on his own. (And he continued to print his newspaper, which was a cash-zapper.) But staying at the

Satterthwaites' came with strings attached, one of them being he wasn't allowed to let angry fathers of the hot girls he posted on his website show up at their front door:

> "Chalk up another milestone for the Stool. Yup, for the first time in the long and illustrious history of Barstool Sports we had an angry dad show up at our World Headquarters in Abington on Saturday. Luckily or unluckily however you look at it, I wasn't around to greet him. But the report I got from the First Lady's family is that he was none too happy about his daughter being featured as a Local Smokeshow of the Day... he decided to take the law into his own hands by coming to beat me up. And people think it's easy being a smut publisher? It's not all photo shoots, gumdrops, and candy canes. Anyway, I still have conflicting emotions over these types of altercations. I mean I kind of sympathize with the plight of angry dads who don't like seeing sexy pictures of their daughters floating around on the Internet. But at the same time I really don't think we're to blame. I mean we don't take the pictures. We don't upload the pictures to the Internet...The fact is that tons of people are already looking at these photos with or without us, but that doesn't stop angry dads from projecting their anger on us.
>
> "As a side note, there is no faster way to get me to take down photos of Smokeshows than to get the First Lady's family involved. I can only take the scowls and disapproving looks for so long. Trust me when I say there is nothing worse than the old 'My daughter dates a smut publisher' eyes."

Several weeks before this incident, Portnoy had begun posting pictures of attractive female college students on his website, under the feature "Local Smokeshow of the Day." While it seemed to be a small addition to his publication, this minor tweak proved to be one of the most consequential moves Portnoy would make while running Barstool. Back in 2008, social media platforms like Facebook made the primal ritual of ogling at *local* girls much more challenging; it required being connected. And though Instagram was an easier place to do this, the platform wouldn't begin melting people's brains until two years later in 2010. Dave's "Local Smokeshow of the Day" filled this void for his mostly male readers.[2]

Much like four years earlier, when Portnoy decided to put local models on the cover of his newspaper, the Smokeshow link was sent along to friends of friends who knew of the girl Portnoy chose to post, and in turn introduced new readers to the Stool. This type of organic marketing helped Portnoy grow his site without a budget, only this time the net effect was magnified thanks to the magic of the internet. And Barstool began to spread outside Boston; by the end of 2010, Portnoy's site would see 2.4M monthly unique visitors, a more than 20x increase from 2006.[3]

The move was part of a broader strategy by Portnoy to overhaul his website—one that looked like a real blog now with a clean background and posts stacked on top of one another—and focus on the one thing he knew his audience wanted...sex. Around 2008, a local Bostonian named Adam Cormack joined the team. Cormack was a heavyset friend of Jerry Thornton and posted under the pseudonym "Uncle Buck"; his role was to hypersexualize Portnoy's site. Buck began posting features like "Wake Up With" which allowed viewers to click through a catalogue of pictures of a particular celebrity or model to start their day. "No one has ever been as good at their job as Buck was at finding pictures of hot women," Portnoy joked. The "Guess That Ass" feature became another staple of Barstool, where users would see a thumbnail of a cropped behind and had to click in to see who it belonged to. And they did. While some would call this

---

2   At first, Portnoy would ask for permission to post the Local Smokeshow of the Day. He eventually abandoned this requirement.

3   This was in part due to the New York expansion.

strategy picking the low-hanging fruit, Portnoy didn't care whether he picked that fruit out of a pile of dog shit as long his site was seeing traffic. He'd deal with whatever criticism came the Stool's way:

"Since the addition of Uncle Buck to the Barstool Sports family, many Stoolies have noticed an increase in tits and ass appearing on the Barstool website. Not coincidently we have received the obligatory emails saying that the Stool is sexist and that we objectify women, blah, blah, blah. We even had "Dr. Degeneracy" launch a craigslist campaign to through [sic] all our smut rags in the trash. Here is my whole take on this issue and if I can succinctly write what I am trying to say here [then] I probably deserve a Pulitzer. Anyway, I don't think there is any difference between great athletes and great looking girls. In my mind they are both just freaks of nature. And they are both worshipped in our society for being freaks. Honestly, what's the difference between being born with the ability to throw a fastball 98 mph or being born with an ass that won't stop? Also, in both cases you need to develop your natural gifts or they'll become useless. And just like how people have stereotypes of hot chicks, people have stereotypes of athletes i.e., stupid athlete, stupid blond. But for some reason nobody ever accuses people of objectifying great athletes when you stick them on a cover of a magazine. You only hear that shit when you stick hot chicks on magazines. If you ask me it's a total double standard and makes no sense. Why would anybody care that we think a girl is hot? How is that objectifying women? We're not saying anything about her intelligence, personality or anything else. We're just saying she's a smoke show and love looking at her. If somebody thought I was good looking enough to be on the cover of a magazine and chicks said they wanted to bang me, I'd be totally cool with it."

Portnoy certainly wasn't afraid to speak honestly about his feelings on women and to defend why he placed them front and center on his website. As captain of the renegade Barstool ship, he could write and post whatever he pleased; there were no governing bodies overseeing what was broadcast over the internet; there were no rules. And while other digital media companies like Deadspin took advantage of this and were also seen as below board by conventional critics, it seemed as if Portnoy went a step further (or lower, depending on how one viewed them), in massaging the male psyche that just wanted to laugh at tasteless humor and stare at hot women. Former Deadspin editor Tommy Craggs reflected on the positioning of the two companies in the digital landscape at the time; "It was hard for [Daulerio, the former Deadspin editor-in-chief] to say that there was something beneath us, and in that way, there was some ground ceded to Barstool."

As Portnoy leaned into smut, with no one to answer to, sometimes his writing crossed lines that he definitely wouldn't cross today:

"Ideally you want to fall somewhere in the neighborhood of 6-8 sexual assault complaints. That means you probably threw a great party.

"Bottom line is that chicks that aren't prepared to be sexually assaulted just a little bit shouldn't go on pub crawls to begin with. And they certainly shouldn't go on bar crawls with the Worm.

"I know everybody thinks I hate women and am a male chauvinist pig, blah, blah, blah. Wrong. I only hate fat chicks.

"Eva Longoria is a little slut bag.

"Paulina is on the right. I need my dick inside of her now. End of blog."

This was sort of par for the course when it came to entertaining a certain faction of the internet during that time. And while Deadspin didn't participate as often, it was still guilty of similar behavior; "I did gay jokes. I did rape jokes," former Deadspin editor Drew Magary admitted. But Magary added, "I don't want to make those jokes anymore." Barry Petchesky, another former editor at Deadspin, wrote the following in a comment on the Deadspin site: "It's not rape, it's surprise sex."

In 2008, Portnoy was not alone in using this sort of vernacular. But as The Stool became more popular in the region, because of his emphasis on "locker-room talk" and plastering his site with attractive women, for those in the Northeast who weren't fans of the site, Barstool Sports started to become a symbol of everything that was wrong with your typical male blog, as this comment reveals:

"To Whom It May Concern:

"I would like to let the webmaster of barstoolsports.com know that he is no better than somebody who runs a pornographic website. This evening, I was looking over my son's shoulder as he was on barstoolsports and I was absolutely appalled at what I was seeing. Elpresidente, or whatever your real name is, you have absolutely no respect for women at all."

And there were others who were concerned about having photos of young, local women on the site:

"Dear Webmaster at Barstoolsports,

"I came across your website and saw an article titled 'Why Don't We Cover Bentley University?' The article mentions one of my players and has a picture of her on the site. Many of the comments are offensive and concern me because I am her coach."[4]

In the spring of 2008, someone who was worried about the number of what they called "prejudiced remarks" made by Portnoy registered the web domain www.bostonbigots.com to redirect to the official Barstool page. Portnoy, as he usually did and still does today, denied his writing was prejudiced:

> "Does anybody know who this is? And is James saying that I write prejudiced shit or is he saying that our readers say this stuff?... I certainly don't think we deserve to have boston-bigots.com redirect to our site. I guess the only thing left to do is just to call up James and ask him to take it down. And we'll have to keep on calling him and emailing him until he does so. Feel free to do the same."

Aside from questionable writing, Portnoy would post items on his website that he wouldn't and couldn't post today, which included leaked nude photographs of college girls who dated popular Division 1 quarterbacks. That was the case with Amanda Marsh at Auburn University:[5]

"From: Amanda Marsh

"Subject: This is Amanda Marsh

"Those images that you are spreading around the internet are me and Max's personal photos and were obtained by a hacker from my myspace account. I'm asking you nicely to please remove all those images. This is unfair and I do not deserve this. I'm writing you this e-mail in tears as I have

---

4   There was also some backlash from Boston College when one of their law students posed for Portnoy's paper.

5   I changed Amanda's name, her boyfriend's name, and their school.

never been so embarrassed and violated ever in my life. Please just be a good person and remove them or this will get very ugly.

"Those were photos I sent to him during one of our several long-distant [sic] stints. Please, it's been hard enough for us due to the previous weekend and please just leave us alone..."

From: randomthoughts@barstoolsports.com

"Obviously with any email like this we have no way to know who we are talking to. Having said that, we are nice guys. But we turn not nice very fast when people include things like 'this will get very ugly' in their emails. We take this as a threat and as a result feel like our hands our [sic] tied since we are 100% legally in the right and can't run our business motivated by baseless threats.

"The pictures were NOT hacked into as you claim. A reader of ours sent us a link of them. It was a PUBLIC gallery that actually has built-in codes to embed and share photos. This is as clear cut as it gets. You have NO legal ground to tell us to take those down.

"So like I said, the last thing I'd be doing is threatening us. We really could care less about you or the photos. But you're all over the Internet. We didn't go looking for you or the photos. They found us. And now with you threatening us, it almost leaves us no choice but to leave them up."

A sobbing 20-year-old college student begging a 31-year-old Portnoy to take nude photographs of her off his website isn't exactly a scene the face of High Noon malt beverages would want to replicate, and Dave eventually took down the pictures of Amanda:

HOW THE JESTER BECAME KING

"Just another day in the life of El Pres. This is where it gets hairy running a blog like Barstool Sports. I'm always faced with bullshit decisions like these. The bottom-line is that anytime we post anything even remotely interesting there is going to be somebody who is pissed and want to sue my ass. So what would you do if you were me? I don't want to be responsible for making some chick cry her eyes out because we posted naked pictures of her on the internet. But at the same time should I really feel guilty about it? I mean it's 100% her fault."

Where was the line? It's a question Portnoy both pondered and at times flat-out ignored when writing from his girlfriend's barn. He had the luxury of doing the latter, for the time being. While there would be several smaller opposition efforts like the one on Craigslist or BostonBigots.com, as the end of the decade approached and Portnoy's site grew larger, there was another much more organized resistance bubbling just under the surface.

7

25-year-old Kevin Clancy was seated in a cubicle at his big four accounting job in Manhattan. He was a typical-looking white male from Westchester, with a borderline square jaw, greenish-blue eyes (one slightly lazy) and a Johnny Bravo-ish haircut. The Fordham grad was peering over to see if the middle-aged woman next to him had a view of his computer; she didn't, she was busy rearranging the company signage on her desk. *Deloitte*, Clancy thought, *where every day is Monday.*

Clancy turned his eyes towards his own screen. He was inconspicuously refreshing a website called ForSureNot.com. As the owner of the ForSureNot blog, Clancy posted commentary on the latest internet happenings, his thoughts on the Mets, and whatever gripe he had that day about being chained to a cube. Clancy had carved out a nice little niche for himself in the last department. He *hated* his job, and he skillfully employed dark humor when documenting that part of his life. Friends of his in New York City and friends of their friends visited his site mainly for Clancy's stories and the stories others would send him, about what it was like being a "cube monkey":

"April Fools' Day in the Cubes…. Tread Lightly

"Today is the best day of the year in the cubes. April Fools. It's the worst fucking day of your life. Tricked you!

"Nothing worse than April Fools' Day strictly because it gives unfunny people carte blanche to try to be funny. And really, when you boil life down, that's the worst thing there is. Unfunny try hards thinking what they're doing is hysterical when really it's just cringeworthy. You wake up to an email that says work has been canceled and 10 minutes later another email that says 'April Fools.' That's not funny man, you actually just crushed some people's souls.

"Put tape over my mouse and rearrange the letters on my keyboard. Cover my office in Post-its. Make airhorns blast off when I sit down. If you do any of those things, you can rest assured everyone in your office—and most likely your life as you know it—hates your guts.

"As always I want you to tweet me with all the pictures, videos, stories, descriptions of your office's most cringeworthy April Fools' 'pranks.' Send 'em and we'll put together a blog of the best/worst bullshit of the day."

As Clancy put the finishing touches on this latest post, he noticed a new email pop into his inbox. It was from Dave Portnoy, the founder of the only website Clancy spent more time on than his own. Portnoy had recently posted an advertisement calling for New York-based bloggers to join his growing company: he was looking to attract a greater audience in the country's largest city, and having a part of his website solely dedicated to what was going on there seemed like the best way to do this. More than 500 applicants had applied.

Clancy's friends had forced him to send Portnoy an application. To his surprise, Portnoy informed the young accountant that he'd been following him for some time and was a fan of his work. Portnoy offered Clancy a job to write for Barstool—which to Clancy was a step up to "bigger and better things…a job with the best blog on the internet." There was one minor hang-up.

Portnoy was only able to offer him a $25k salary, which in Manhattan would last Clancy about a month. Dave was providing an additional $25k to a young blogger named Keith Markovich, a recent Emory University grad who was also NYC-based. Markovich had sent an application to Portnoy only after his former babysitter forwarded him the Craigslist link for it, and after receiving an offer from Portnoy, he decided to forgo journalism school and write for Barstool because "Blogging for El Pres seemed like it would be way more fun." Since he couldn't decide between the two writers, Clancy and Markovich would essentially be splitting a $50k/year salary, Portnoy said in his email to the ForSureNot blogger. And they would co-run the new NYC arm of Barstool.

This wouldn't be an issue: it wasn't about the money to Clancy. At least not yet. Like the others who joined Portnoy before him, it was about the chance to entertain people and have meaning outside of a monotonous nine to five. It was fun to be creative, to have *talent*. Clancy certainly wasn't going to pass up that opportunity; the last semblance of fun he had at work was when he watched his boss trip over his chair and break his wrist. Even if it meant secretly working a second job, which he did for the next two years before quitting Deloitte and going full-time with the Stool, Clancy was in.

On August 14, 2009, the Barstool NYC site went live. Clancy, writing under the pseudonym "KFC," and Markovich using the moniker "Kmarko," posted their first blogs for the Stoolies. Portnoy's empire was expanding.

8

Chants of "Barstool" rained down from the frat houses lined up along North Pleasant Street at the University of Massachusetts at Amherst. "VIVA LA STOOL" and "Portnoy for President" signs were drawn in large red lettering across bed sheets and hung over outside balconies.

UMass Amherst was hosting Barstool's "Back to Stool," a concert series Portnoy & Co. were throwing across several campuses in New England. And although famous singer Mike Posner wasn't set to perform until later that night, the Stoolies at ZooMass (an apt nickname) were already partying.

Anyone walking by would have thought the school had traveled back in time to Woodstock '69. Flocks of 18- to 22-year-olds gathered at Hobart Lane in a large field behind frat row, spraying each other with beer and flinging bottles high into the air with no regard for where they landed. Students were taking turns sliding through the mud. Dave and his crew were in the thick of it, tossing ping pong balls into red Solo cups and appeasing the large crowds that gathered around them by chugging whatever they were holding. He wasn't a big drinker, but on that day, Portnoy drank like the plane was going down.

It was both a raucous and bizarre scene, and a sign the internet had officially changed the entertainment landscape. At the time, bloggers were typically thought of as low-life basement dwellers, typing with Cheetos dust on their fingers while lounging in their underwear. And now here was Portnoy, a 33-year-old blogger—whose fanbase up until recently consisted of Stoolies mostly around his age—showing up to a college party where he had at least ten years on everyone in attendance, and he was being treated like a rockstar. *What planet was he on?* Portnoy thought:

> "The college tour was one of the first eye-opening moments. We had never been to a college campus before, and it was like the Beatles showed up. People had Barstool signs in the windows, and they were rushing at the buses. That's when I knew we had another way to make money."

As nighttime approached, drunken students began to stagger en masse over to the Mullins Center, where Posner was set to perform. Just before taking the stage to introduce the musician to the 5,000 person-crowd, UMass police told Portnoy to calm down his fans and demanded he order them to return to their dorms immediately following the concert. The chaotic situation was bordering on dangerous. Portnoy, wearing a neon-yellow Barstool hat at a slight angle (whether to appear younger or because by that point he was more than a little buzzed), walked out and grabbed the microphone.

> "The cops told us to not go out...we're fucking going out!"

The crowd erupted. And for the next five hours, Portnoy and Barstool burnt down UMass. The local paper reported on the aftermath:

> "Police arrested 15 UMass students in Amherst on Friday. '[The students] developed a mob mentality and started standing their ground, chanting, throwing bottles at police,' said Amherst Police Captain Chris Pronovost. Police used pepper spray to tame Friday's unruly crowd."

In the days following what can only be described as a bacchanal, police informed the Barstool founder that if he ever stepped foot on campus again, he'd be arrested on sight.

♣

By the fall of 2010, Portnoy was working out of an actual office in Milton, MA. The outside of the nondescript, two-story building looked like a duplex apartment one might find on the outskirts of a major city, with a simple white wooden roof and a red brick base. Portnoy's new workplace sat close to the main road that ran through downtown—so close, in fact, that an old woman crashed her car into the front steps twice. Yes, it was the same lady.

The $900/month space fit the bootstrapped company perfectly. There were squirrels living in the walls, and because Portnoy decided an old dentist's office would be his new headquarters, there were random sinks in every room. On the first floor of Barstool HQ was a narrow common space with desks lined up along the wall, above which hung posters of *Maxim* girls and Barstool paraphernalia. A short, carpeted staircase led up to Portnoy's office, which featured a desk, an air conditioner from the 1970s, a side-room where he stored all of his unsold Barstool t-shirts, and a dimly lit bathroom. (Dave did not let his employees use his bathroom; they shared a tiny one downstairs.) But most noticeable was the random assortment of trash, food, and clothes scattered throughout both floors. The office was a dump, but it was still an office, one Barstool would call home for the next six years.

"The Milton working conditions were less than ideal," according to Paul Gulczynski (known as Gaz), one of Barstool's first paid employees. "We had no AC. No internet (pretty much). In the summertime, stink bugs would just take over the lights in our ceilings."

"One day, it just rained bugs," John Feitelberg, another Milton office employee said.

"There are no worse conditions to start a company in that what we had," Gaz added, "So when I come into our office now and I see snacks and water, I'm like holy shit, we fucking made it."

The success of the Barstool-produced "Stoolapalooza" concert series several months earlier had allowed Portnoy to make this move. Ever the entrepreneur, Portnoy decided to start throwing concerts at local colleges due to the growing number of younger readers that visited his website: by now, the 18- to 34-year-old demographic was his largest audience. It was an unexpected development for Dave as he peered through web traffic statistics, and one Portnoy knew he needed to monetize.

> "**STOOLAPALOOZA TICKET UPDATE**—In case you've been living in a cave, Stoolapalooza is getting ready to kick off this Friday at Lupo's.[1] Tickets are starting to run low at Lupo's, so if you haven't bought them yet, I highly suggest doing so. Also UMass already basically sold out. We had to revamp our entire plan and add more seats. In other words, tickets are starting to fly everywhere."

It was an outside-the-box move for an internet company to throw in-person concerts, but Portnoy needed to make money; he didn't care how. And in setting up that first concert series, the Barstool founder paid local rapper Sam Adams $20,000 to perform a total of six shows, at UMass Amherst, University of New Hampshire, Providence College, and University of Rhode Island—as well as two others in New Haven and downtown Boston. All six were low budget, produced by Dave and his crew. All six sold out.

> "[The first show] was fucking bonkers. Bottom line is this, when the Pres says something is fucking hot, you better fucking believe it's hot. That's what I do. That's my business. Fuck underground rappers and paying your dues. We're above ground, motherfucker!... Is it possible I'm a better

---

1   Lupo's was a live music venue near Providence College; it's now called Strand Ballroom.

promoter than blogger? Bottomline is Stoolapalooza is rapidly becoming the toughest ticket to get in New England."

When the venture was over, Portnoy walked away with a six-figure profit, by far the most money he'd ever had in his bank account. Not that he knew what to do with it:

> "I [now] just have a mishmash of bills, expenses, and invoices that all blend together. And like any good businessman, I combine my personal expenses with my business expenses, so it's almost impossible to figure out what's going on."

Portnoy was becoming a hit among the younger generation because unlike their parents, or even Portnoy himself, those college students were much more internet savvy, having been raised in front of a computer. And by 2010, they were increasingly turning away from the TV and towards the web—where Portnoy had planted his flag—for their entertainment, which by that point was a much more content-rich experience.

Following the rise of the smartphone, now everyone carried a camera in their pocket, which meant the number of entertaining videos on the web exploded. Every other blog post now featured a video embedded inside; there was more to comment on, more to shock readers with, more to post about. And thanks to the loyal community Portnoy had built the Barstool brand around since he wrote that first newspaper article, and almost as an "F-you" to larger, more mainstream media sites, Barstool fans sent clips they either took or found in a remote area of the internet exclusively to Barstool. Portnoy's site featured videos no one else had.

Even if Barstool wasn't the only blog with a certain compelling video, like the infamous Grape Lady Falling (*owwwwwwww ow ow ow ow*) or a man with no arms freaking out in the lobby of a Miami hotel, the commentary from Portnoy—who while nearing the end range of the 18-34 demo could still relate to younger readers—was going to make them laugh.

Another reason this audience tuned in so heavily was Dave's growing commitment to the El Presidente persona. Video turned Dave into a true *character*. In one of his more famous productions, Portnoy dressed up in a tuxedo and surfed the then-popular web app Chat Roulette, which matched people up with strangers via video chat. This led to several ridiculous interactions, as those paired with Portnoy were repeatedly outwitted by what appeared to be a butler with a Boston accent.

These types of videos would become more and more popular on the Barstool Sports site: whether it was a fat Portnoy training for a Spartan race, him slowly falling over into a pool and asking viewers to rate his "dive," or Dave confidently blind taste-testing McDonald's, Burger King. and Wendy's only to be completely wrong, the Barstool founder officially became an internet personality. Unlike the writers at Deadspin or BroBible, Portnoy wasn't just a byline.

"El Pres is a character Dave plays," Thornton has said. "Dave's one of the most regular, nondescript guys going, and I mean that as a compliment."

"There are times when you talk to Dave and there are times when you talk to El Presidente," Mo Peebles, another eventual writer for Barstool, added on this dynamic. "And you can kind of see those differences."

"I would get emails from Dave where he would be like 'Jesus Christ Feitelberg, you might be the first person to actually get fired,' Feitelberg explained, "And I would laugh at them because I only knew Dave as the character. And then I met him and I was like, oh no, those emails were dead serious, and I just skated by them."

And as internet culture began to bleed into real life, Portnoy was now getting stopped in downtown Boston by fans of Barstool. Dave was locally famous thanks to his site garnering over two million unique visitors a month—which was more than that of national magazine websites such as *Rolling Stone* or *GQ*—with a majority of them coming from the greater Boston area. "It takes me 45 minutes to walk down Lansdowne Street," Portnoy said at the time. His fans wanted to see what El Pres was like in the flesh. But Portnoy, when reflecting on this development, states he never intended to become an internet celebrity, a title that was still in its early days of existence: "I always looked at [Barstool] from a business perspective, like, 'How can I make money from this?'" Being a personality that fans were invested in was an unplanned happening; "The things that people responded to the most were stories from my personal life, so I just followed [that]."

Following the move to Milton, and with the growing sensation of his now multi-city website, Dave began winding down his once heavily read newspaper. The time and cost of that operation when compared with the blog eventually made this decision an easy one (he probably could have made it sooner), and the last physical issue of *Barstool Sports* would be released towards the end of 2011 after an eight-year run.

Two of the original four newspaper writers, Jamie Chisholm and Pete Manzo, never made it to Milton. As the website became the sole focus of Portnoy's operation, Chisholm and Manzo had struggled to keep up. Both were extremely skilled in long-form writing, which fit the paper nicely but wasn't ideal for blogging. The posts being deployed onto the Barstool Sports website became much shorter and more frequent, and the pair's skillset didn't translate to Portnoy's new formula. Ironically, it was the 40-year-old core-four member Jerry Thornton who adapted best to this new style of writing, and Thornton, who never physically worked out of the Milton office, remains with Barstool to this day.[2,3]

---

2   Both Manzo and Chisholm would return for a short stint in 2011 but would leave again.

3   Uncle Buck left the site in 2011.

Aside from the squirrels, in 2010 Portnoy shared the dinky office in Milton with several new faces, starting with Devlin "The Intern Slave" D'Zmura, a student at UMass whom Portnoy had hired before Stoolapalooza to help sell tickets on campus. D'Zmura, a roundish 20-year-old with dark hair and a scraggly dark beard that screamed 'I play video games,' landed the gig with Dave because he showed up to the interview wearing a tuxedo, an homage to his "Chat Roulette" videos (he was also able to locate an obscure online video for Portnoy). D'Zmura broadened Portnoy's portfolio of posts by providing "Devlin's Links of the Day," a set of URLs that led to content he knew people his age would enjoy. Besides basically doubling his employee count, Devlin's addition reaffirmed Barstool's newfound focus on catering to the college crowd.

Portnoy also made his first attempt to capture the female audience around this time when a young woman named Jenna Mourey joined the Milton office. Known as "Jenna Marbles" in the Barstool world, Mourey was a recent grad of Suffolk University; before meeting Portnoy, she "worked in a fucking tanning salon." Or at least that's how Dave described her.[4]

At first, Mourey was a perfect fit for the Stool: she was an attractive blonde with a sailor mouth and was tough enough to take any harassment or overly aggressive compliment (depending on one's interpretation) from the male-dominated keyboard warriors known as Stoolies. When Portnoy realized Marbles was actually a solid writer, he put Jenna in charge of her own website under the Barstool umbrella.

> "Well stoolies, it's been real. I will be parting ways with Barstool Sports, but not completely. Dave has decided to give me my own blog on our new site Stoollala.com. It's basically a girl version of Barstool but with more gossip

---

4   Barstool had a female writer before Marbles. A woman named Kati Cawley wrote for the newspaper for a while.

and girl stuff that none of you guys care about. The good news is you never have to read another one of my terrible posts again on Barstool. Thank you for those of you with enough hate in your hearts to let me know how retarded I am and how I should just show you my tits and shut the fuck up. Well, your wish has been granted, minus showing you my tits."

Around the time of launching Stool-La-La (stoolala.com was the URL), Marbles posted a video on YouTube called "How to Trick People into Thinking You're Good Looking." It was a makeup tutorial, the premise of which was pretty self-explanatory. To the shock of both Marbles and Portnoy, the video went immensely viral, racking up 3 million views (a massive number back in 2010) over the first few days it was online.

While YouTube had become an important platform, the idea of a video "going viral" was still a relatively new phenomenon at the time; there simply hadn't been many that achieved such status, unlike today where all one has to do is open TikTok or Instagram and see hundreds of clips with view counts well into the millions. Because it meant so much more to accumulate that many impressions, Marble's video became somewhat of a sensation: news outlets across the country, and even abroad, were calling to speak with her.

After the first phone call came in, Marble's relationship with Portnoy was never the same. She began focusing her attention on her own YouTube page, which drove Portnoy bonkers. The pair argued both in the Milton office and on Portnoy's website about who was responsible for her sudden success: was it Jenna or Barstool? She was propped up by the platform Dave had built with his bare hands—Portnoy had made Jenna post the video on Barstool's site—but would she have gone as viral as she had without Portnoy's ready-made following? Jenna believes she would have:

"So me and Prezzy have always had this debate: would my "How to Trick People" video have gone viral without Barstool? Prez always says that if Barstool hadn't posted it, no one would have seen it and that's the whole reason it went viral…. The first place the video was ever posted was on my Facebook wall and didn't go up on Barstool until later that evening… But I will say that I know the majority of people who watch my videos are female, I tell you guys all the time I have the hottest girl fans on planet earth. If Barstool made this video go viral, yet made up a whopping 1% of views in the first week (when it quote "went viral") then how did so many girls see and share the video via social media…Last time I checked, I didn't know Barstool Sports was mostly female readers…"

This would become a central battle Portnoy fought on numerous occasions while growing his digital media company. As social media and other online technologies advanced, content creators began to have more direct access to their audiences, which gave the companies they worked for less leverage over them. Portnoy walked this line more carefully in later years, but in this first instance, after offering Jenna 100% ownership of the Stool-La-La site, Portnoy wasn't able to keep his talent from leaving Milton in 2011.

"Per Jenna's blog trashing me yesterday Stoollala is dead. I actually wrote a long rant in response, but I didn't want to make people cry so I just bit my tongue on this issue which I never do. I'll just wish Jenna best of luck in her new endeavors. Peace out, homey…Nobody better than you…."

And Marbles ended up being quite a large talent at that. She became one of the most famous internet personalities in the country and one of the biggest stars to ever work at Barstool. Portnoy definitely in no way was bitter about this:

"This whole Jenna Marbles thing is an act. It's a fake person. Somebody she apparently has to pretend to be every time she goes outside in public. It would be like Will Ferrell having to be Ron Burgundy in public for the rest of his life. I'd hang myself. That's the good thing about Barstool…. There is literally no acting involved. What you see is what you get. Jenna has to morph into this fake weirdo character that 12-year-old girls expect to see. I wouldn't wish that on my worst…. Wait a minute…. She made 10 million dollars this year? 10 million fucking dollars! Fuck me. Umm, never mind. Now excuse me while I go claw my eyeballs out. Somebody buy a freaking t-shirt."

Aside from a carousel of less-than-brilliant interns rotating through (one tried fixing Portnoy's air conditioner by stabbing it with a pair of scissors), the eclectic foursome that occupied the Milton office in 2010 was rounded out by one of the first employees Portnoy ever officially hired, Paul "Gaz" Gulczynski. Portnoy met the tall, thin, balding Gulczynski through his then-girlfriend Renee (Dave and Renee would get married in 2009). "I went to high school with Renee, and she told me she went out on some date with some guy named Barstool-something, and I was like 'Oh I know that newspaper, it's kinda shitty: they don't do like any editing or anything like that.'" Gaz was a few years younger than Portnoy and eventually became a serial attender of Barstool's parties in downtown Boston. "As it got bigger, I was like do you need help like operationally? And he's like 'I can't pay you, so you'd have to do sales to be able to pay your salary.'"

By the time Portnoy moved his operation to Milton, Gulczynski had been working at Barstool for a short while as the only non-writer to join the crew, and as he explained, one of the first to be "paid" by Portnoy. Gaz became known as *Sales Guy* to the Stoolies, though Portnoy would often state he didn't really sell anything, ever. "This is our sales guy, but he hasn't sold anything yet," Portnoy relayed to his fans while giving a tour of the Milton office. It became a recurring joke later on that Gaz rode Portnoy's coattails. Because Gaz attended Figawi, the largest party weekend in Nantucket, well into his 30s, Portnoy often declared, "I work hard so [Gaz] can enjoy his life."[5]

Despite the ribbing from Portnoy, Gulczynski did take his sales role seriously, going door-to-door pitching the Barstool newspaper to local businesses and cold-calling larger advertisers as the website grew. Gaz had his work cut out for him; Centerfolds Strip Club in downtown Boston told him they would only advertise if Barstool could wrangle 40 people to go to its club that weekend, and Boston.com wouldn't let him pay *them* to advertise Barstool on *their* site. Similar to when Portnoy was pitching on his own when he first started his company, the Barstool sales role at the beginning of Gaz's tenure was still very much an uphill battle.

Portnoy provides an anecdote to explain Gaz's rocky start:

"Paul came in and was like, 'Hey, I'll sell t-shirts for you.' Alright, Paul, here's some t-shirts: go sell 'em. He walked to Fenway Park, where they told him he needed a license to be there. He came back 10 minutes later and said, 'Oh, I can't sell t-shirts.' And I was like, 'I had 3,000 t-shirts made, what do you want me to do, Paul? I bought them for you to sell.' He was like, 'Oh. I can't do that. I thought I could.'"

But as time went on, "Sales went well, comparably. It was a little bit of a chase for a while, and then I came on full-time," Gaz explains. By 2010, advertising for the Barstool website had begun to increase, thanks to total ad spend online hitting $28B that year, but more important was Barstool's positioning inside the growing industry. As Portnoy explained at the time, "There are almost no other websites that have

---

5   Portnoy hired a man named Phil Norton for sales before Gaz was in charge, but he didn't last very long.

the type of readership we do. [Advertisers] should be like, 'That's why I need to be on that site. Because if he [Portnoy] says something or does something, the readers react to it."

The number Portnoy was starting to be able to demand for space on his site wasn't insignificant, as seen in the email he sent in August to Clancy and Markovich, the New York-based bloggers:

"I met with NY guy today. Kind of a weird bird and all over the joint but definitely interested. I think they'll make a significant buy for 2011. Maybe "fingers crossed" enough to pay a good portion of both your salaries. 40-60K range with parties. Here is his email to follow up with him in NYC."

Of course, Dave accidentally sent that email to the advertiser himself, and in an unexpected turn of events, he didn't end up spending with Barstool.

Portnoy wouldn't hit reply-all on every ad deal however; thanks to the ones that actually materialized, and as previously mentioned, the ticket sales from his college concert series, by the end of the decade, Portnoy's website was making enough money for him to move out of his in-laws' and into an apartment in Dorchester—a five-minute walk from the new Barstool headquarters. (Portnoy was also now driving an Audi Quattro.) As more and more eyeballs turned toward his digital content, the financial prospects of the Barstool venture were looking up:

"Wait, what? The Big Lead just sold for over a million dollars? Umm, I'm pretty sure Barstool Sports has more traffic than them. Not a shit-ton more, but more. At least by all the metrics I see. So does that mean I'm worth a million bucks? I think it fucking does, right? HAHAHA, Manzo, you fucking idiot! Way to bail after 5 years, right when the going is getting good.

"So what happens now? Do I just sit by my phone and wait for the offers to roll in? I think that's how it works, right? I mean, after all, I'm rich with writing abilities, flush with blogging expertise, and extremely well off when it comes to smut. So I guess if you're interested, just call 1-800-Pay Me and let's get this shit done. And if you don't mind Mr. rich dude who is going to make me a rich dude please hurry. I'm sick of entertaining these assholes. Just kidding. I love our readers. At least until I sell this bitch."

9

Two hundred miles south down I-95, Clancy and Markovich were beginning to hit their respective strides as co-heads of Barstool's New York arm. As Clancy explained:

> "It was the golden years of blogging, when you'd put up a post and people would give you positive feedback. Now the internet and Twitter, everyone is so negative, but [back then] we knocked it out of the park."

This was no easy feat: The Big Apple was a completely different animal than Beantown. NYC didn't have the same local feel as the much-smaller city of Boston, where happenings such as Barstool spread fast among like-minded residents. New York was a much more diverse community, and that made the process of building an audience slower and tougher.

But Portnoy's bi-city model provided a new element of entertainment, one that KFC, who would become the #1 guy in New York, and Kmarko utilized in those initial days: a rivalry between the Boston and NYC bloggers. More specifically, between Portnoy and Clancy.

> "You have gotta be the biggest asshole in the history of Boston, Dave."
>
> —@KFCBarstool

> "Only way that asshole gremlin Portnoy has had the success he's had? Sold his soul to the devil."
>
> —@KFCBarstool

"Don't mean to make this philosophy class, but world is about balance. KFC is a loser. His teams should always lose. Everything at peace now."

—@stoolpresidente

"@KFCBarstool And I get the hate. When your entire life is a punching bag, you need to get your punches in when you can. That's what the peanut gallery does."

—@stoolpresidente

Ever since he posted the infamous John Dennis voicemail on his website, Portnoy had envisioned Barstool living in a WWE-like world. And now he had created one. Fans were enamored with the faces of the Stool sticking by their respective cities, ripping each other when the opposing side lost, because that's exactly what they did with their friends at the bar. Though it was very much a one-sided battle; Clancy's Jets and Mets were consistently horrible, and he became—as Portnoy put it—a punching bag for Boston fans, whose Patriots and Red Sox (and Bruins) dominated during that time.

And the pair's battle would transcend sports; KFC became Portnoy's foil, and vice-versa. Since he was technically the second guy behind Portnoy, fans looked to him to push back against Portnoy and he did, mostly during their eventual face-to-face Barstool Radio show: "I hated Kevin during that," Dave said on an episode of *The Dave Portnoy Show*. Clancy would continue to call Portnoy "an asshole," and though on one segment of radio in 2018, Portnoy would go so far as to call KFC, "a friend" (in a reluctant tone), outside of Barstool Radio, the two rarely interacted. And that continued to the present day. When Clancy went on Portnoy's show in 2022, the pair had the following exchange:

Eddie (host): So where are you two at, how often do you guys interact?

Portnoy: Never.

Clancy: The Monday rundowns are the most interaction we've had in a couple years. The best way I can put it is Monday of Super Bowl week he was like 'Where are you? We need to do the rundown,' and he didn't even know I didn't travel out with everyone to the Super Bowl.

Back when the New York site launched, Clancy and Markovich sent Portnoy blogs they were planning on posting. Dave edited them, gave feedback on what jokes he thought worked, and provided tips on how to craft their Barstool voice. That lasted about a week. Much like how he operated with his three original newspaper writers, Portnoy was hands-off as a boss, an approach that gave his employees creative freedom and at the same time occasionally landed the company in hot water—at least hotter than what the Vince McMahon wannabe was looking for.

Left to his own devices, Clancy adopted a "I don't give a shit" attitude about offending anyone who read his writing. He cornered the market on white privileged male humor. At times even more so than Portnoy, Clancy tested the limits of what was politically appropriate to post on the internet in the name of comedy:

"If I was Jewish, I would kill myself"

—@KFCBarstool

"Why I love Barstool. I point blank said I don't like Jews in my Xmas movie blog and the thing that has ppl angry is not liking Xmas vacation."

—@KFCBarstool

"We lost to Honduras in soccer? Do they even have food in Honduras?"

—@KFCBarstool

"So the US Soccer team lost yesterday to fucking Honduras. They're like the worst team in the United States' group and now we gotta play all the good teams and we might not even make the World Cup or some shit. Fucking Honduras! I think I "sponsor" their goalie for like 60 cents a day! Anyway, I sent this tweet out, and the people of Honduras are none too pleased with me… Fuck you, Honduras! All your plantains and huts and shit. Kind of a milestone for me. First time I've taken my hate international…Just taking this hate fest overseas one ignorant comment at a time."

Clancy also directed this "hater" persona towards other communities. One memorable battle he fought was against probably the most unlikely group a writer could offend: the blind. An online article described how a baby of two hard-of-seeing parents was being taken away from them by the state, and Clancy sympathized with the government, agreeing with them that the parents were unfit to raise the child. To his surprise, there were a number of blind fans who followed Barstool and were actually able to read his writing. This group rallied against him in the comment section of Portnoy's site. *You can't make this shit up*, Clancy thought. When he learned these readers, or "Blindos" as Clancy called them, were using a text-to-speech software to consume Barstool content, he posted a blog containing sentences with misspelled letters that people with normal eyesight could understand, but those using text-to-speech would not. "Here's a completely misspelled sentence, good luck reading this," he wrote.

While this sort of humor was mean-spirited and undoubtably nasty, the 20-something-year-old white males living in the greater NY area who read Barstool found it mostly hilarious. "The Blindos blog set the tone early on for me," Clancy says. But eventually, Clancy's writing would drag Barstool into the one arena Portnoy did not want to do battle: the courtroom.

A Jersey City man was in the local news for losing a $4M lottery ticket on the city bus, and Clancy decided to put his own comedic spin on the situation for the Barstool readers. After the man, Isaac Mendez, sued the state over the lost winnings, Clancy posted the following headline:

"Jersey City Pedophile Loses His $4 Million Lotto Ticket, Sues the Whole World."

To Clancy, it was just another anecdote that would make his readers laugh: he thought the man looked like a pedophile. Mr. Mendez didn't get the joke. Instead, he sued Clancy and Barstool Sports to the tune of $100M, for "defamation, negligence, and intentional infliction of emotional distress." (It was really his only move after losing a $4M lottery ticket outside of evaporating into thin air.)

Clancy's "Pedophile sues the world" headline went from offensive to self-fulfilling, and for Portnoy, it became problematic. He consulted with his father, Mike Portnoy, Esq., who reassured him the man had no legal grounds to stand on. Still, being sued for more money than the average person could make in a thousand lifetimes wasn't the best feeling in the world. Meanwhile, in response to the lawsuit, Clancy posted the following:

"I wrote a blog about Isaac Mendez who was suing the NJ Lottery for a lost lotto ticket. The headline of the blog at the time was "Jersey City Pedophile Loses His $4 Million Lotto Ticket, Sues the World." In the first paragraph, I clearly state that I was being satirical in nature with that description of Mr. Mendez. In no way did I intend to infer that Isaac Mendez was ever accused of any deviant behavior or has any criminal record of any sort. For anybody who misunderstood the satirical nature of that blog, please excuse the inconvenience."

It was the first time Dave had been sued for a seriously large amount (he had had some small DCMA copyright squabbles in the past), and if he had to pay anywhere close to that number, he'd be back in Swampscott.[1] But in just one of several lucky breaks Portnoy & Co. received while building Barstool, Mr. Mendez—who was no pedophile—waited too long to file the remaining paperwork for the lawsuit, and by the time he got around to it, the statute of limitations had passed. Clancy was right: Portnoy had made a deal with the devil.

---

1   DCMA stands for Digital Millennium Copyright Act.

10

After seeing the success of the first "Stoolapalooza" concerts with Sam Adams in May, Portnoy doubled down on a second concert series, "Back to Stool." It was no surprise to anyone around him when Dave decided to put pretty much all of his money into this second act. As Dave said in Barstool's documentary series, "I have a gambling personality, [so I thought] if we did 3,000 people with Sam Adams, I'm gonna go hire real talent and go do 8,000 people, and I'm gonna do more shows and bigger venues, and we came back with 'Back to Stool.'" He spent upwards of six figures on booking real talent and an outside production company. Mac Miller, Wale, Chiddy Bang, Mike Posner, and White Panda were some of the famous artists on the Barstool bill. Renee confirmed the cost: "I think we had put up every single dollar known to Barstool sports including our savings, which was Barstool Sports—literally everything was on the line for this."

But unfortunately for Portnoy, the concert series was doomed from the beginning. For one of the first shows in Providence, Chiddy Bang was late showing up to perform. Just hours before they were set to go on stage, Portnoy discovered the group was still in Manhattan. To make matters worse, the band was giving Portnoy shit for not being able to find them a ride. After several unsuccessful attempts to communicate through their agent, Dave blew a gasket: "I yelled at him more and dropped more f-bombs to this guy 'Jessie K' in the span of a five-minute conversation—I was just screaming 'Fuck' at him." Here's how he explained the situation to the Stoolies:

"So 'Back to Stool' sucked last night at Lupo's [the music venue]…it was a total disaster. The crowd sucked. Chiddy Bang didn't show up. Posner's road manager gave me an invoice one second before Posner was due to go on stage for $4,000 in expenses, which I'd never seen before and didn't know was coming and threatened that Posner wouldn't play if I didn't pay it on the spot. Keep in mind, I never disputed that I owed expenses. I just wanted to check their invoice with my records like a normal human being before paying. And then to top it off, I get home and see Chiddy Bang is bashing me on Twitter for 'screwing the fans and being unorganized.' All in all, probably the most aggravating sur-real life of my night."

While the UMass "Back to Stool" show was bananas—as a result, Dave wasn't allowed to go back there—the rest of the slate was an unmitigated disaster. Portnoy had made a massive miscalculation: although the musicians were much more famous, the same number of people—if not less—bought tickets. "He was hitting that refresh button on the ticket sales and like one would get sold in a day," Renee explained. "And I just kept saying 'it's gonna be ok, it's gonna be ok,' and for the first time, he was like, 'I'm not sure it's actually going to be ok.'" Also, because he had hired better-known talent, Portnoy had spent a fortune booking larger venues, at around $100,000 per spot. "We got fucking wiped out. It was a disaster," he says.

After the Providence show meltdown, Dave continued to torch Chiddy Bang on his blog: "You're not the fucking Beatles!" And Mike Posner, who he claimed had the stage presence of *an ant* and didn't promote the show at all. Portnoy trashed pretty much everyone involved in the catastrophe:

"If you don't like hearing me bitch about shit, today is not the day to read the Stool. I'm just getting going, mother-fuckers. I'm just getting going."

While Portnoy would vent his frustrations, the hard truth was that sometimes when you bet big, you can lose. Defeated, Portnoy ended up cancelling the remainder of 'Back to Stool.' "There were definitely times Dave was discouraged," Renee says, "I mean, this has been like the craziest evolution ever, so there have been times when things were really scary and we were like very much questioning, was this gonna go bottoms-up?" This was, in fact, one of those times. Devlin described it similarly:

"Dave would like walk into the office. I was like the first one he'd see and, he would just start saying like 'Yeah, well, we're going under. And my wife's certainly not happy. Yeah, no, we're bankrupt. And he'd like say these things not to … scare us; it was just matter of fact Dave [saying] 'oh yeah no, this is over.'"

Following the disaster that was 'Back to Stool,' Clancy, Markovich, Gaz, and the rest of his crew had begun thinking about other employment. It was a fate they all were mentally prepared for: even when things were going relatively well, most everyone working at Barstool thought the venture wasn't going to last—that is, everyone besides Portnoy. It's not that they didn't take it seriously; it's just when they thought about what they were actually doing, posting smut-blogs on a website, well, that didn't exactly scream solid five-year plan. Clancy reflected on this predicament to his fans:

"About every 3 months, I lose my fucking mind because all the shit that bothered me day in and day out finally explodes. It's a quarterly thing. Yesterday was a big one. Realized I'm turning 27 next week and my life is a complete and utter joke. I realized all I do is write blogs all day and then I go out to dinners that are way too expensive for my bank account, booze way too much, and then I wake up and do it all over again. Empty wallet, fat stomach, brain cells diminishing by the millisecond."

At one point during the calamity that had become just trying to survive, Renee made the executive decision that Dave needed to get another job. Portnoy admitted this on an episode of the *Spittin' Chiclets* podcast: "One day, I got a job because we had no money. I took a sales job…and was like, I cannot do both. Barstool has no chance if I have this job. So on day one, I'm like 'alright, I'm going to lunch' and [I] drove away and never came back. That's as close as I was to 'this just isn't working.'"

The "Back to Stool" disaster had put Barstool in a dire financial position. But although they thought about leaving, Portnoy's guys stayed; as Gaz explained: "At the end of the day, 'Back to Stool' was an eye-opening experience. The trajectory of Barstool was something we had to learn, and with failures you learn things; it actually woke us up to like being smarter about what we're doing."

Portnoy also took something from the failed concert series: "I realized then that people weren't showing up for the talent, they were showing up for Barstool." That was a key insight that Portnoy utilized in his next venture. But in the short term, despite what Gaz said about getting smarter, Portnoy would make another misstep at a time when they could least afford it.

11

It was 80 degrees in Boston, which meant it felt more like 95 in the cramped, now-borderline-disgusting Milton office. Portnoy assumed his normal position upstairs, sitting in his black leather swivel chair, neck bent, staring at his computer screen. Empty Dunkin' Donut cups flanked his laptop, along with random assortments of papers and t-shirts.

Summertime meant fewer sports, which meant fewer stories. Portnoy's Red Sox were the sole Boston team in play at this point, sitting atop the AL East at 72-44, just a game ahead of the Yankees. One could only blog so much about baseball, however, and Dave found himself once again browsing through paparazzi photos he could post and dissect for his followers. Barstool readers cared about pop culture as much as they did sports, even if they didn't like to admit it: clicks never lied.

After several minutes of perusing the usual celebrity couple pictures, Portnoy came across one that caught his eye. It was a photo of Gisele Bündchen, Tom Brady's supermodel wife, and their two-year-old son, walking along the water on a beach in Chile. Wearing a scant purple and white bikini, Gisele was holding her toddler's hand, who, because he was a toddler, was naked.

It was innocent enough at first glance. But as Portnoy examined the picture further, he realized he had his next blog:

"Check Out the Howitzer on Brady's Kid," the title of Portnoy's post read.

"That's a big fucking hog for a 2-year-old, right? Just swinging low like a boss. I guess we shouldn't be surprised, though. That's what MVP QBs do. They impregnate chicks and give birth to big-dicked kids. Does Peyton Manning have any children? If he does, I bet they got pencil dicks."

"PS—The mom's ass ain't bad, either. I was going to try to save this for 'Guess That Ass' tomorrow, but just couldn't do it. Not with Brady's kid's dick staring me in the face."

Portnoy checked the time—12 p.m.—and hit *publish*. Onto the next blog.

WEEI's radio station had long been a fixture of Boston. Its history dates all the way back to June 20, 1929, when Ralph Matheson founded the station in Gloucester, Massachusetts. Given Gloucester's presence as an important fishing port, the programming was originally geared solely toward fishermen, mostly providing updates about the weather and where the fish were hiding. Slowly, sports began to make their way onto the station, however, and from 1949 to 1975, WEEI (then known as WHDH) served as the home for Boston Red Sox games.

As sports talk radio began its rise to prominence in the 80s and 90s, in September 1991, WEEI rebranded to an all-sports radio station. Throughout greater Boston, sports-hungry listeners tuned into WEEI in droves to hear discussions (or incoherent screaming, depending on the day) about the current state of their beloved Red Sox, Patriots, Celtics, and Bruins. Two shows in particular, *Dennis and Callahan*, with John Dennis and Gerry Callahan in the morning drive slot and *The Big Show* with Glenn Ordway in the afternoon time frame, helped solidify the station's popularity among local listeners.[1]

Jason Wolfe had been the programming director at WEEI since 1997 and was a driving force behind this growth. A short but broad-shouldered man with thin-rimmed glasses, Wolfe knew how to navigate the passionate and often unforgiving Boston market. Under his guidance as director, for six consecutive years starting in 2002, WEEI finished first in the ratings book. The station conquered new entrants such as WWZN 150 and ESPN 890 with ease; in the 2000s, when someone wanted to listen to Boston sports talk radio, they turned on WEEI.

By 2011, however, another upstart, "98.5 The Sports Hub" had finally become a serious threat to Wolfe and WEEI's reign. The rival station had launched only two years earlier and was already tied with WEEI in the ratings. Wolfe knew the catalyst for this was his station's declining relative performance in the coveted 18- to 34-year-old demographic. He also knew he needed to reverse this alarming trend, before it was too late, and in his desperation, he turned to a man he didn't fully understand.

Starting in the summer of that year, Dave Portnoy was brought on as a regular Friday morning guest on the *Dennis and Callahan* show.[2] Portnoy had a reputation for always speaking his mind; Wolfe had seen the not-so-PG writing in his blog and he wasn't a huge fan. But this wasn't 1997; times had changed. Like it or not, the man had an audience.

The past few months with Portnoy had progressed without any major hiccups. But on the morning of Thursday, August 11, *The Big Show* with Glenn Ordway was on the air when WEEI first caught wind of Portnoy's post about Tom Brady's son. Without hesitation, Ordway began to lambast Portnoy for the blog. The lines lit up with angry callers phoning in to rip Portnoy as a pedophile; while he may

---

1   The same John Dennis from the voicemail.

2   It's unclear whether Dennis knew about Portnoy posting the 2005 voicemail.

have amassed a large following of Stoolies, the Bostonians calling in were incensed. And Ordway did nothing to stop the bleeding. Who cares if Portnoy was a guest on the station's afternoon drive show? Ordway understood what the ratings would be if they kept this story rolling. For the next four hours, the entire show revolved around Portnoy's seemingly despicable lack of judgment and character.[3]

Back in his office, Portnoy was tuned into the debacle. He listened as Ordway declared this the end of Barstool Sports and wondered aloud about the possible jail time Dave may have been facing. Despite Ordway's rant, Portnoy wasn't distressed; instead, he was confused. The picture of Brady's kid was already online: Dave hadn't hidden in the bushes and taken it himself. In a phrase he would often have to repeat, "it was just a joke":

> "I stand by Brady blog 110%. People who don't get
> it probably shouldn't visit the Stool to begin with.
> Ordway needs ratings. He got 'em today."
>
> —@stoolpresidente

Like Ordway, Wolfe appreciated the ratings boost this controversy brought, but as director of the station, he couldn't stand to have Portnoy's recent actions associated with the WEEI brand. Hell, Wolfe had people from *out of state* calling for Dave's head. He sent out a tweet the following morning:

> "For those of you who've been tweeting at me: No,
> we will not have Portnoy on again. What he did was
> completely irresponsible. It's not about whether
> he was allowed to do it or not. It's about common
> decency. And he showed none."
>
> —@jasonwolfe

---

3   Ordway would later become a Portnoy nemesis.

That same morning Portnoy woke up to a press release from WEEI saying he had been let go. No call, no text. Sitting at a table in his apartment, wearing a faded blue *Jaws* t-shirt, Portnoy looked directly into the camera for his fans—his befuddlement had devolved into anger—as he listened to Dennis and Callahan explain how they had nothing to do with his firing. "Now again, I repeat, we have no say in whether he is on the air or not on the air," Dennis explained.

"BULLSHIT!" Portnoy screamed. "Talk about Jason Wolfe taking the sword for you. It wasn't even an issue until you talked about it!" Whether or not this was true, Portnoy was out. He'd been kicked off Boston talk radio, again.

Later that night, Renee Portnoy was reclining on the off-white couch of her and Dave's Dorchester apartment when she heard a loud banging on the door. "State police, open up!"[4] It was a four-word phrase she thought she'd only hear in movies and at bachelorette parties. Startled, Renee rose slowly off the couch and became the second Satterthwaite woman to answer the door on behalf of a Portnoy blog post.

"We need to speak to the founder of Barstool Sports," declared the officer, wearing dark shades and a tan circular hat. A second officer in matching attire stood behind him, and Portnoy eventually made his way over to meet them. The Massachusetts Attorney General's office had been inundated with complaints about the Tom Brady post, the officers told him. The AG wasn't used to dealing with local bloggers—the officers themselves weren't really sure why they were there—but after looking over the website, it was determined Portnoy had to be paid a visit. As Portnoy blogged later:

---

4   The quotes from the officers are based on Portnoy's explanation of what happened.

"The police just said they were getting lots of complaints from the lunatic fringe…and it would be in the best inter- est of everybody involved [for me to] just take them down. When Staties show up at your door, it's hard to say no."[5]

Portnoy took down the blog post, and no charges were ever filed against him. As he glanced over at Renee, he knew that didn't mean he wasn't in serious trouble. And later that night, after calming down a bit, Renee decided to take a walk outside to clear her head; as she opened the door to her apartment, a blue object landed at her feet. Someone who clearly wasn't happy with Portnoy's Brady post had broken into their building, found their apartment, and attached a blue dildo to their front door. Terrified, she ran inside holding the rubber phallus. Dave was lying in bed when Renee, who by now was sobbing, violently opened the bedroom door and chucked the dildo at him.

"Are you happy now!?!?"

The failed "Back to Stool" venture had Portnoy once again squinting at his bank account, and to make matters worse, the backlash to the Brady blog had not subsided following Ordway's show. In fact, it was growing. National news outlets, including NPR and NBC Sports, were covering the story. One popular headline read:

"Boston Blogger Posts Naked Picture of Tom Brady's Son"

Also, a local attorney and former sex-crimes prosecutor was not finished with the much more consequential legal side of things. Wendy Murphy was campaigning for action by the Attorney

---

5 This quote is a combination of two separate quotes from Portnoy. You will see in the back of this book that there are two different sources listed. You can copy- paste the link to see where each part came from.

General's office—even after Portnoy wasn't being charged with a crime. In an interview with another local radio station, WBZ 1030, Murphy asked:

> "So the question is, do we want to encourage or discourage this behavior? Obviously, it seems to me, we don't want people doing this sort of thing with children...Why wouldn't an elected District Attorney take this case on....make no mistake about it, if you're asking the public to look at the photograph, and to have a certain feeling or reaction to the size of a little boy's penis, you ARE sexualizing the child, period. End of discussion."

Portnoy knew he needed to rebuke this sentiment and eventually went on with Carl Stevens from WBZ to respond to Murphy:

> "I said he had a big 'howitzer.' So that's not sexual. If you're making a connection to that being sexual then I would look into the mirror is what I would say, because it's not sexual at all. I don't know how anyone with a rational brain could say, 'Oh, because I said that, that's sexual.' It's a *Curb Your Enthusiasm* joke."

Much like Clancy and the $100M lawsuit (for calling a lottery winner a pedophile) that never actually became a lawsuit, however, this didn't either. But Portnoy flew too close to the sun on the Brady blog; although he may have failed to realize it after watching hordes of college students pile into a concert, or getting a call from his in-laws about someone's father wanting to murder him, it was clear now that Portnoy wasn't just writing to the local Bostonian who worked at the airport. More people outside this digital world he had created were starting to be touched by it.[6]

---

6   There were rumors that Brady and Gisele weren't happy about the post.

One of those people happened to be someone Portnoy idolized. When the Barstool founder received an email from Howard Stern's production assistant asking him to call into the show, Dave was ecstatic. And also somewhat relieved. Stern had made his living crossing the same boundaries Portnoy sailed over: the famously crass talk-show host would amass a total of $2.4M in fines from 1986-2005 from the FCC. If there was anyone in media who understood what Portnoy was doing with the Brady blog, it would be Stern, Portnoy thought. And as he tweeted to his followers, "Going into the Stern interview, I would have said there was a 20% chance he disagreed [with him posting the blog]."

Then Howard Stern opened the show with this:

"We now have Dave Portnoy on the line to hear his side of it. Dave is the founder of Barstool Sports, Barstoolsports. com, the blog that posted the picture of Tom Brady's son. Dave, people said you must take this down, it's kiddy porn, and I saw the picture, and quite frankly, I *do* think it's kiddy porn. I don't think you should put a picture of a two-year-old nude on your site."

Stern's words blindsided Dave. He took a moment to gather himself before responding. "My issue is, I know I'm legally within my rights to do it," he replied.

"Well, why did you take it down?" Stern asked.

"I was torn on it, to be totally honest. Because I kind of felt like, in a way, I was selling out by taking it down, but I wasn't ready to fight that fight," Portnoy stated. The Barstool founder was deflated. Stern was supposed to have his back. Instead, he essentially called him a pedophile on national radio.

And while the fallout from Bradygate continued, Dave's financial situation worsened when the one thing that couldn't happen started happening: advertisers began to drop. Quirk Auto, a well-known car dealership group in greater Boston, was out. So was

Daisy Buchanan's and Roggie's, two popular restaurants in Back Bay and Brighton. Coors Beer, Portnoy's most recognizable advertising partner, called and told him they needed to rework their agreement. From now on, he was not allowed to talk about anyone under the age of 12 on his blog. "Nope," Portnoy replied. "What if something funny happens involving a person who is underaged? As a comedy site, I need to cover it. I'll agree to not talk about the private parts of anyone underage, but I can't agree to that," he told them. See ya, Coors.

Miltons, a large men's clothing store in the greater Boston area, was one of Portnoy's best sales accounts. The President and CEO of Miltons, Dana Katz, was a fan of Portnoy and recognized Barstool as a key sales driver among younger men. However, this whole posting a nude photo of a two-year-old had put him in a difficult position. His grandfather had started Miltons in 1947 before it was passed on to his father and then to him. The store had built a solid reputation that spanned three generations, and he was now entrusted with upholding it. It pained Katz to do this. He picked up the phone and called Portnoy. Miltons was going to pause spending with Barstool for now.

One can't really ever be sure why Dave didn't just give up then and there; though Renee tried her best to answer this:

> "Dave has an unbelievable ability to be comfortable with risk, so even when the going gets tough, he doubles down. He would wait until he had sold his last shoelace… there would be no giving up."

Clancy explained: "Dave just kept going, even when there were failures. If it were me, I probably would have taken my ball and gone home."

"He was relentless," Renee added about Portnoy, who once was hospitalized for a mild heart attack while running Barstool. "No one else could have done what he did."

Portnoy made a few strategic moves that allowed him to stay on life support. For starters, he tightened his proverbial belt, which is another way of saying he just stopped paying his employees. John Feitelberg, who had been with the company making a meager salary, was back to working for free. (Before writing for the Boston site, Feitelberg actually wrote for the NYC crew, and was making such little money that Clancy got Feitelberg guest-bartending gigs at Saloon, a dive bar in lower Manhattan. Feitelberg actually lost money on his first appearance when he spent more on his all-black uniform than he made in tips, because no one showed up. Clancy, in an act of support, eventually stopped by and slipped Feitelberg $200.)

Several paychecks were also late getting to the New York guys, who didn't have healthcare and were very much reliant on Dave to make payroll. But if anyone complained, Portnoy pulled out the world's smallest violin; back during the newspaper days, the original four writers had worked for free for four years.

Dave also decided to give his website a significant upgrade. Before, when readers landed on the Barstool homepage, they would be greeted by a chalkboard background with two options to click into, Boston or NYC. Now when they entered, they were met with what Portnoy called "The Superblog," one singular page of all the blogs from each city chronologically stacked together. And by this point, Dave had expanded to include two more sites for readers to choose from, Barstool Philly and a college-focused BarstoolU (more on both later). This consolidation helped readers stay on the site longer while they explored posts by writers from different cities (as opposed to just staying on their hometown site), and as they followed more writers, they visited more frequently. The increase in Barstool's web stats put Portnoy in a better position to replace those lost advertisers, which he would, and The Superblog was a harbinger of how Barstool would operate down the road, as a single, more unified company.

One key revenue stream Portnoy tapped into during this time was merchandising. Technically, Portnoy had been "in the merch game" since he started selling his appropriately named "ugly T-shirts" in the very first issues of his newspaper. His product line eventually expanded to include hats, sweatshirts, flags, and all the other gear a fan might expect to see in a company's online store—but with a Barstoolian twist, which usually caused heads to turn when worn. Gaz's go-to shirt, the Ben Roethlisberger "Throwin' picks assaultin chicks" tee was a prime example of this.

And the Barstool boss didn't have to tell his employees twice to work the merchandise angle, because they received a cut of whatever stock they designed and sold. One popular t-shirt could net the team $50k in one week, which is exactly what happened with Clancy's "Let's Go Eat a God Damn Snack" Rex Ryan shirt.[7] With sales like this, the ability to push product out the door became essential to Portnoy's operation, mostly because moving t-shirts meant the company didn't have to be completely dependent on advertisers like Quirk Auto.

While there's no denying Barstool's ship took on water during those early times in the Milton office, Portnoy kept his shoelaces thanks to The Superblog and his ugly t-shirts. As for the heart attack, "I ate too much popcorn," Portnoy explained. And following this downturn, the founder came up with yet another ploy to make his company money, *a lot* of money, in fact, one that would give the Barstool name a national reputation.

---

7   This was a quote by the head coach of the New York Jets, from the HBO Series "*Hard Knocks.*"

12

"A Huntington, Long Island event billed as a 'Barstool Blackout Party' landed nine young people in the hospital over the weekend and has prompted criticism of the party planner. About 1,600 people attended the party Saturday night at The Paramount Theatre…nearly all of those taken out by ambulance crews suffered from alcohol poisoning, said Lt. Joseph Condolff…"I think they were there to drink a lot and party heavily."

—NBC News

"Thousands of young partiers tried to cram into the Wellmont Theatre in Montclair, New Jersey for a beer-fueled dance party called 'Barstool Blackout'.…Six people were arrested; nine were hospitalized."

—CBS News

"A destructive, roving dance party that led to a slew of arrests and injured partygoers in New Jersey and Long Island last night is set to hit New York tonight. Police Commissioner Ray Kelly said the NYPD could take on the party. 'We are a big department. We handle a lot of different events every year, certainly in Manhattan,' said Kelly. 'I think we're in a position to handle this type of event. We'll see."

—*The New York Post*

By now, Avicii and The Electronic Dance Music craze was sweeping across America, and Portnoy watched as other organizations not named Barstool cashed in on the trend:

"Usually I'm not into techno, doing ecstasy and rolling balls, but I got to admit that Dayglow at UMass looked fucking bananas…And that's not only at UMass. As far as I can tell, Dayglow is just about the toughest college ticket in America and maybe the world. My fucking question is, how the hell do they pull this off? I mean Barstool got fucking banned at UMass for bringing Mike Posner who is so fucking soft that if you cut him with a knife, he'd bleed light pink. Dude seriously put half the crowd to sleep by intermission and yet we get banned for basically bringing Kenny G to town and Dayglow gets 2 fucking shows of lighting the campus on fire. Again, I got nothing against Dayglow. They fucking do it right and UMass does it right. Just kind of seems like a double standard that they get to come, and I get arrested if I enter town lines. Seriously, that's what they told me."

It wasn't until DraftKings, who was a client of theirs at the time, told Portnoy they wanted to advertise more directly to frat guys that Dave threw his neon hat into the ring. "So, we said [to the fraternities] why don't we just say Barstool is throwing a party. You wear white, [we'll bring] black lights. We'll throw you the party." And with that the regrettably named Barstool Blackout Tour was born.

The Blackout Tour was a different undertaking compared to the two previous concert series Portnoy had organized. There was no musician performing. Instead, as Portnoy explained, the premise of Dave's newly conceived business plan was simply to get college students to show up to a Barstool-sponsored party at their campus. "It was a party you did in your house, but it was just in a professional venue. So, what I mean by that is it had no rules. Like you go to concerts and there were rules. This didn't have them," Portnoy elaborated.

Before reaching those professional venues, however, the rave tour had the standard Barstoolian humble beginning. Gaz, Devlin, Feitelberg, and two newcomers: Tom Zollo, an intern from Harvard (one might think his IQ would have brought up the average for Barstool, but Portnoy might argue otherwise) and Dante Deiana, aka "Dante the Don," started the junket in the basement of a frat house. The crew had practiced setting up the black lights they bought from Spencer's in Gaz's dad's warehouse, and with Dante DJ-ing, Barstool began throwing these parties at schools along the Atlantic coast. That didn't mean they knew what they were doing; the guys had nearly killed an entire fraternity at UVA after they noticed the students' eyes started turning bloodshot red. Turns out running a gas generator inside a tent is a fairly efficient way to poison people with carbon monoxide.

Clancy thought the entire plan was ridiculous. They were an internet blog: they wrote funny articles and posted them online. This, in his mind, couldn't be further from an actual production company. "I remember [thinking] this is a terrible idea, we're not going to make any money off of this, what are you talking about Dave…we're gonna run a techno tour?"[1]

Feitelberg also shared this sentiment. "One day Dave just said, 'You're going on tour' and…I thought 'I'm a blogger,' but I was like Ok, I'm going on tour. Here we go."

Adhering to the Barstool ethos, Dave's crew figured it out on the fly. As Zollo recalls, "We had one of everything, we had no backups. I had no idea how to do any of that shit before until it was just on our plate." But eventually, as Portnoy mentioned, the Barstool Blackout Tour went from frat basements to legitimate venues, and for the first real show of the tour in Albany, they somehow got Avicii to per-

---

1   Portnoy would form a production company called Purple Starfish Productions.

form. Gaz explained, "They [the group working with Avicii] were having trouble selling tickets, and we just slapped the Barstool name on it at the last second." And the Blackout Tour, more officially, was underway.[2]

But it wasn't the famous Swedish DJ who turned the Barstool Blackout Tour into a phenomenon, however: for the first stretch of shows, the turnout was pretty average. The Barstool guys thought they would be doing this for the next couple weeks, and they'd be done. As Devlin said, "We rolled into Iowa in November, we had done it for a couple months and I remember we all went to Iowa and were like 'It's been a good run, guys, we're not selling tickets for the next show, this is over, let's just have fun tonight.' And they had these CO2 cannons shooting down from the top, and that changed everything. So shoutout to the CO2 cannons because that is quite literally what may have built this company."

Following the show at the University of Iowa, Gaz put together a video of the party, and the trailer he came up with was mesmerizing: attractive girls in bright and tight clothing, dancing, being blasted by C02 steam (eventually they would add foam to their repertoire, which was also a huge hit) with strobe lights and black lights everywhere, while people crowd-surfed near the stage. The party looked wild, and it looked *awesome*. After Gaz released the promo video, the Barstool Blackout Tour exploded. The shows began to sell out at a somewhat alarming rate, depending on how one looked at them. As Zollo put it, "I can't explain how crazy the Blackout Tour was compared to anything else I'd seen in my life without just sounding like a dickhead, but it was, like it was intense in those buildings, it was fucking bananas."

During the shows, the Stoolies went nuts, unsurprisingly: seeing two girls make out with each other while the Barstool guys, dressed in full mascot costumes, jumped off stage over them into the crowd

---

2   The rest of the Blackout Tour shows were played by Dante.

was a common occurrence. Feitelberg said, "It was incredibly dangerous, it was crazy, it was a drunk children's birthday party, it was, I dunno, it was chaos."

Portnoy saw he had a hit on his hands. But it wasn't Dave who would spend his days and nights traveling from campus to campus, setting up and taking down the shows; that fell to his crew. And they did so at first with excitement—it was fun being the center of attention at one of the hottest parties in the country. But as the shows wore on, that excitement turned to ambivalence, which turned to dread. As Gaz reflected:

> "At the beginning, we were kind of fired up because it was fun. We were going to campuses and we had energy. So, we'd be drinking every night. [But] we ended up burning the candle really quickly…you know, you're drinking 'til 3 in the morning, you'd have to pack up all these lights, there'd be drunk kids passed out everywhere, then you'd have to go from Indiana and drive to West Virginia…we would drive nine hours overnight and we'd get to a venue at 11 in the morning, set up, do it again 'til 4 in the morning."

Gaz & Co. were always on the move, throwing shows Wednesday through Saturday night every week. And to save money (not that they had a say in it), the Blackout team shared one hotel room, and what was probably worse, ate McDonald's every night. "It was a big deal if we were able to get Subway," Devlin explained.

Barstool did three different Blackout tours, 170 shows in all, and by the third tour, Devlin wasn't drinking anymore; Feitelberg had refused to participate; and Gaz…well, Gaz was still allegedly trying to hook up with college groupies. "If Paul (Gaz) wanted to see a girl, the crew would have to wait and stay extra time: everything was based on Paul and whether he was trying to hook up with a girl after. If he didn't have any girls, they'd be out of there in a minute, but if he was interested, they'd stay," Portnoy said.

This led to several arguments, and the crew went at it on more than one occasion—four to a hotel room will do this—with Dave hearing gripes about everything from infighting to the conditions they were forced to put up with. As Dante recalled about a conversation he had with Portnoy: "I remember pulling down the bed sheets in the motel at Vanderbilt and there were blood stains, and I remember complaining to Dave, and him being like 'I don't fucking care, deal with it.'"

Portnoy wasn't necessarily easy on the Blackout crew, and he often rebutted any complaint with something along the lines of 'Why are you whining? All you guys do is party'—which was partly true, but it also diminished the grueling aspect of being on the road (under those circumstances) for an extended period of time. As Feitelberg recalled, "Every morning, you'd get in the car and be like *I don't know if it's my back or my liver but something is wrong, I'm hurting*...we did it for fucking...months straight." On their way up to a show in Connecticut, the crew got stuck in a massive blizzard, with a flat tire, a downed powerline in front of them, and a tipped 18-wheeler behind them: they were literally trapped in their car. The group called Zollo's dad who knew a guy who could help tow them out, but that wasn't happening for several hours. With nowhere to go, the four of them were reduced to eating leftover fries out of a McDonald's bag and drinking snow they melted on top of the car heater. Eventually, they dialed Dave to inform him they weren't going to make it to the event. But the boss wasn't having any of it: he told them in no uncertain terms that they needed to figure out a way to make it to UConn. It wasn't until local authorities shut down the campus and the Barstool party due to hazardous weather that Portnoy let them off the hook.

Dave was pushing his guys because he knew this venture wasn't going to last forever. "It's something that could exist only for the short time it did. It was too volatile to exist long term," Portnoy recalled. As the money came rolling in, Dave needed to squeeze every last drop out of this phenomenon he had concocted, one that could have only been spawned from the bizarro world of Barstool. As Dave said:

> "We went from a couple people in a frat basement to I was on a conference call with Live Nation (a large production company) to close out Bamboozle—which is a huge festival in New Jersey—we were going on after Bon Jovi—and they were trying to get us a $150k-$200k guarantee, like we just show up and they cut us a check for 200 grand. And they thought it was… low. They [said] 'we know you probably should be getting more money…but all these people will get to hear your music who haven't ever heard it'…and I was like, uh, we don't have music. They didn't even know what we were, all they saw is the ticket sales whenever the Blackout Tour went on sale: they sold out instantly…the Blackout Tour was the most popular event going on in the country: it was insane."

Portnoy was clearing $250k a night for their bigger shows, which meant the Barstool founder was no longer in financial distress; actually, quite the opposite. But unsurprisingly to Dave, more of the late-night phone calls like the one during that snowstorm began pouring in. As the Blackout Tour's popularity grew, local police started receiving advanced notice about the Barstool parties arriving in their towns, and underaged concert goers began getting in trouble. Devlin paints a picture of when things began to turn: "I remember Zollo walking up to me being like 'There's thousands of people out there, there's 800 already in.' And I was like 'oh my God, we actually did it, we did this thing.' And then five minutes later Zollo comes up to me again and is like 'someone just punched the chief of police.'"

This pretty much sums up the demise of the Blackout Tour. Shows began getting shut down—one venue employee pulled the fire alarm because he thought things were getting too out of control—and some venues such as Roseland Ballroom in NYC started banning alcohol. But it was the growing amount of negative media coverage they received following shows like the ones in Huntington, New York and Montclair, New Jersey that did the tour in. "The more the media portrayed this as... an out-of-control drug-fueled sex orgy rave, the more PR problems we had...that is when this thing became a PR disaster..." Portnoy said.

"We became the face of EDM [electronic dance music] danger," Clancy added.

While Portnoy argued that his shows were, statistically, just as safe if not safer than other comparable events, he also bemoaned the press for singling out Barstool as the face of underaged drinking and partying, which went on at pretty much any concert or event in America. But, as Clancy explained, there was some truth to what the media was writing. "There should have been, like, multiple deaths," he admitted. As the negative media attention went through the roof, so did Portnoy's insurance, and eventually in 2014, Barstool shut down the Blackout Tour.

13

Dave Portnoy was seated in the back of an SUV, wearing a black winter jacket and a dark green beanie hat, the camera pointed directly in his face. He was getting pretty used to this set up. "I don't know what to expect right now, my life is like, it ain't boring. Right now, we're driving over to a mass protest, about *me*...Who would have thought that seven years ago?" Portnoy said, with a hint of excitement.

Dave stepped out of the car and walked toward the Freshman Quad at Northeastern University. Despite the unforgiving Boston winter night, in front of him stood a group of 200 mostly female students from the surrounding campuses of Boston College, Boston University, UMass Lowell, and other nearby schools. A young woman was perched on the two-foot-high ledge that wrapped around the grass in front of a large tan building, the crowd standing together as one on the brick plaza beneath her. Holding a megaphone, she was chanting one-line phrases and pausing to let the audience repeat what she said:

"University Health and Counseling Services has been amazing, *University Health and Counseling Services has been amazing*, if you've been raped, *if you've been raped*, if you've been sexually assaulted, *if you've been sexually assaulted*...you can go to them, *you can go to them*."

Portnoy slinked up behind the crowd, unnoticed. Underneath his right arm was a Pirate Dog sign, the unofficial Barstool logo of a dog with a patch over its eye. He slowly raised it in the air, until finally the woman recognized him. "Dave, is that you?" she bellowed into the mic.

The crowd turned toward where the woman had directed her question, and Portnoy, unalarmed, cautiously began making his way up to the front of the group. As he approached, she continued: "I just want you all to know that when you can identify people in your community and outside of your community that are perpetuating rape culture, victim-blaming, sexism, misogyny, homophobia, racism... you need to identify them and make them known."

Dave turned to the crowd and mouthed an inaudible "we don't condone rape" after she finished. A man in the back shouted "let him talk!"

"Are you going to let me talk?" Portnoy asked her, only half-picked up by the mic; he was now standing directly in front of her on the ledge.

"I hope you have a horrible night!" the woman screamed in his face. That was a *no*.

Portnoy, shaking his head, again mouthed, "We don't condone rape," and turned to walk away. Out of nowhere, a young woman jumped in front of him, stopping him mid-stride. Wearing dark-rimmed glasses and an oversized green wool hat, the young woman came face to face with Portnoy.

"You think I like doing this?!" she yelled at Dave. She finished by shouting, "You can fuck off!" The crowd began chanting, "Fuck off, fuck off, fuck off!"

Portnoy, who at one point started tapping his feet sarcastically along with the chant, shrugged and walked away. The Barstool founder never got a chance to speak to the crowd.

The woman who jumped in front of Portnoy was a young college student by the name of Anna Siembor. Siembor started the group

Knockout Barstool—most of those protesters were members—as an opposition to Portnoy's company, which she believed promoted rape culture. A few months earlier, Siembor had first come across inflammatory comments made by the Barstool founder. A report had described how a fraternity at the University of Vermont was in hot water for handing out a survey that asked its members to answer which female students they would want to rape the most, and Portnoy had commented on the article at the end of one of his blog posts:

> "Just to make friends with the feminists, I'd like to reiterate that we don't condone rape of any kind at our Blackout Parties in mid-January. However, if [a] chick passes out, that's a grey area."

Siembor kept digging. She discovered another post by Portnoy in a May 2010 blog in which Portnoy again joked about rape, referring to an Australian court that had acquitted a man accused of raping a 24-year-old woman. The man's lawyer argued that because the plaintiff was wearing skinny jeans, it would be too difficult for his client to rape her without her helping to take them off, i.e., implying consent. The man wasn't charged, and it was an obviously absurd ruling. When commenting on an article about this case, Portnoy wrote:

> "Even though I never condone rape, if you're a size 6 and you're wearing skinny jeans, you kind of deserve to be raped, right?"

The deeper Siembor dug, the more she found. Appalled, Siembor decided to use Portnoy's weapon of choice against him. In early 2012, the Knockout Barstool blog first appeared on the internet. As users entered, they were greeted with the following message at the top of Siembor's homepage:

"Barstool Sports has perpetuated their cycle of misogyny and rape culture for far too long. We will not sit idly and allow this to happen to the women of our community. We will knock out Barstool!"

And the site quickly gained a following. Female students from neighboring colleges began posting on the site:

"I would love to get to know whoever is running this blog. You are all absolutely brilliant and reading all of these posts and learning about the KO Barstool movement is completely inspiring."

—dashuri

"I'm a recent Northeastern grad, and I'm behind you completely. This sort of thing has gone on far too long, and conversations need to be started and sustained in order to spread awareness. Keep up the great work!"

—ladyshipwreck

"Totally support what you guys are doing. The Barstool site could be just as successful without supporting rape culture, it's just unnecessary!"

—kmerry

KO Barstool was the first organized resistance to Portnoy's website. Yes, there had been cases of individuals pushing back against Dave, and several articles in the news (both locally and nationally) that didn't paint Barstool in a flattering light. There were the angry local callers who had dialed into Glenn Ordway's show about the Tom Brady post and moments like the Howard Stern interview. But all of that opposition was, for the most part, individual instances of anti-Barstool sentiment; in contrast, KO Barstool was a coordinated movement going after everything Portnoy and Barstool represented.

Siembor's group argued that the culture Portnoy perpetuated had real-life consequences, citing Barstool's Blackout parties as the prime example. The group believed they were dangerous, because the videos Gaz released were sexual and suggestive in nature, featuring college females dancing in tight outfits, and while Barstool fans perceived this as a great time, Siembor and her team saw a hunting ground. Here's an excerpt from an interview Siembor gave to Boston University's online magazine:

"Q: What is the ultimate goal of Knockout Barstool?

"A: Originally, we wanted Northeastern to publicly disassociate themselves from Barstool Sports, and this is still one of our goals. But because of all the attention and support we've gotten, because other universities are getting involved, we want to create a dialogue about the epidemic of rape on college campuses. … Ultimately, no Barstool Blackout Tour [event] will go unchallenged in the eyes of a student body.

"Q: How do you think organizations like Barstool contribute to rape culture?

"A: Joking about rape normalizes the idea of sexual assault. From a recent BS article: 'we don't condone rape of any kind at our Blackout Parties in mid-January. However, if a chick passes out, that's a grey area.' That's supposed to be a joke, but women (and men) have been raped when [they] passed out. It happens every weekend, at parties, bars, and clubs. Why is that OK to joke about? Because rape has been normalized. Because people don't understand the psychological trauma a sexual assault victim must go through…"

As KO Barstool gained momentum, the CBS newsmagazine show *Inside Edition* caught wind of Siembor's movement and asked to interview Portnoy about the Blackout Tour. At first, when correspondent Lisa Guerrero and her production team showed up at the Milton office, they were cordial. Portnoy wasn't sure what sort of interview this was going to be, or how to dress for it:

> "Do I play it straight on *Inside Edition* today or rock the purple starfish?"
>
> —@stoolpresidente

His purple starfish lacrosse jersey meant "I was getting ready for war," and Portnoy decided to don it that day. For good reason.[1]

> "Lisa Guerrero just brutalized me on *Inside Edition*. Ambush city."
>
> —@stoolpresidente

Guerrero and Portnoy had the following exchange:

Guerrero: You posted the following on your site. 'I never condone rape. But if you're a size six and you're wearing skinny jeans, you kind of deserve to be raped.'

Portnoy: Correct. I stand by that. I think it's a funny joke.

Guerrero: You think rape is funny?

Portnoy: No, I didn't say that. I think it's a funny joke.

Guerrero: Do you understand how offensive that is?

Portnoy: No, I obviously don't.

---

1   Portnoy would make the purple starfish bathing suit part of his brand. He bought it when he needed a bathing suit while on a vacation. When he brought it up to the register, he had no idea it cost $400. But he was determined to not look broke to the cashier, so he purchased it anyway.

The back and forth was contentious, but also ridiculous considering Portnoy's outfit. And the interview became a rallying cry for Stoolies, who had begun to fire back at Siembor and the other Knockout Barstool organizers. It would be an unfortunate consequence that most Portnoy adversaries would have to deal with in the coming years. Below are two examples of comments made by Barstool fans on Siembor's KO Barstool website:

"You people are fucking pathetic. I see what you did: you just searched [for] the word 'rape' in Barstool's search bar and found the three out of a million blogs that glorify rape. If you [had] any sense of humor and removed the large stick out of your ass, you would realize it's a joke and el pres is writing to entertain for the masses, not just you and your sensitive faggot friends. If you're from Boston and go to school in Boston, you should smarten up and take pride in the Stool. Go Fuck Yourselves, Stoolie For Life"

—[username was deleted]

"'We don't condone rape of any kind at our Blackout Parties in mid-January. However, if a chick passes out, that's a grey area' is so obviously a joke. Anything is open to being made fun of. It's called 'free speech,' and we have it here in America, you terrorist bitches."

—penn99

Eventually, Portnoy began responding to Siembor on his website:

"When will KO Barstool come out and admit it? Their hatred for us really has nothing to do with rape. They are all ugly dykes who hate pretty girls, partying, and me. They can't stand the fact that our parties are safe. They can't stand that they are fun. They can't stand that girls actually come home from these and say it was the best night of their lives. It drives them nuts."

Aside from trying to tear down everything he had built over the past nine years, Dave believed Siembor was working with the local government to shut down his parties. When *Boston Globe* reporter Dave Wedge interviewed Portnoy about underaged drinking Barstool Blackout events, Portnoy asked Wedge where he heard about that, because he hadn't heard any previous complaints on the subject. Writing to his fans, Portnoy claimed Wedge responded with, "KO Barstool…complained to Menino[2] about the underage drinking and said it was dangerous, so I started snooping around and calling venues." This riled Portnoy:

> "What [does KO Barstool] do once people dismiss their ludicrous rape-culture bullshit? They just shuffle along to the next thing to complain about. They claim college kids wouldn't drink if it weren't for these parties. That we are now responsible for all underage drinking in in the world. Like this is a new phenomenon. That fake IDs didn't exist until Barstool started. It's literally looney tunes. Next thing you know, it will be that our black lights give off radiation and give people cancer. That's how crazy it's getting…They are just looking for anything they can grasp onto that stops us from being awesome."

Portnoy finished this declaration with a line he'd use again on another prominent female adversary years later:

> "I'm sorry, Anna Siembor, I know you want me so bad it's like acid in your mouth. But not this time."

Back at the Barstool protest in March of 2012, as Portnoy headed towards the SUV he arrived in, Siembor signaled to the KO Barstool

---

2   Thomas Menino, Boston's mayor at the time.

crowd to begin the ten-minute walk downtown from Northeastern's campus to House of Blues, where Barstool was hosting one of its Blackout parties. With the Boston Police Department blocking traffic along the way, Siembor's group carried signs, blew whistles, and continued their chants of anti-Barstool rhetoric: "Hey, hey! Ho, ho! Rape culture has got to go!" At around 7:45 p.m., this chorus for social justice turned onto Lansdowne Street. There, they were greeted by what appeared to be one thousand Stoolies lined up, mostly drunk, all in white and bright apparel, waiting to get into Portnoy's party.

Portnoy's fans began shouting at the protesters, cheering sarcastically and laughing; others hurled obscenities. Several meathead-looking concertgoers started chanting "Stool! Stool! Stool! Stool! Stool!" while female line members hid somewhat sheepishly behind them. One person stepped out of the crowd to scream "Viva La Stool!" Meanwhile, the Boston cops watched calmly from the sidelines, waiting to move in if any semblance of violence broke out. With the bowels of the Fenway bleachers as the backdrop and blue police lights flashing across their faces, the protestors and Stoolies stood toe to toe.

After several minutes of yelling from both sides, Portnoy's fans eventually made their way into the House of Blues sans any major altercation. As he had done before and would do at many of these shows, the Barstool founder took the stage and looked down on his massive college crowd, sardined shoulder to shoulder. Wearing a neon pink trucker hat with HARDO in black letters on it, pink sunglasses, a glowstick around his neck, and a white Barstool t-shirt, Dave grabbed the microphone off its stand. Chants of "El Pres" began to break out.

"Northeasternnnnnnnnn."

The crowd cheered loudly.

"So I went to a Knockout Barstool rally today."

A chorus of boos ricocheted off the venue walls.

"They got in my face, to be honest, they said they were gonna kill me, lotta f-bombs, lotta shit, I'll tell you this, there were maybe 10 Northeastern students there, we got 3,000 here! We like to party, and we're not going to apologize for it!"

The crowd let Portnoy know they agreed. And as the students began to drown him out, Portnoy leaned into the mic for his sign off:

"Thank you, Northeastern! Fuck KO Barstool!"

14

"God I love you HotGlove when you gonna stop being a
pussy @TheHotGlove"

—@devlinbarstool

Dan Katz stared at the tweet from Devlin. The message hit the
27-year-old Chicago real estate analyst harder than a 5 p.m. Friday
meeting invite. Katz, who was tall, dark-haired, and at the time both
fit and handsome, was a massive fan of Barstool and a regular caller
into Portnoy's now-defunct Barstool Power Hour radio show. Much
like Clancy, he moonlighted as a blogger while working in a cube
farm, running his own site called *The Hot Glove*. While it might
seem by now as though a prerequisite for starting a blog was pas-
sionately hating one's job, Katz's motivation was much more about
creative expression than it was a plan to leave the well-paying gig he
landed after graduating from the University of Wisconsin.

Regardless, Katz was *talented*, and Portnoy recognized this
immediately. As he followed *The Hot Glove*, it became clear to Dave
that Katz's writing style differed from his and Clancy's, whose humor
was at times cloaked in cruelty. Katz's angle was usually much more
benign, but also much weirder, a combination that would leave the
followers of *The Hot Glove* (friends of friends) strangely amused.
Take his obsession with the head of communications for the San
Francisco 49ers, Bob Lange: the head of PR for an NFL football
team should be the last person a fan thinks about, let alone writes
about, but not for Katz, who became fascinated with the man after

he watched him haplessly attempt to break up a post-game scuffle between people much, much larger than him. From *The Hot Glove*:

"Robby Lange Will Not Respond to My Emails Anymore and that Makes Me Want to Kill Myself

"To say I'm heartbroken would be an understatement. I'm despondent. I needed closure. Instead, every time my gmail tells me I have an email, every time my phone lights up with a new message, every time I log on to my computer, I think... *maybe it's Robby. What if he just wanted to talk? What if he was in town and wanted to grab a beer? What if he needs a mortal lock for this weekend's games?*

"I'm like Ben Affleck in *Good Will Hunting*. You know what the best 10 seconds of my day is? When I log into gmail and the page loads. Because I think maybe I'll get to my inbox and Robby will be there. No 'hello.' No 'how you doing?' No nothing. Just a simple email asking me to drop everything and move out to San Francisco so that I can be his best friend. I don't know much, but I know that."

Later, Katz took the same aim at Adam Schefter, a well-known ESPN insider, when he started a long-spanning online investigation into whether Schefter was a midget. (Katz now calls Schefter a friend.) It was the kind of humor Portnoy was looking for, the exact internet niche comedy that Barstool trafficked in; Dave knew Katz would slot nicely alongside Clancy.

But when Portnoy reached out to Katz toward the end of 2011— around the time of the strategic shift to the Superblog formatting (and the addition of Philly)—Katz declined Dave's invitation to join the Stool. He was reluctant to start working a second job, particularly one as risqué as writing for a site like Barstool. To Katz, it simply wasn't a safe career move.

Portnoy wouldn't give up on recruiting Katz. But as the Knockout Barstool drama played out, and as Barstool earned a reputation for being the bad boys of the internet thanks to the wild Blackout parties, Katz remained deterred. Then, in the spring of 2012, he gave up blogging altogether:

> "Well, this is it. I started *The Hot Glove* 2 years ago in hopes that it could be a small respite in the otherwise monotonous life of cubicle monkeys everywhere. Hopefully, that's what it provided as well as some of the more important life lessons, like *never go to Florida; more people masturbate in public than you could ever imagine; all Russians are fucked in the head;* and *the internet is literally wall to wall with weird.*

> "I never imagined *The Hot Glove* would grow to the point it has, and although it sucks to pull the plug, I think we can all agree it's been a blast. Writing a blog and keeping it constantly updated is really hard work. It may seem easy, but it takes a lot of time. Not to sound all sappy and shit, but the reason I kept it going and put in the long hours was because of the readers. So if you have ever read, shared, commented, or emailed *The Hot Glove*, thank you. It means more than you can imagine.

> "Seriously, though, that was way too sappy. What I really meant to say is go fuck yourself. Bye, haters."

By June, however, Katz had a change of heart about contributing to Barstool. Maybe it was because it had been several months since he gave up his own creative outlet. Or maybe it was because it was warm in Chicago and he was in a good mood: Katz and pretty much everyone else from the area will argue to the point of exhaustion that Chicago is the best summer city in America. Whatever the reason, when Devlin fired out that tweet ripping Katz for not joining the pirate ship, it landed. Katz responded to Devlin: "How about I'll just write a few Cubs blogs?" He was in.

On July 16, 2012, the Barstool Chicago website went live, joining the four other sites under the Barstool umbrella. Because Katz was only going to be part-time, Portnoy hired a mysterious figure named Neil to head the Chicago site. No one knew much about him, and he didn't last very long. That's because Katz (known as "Big Cat" to Barstool readers) quickly eclipsed Neil as the main writer for Barstool Chicago, becoming the second most important person in the company behind Portnoy and an influential figure in internet culture today.

15

It was a brisk 40-degree day on April 15th in downtown Boston. Dark bars overflowed with patrons wanting to grab a cheap drink or five before turning to watch 23,336 participants run longer than any person really should. The Boston Marathon, the country's oldest race, is an official Monday holiday for the city, and that day Bostonians were treating it as such.

At 2:49 p.m., race clock time 4:09.43, two explosions occurred near the finish line. The loud blasts happened exactly 14 seconds and 210 yards apart. With everyone unsure of what had just transpired, it took several moments before the scene devolved into a chaotic frenzy as police officers rushed in to assist disoriented and fallen runners. Three spectators were killed and 264 others were injured from what would later be determined to be a pair of homemade pipe bombs built by radicalized brothers Dzhokhar and Tamerlan Tsarnaev.[1]

What ensued captivated the nation. America watched as authorities took to the surrounding Boston neighborhoods in a surreal manhunt for the two brothers at large. After President Obama bluntly declared, "We will get to the bottom of this," the city of Boston became the center of the universe. And in some ways, so did Barstool Sports.

It began with Portnoy tweeting the following message:

---

[1] Krystle Campbell 29, Lingiz Lu 23, and Martin Richard 8, were tragically killed in the blast. Sean Collier, 27, an MIT police officer also was killed by the two brothers. Boston police officer Dennis Simmonds, 28, died a year later after succumbing to a head injury he suffered during the shootout in Watertown.

"What the fuck is going on? Did the marathon just get bombed by terrorists?"

—@stoolpresidente

Over the next few days, Portnoy and Barstool provided real-time updates for their followers about what was happening in greater Boston; several Stoolies sent them local police scanners, and Portnoy's crew was relaying what they were hearing via Twitter:

"Current situation. Guy on boat still moving. Police still waiting to move in. Still securing perimeter."

—@stoolpresidente

"All units stand by for flash bang. Don't return fire."

—@stoolpresidente

"Police say he is very likely wounded and has been there all day."

—@BarstoolBigCat

Barstool wasn't in the business of breaking news, but on this occasion, it happened to be in a prime position to do so. Aside from the police scanners, Portnoy had Stoolies on the ground providing valuable information that he could relay to a captivated public. More Americans began to tune in to the blog's updates as they spread across the internet. When the climactic gunfight broke out in Watertown, a suburb of Boston, a Barstool fan sent Portnoy the video he took of the exchange which occurred directly in front of his house. Barstool was the first to post it; CNN, FOX, and NBC picked up the video, crediting Barstool Sports. Another Stoolie who worked at the hospital where police brought one of the terrorists took a picture of him on the operating table and sent it to Portnoy. Again, Barstool posted it and other major news networks used it and credited his company.

Throughout the saga, it seemed the national media was routinely 20 minutes behind Portnoy and his crew, who were faster and more accurate in their reporting thanks to info from the loyal Stoolies.

> "Anybody who reports anything other than he is alive in the boat and police are waiting to make their move is wrong"
>
> —@stoolpresidente

> "The boom that the tv stations didn't know what it was is the flash bang. Wake up fellas."
>
> —@stoolpresidente

> "Head lifting. He's alive. Fox and CNN need to shut the hell up calling him a body."
>
> —@BarstoolBigCat

It was the same formula Portnoy used to gain a competitive advantage when it came to his content, but this time the scenario was playing out on a national level. And the subject matter was a tad more serious than a video of people in Alabama claiming they had seen a Leprechaun. But Barstool was still in fact a comedy site, and it did provide some comedic relief in its coverage:

> "I hate how when my wife calls and asks me what I'm doing and I say 'catching the terrorists,' she doesn't take me serious. #respectthegame"
>
> —@stoolpresidente

> "Holy shit: is it back on? Are we manhunting again? I feel so alive"
>
> —@BarstoolBigCat

"Completely aside, House Boats are so awesome. Totally underrated."

—@BarstoolBigCat

Portnoy and Katz provided some levity to a dire situation, which was appreciated by newcomers to Barstool who came across the site because of their reporting: Katz gained 20,000 new Twitter followers basically overnight, a significant number back in 2013. The exposure Barstool received as a whole during this time was more lucrative than any expensive marketing campaign could generate. And Portnoy would lean further into this type of organic promotion.

Marc Fucarile was standing directly next to the base of the tree where the second bomb was stashed inside a black backpack. The blast took off his right leg, and as paramedics carried him away, the local Bostonian remembers handing someone his foot to take to the hospital. Fucarile spent 55 days in Mass General, undergoing more than 50 surgeries.

In the weeks that followed the disaster, Fucarile's sister emailed Dave after learning the Barstool founder was using his platform to raise money for the victims of the marathon bombing. Portnoy had called upon his fanbase to buy Barstool's "Boston Strong" t-shirts at $24 each, with all proceeds going to benefit a single Bostonian who was injured in the attack. Portnoy figured this was the most streamlined way to handle the funds, and he had looked to find a victim who fit the Stoolie profile—someone who might not have gotten the money from the usual fundraising orgs.

Marc's sister explained his story about the physical struggle he went through following the bombing—he was trying desperately to save his other leg—and about how he was just a normal guy, a typical Masshole Red Sox fan, and what he would do with the money. Fucarile was going to put it towards buying a new, handicapped-accessible home for his family; he had a son and a fiancé who was just starting nursing school, she explained. When Portnoy read the email, he figured he might have found his guy. And when he learned Marc asked for a laptop while in the ICU because he had so many bills to pay, the money was his.

The video of Portnoy giving Fucarile the $250,000 Stoolies raised—when he first read the amount Fucarile thought it was $2,500 and was still elated—made its way across the internet. Viewers watched as a stunned Fucarile asked, "Are you kidding me?"

"As much as I'd like to take credit, it's just all the readers," Portnoy responded. Barstool fans, for the first time, had a reason to be portrayed in a favorable light by the national media, and these news outlets ran glowing headlines about Barstool's efforts. The community that Portnoy built was never more important than in the months that followed the bombing, and Dave used the event as a rallying cry for Stoolies and the people of Boston:

> "Obviously on a day like today, everybody takes time to look back at the events of 1 year ago. But for most of us, we'll just move on with our lives after this coming Marathon Monday, not giving the bombings too much thought over the coming months and years. Not Marc Fucarile, though. Not Krystle Marie Campbell's family. Not the Richard family. Not Lingzi Lu's family. Not Sean Collier's family.[2] Not every single person who lost a limb or was severely injured. Their lives changed forever. Every day, they will deal with the actions of these two cowards. That's why we can never raise enough money. Never forget. The Marathon Bombings will be with us forever. In a weird way a rallying point for

---

2   As a previous footnote mentioned, Krystle Marie Campbell, Martin Richard, and Lingzi Lu were killed by the bombs at the Boston Marathon; Sean Collier was an MIT police officer who was shot and killed by the Tamerlan brothers 3 days after the bombing.

the city. A tragedy that brought us together and made us stronger in the end."[3]

For those who were vehemently against Barstool, the well-covered fundraising effort was a bit of a curveball. And these detractors might have been surprised to learn that Barstool had in fact been raising money for good causes as far back as 2008, when Portnoy asked Stoolies to donate to WEEI's Jimmy Fund drive supporting the Dana-Farber Cancer Institute:

> "As much as we make fun of WEEI here at the Stool (still can't believe they hired [Ron] Borges), what they and NESN do in their two-day Jimmy Fund drive more than makes up for it. It's really one of the great things about living in this area. So we're asking all Stoolies to join the cause and donate whatever you can if you haven't already."

Raising money for charity would become a staple of Barstool up until present day. Here are some of the notable campaigns led by Portnoy:

- $15,000 for wounded warrior Zach Parker in 2012 so he could purchase a wheelchair: Parker was an Army Medic who lost both legs and one arm in an IED explosion in Afghanistan;

- $68,000 for the families of two firefighters who died in a nine-alarm fire in Back Bay in 2014;

- $104,000 for the families of two NYPD officers who were shot dead in 2015;

---

3   Portnoy was known to make fun of marathoners before this. After the 2013 tragedy, he'd tell his fans the situation put him in a comedic pretzel.

- $85,000 for Denna Laing, the women's professional hockey player who was paralyzed during the NWHL Winter Classic in 2016;

- $50,000 for families of victims of the shooting at the nightclub in Orlando in 2016;

- $30,000 for K9s for Warriors in 2017;

- $50,000 for the JJ Watt Foundation, supporting school athletics, in 2017;

Two of Portnoy's charity efforts stand out among the rest: the first being the hundreds of thousands of dollars Barstool helped raise for the Peter Frates Family Foundation, which aims to help find a cure for ALS. Pete was a former Boston College baseball captain, who was diagnosed with ALS in 2012 at the age of 27. With Portnoy's promotion, Barstool became a massive champion of the Ice Bucket Challenge, a viral act started by Frates to raise ALS awareness in the summer of 2014. Dave quickly became close with the Frates family, and he often posted about his visits with Pete on his site.

The second and probably best-known cause was the Barstool Fund, which raised millions for small businesses in 2020, during Covid.

It was in these moments where Barstool fans saw a different side of Dave. While he employed self-deprecation in his humor, by now Portnoy had built his El Pres brand by harnessing a tough exterior; having thick skin was table stakes when it came to surviving ten years on the internet—"Portnoy's late, but his nose is on time" was just one of the many jokes crafted by the Barstool comment section, a group that both admired and ruthlessly ripped him. Portnoy said of these daily insults, "I read 'em a decent amount. Smokeshows couldn't exist with comments on. Girls are sensitive. I am not." And of-course there was his inclination to tear down anything and anyone he deemed in his way, a tact that he now referred to as going

"Grudge Dave." But when it came to the Frates family or any other of the charities he posted about, Portnoy let his guard down, dropping the El Presidente persona for those several paragraphs.

But opponents of Barstool still begged the question, is a company *good* because it raises money for a good cause, even if that company continues to advance a culture some might perceive as hateful? Portnoy often pointed to his company's chartable efforts when rebutting criticism from opposing groups, who in turn dismissed those efforts as whitewashing. Regardless of whether one believed Barstool promoted a culture of misogyny, it was arguably difficult to reconcile the Dave Portnoy speaking in those early offensive blog posts—which he defends as poorly aged comedy—with the Dave Portnoy leading his charity drives, and for many, it remains this way at the time of this writing.

By the middle of 2013, Knockout Barstool, the group whose answer to the previous question was a resounding *No*, had lost traction, with Anna Siembor graduating from Northeastern and eventually heading to the University of Washington to earn a master's degree in social work. And thanks to Barstool's profile being lifted during the marathon bombing—and the organic marketing from the thousands of "Boston Strong" t-shirts sold by Barstool—Portnoy's company was becoming more established both in the Northeast and across the country. "Viva La Stool" signs—a phrase Portnoy had coined back in 2006—had begun appearing in the background of ESPN's College Gameday show. Eventually, Portnoy began posting a collage of the best ones Stoolies sent to him, which included places he'd never thought he'd reach:[4]

---

4   The troops were reading Barstool as far back as 2007.

"Viva La Stool from Ghana to the Great Wall of China to the Holy Land to the Jets Locker Room and Beyond"

And there were certain Viva La Stool sightings that were particularly meaningful to Portnoy and the Stoolies:

"Soldier from Brockton Gives a Christmas Viva La Stool Shoutout on Fox from Afghanistan"

As Barstool became popular with the military, his "Viva La Stool" posts featured signs from marines in warzones like Afghanistan or Iraq, and these signs became the backbone of his annual "Memorial Day Tribute to the Troops." But international sightings were not limited to the military. "The moment I realized that something was going on was when there was a Barstool sign at Buckingham Palace when Kate and William got married," Clancy says.

While the Boston Marathon certainly drove eyeballs towards Portnoy's website, it was Barstool's unique multicity model that was most significant in growing its audience during that time. In May 2013, when visitors entered the site, they chose from Boston, NYC, Chicago, Philly, and Barstool U to read from.

Following the addition of Clancy and Markovich, in 2011, Maurice Peebles, also known as "Tall Mo," was brought on to run the Philadelphia site. Unbeknownst to some readers, Mo was African American; Barstool, which would later be criticized for the company's lack of diversity, in fact had some (to some degree) until Peebles took another job in 2014 as an Associate Editor at Complex Media. Mo was joined by Adam Smith, a block-headed former college football player from the Philly area who would become a punching bag for Portnoy. And following these two (and Katz), another writer in his mid-20s named Eric Nathan was hired to oversee the D.C. expansion in the back half of 2013. Nate, a small and wiry figure, would also become a punching bag for Portnoy, as most of Dave's employees would, at one point or another.

Here's a quick synopsis of who led what city/site for Barstool in 2013:

- Boston: Dave Portnoy, "El Presidente" (Feitelberg and Devlin are part-time)

- NYC: Kevin Clancy, "KFC"

- Barstool U: Keith Markovich, "Kmarko" (who moved from the NYC site to run this)

- Chicago: Dan Katz, "Big Cat" (who was full-time by now)

- Philly: Maurice Peebles, "Tall Mo," and Adam Smith, "Smitty" (#2 behind Tall Mo)

- D.C.: Eric Nathan, "Nate"

Portnoy's cast of characters grew larger, and aside from attracting new readers from different cities, having so many personalities amplified the WWE dynamic he set out to create online. It was so successful in generating almost daily buzz that ESPN attempted to copy the model by dividing its site into sections by city. Shockingly, ESPN wasn't able to generate the same results, mainly because the individuals at Barstool—and the storylines of their lives—leading their respective city's website were more interesting to readers than the news about the region they were covering. Portnoy recognized this even before he expanded his team, as far back as the newspaper days when his readers followed the ups and downs of his paper. And he'd lean into this theme heavily throughout his time running Barstool.

By the end of 2013, Portnoy's website would generate more than 5M unique visitors a month, up from 2M at the end of 2010. And while the multicity model strategy was clearly paying off, Portnoy's decision to expand to a new city wasn't one he took lightly: it was completely dependent on whether he could find someone talented and interesting enough to lead it. Portnoy would have started

Barstool Cuba if a worthy candidate emerged from there. As he put it, when asked about where he would expand to next during that period, "We're like Pat Hill. Anytime, anyplace, anywhere. [Just] need to find the writers." That wasn't easy. Portnoy constantly asked for submissions from hopeful writers and sifted through hundreds of blogs, most of which were unreadable; he was extremely selective in who he brought on to write for him, and even when he did decide to greenlight a new city like Barstool Los Angeles, it didn't always work out.

Portnoy had been eyeing a west-coast expansion for several years. It made sense: apart from Chicago, Barstool's digital footprint remained centered around cities along the Atlantic. Los Angeles was his primary focus for this move for obvious reasons. In 2013, he found a writer by the name of Nick Hall who wrote under the pseudonym NickInsider. After watching one of Hall's YouTube videos, in which he plays a Little League head coach who berates his team of 10-year-olds, Portnoy hired the out-of-shape young comedian.

Hall's honeymoon at Barstool lasted all of one week. Much funnier in videos, Hall simply wasn't a great writer, and Barstool fans quickly called for his head. Portnoy addressed the situation a week after Barstool LA went live in a video to his fans, holding one of his patented Emergency Press Conferences:

> "A lot of people have been asking for an LA press conference [about] the state of the LA blog. I'm gonna give you the press conference, it's gonna be the truth, and well go from there… Am I happy with the LA week 1? No, I am not. Do I think it was a great blog week for him? No, I do not. Am I gonna fire him? No, I am not. I firmly believe that Nick Hall is a funny dude. Met him in California, he's funny looking, he's kinda fat, he's got a great vibe about him, fairly new to the

blogging thing but I wanna make one thing clear...we look *everywhere* for writers. I don't hire people lightly. I think it's very difficult to find funny people, I think he's funny, I think he's gonna get it, it's day fucking five, so people gotta give him a little time to get his feet wet."

But unfortunately for Hall and Portnoy, Hall wasn't cut out for blogging. Just one week later, a sheepish looking Portnoy again addressed his fans:

"This will be a brief press conference. This is on the LA office of Barstool Sports, which essentially is no more. So, what I said in the last press conference was we'd give him time to see if we could make it work. I think everybody has seen it's not working the way we need it to work."

Maybe it was because California cool didn't jive with Barstool's common-man approach. Whatever the reason, the Barstool LA office would remain permanently on pause, as Portnoy has yet to establish a presence in a city west of Chicago.[5]

In 2013, Chicago became the most followed site behind Boston. By that point, Katz had rid himself of his corporate inhibition and joined full-time to run the windy city's website. He recalled the day he made the decision:

"I remember walking into my boss's office to tell him I was going to leave...I [asked him], 'Can I talk to you for a sec, privately?' And he said to me, 'Either you stole money from me, or you found something you're passionate about and

---

5   Technically, there is a presence west of Chicago: Barstool Iowa.

you're leaving us.' And I [said], 'Well, I didn't steal money from you."

It was an inevitable development: Katz was born to blog. As Peebles explains:

"Big Cat was the most interesting [writer] because when he first came on, he was writing like he was this big personality. Immediately, you felt a bit of a sea change, like this guy has something. But up until that point, he was just writing and had done a few videos. And Dave invited us to Boston for a 'holiday party.' Whatever that means. So, it's like ten of us going to a Celtics game. But afterwards, we went to a club, and Big Cat was in the middle of the dance floor, being 'that guy.' And in that moment, it's 1 a.m., and I've had a few drinks, and it was like, 'It's not a lie'. He is that guy. So that was interesting early on to see 'ok, they've got something here.'"

Although popular, Big Cat's writing wasn't nearly as mean-spirited as Dave's, which provided a balance to the more bombastic Barstool founder, who described the difference between him and Big Cat this way: "Dan doesn't really love controversy. He doesn't seek it out. I do." Having Big Cat as part of Barstool opposite El Presidente became a winning formula. Portnoy brought the attention, and Katz closed the corporate sponsors. "Dan is much easier to advertise around," Portnoy says. "He could open doors and have relationships that I probably couldn't have because overall he's just a more pleasant person."

While Katz would play the good cop in this routine, when he first joined Barstool, the Chicago-based writer shared a silent rivalry with Clancy as to who was the number two blogger at Barstool behind Portnoy. Yes, they were posting about asses and funny internet videos, but they are human, they were still competitive, it was still a *job*. After several hangout sessions on Google Chat, that sentiment faded, and Clancy watched as the more talented Katz surpassed him as the other face of the Stool. As Clancy put it, "The story of *me* will be not the funniest, not the most talented, but I just grinded and built an audience. Dan, however, is this comedic gift to the world."

Katz's rise to #2 at Barstool happened in part because he gelled comedically with Portnoy. Despite being sometimes viewed as counterparts, the pair shared a similar sense of humor when it came to what they found funny on the internet: both were huge fans of internet personality Danny Boy Cane, the unintentionally hilarious Miami Hurricanes superfan, or Billy Mitchell, the villain in the YouTube documentary about Donkey Kong, *The King of Kong: A Fistful of Quarters*. However, it was sports gambling that brought them together above all else; Katz, like Portnoy, harbored a gambling addiction, and the pair commiserated more often than they liked over their losing bets.

In a memorable moment for Barstool fans, when the Blackhawks played the Bruins in the 2013 Stanley Cup Final, Portnoy and Katz dressed up in the gear of their respective teams; this led to a ridiculous visual as they sat in full hockey pads alongside spectators. In another often-referenced video, the duo took on King Richard's Faire (an annual New England Renaissance fair), where Barstool filmed them—joined by Clancy—dressed up in medieval garb and participating in a live-action role play. (Katz was later reprimanded by the event organizer for fake-killing too many people.)

But the most noteworthy bit between El Pres and Big Cat began when Katz challenged Portnoy to see who could eat their favorite food every day (all day, literally nothing else) for longer than his opponent. Katz posted the following announcement to Barstool fans tuning in:

"El Pres and Big Cat's Burrito/Pizza Challenge. Official Rules and Updated Odds.

"I feel like Ron Burgundy right now. I had a simple hypothetical that my friends and I were talking about at the bar on Sunday, and next thing you know, I'm a Mexican Day Laborer eating Burritos for breakfast lunch and dinner for the rest of my life. Not sure how we got here, but we're here. You know back in college when you and your friends decided that it would be awesome to do a case race or play Edward 40 hands[6]? You get all jacked up and excited, then you start and after about 90 seconds, that wave comes over you where you're just sitting there saying to yourself, "Why the hell did I agree to this?" Well, that's me right now. But a bet is a bet, and when I agree to something, I don't back down. I made my bed, now it's time to eat burritos and shit my pants in it.

"So here are the official rules.

"First, what we are eating: Dave will eat only plain cheese pizza; I will eat only Burritos."

Katz won the battle, eating a disgusting number of burritos in a short period of time, but Portnoy won the war. It was from this contest that his idea for reviewing pizzas emerged—a part of Portnoy's act that he is probably most well-known for, at least when it comes to people who don't follow Barstool (*one bite, everyone knows the rules*). In the end, though, they both lost: following this contest, Katz and Portnoy became increasingly fat. For the next several years, both embodied the typical out-of-shape blogger, with Katz never relinquishing that title.

Regardless of any health consequences, it was clear Portnoy had struck gold with his hiring of Katz, whom he had been able to

---

6   For those of you who are ignorant of these, they are drinking games, involving cases of beer or 40-ounce bottles.

talk into becoming full-time thanks to the $60,000 per year salary
Portnoy was now paying the heads of each city. It wasn't a fortune,
but relative to what other bloggers were making at the time at companies like BroBible and Bleacher Report, it was above market. As
Clancy explained, "Dave is a motherfucker and we don't see eye to
eye on a lot of things, but one thing I can say about Dave is he's never
been cheap. He's always paid people well. No one else in the industry
was getting paid, SB Nation, all the other networks that tried to exist
were paying people pennies and Dave was giving people $60,000 sal-
aries." That's because thanks to the Blackout Tour, at the end of 2012,
Barstool Sports netted $500,000 in profit. As Dave said of his 2013
financial situation, "It was the first time I had *real* money."

16

In 2013, while the other Barstool cities were working remotely, back in Milton, Portnoy's Boston crew reconciled being popular on the internet with the reality that they still were a bootstrapped company operating out of what was basically a shithole. "Name another mogul that has a squirrel living in its office; you can't," Portnoy wrote. Dave wasn't broke anymore, but he wasn't filthy rich, either. Still, with half a million in the bank, he could afford a few luxuries he certainly hadn't been able to enjoy while he was living at his in-laws' five years earlier. When he was asked during that time (on a Reddit AMA)[1] whether Renee was happy with her husband's career choice, Portnoy stated, "Her last two presents for her birthday and Christmas came from Chanel. We're going to St. Bart's in March. She has 2 horses. She's okay with it as long as that shit keeps happening." And it did. The following year, Dave and Renee moved out of their apartment in Dorchester and into a spacious new condo in downtown Boston, with two floors and a rooftop that had an impressive view of the city.

But while Portnoy was able to afford more space to live, his employees in Boston were still stuck with him inside that tiny dentist's office, which wasn't always ideal. "Everyone was in tight quarters," Dave said, "at times getting on each other's nerves. It was a bunch of people who've never had a real job in their life."

By this time, Dave, who was never a pat-you-on-the-back guy to begin with—Feitelberg said he can count how many times Dave has said 'good job'—had become a notoriously tough boss: there was a sense of fear among his guys in those days, and no one wanted to be

---

1   A Reddit AMA is Reddit's "Ask Me Anything," where users on Reddit.com ask the host of the AMA questions and the host answers them.

on the other end of a Portnoy lashing. "I was terrified to go up to his office," said Henry Lockwood, an early Milton employee.

"I never really had a long conversation with him," Feitelberg added.

"Milton Tough" is a badge of honor still worn by that early Barstool team. "Being 'Milton Tough' in the Milton days was being able to work in prison-like conditions," explained Gaz. "You were in Dave's crosshairs every day. And 90% of the time, you were going to have a pissed-off ornery Dave, and he was going to take it out on us."

"It was like being in the middle of a firefight 24/7," Feitelberg stated. "It was a place of torture."

"What do they say about dickheads? Mercurial?" asked Coley Mick, an intern during the Milton days.

Dave explained his approach as the boss during that time: "You are essentially proving yourself as a slave of Barstool Sports; if I yelled at you, it meant I liked you and knew you could take it." He also provided his own definition of the mantra: "'Milton Tough' [means] you work around the clock. I expected a lot from the guys, and nobody was making a lot of money for a long time."[2]

While it wasn't certainly wasn't fun being torn apart by Portnoy, his employees eventually realized what kind of pressure the founder was under, running his own operation. "As time went on," Peebles explained of Portnoy's austerity, "I think Dave felt like maybe he had a lot more riding on [Barstool], a lot more at stake."

"In hindsight, he was probably just really stressed trying to make it all work," Coley added.

Being tough on his guys was a strategy that they acknowledge was probably needed. As Markovich explained, "What it takes to turn this blog of us—these idiots, just typing our thoughts—to turn

---

2   "If I yelled at you..." is a summary of Portnoy's thoughts on screaming at his employees, one he has repeated many times. It's also a paraphrase of an *Awful Announcing* article where he wrote about how he likes the people he works with, and that they have "adjusted to me yelling and hanging up on them."

that into what it is today, you can only get that a certain way and that's doing the Milton Tough way, [both] physically being in that office and mentally having that mindset."

Gaz added, "Milton is something that I think we're all proud that we went through. I think we all became way better for it now. I wouldn't change a single thing about it, the work ethic Dave instilled in all of us."

Despite going through hell, those early Milton employees still respect the founder. Perhaps Markovich summed it up best in a happy birthday video to Portnoy; "Dave, you're an asshole. Happy birthday."

That year, the addition of another newcomer gave Portnoy someone else to take out his frustration on: Henry "Hank" Lockwood. Lockwood was a skinny, slack-jawed 19-year-old from Scituate, MA, and as Portnoy admitted, "I used to torture Hank," which probably explains why Lockwood said he was afraid to go up to his office.

In what was actually quite fitting for Barstool, Lockwood had sent an email to Portnoy—one that was riddled with lies and spelling errors—about how his unique access to free camera equipment at the school where he was studying (which may or may not still be in operation) combined with his experience in production (he didn't have any) would make him a potentially valuable employee for Portnoy. Luckily for Hank, Portnoy's crew was looking for someone to shoot a video that week and was in need of equipment.

After showing up to record at a local park—Barstool was filming a video with the bloggers participating in a series of athletic challenges—everything went smoothly that first day besides the fact that the video he took had no audio (as a horrified Lockwood discovered). Somehow, though, in very Barstoolian fashion, he was invited back the next day. But that didn't mean the same scenario wouldn't play out again.

"Odds Hank ever figures out how to use a microphone?"

—@stoolpresidente

"After 10 minutes of saying 'that's as fast as our high-end camera zooms,' Hank casually mentioned he didn't press the right zoom button."

—@stoolpresidente

"I gotta say Hank outdid himself with the producing on this. I sound different every time I talk. Unreal ineptitude."

—@stoolpresidente

"There is nobody on earth who disappoints me more than Hank."

—@stoolpresidente

Dave berated Hank like a dog for messing up whatever task he was assigned by Gaz, with Lockwood standing there blankly and taking it. Lockwood wasn't the brightest bulb, though his mother put it more delicately: "Henry was never a lover of academics." And she didn't approve of him working at Barstool: "I told you not to trust that Dave Portnoy; he's gonna lead you straight into the ground!" she exclaimed after Hank went to the hospital when a drone blade sliced his finger. But Hank soon became an endearing idiot to the Barstool fanbase, and Portnoy kept him around.

Lockwood explained his reasoning for staying at the Stool, despite becoming Portnoy's whipping boy:

"...most of the time, it was normal Dave, the absolute man, loved working for him. And then some of the time, he'd lash out or bitch at me on camera. If you're weighing the two things of on one hand, you have the best job in the world, but you have to get bitched out by Dave Portnoy once a month, you take that every time."

In one of the more memorable videos to come from those early days, Lockwood was ceremoniously duct-taped to the wall. Portnoy also eventually fired him, but when Dave arrived at the office the next day, he walked in to find Lockwood pulling a *George Costanza*, sitting at his desk, acting as if nothing happened. This would become a well-known quality of Portnoy when it came to being the boss. He was rough at times, but he never actually fired anyone, even when Portnoy found out that Lockwood, while working five feet away from him, would bash him anonymously in the comments section of the website. Again, Hank was not the brightest bulb, as Dave later reported:

"The Most Mind-blowing Fact I Found out about Handsome Hank this Past Weekend Is that He Used to Trash Me in the Comment Section While Working Here

"So this was by far the most mind-blowing fact that I learned about Handsome Hank this weekend. Back in his early days, he used to comment under the name "Frannie" and just eviscerate me, Big Cat, and Feitelberg in the comment section. He loved KFC but hated the 3 of us...[He] just crushed us day in and day out. Like one second, he'd be sitting in my office, and the next second he'd be calling me a "Heeb" and inciting the trolls. And keep in mind this wasn't a joke.... He had no intention of ever stopping or telling us. The only reason he stopped is when another intern busted him because he was using his ex-girlfriend's email address....

And apparently, everybody in the office has known about it for months, but [they] promised to keep it a secret from me because he almost cried when people found out. He even wrote me a long apology letter because he thought I was gonna fire his ass (for the 3rd time). I honestly still don't even know what to think or make of this move? I tried to go back and find all the shit he said, but Hank went in and deleted it before I even knew this happened. It's just Hank being Hank, I guess? The only thing I'm left to do is try to let him explain it himself."

Instead of letting Lockwood go, Portnoy opted to make him wear a t-shirt that said "I am an internet troll" for 30 days; if Hank took it off at any point, he would be fired. Lockwood kept it on and stayed at Barstool for the next ten years. In a shocking development to most people who followed those early days, Hank went on to be one of the highest-ranking producers at the Stool: as Portnoy described, "I turned Hank into a man." Lockwood credits his time in Milton for making him a better worker, saying, "No one gave me direction, you just had to figure it out because no one was gonna help you. If that person who was an intern tried to become an intern at Barstool now, I never would have gotten through the door." Hank was Milton Tough.

These mini controversies, like the ones with Hank, were a staple of Barstool. In August 2014, Dave discovered one of his employees had anonymously downloaded a pornographic video titled *Stagnetti's Revenge* while at work. Portnoy spent the next week interviewing everyone in the office under a hot lamp, interrogating his guys on camera to find out who had downloaded the pirate-themed porn (*arrrrrrr you the culprit?*). A young 20-something named Simon who had joined the company that year in a behind-the-scenes role ended up confessing. From that day on, he was known in the Barstool World as Pirate Simon.

This type of content was completely organic. Most times, Portnoy lit the fuse and the rest played out as unpredictable entertainment (NFL quarterback Jared Goff said the pirate porn saga is what drew him in to Barstool). One of Portnoy's greatest strengths and probably the most important characteristic he possessed as the head of Barstool was his ability to recognize what kind of situations his audience would laugh at. "I've always thought I've known what our fans would find funny," Portnoy said, "Even if it wasn't necessarily my cup of tea." Though at times this would involve others in the office, Portnoy often was the center of the production, as when he ran for Mayor of Boston, an initiative Portnoy took seriously for several months, for the sake of content and because he hated then-Mayor Menino. Dave even hired a campaign manager he nicknamed "Weird Haircut Seth" due to his receding hairline. Here's how Portnoy explained his decision to run:

> "I just wrote that blog saying I wasn't going to run for mayor, but then Stoolies started calling me a pussy: 'oh, you never meant to do it.' What the fuck are you talking about? Of course, I meant to do it. I set up the bank account, anyone who is doubting that I was serious about this is an asshole. Now you want me, now you got me, you better register to vote, you better do the signature, and I'm going all out, so that's it...fine, I'm in."

In a typical Barstool ending to his mayoral run, the signatures Portnoy collected to officially be put on the ballot were invalid, and he was disqualified from the race. Still, in its coverage of the election,

The Boston Globe mentioned Portnoy as a candidate, listing his profession as "unknown."[3]

But probably the biggest stunt Portnoy pulled during that time involved his New England Patriots. In 2015, Brady was suspended four games for intentionally deflating footballs, according to the NFL. And the saga of Deflategate was born. To say Portnoy went absolutely bananas about NFL Commissioner Roger Goodell's decision is an understatement:

"I'd Die for Belichick

"I LOVE IT. Deflategate. Spygate, we're-better-than-you-gate. 11 of 12 balls were deflated by 2 pounds per square inch blah, blah, blah. SHUT UP and listen, you peasants. You're not gonna do shit about it. You're gonna run back to your little shanty towns and throw stones from the valley and hope and pray we don't knock on your door. We're going to the Superbowl, and there ain't shit Bob Kravich or Jerry Rice can do about it. Any sumbitch takes a shot at us, we're not only gonna kill him, but we're gonna kill his wife, all his friends, and burn his damn house down. Alpha males take what they want."

Channeling his inner Vince McMahon again, the founder rounded up the Patriots fans in the office—Gaz, Hank, and Feitelberg—and the four of them hopped in a car and made the four-hour drive down to New York City. When they arrived, after marching around outside in a small circle holding signs that read *Fire*

---

3   In Boston a voter can only sign one mayoral signature petition and if the voter signed more than one, the campaign to file the petition first officially gets the voter. Portnoy stated that other candidates had submitted signatures from people who also signed for him before he filed his signatures, which made their signatures for Portnoy invalid and he did not reach the signature threshold to make the ballot. And this happened despite hiring a campaign manager and a consulting firm to help him.

Goodell, the crew entered the NFL's office at 345 Park Ave and hand-cuffed themselves to each other, taking a collective and symbolic seat on the office lobby floor. Although the cops weren't actually upset with the group—they recognized this was some sort of harmless gimmick—and let them sit there for 15 minutes, the Barstool crew was eventually arrested. "The Brady Four" spent the night in jail, becoming martyrs to Pats fans everywhere.[4]

> **"Pats fans arrested protesting Brady ban at NFL offices"**
>
> —*The New York Post*

> **"Patriots' fans stage Deflategate protest at NFL offices, get arrested"**
>
> —*CBS Sports*

> **"Deflategate Protest by Barstool Sports Leads to Arrests NFL Offices"**
>
> —*Bleacher Report*

Following the sit-in, Dave became the leader of his own "Defend the Wall" movement, printing his infamous blue Roger Goodell clown t-shirts and generating more buzz about Barstool's resistance to Brady's suspension than the actual suspension itself. The crusade cemented Portnoy as the face of the Pats fan, a development that was obviously beneficial to his company. The attention that the success of the Patriots (and of Boston sports, in general) brought to the city—which began pretty much exactly when Portnoy started Barstool—was a fortunate catalyst for the growth of his website. And in 2016,

---

4   According to the NY Post, they were charged with criminal trespassing, and were given "adjournment in contemplation of dismissal deals." And according to Feitelberg, the judge they appeared before laughed and sentenced them to six month of probation (if they didn't violate it, the incident was off their record).

Pats owner Robert Kraft would tell a grinning Portnoy, "It's Brady, Belichick, Portnoy."[5]

It wasn't only Dave who capitalized on unique content like this. Clancy got himself into an internet rap battle with a female rapper from Houston named Tiko Texas; Katz, a Bears fan, dressed up with Lions superfan Detroit Don as they both watched their mutual arch-nemesis Aaron Rodgers throw a game-winning Hail Mary directly in front of their fully painted faces; these spontaneous events helped Barstool stand out among the millions of other blogs now on the internet. There weren't other companies that saw their founder go toe to toe with a grilled-cheese company, as Portnoy claimed the restaurant never acknowledged him shouting them out on Twitter:

> "Cheeseboy is a punk ass sucker bitch"
>
> —@stoolpresidente

> "I appreciate it. @tag_11: @stoolpresidente so hard to resist cheeseboy. Shit looks so good...but I did it for you"
>
> —@stoolpresidente

> "Fuck you, cheeseboy, you cunt @gocheeseboy"
>
> —@stoolpresidente

Barstool did have several regularly programmed shows during those Milton days, operating like a traditional media company in that sense. As podcasting began to find its footing, in 2012, Clancy

---

5   Aside from the success of the Boston teams, pro athletes in Boston and other cities (NFL QB Jay Cutler in particular) reading Barstool helped grow Portnoy's site. They could be seen wearing a Barstool shirt at a press conference, and this helped boost exposure.

launched *KFC Radio*, where he and Feitelberg answered voicemails and wild hypotheticals from their fans. In 2013, "The College Pick Em'" show arrived, with Portnoy and Katz hosting: the pair leaned into their respective gambling addictions and made their picks for their fans to follow (and they often lost). One fan, a crazed caller named Rico Bosco, became a mainstay of the show, screaming mostly nonsense about his picks, but it was entertaining enough that eventually Bosco joined the program full time and remains a host today. Although podcasting hadn't yet exploded—that would happen a few years later—both vehicles were popular with Barstool fans, raking in thousands of listeners.[6]

But the most important production Portnoy & Co. developed during the Milton days was one that became their flagship show for the next five-plus years: "The Rundown." On May 17, 2013, Portnoy posted the following announcement on his website:

"It's the Bro Show Yo...Recapping the Week at Barstool

"So as I said in this video, this is a new concept for us. We still haven't come up with the name yet. We still need a set. We still need a lot of things. I'm sure everybody is gonna say it sucks. Well, fuck that noise. We're doing it. I haven't even watched to see how Sales Guy edited this shit yet. I'm sure I'll hate it."

Originally called "The Bro Show," the formatting was simple: Dave, Clancy, and Katz talked about happenings on the internet, with the topics appearing in a visible list on the right-hand side of the screen à la the sports TV show "Pardon the Interruption." It was a premise that had roots in Portnoy's original company thesis, designed to cover what your friends would talk about at the bar.

---

6   There was also the weekly animated series "Barstool Shorts" by a contributor named Milmore. It was a popular show for the Stoolies, usually depicting the Barstool drama in a cartoon format.

Fans tuned in at 6 p.m. Monday to Thursday to watch the Big Three of Barstool on Skype, with KFC and Big Cat dialing in from their apartments and Dave from his office in Milton. The dynamic that was immediately established featured Katz and Clancy teaming up against Portnoy. For Barstool fans, it was refreshing to watch the brash founder be put in his place, which occurred often:

> "Just rewatched the Rundown, never do that, @ KFCBarstool and I decimated Dave with reason, wit, and guile #GetUpDave"
>
> —@BarstoolBigCat

> "I legitimately thought @stoolpresidente was going to cry on the Rundown today. Thought we'd see tears."
>
> —@KFCBarstool

Portnoy, of course, was a formidable opponent—diehard Dave fans, or #GoPresGo supporters, would have his back in the comment section during heated debates with Katz and Clancy—but the pair did wear him down. "When he turned around and went back to typing on his computer, that's when you know you've got him," Katz stated.

The show was a low-budget operation, but that's what the fans enjoyed. Portnoy, Katz, and Clancy weren't sitting in a slick, multimillion-dollar studio wearing suits their audience couldn't afford; this sort of production value came to be known as "The Barstool Difference." Usually things went wrong: for instance, Portnoy almost never got the date correct when opening the show; he often struggled with pronunciation; and sometimes, he didn't save the Skype video. "Dave forgot to record the Rundown again. Unbelievable," Katz wrote several times to his fans. But Barstool followers didn't care: mistakes were a feature of the show, not a bug; they were what made Barstool *Barstool*. They enjoyed listening to Portnoy rip on Lebron from his tiny office, or Hank joining to tell a story about how he accidentally drank his aunt's breast milk from the fridge. During one Rundown, Portnoy's bookie showed up, handed him a Dunkin' Donuts bag full of cash, and left.[7,8]

Fans also viewed the show to learn about the inner workings of Barstool: what was happening behind the scenes often seeped through the cracks in the form of banter between the three leaders of the company. This sort of content was particularly attractive to Stoolies, who relished hearing about the company's profitability just as much as the opinions doled out by its personalities. Unsurprisingly, The Rundown would become the most important piece of content Barstool produced, and in 2017, the crew brought the show to Comedy Central for a week-long trial run leading up to the Super Bowl. In what probably should have been foreseen, the grassroots feel of the show didn't translate well to TV, and Comedy Central declined to pick it up full-time. But the big three of Barstool remained unfazed and carried on with the vehicle in its true internet form, and The Rundown remained a pillar of Barstool for the next several years.

By the middle of 2015, Portnoy's company was still humming out of Milton. According to an article in *Adweek* magazine, in August of that year, Barstool Sports saw the highest growth of any online publisher for that month:

---

7 The Barstool Difference included Katz and Portnoy filming clips from their home TVs and posting them to Twitter.

8 Probably the most memorable Rundown moment came after the Patriots defeated the Seahawks on a last-second interception by Malcolm Butler. Portnoy, who lost his voice during the game, appeared poolside and shirtless with a cowboy hat and sunglasses. He proceeded to smoke a cigar and gloat in KFC's and Big Cat's faces.

"125 percent growth, suckers! Most growth in the history of the internet. Brick by brick. That's how you do it! That's how you lead, motherfucker! Most growth ever! Pageviews! Pageviews! Pageviews! BUY! BUY! BUY!"

Davey Pageviews (a nickname Portnoy had given himself) was continuing his trajectory towards becoming a digital media mogul. But despite the steadily growing audience size, the health of the company as a whole was a bit more nebulous. The EDM craze had officially died off in 2014, and Barstool's largest revenue stream, the Blackout Tour, had disappeared. More significant, morale had begun to dip.

Portnoy's top guys were growing restless. Clancy was coming up on six years at Barstool, Katz four. That was a lot of blogs, and always having to be plugged into what was happening online had begun to wear on them. As Katz explained:

"I'd be home at my desk, I'd have a different blog up every 40 minutes from 7:30 in the morning basically until five at night, and at five I would maybe take an hour to take my dog out, decompress, and as soon as games start, I'm back on the couch for the rest of the night, interacting, always being on, because people would watch a sport and they're on Twitter and want to interact and see a blog about it and want to know no matter what happens, you'll have my thoughts about it within ten minutes. I didn't have much of a social life."[9]

Dave was the only one with equity in Barstool; he owned the entire operation. And this was a point of contention for both Clancy and Katz, who began questioning what the end game was in the routine Katz described. "I remember [thinking], 'Alright, another pod-

---

9   Despite the grind, Barstool bloggers usually didn't post on the weekends.

cast, another Rundown, a few more blogs. What are we doing here?'"
Clancy said. By now, both were somewhat established digital media
personalities, and both began assembling backup plans. Having a
plan B was one of the main reasons Clancy started his KFC Radio
podcast, and it made sense, given New York was the largest talk radio
market in the country. For the former accountant, who was married
by now, a move to a more traditional company like popular NY radio
station *WFAN* was becoming more attractive.

Meanwhile, Katz began making appearances in front of the
camera on Fox's *Good Day Chicago* and became a contributor to the
ESPN Chicago radio station, calling in to provide his thoughts on
the Bears and the overall climate of the local sports scene. Katz even
started a sports podcast with WGN Radio's Sam Panayotovich called
The Shootaround, but Portnoy shut it down: it was a conflict of interest, given it was being hosted at WGN, not Barstool, and they were
a competitor.

As for the chemistry between Portnoy, Katz and Clancy,
although Portnoy's multi-city model was fruitful for the leaders of
the Barstool cities, it also isolated them. The top three guys weren't
ever working in the same room—"We were all separate," Katz said,
"Our only interaction was on Google Chat"—and it was as if each
site began drifting away from the others. "It was just all stubborn assholes, all working on their own thing," Devlin said. "And then Dave
at the top, who was poor and fat and not the guy you know today."

Despite what someone from *The Phoenix* or *Inside Edition* may
have argued, the Barstool founder wasn't an idiot. Dave could sense
there was dissension brewing:

> "We were at a breaking point. And we'd been doing it for a
> long time. And it was like a band that's been together for a
> decade. While Big Cat and KFC had carved out their own
> niches, I was the lead singer. And if you watch the Rundowns
> during that era, I could say the sky was blue, and Dan and

Kevin would [say] 'Fuck you, it's grey and raining.'…we were just at each other's throats."

Eventually, the situation came to a head: Katz and Clancy held a meeting with Portnoy to let him know something needed to change or they would be gone.

17

Mike Kerns was nervous. He was about to pitch his boss, Peter Chernin—a colossal figure in the media business—on investing in a website whose latest article was titled "Guess that Ass," asking its readers to identify which celebrity they were referencing based on close-up photos of that woman's backside. He wasn't sure what Chernin would think of Barstool Sports. Kerns himself was a fan of the site. He believed that unlike other media companies, "They spoke 'the real talk.'" Moreover, Barstool had bootstrapped its operation for the last 12 years, which was both unusual and impressive. But the timing of his pitch also made him hesitant: he had been at The Chernin Group only since the beginning of the month.

Kerns's first foray into the entertainment world began in 2001, when he joined Leigh Steinberg, a legendary American sports agent (Tom Cruise's 1996 hit movie *Jerry Maguire* is based off of Steinberg's career), to work as his VP of Business Development. Kerns was likable, with cherubic looks that often masked an unrelenting drive, and he excelled under Steinberg. But like Portnoy, Kerns also had the desire to start something on his own, and in 2004, he left to launch ProTrade (later renamed Citizen Sports Network) with co-founder Jeff Ma. Continuing Kerns's theme of having colleagues in movies, Ma was a member of the infamous MIT Blackjack Team and became the basis for the main character of the well-known film *21*.

Citizen Sports Network built sports apps for the emerging social networks, including Facebook and Myspace, and the company created a popular iPhone app called Sportacular, which became the most downloaded sports news app at the time. Social media and smartphone growth exploded, and advertising revenue began to pour in. In 2010, internet giant Yahoo! was looking to expand its reach across sports tech and eventually acquired Citizen Sports Network for between $40-$50M. Following the acquisition, Kerns joined Yahoo! full-time.

During his time at Yahoo!, Kerns was in charge of leading the company's Homepage, Video, and Global Media properties. It was an important role: the three business units handled more than one billion monthly users combined and included Yahoo!'s flagship products Yahoo! Finance and Yahoo! Sports. But by 2015, Kerns had grown tired of the corporate politics that plague a company of Yahoo!'s size, and he eventually made his way over to The Chernin Group, where he was hired as Head of Digital for the media investment firm in July 2015.

By this time, Kerns was well versed in the fast-moving internet landscape. He had watched Portnoy's rise with admiration. At one point during his tenure at Yahoo!, Kerns had even attempted to buy Barstool, but he was shut down internally before he ever had the chance to speak with Dave. Corporate politics.

Kerns kept this move in his back pocket, however, and when he arrived at his new company, he revisited the idea. Kerns loved the humor, and he believed Portnoy was operating in a totally unique space. Barstool's brand of humor and commentary was different from everything else out there: it was unfiltered, authentic, and ran counter to the buttoned-up product delivered by the traditional sports networks. "The world didn't need another person in a suit asking athletes canned questions," he said. Kerns thought Portnoy was on to something.

Barstool's audience engagement was particularly attractive to Kerns—because it was unlike anything he had ever seen. Other digital sports companies didn't come close to having a connection with their fans the way Portnoy and Barstool did: users came back over and over and over again, sometimes 20 times a day. "The interaction was analogous to a social networking platform—like Facebook or Snapchat," Kerns said. "It was incredible."

This meant there was value to be capitalized on. Kerns had never met Dave Portnoy and had no idea what he was like as a business owner. Nor did he have any inkling of whether he wanted to keep Barstool Sports as an interesting lifestyle business for himself, or if he wanted to grow the company into a larger entity, which was the only way The Chernin Group would get involved with an investment. But he knew how loyal Portnoy's followers were and how compelling the brand was.

Kerns approached Jesse Jacobs, the President of The Chernin Group and a former Goldman Sachs banker. "Jesse's also a big sports fan, and he understood the comedic nature of the content," Kerns said. Jesse thought the idea was a good one. They would just need to run it by the man whose name was on the door.

Their boss, Peter Chernin, had become a titan in the entertainment industry, and he looked the part. The Hollywood executive was tall and handsome, with a flashy smile, well-kept dark hair, and square glasses that matched the outline of his face. During his time leading Fox and News Corp as Rupert Murdoch's right-hand man, Chernin oversaw the two highest-grossing films of all time, *Titanic* and *Avatar*. Under his reign, Twentieth Century Fox Television became the number one television studio in the country, producing hit shows such as *24*, *Modern Family*, and *Glee*. Chernin also successfully ushered the company into the digital age by launching Hulu, the popular subscription-based video-on-demand service.

In 2009, Chernin left Fox after a successful 20-year run, and the following year founded The Chernin Group, a multifaceted media company that served as a production studio and investment firm, providing capital to organizations that either built new technology or created original content. Despite his apprehension, Kerns knew his boss had seen a lot throughout his time at Fox: Hollywood tends to produce some interesting characters. So when he worked up the nerve to walk into Chernin's office, Kerns had convinced himself that Chernin would find his Barstool proposition interesting at worst.

And his instincts were correct. Chernin was keen on pursuing an investment. "You go to sports talk for attitude and fun, and I felt Barstool had a huge opportunity there," Chernin explained.

"Peter is a big believer in unique content and original voices, which Barstool had," Kerns said. Chernin agreed with Kerns and Jacobs that there was something exceptional about the Milton-based group. But more important, he wasn't deterred by the company's controversial reputation. "They knew about [things like] Babygate [when Portnoy posted the pictures of Tom Brady's son]... They got it. They understood it," Portnoy said.

Kerns added, "We certainly understood that there was an element of controversial topics and off-color content and programming ... and we talked a lot about it. So, there was certainly an element that isn't going to be for everyone."

Chernin's company did have close relationships with the NFL and several of its owners, and Dave had declared commissioner Roger Goodell his arch nemesis following his Deflategate protest: "This is America! You can't lie lie lie! Hitler! Hitler!" Portnoy (who is Jewish) once screamed at the NFL Commissioner as he was escorted into a New York courthouse for the final hearing over Tom Brady's suspension. But as Kerns explained, "Barstool was a comedy site: if people took them too seriously, that was their problem."

All three Chernin guys were also interested in the gambling aspect of the venture. Barstool Sports was the first media company to take the popular but still taboo pastime mainstream, and Kerns was adamant that the legalization of sports gambling in the U.S. was inevitable. If this were to happen, Barstool would be in a perfect position to take advantage of that development.

But when it came down to deciding whether to invest, what stood out most to the man cutting the checks was Portnoy's resilience. "I was really impressed by the journey," Chernin said. "Giving out newspapers, then morphing into the concert business, I was really impressed with his willpower, and the people who are successful are the people who just *keep* at it."

Chernin gave Kerns the greenlight to contact Portnoy. Fortunately for Kerns, he had a loose connection to Barstool's founder. His good friend from high school was NFL QB Jared Lorenzen's agent. Nicknamed "Hefty Lefty," at 300lbs, Lorenzen was by far the heaviest to ever play the position in the NFL. This garnered him notoriety and led to several appearances on the Barstool website, including facing off with Katz in a Burger King Chicken Fries eating contest. (Lorenzen lost.) From this, Lorenzen had become friends with Portnoy. "I called Jared… and said 'Hey Jared, my name is Mike Kerns. I'm sure people try to get in front of Dave all the time.' I told Jared my background and he said, 'I'll introduce you to him.'" When Kerns phoned Dave asking if he would be interested in discussing a possible investment, Portnoy told him he would be willing to take a meeting.[1]

"I wasn't desperate for an investment," Portnoy says. Despite Devlin's "poor and fat" title, Dave wasn't poor. In fact, after surviving the Blackout Tour shutdown, thanks to the continued growth of his website, the Barstool founder was on pace that year to take home close to one million dollars personally after taxes. One million dollars! It was more money than the former paperboy ever imagined making after accepting that tuition check from his father. He'd even begun looking at property on New England's crown jewel, Nantucket Island (and that November, Dave did indeed close on a $2M house).

But Portnoy was a gambler. He often took risks not because it was in his interest, but because it was in his *nature*. Ceding control of

1   Sadly, Lorenzen passed away in 2019.

Barstool through a majority investment by Chernin—which is what Chernin's company would demand—certainly was a more uncertain path than just fucking off to Nantucket; anything can happen to a company once it hands the keys to new ownership. Still, he knew the final payoff would be much, much greater if he took their money and successfully grew the company: "It wouldn't have even been close."

Also, Dave had come away from his five-alarm meeting with Clancy and Katz, the two other legs of the Stool, knowing that keeping things how they were for the next decade wasn't a realistic option, even though it would be nice for him. Both Clancy and Katz were ready to leave. Taking Barstool to the next level was the only way they would be enticed to stick around, and he knew this would only be possible through a partnership with a company like Chernin. "We would have never been able to make that leap without them."

Fortunately for Dave, Kerns seemed serious about making a deal. "I can always tell who's really interested. Because we've actually had a lot of people throughout the years who've dipped their toe in the water and want to speak, but when push comes to shove, they'll be like 'hey why don't *you* fly yourself out *here?*' And when I spoke with Mike, he jumped on a plane from San Francisco almost instantly, so that was a good first step."

When Kerns arrived in Boston, he wasn't sure if they were going to have dinner at a high-end restaurant or a local sports pub. What was El Presidente like in real life? What did he do for fun? Where did he eat? "I wanted to see what kind of person Dave was," he said. "I knew him as his on-camera personality, but I wanted to see if he was someone I thought we could work with in terms of his character." Dave let Kerns know they were going to meet at Mistral, an upscale French restaurant in the wealthy South End neighborhood of Boston. If Kerns was going to take him seriously, Dave would return the favor.

The pair sat down and immediately had a rapport, bonding over what it was like starting a company and laughing at Portnoy's abysmal horse-racing record. But as dinner wore on, Kerns had to reel himself in: "Part of the thing for me was because I was a fan, throughout the whole process of getting to know Dave and Barstool, I always had to check myself and say, ok are we doing this because I think Dave and Big Cat and KFC are funny? Or do I think there's a real business here?"

Then Dave laid out his vision for Barstool: he wanted to move all of his employees to one office in New York City, the media capital of the world, to create a fantasy-factory, 24/7 comedic reality show. Having the Barstool personalities, in whom his audience was so heavily invested, interacting together under one roof would amplify the WWE-like world he created, Portnoy explained. And the founder finished on a more grandiose note, declaring to Kerns he wanted Barstool to be "this generation's *SNL*."[2]

Kerns was relieved. Not only was Dave absolutely someone they could work with, "Dave was direct and professional," but he also shared a similar vision for what the company could be, one that was large enough for Chernin to invest in. Portnoy did have one demand, and it was non-negotiable: Barstool's content wouldn't change. Chernin was not allowed to have a say in what Dave produced. For Kerns, this wasn't a dealbreaker, in fact, quite the opposite. "The fundamental reason we invested in Barstool was because of the guys— the talent and the content—we didn't invest because we thought they had a great sales strategy, or a great product; it's the guys, so we'd be pretty stupid to try to change the content," Kerns said.

Peter Chernin backed this up: "Not only were we comfortable with edgy content; I viewed it as being really important and something to encourage and protect."

Dave knew then that Chernin was the right partner. Portnoy didn't want his fans thinking he'd sold out—for a while, many would think this anyway, but such is life with the Stoolies, who are just as

---

2   This quote is based off of the numerous times Portnoy has made this comparison to SNL, and both Kerns's and his explanation of that meeting.

cynical as their founder—not just because he didn't want this label personally, but because it wasn't a smart move business wise. As Chernin realized, his fans would just stop visiting his site if they diluted his content. When asked later if he worried about this scenario when giving up a majority stake, Portnoy said, "I didn't fight all that hard at giving up full control. Don't get me wrong: the equity was a huge part, that I still had a huge stake, I was trying to get uber rich compared to what I had before, but my biggest takeaway was I was 100% convinced the content wouldn't change."

Kerns told Portnoy, "There are some things that you and I will talk about business wise that I think would be useful that you didn't share, but at the end of the day, you can do whatever you want content wise." With Chernin, Portnoy had full editorial control.

In his attempt to bring Barstool to a nationally known media brand, Portnoy needed not only Chernin's money, but also The Chernin Group's business expertise. Badly. Barstool had no payment-tracking system, no data reporting, no real infrastructure. No other popular media company had its head writer simultaneously handling all business operations, and this wasn't a recipe for success. Dave didn't know how to open a Google Doc. "For all I know, advertisers could have owed us hundreds of thousands of dollars over the last couple years because we didn't know when people paid."

Much like Hank hanging off the Milton office wall, Barstool was being held together by duct tape. "It was a miracle they had gotten as far as they had," Kerns said. Because Portnoy often conflated his personal bank account with his business account (they were essentially the same), attempting to navigate Barstool's exact financials was a journey unto itself.

"I'd pay everyone their salary and whatever was left would stick in my bank account. And then as crazy as it sounds, I'd lose money gambling and the account would go down, and then I'd sell t-shirts, it was like pulling levers, like the Wizard of Oz." At one point during negotiations, the Chernin guys found themselves discussing who would take ownership of Portnoy's two racing horses, which were technically under the company's name. Dave insisted Chernin get them, and he would keep the RV he had purchased for the Barstool Dixie Tour, which was of roughly equal value. "I didn't want the horses because I knew they were losers," Portnoy said with a grin.

It was clear Dave needed support, and if he were to move his employees to a central office in NYC, he would need help negotiating a lease, buying a multimedia set up—the list was never-ending. Both The Chernin Group and Portnoy agreed Barstool had to bring on a CEO, someone who could do this—and build out a sales and marketing team, sign new partnerships, improve Ecommerce, "Someone to capitalize on all the commercial opportunities I knew were missing out on," Portnoy said.

Portnoy also needed the legitimacy the Chernin brand brought to his operation. When he met with potential advertisers, at times, Portnoy had difficulty convincing them to spend with a company like Barstool: "They would see me as this crazy internet guy; it was sometimes tough to be taken seriously." The conference room was an away game for Portnoy; not so for Chernin, and he understood these sorts of intangibles The Chernin Group brought to the table would be invaluable.

Before any offer was made, Peter Chernin still needed to meet with Portnoy. When Dave sat down to dinner with Chernin at The Four Seasons, Kerns still wasn't sure if a deal was going to happen. He didn't know if Dave was willing to give up full control of his company—Barstool was his baby, and he had spent the last 12 years bootstrapping the company—and Kerns wasn't sure if Chernin would officially sign off. Kerns still didn't know Dave *that* well. But reassurance came in the form of a brief phone call from his boss.

"Dave is brilliant. Let's figure out a way to make this happen."

18

On January 1, 2016, The Chernin Group bought a 51% stake in Barstool Sports at a $12.5M valuation. "I think I got around $5M directly in cash, and the rest went into the company's bank account or something like that," Portnoy said. Dave had given up control of his baby. "I wanted to take Barstool to the moon."

But like any founder who sells their company, Dave would look back at the deal and believe he left money on the table. In numerous podcasts and interviews over the next seven years, Portnoy lamented the price he received—mostly because he had no idea what he was doing. "I wasn't a business guy. Mike was a business guy and an agent trying to get the best deal." Others in the industry claimed The Chernin Group, who unlike Portnoy were professional negotiators, basically stole the company at that price.

But Kerns, who now calls Portnoy a friend, defends his company's position:

> "I thought the offer was genuinely fair, primarily because Barstool's growth had plateaued. And basically when these digital media companies get bought, they get bought as a multiple of growth. Whether it be topline revenue or profit."

While Barstool brought in a healthy profit of $1.5-2M the previous year, its revenue had stalled at mid-seven figures, thanks to the Blackout Tour ending. (For context, internet content companies at the time were trading at a 2.5x multiple. And as a benchmark, Portnoy's website had half as many monthly unique visitors as Grandex, which owned the popular college humor website Total Frat Move. In June of 2015, Grandex raised money at a $20M valuation.)

"What I would have done differently, we were super profitable, if I had focused the business on growing top-line revenue more, I could have made more money from Chernin or someone else." Portnoy said. "With the Blackout Tour shutting down, a huge part of our revenue went away." Portnoy argued that his audience size was growing, and he was right:

> 2006: 100,000 monthly unique visitors (MUV)s
> 2010: 2.4M MUVs
> 2013: 5M MUVs
> 2015: 7M MUVs

But Kerns provided a friendly counter to the argument of audience growth. "The ad growth was put at risk long term based on ad blockers and the fact that they were largely web and not on app and not on TV." And he did have a point. Dave was late to create any sort of useable Barstool app for the iPhone, stating his aversion to building one early on:

> "Maybe the #1 request I get here at Barstool Sports is to create some sort of iPhone or Droid app or something like that. Well, I'll let you in on a little secret. I honestly don't know what the fuck that means. In fact, I've gotten so many emails about it over the past couple years that I've actually hired two different companies to build me this mythical application. Guess what? Both times they sucked. It looked way worse on the app than it did just normally. So basically, I've flushed [about] 2 grand down the toilet, and I still don't have anything to show for it, and I still don't even understand what people are asking for. Can somebody explain to me what this means? Our site works fine on PDAs, right? What's the fucking difference? Fuck apps.[1]"

---

1   PDA stands for Personal Digital Assistant aka Palm Pilots.

(Sidenote: Barstool eventually built an app, but it often crashed and wasn't easy to use. In fact, an app would be a feature the company never really nailed down. Even to this day. Second sidenote: During an attempt to build an app, the entire historical catalogue of Barstool blogs was accidentally deleted. This became known as The Devnest Disaster.)

Before signing the deal, one thing Kerns had mentioned to Dave was he believed his original crew—Katz, Clancy, Gaz, and Kmarko—should hold some equity in the company going forward. Portnoy more than agreed. Up until that point, they didn't own any shares of Barstool. And they deserved to. (Portnoy also needed to keep them incentivized.) The Chernin Group told him they could figure something out on this end. They were going to create an employee option pool to give equity to new hires and could take shares out of that. Dave, however, offered to give the guys a piece of his 49% directly.[2]

"This was above and beyond. The way Dave looked out for his team, that was the thing that gave me the most confidence that in two years when we would be going through ups and downs [that this would work]. That was a sign of his character. I don't even know if those guys fully appreciate how much he gave from his part of it," according to Kerns.[3]

While there certainly was friction right before Chernin showed up, at the end of the day, Portnoy had his guys' backs. "We were in it together. I do, for the most part, try to be very fair with all our employees. I want them to be their best with us or with someone else. When I feel like I've been crossed, though, I hold a grudge against them for 3,000 years."

And just as the deal had reached the finish line, Portnoy did end up feeling crossed, not by one of his employees, but by Mark Kamal, SVP of Digital for The Chernin Group. A numbers wiz, Kamal was

---

2   This was more concrete than employee options that usually take time to vest.

3   The Milton guys would end up getting a small percentage of Barstool, which would end up being worth a lot of money.

in charge of cost control inside the deal and was tying up the last loose end in the transaction: the lawyer fees. When he picked up the phone to let Portnoy know he still had to pay $50,000 to cover this, Portnoy responded, "Uh, no, I don't. You guys said you would pay for it. We had a verbal agreement."

There had been a miscommunication, and Kamal would go back and forth with Portnoy, trying to find a middle ground. "We can cover most of the cost, if you step up and make a contribution." The Barstool founder was not having any of it.

"Kamal, I don't think you are fucking hearing me. I am NOT negotiating with you. We had an agreement. I will walk away from this deal right fucking now if you don't pay it!" Dave shouted into the phone.

Kamal was taken aback by this sudden outburst. "You are going to walk away from the deal, after 6 months of negotiation, over this?" he asked quietly. Dave was. And it wouldn't be the last time he threatened to do so.[4]

Though he trusted Dave to think rationally about his business, this was Kerns's first glimpse into how Dave operated: if he felt slighted, Portnoy was stubborn and absolute. It's a trait he'd built his company on. But Kerns and Dave, in this instance and other disagreements going forward, would lean on their mutual understanding of where they wanted to take Barstool. And Kerns wasn't about to let this fall through at the last second. He let Dave know Chernin would pay for the fees.

With the deal signed on New Year's Day, The Chernin Group officially legitimized Barstool Sports. Portnoy and his free-wheeling style of entertainment were now backed by an established organization. It was a paradoxical partnership: Portnoy had spent his entire life ripping down buttoned-up suits like Chernin; and likewise, the polished image Peter Chernin presented stood in stark contrast to

---

4   Kamal's quote is based on Portnoy's explanation of their conversation, which he gave on an episode of The Dave Portnoy Show.

the one Portnoy had peddled over the last 12 years. But Chernin was savvy enough to see where media was heading, and Portnoy wanted to "take Barstool to the moon."

Later that day, Portnoy let his followers know there was big news dropping on January 7th. Stoolies buzzed on Twitter wondering what their mercurial leader was up to now. On The Chernin Group's side, Kerns hired a PR firm to coordinate the large press release about the partnership, one that would include a number of established journalists and media outfits. With their respective ducks in a row, all that was left to do was make the announcement.

On January 7, 2016, Mike Kerns was standing outside The White Horse pub, in his wife's hometown of Cork, Ireland. He was leaning up against one of the large glass windowpanes next to the entrance, behind which there were several neatly displayed antique pieces of furniture. The place had the appearance of a storefront, like you were about to enter a Ralph Lauren instead of a local watering hole. Kerns was damp from the usual mist that permeated the area and was having trouble opening his iPhone, which had begun buzzing wildly.

Glaring at his phone, Kerns was confused. The press release about Chernin's investment in Barstool that he had organized was scheduled for later that day. It hadn't happened yet, why were people calling him? He fumbled through a quick google search and found the headline from *Sports Illustrated*, one of the most reputable brands in sports media:

"How Barstool Sports Uses Social Media as a Weapon."

Kerns couldn't believe it. Of all days, this article had to drop *today*?

As it turned out, *Sports Illustrated* hadn't the slightest idea that Chernin had invested in Barstool, nor that they were about to let the world know it that day. Portnoy didn't care. Back in the states, and livid, he immediately took exception with a man named Jamie O'Grady, who owned *The Cauldron*, the subsidiary under SI, which had posted the article. "I hate this guy so fucking much. Fuck this fucking guy!" Dave told his fans about O'Grady. "Jamie O'Grady is a loser nobody bum!"

Katz, on the other hand, found the timing slightly amusing: "It was the most Barstool thing of all time," Katz said. "It was supposed to be this beautiful PR moment, and there we were, in the fucking muck, fighting like we always do."

As for the article itself, the piece was written by a contributor in his early 20s named Nick Stellini and was a major critique of the way followers of Barstool Sports would galvanize online against detractors of the website (re: Knockout Barstool). How they would attack anyone who opposed the leaders they looked up to—Dave, Clancy, Katz, and Kmarko. And how they were vicious.

Stellini highlighted a tweet from Barstool's Kevin Clancy:

> "Al Jazeera = Al Qaeda in my mind and in the mind of everyone with a brain."
>
> —@KFCBarstool

The article followed with a tweet from Jen Mac Ramos, who was a journalism grad student at USC, contributor to SB Nation (another Barstool competitor) and most important, a friend of Stellini.

> "Man who tweets ignorance Al Jazeera/Al Qaeda has 127K followers and writes for Barstool Sports. Meanwhile I'm still job hunting."
>
> —@jenmacramos

Stellini then highlighted the chaos that ensued. Barstool supporters flooded Ramos's Twitter page, bashing her with nasty comments that Stellini reposted in his article:

"@jenmacramos Lose some weight and pretty yourself up and you might get lucky"

—@just1hanna

"@jenmacramos do you mean there is no job market for ugly broads with an extra chromosome?"

—@dpfleck04

"@KFCBarstool @jenmacramos with that fuckin' gross fat frog ice cream looking ass face, I'm not shocked she's job hunting with 0 success. Woof"

—@DCaruso83

The piece ended with a conclusion by Stellini:

"Not surprisingly, Barstool Sports never said anything to condemn the harassment and abuse levied by their community. All the while, the Barstool crowd—"stoolies," as they refer to themselves—laughs it all off. To them, it's all just a bad joke that we don't get. It's satire. Good clean fun that falls on the deaf ears of the church of politically correctness. It's not. It's not funny. It's not a joke. It's not satire. It's *actual* harassment."

The article brought to mind a question that could be asked of any popular media outlet: are its leaders responsible for what their fans say online? The comment section of Barstool was one of the major lifebloods of the company—often, readers clicked on a blog just to read the comments—and until technology improved and allowed Portnoy to remove hateful posts made by commentators, it was at times a disgusting underbelly of Dave's operation. Still, Portnoy used to value this aspect of his website, writing in 2013:

"See, I understand that the comment section is littered with morons. I understand that many of them probably haven't fucked a real chick in the past decade. But guess what? Deep down in places I don't talk about at parties, I love our comment section. I wouldn't trade 'em for the world. Sure, they say a ton of stupid shit, but they also say some pretty funny stuff."

By 2019, he changed his tune, however, even going so far as shutting down it down for an extended period of time:

"So I've noticed the comment section, which I fucking despise and have despised for a long time, is getting worse and worse. We try to stop it. We try to ban people. We can't stay ahead of it. I'm talking N bombs in every post. The last post I wrote there was a comment that said, 'I hope N bomb blow their heads off with a gun.' Are you serious? Well, I've had enough. I've made the decision to shut it down effective immediately until we can regain control of it. And if we never bring it back, I don't care. I don't care if you hate me, hate Barstool, etc. I don't care. The racist shit has to stop. If we can't stop it, I'll just eliminate it, and that's exactly what I just did. I'm told it will cost our company money with clicks. Guess what? I don't care. It's trash. The people in it are trash. Go read some other site. Don't care. Bye, losers."

Once Twitter became prominent, the underbelly of Portnoy's website was now activated; aside from being in a public forum—they weren't just writing at the bottom of a Portnoy blog post anymore—and thus more visible to people like Stellini, the tools at these Stoolies' disposal allowed them to direct their anger (and whatever other sentiments they held) towards Barstool detractors in an efficient manner, usually by swarming the social media profiles of writers like Jen Mac Ramos. The real-world consequences of these kinds of actions led critics like Stellini to believe that even if they weren't the ones doing it—opponents said these fans were simply emulating their leaders—Barstool was wrong for letting it happen.

Katz seemed to recognize this when commenting on the 2016 *Sports Illustrated* article: "He said we never condemn anyone…how many times do I say we lose when we go around calling people cunts for no reason? I've said it a million times."

But Portnoy had a more aggressive response to the article than Katz did. He explained his reasoning for this as follows (without specifically commenting on the Stoolies who went after Ramos or were now going after *Sports Illustrated*):

"I don't like this philosophy that people think it's fair to attack us but we can't say anything back. It's bananas; we didn't go looking for this fucking fight…They think you can trash Barstool in an internet safe space."

And in going after O'Grady (who published Stellini's article), Portnoy said:

"I don't care if I harass them. Or am mean. If you come at me—I just go how much blood pressure is going, and this person [O'Grady] got me fucking mad. I'm gonna try to rip your heart out and fucking eat it!"

Back at the pub, after reading the article, Kerns quickly dialed Peter Chernin. They both agreed that a change in plans was needed. One notable journalist Kerns planned on sending the release to was Kara Swisher, a prominent tech reporter who had been covering internet companies since 1994. She founded All Things D and Re/code, two very popular websites that specialized in technology and startup news, and The Chernin Group had a good working relationship with her.

Before Kerns could send her the announcement, Swisher tweeted about the *Sports Illustrated* piece. Asked why she cared about the article, Swisher replied:

> "You think I like women being called vile names
> for amusement of dolts?"
>
> —@karaswisher

Well, there was no way in hell they could ask Swisher to run a story on the Barstool deal now. Not after that tweet. Kerns and Chernin decided to scrap the entire plan. The Chernin Group's PR team called every single outlet that had been prepped on the story and told them they were not moving forward with it. Kerns, who was continuing to serve as the liaison between Chernin and Barstool, then phoned Dave.

Here's how Portnoy described that phone call:

> "Kevin Clancy had just called me and said 'Can you believe this timing? It's perfect. This just broke, and we're going to say we just got invested in an hour later.' I hung up the phone and then Mike Kerns called me and said 'Can you believe this timing? It's the worst timing ever. Can we delay the announcement?'"

It was a tale of two companies.

Portnoy's response to Kerns's request was unsurprising. "I am not fucking doing that," Dave basically shouted through the other end of the phone. "I already told our audience that it was coming today—and I'm not changing it. You guys can do whatever you want. I have full editorial control. I am going forward with it."

"Sounds good," Kerns replied and hung up.

For The Chernin Group, this was their "Welcome to Barstool" moment: the first real test of whether they could stomach a partnership with Portnoy's company. And that test happened to come less than a week after their agreement was finalized. But this is what the Chernin people had signed up for, and although they ended up never sending a press release to the 100 reporters they had planned to contact, Chernin eventually gave Dave the greenlight to go forward with his announcement. Kerns explained why: "If anyone with a rational mind examined what that author had written and used as evidence, the problem was what the commenters and people who followed Barstool were saying, not what Dave, Katz, or Clancy were putting out there. Everyone, including the press, needed to look at where the misogyny was actually happening: it wasn't coming from anyone who worked at Barstool." In an unexpected turn of events, the buzz that developed online from the hit piece only furthered the investment firm's excitement about the deal.

For Portnoy, this was just another day at the office. And at 2 p.m., the blog post went up on Barstool's website, as scheduled. It was a video of Dave in the middle of Times Square on a cold January night, dressed in a tuxedo, with Clancy, Katz, and Kmarko behind him.

"Barstool Emergency Press Conference—New York, New York

Music. Ok, Live, Emergency Press Conference. Probably the most important press conference to date. We are in Times Square, Elmos around, it's negative five degrees, and we have what I would say is shocking news. I am no longer the majority owner of Barstool Sports. We have taken investment from an investment company called Chernin Digital—Peter Chernin, big swinging dick at the cracker factory—[after] 6 months of negotiation, they said we're the guys, we're the people that are gonna take this thing to the next level. So, we accepted this investment. By the way, people are [saying] I sold out [and] this is cheap. I didn't fucking sell out—if I sold out, I'd be in Nantucket, surfing

24/7; instead, my hands, I can't feel them. This is for you, the readers. I don't think you guys owe us a thank you, but we're trying to take this site and crank it the fuck up. Music!"

At the bottom of the blog post, under the announcement video, Portnoy ended with a captivating assertation to his followers:

"P.S. I'm kinda rich now."

19

FEBRUARY 2016

If Barstool fans were worried about Portnoy being neutered after the takeover by Chernin, the headline of an online article the following month should have eased any concerns:

> **"A sports blogger with 250,000 followers barged into Twitter headquarters demanding to be verified."**

Portnoy & Co. were out in San Francisco for the Super Bowl, and still unverified by Twitter, Dave decided to pay them a visit. "There was just no explanation why we couldn't get verified. I said you know what, I'm gonna storm into their headquarters, I use 'storm' loosely, but we're gonna try to talk to their verification department and get an answer."

When they entered the lobby (peacefully), Barstool was greeted by Twitter's head of security, an ex-FBI agent who didn't know whether the unkempt-looking bunch was lost or homeless. He ended up escorting the crew to the cafeteria, asking them for their Twitter names and if they knew anyone at the company. "I said 'well, my new boss is on the board. Peter Chernin.'" Portnoy recalled the surprise on the man's face. "He looked at me like I had six heads." Five days later, Barstool had a blue checkmark next to its name.

It was symbolic of the legitimacy Portnoy sought to achieve with this new deal. And in the case of Clancy and Katz, the investment from Chernin worked just as Portnoy hoped it would. "That's when I realized this would be a 'safer' job, that this could be a career," Clancy said of teaming up with Peter Chernin.

For The Chernin Group, one aspect of a partnership with
Barstool it hadn't fully thought out was how closely aligned publicly
it would be with Portnoy and his company. "Every other word was
'Chernin' on their podcasts," Kerns said. The VC firm was accustomed to being the silent partner, investing in a company and
disappearing into the background. That wasn't going to happen
with Portnoy.

"You can't get in bed with us without our stink getting all over
you," Portnoy said. "It's just the nature of Barstool Sports." And he
was right. Soon after the investment, *Sporting News* wrote an article titled, "No defending caveman Chernin's investment in Barstool
Sports," with a photoshopped Peter Chernin dressed like Fred
Flintstone holding a red stool:

> "I can't decide what's worse: Sports 'comedy' sites that
> routinely demean women or the corporate enablers who
> reward them…. So here's the question for Peter Chernin:
> How would he feel if it was his wife, daughter, or grand-
> daughter who was being harassed online by fans of a com-
> pany he invested in?"

Chernin wasn't fazed by some of the negative response to his
backing of Dave, however. "I liked the caveman suit," he joked.
Though the timing of the *Sports Illustrated* piece had been less
than ideal, he knew at least some criticism was coming, and with
Portnoy at the editorial helm, there would eventually be more. But
throughout its time with Barstool, The Chernin Group would roll
with the punches.

"For the Chernin guys, the biggest thing that they really lived up
to was they didn't really interfere with content at all," Portnoy said.
"They never said 'you can't say this' or 'you can't say that.'"

The big swinging dick at the cracker factory would let Portnoy
entertain his fans. "I thought that was the funniest thing I've ever

seen," Chernin said of the nickname Portnoy gave him in his announcement video. "It sort of shows you what kind of genius Dave is because it was completely spontaneous. The 'cracker factory' part makes it so weird and funny."

After Portnoy returned from the west coast, he began convening with the Chernin team on a regular basis. Barstool wouldn't move into its new Manhattan office until September of that year, and there was much to get sorted out before they could make that happen. Finding a CEO was at the top of that list. But with Kerns's and Chernin's business acumen, along with Portnoy's vision, all three were confident they'd be able to find the right man for the job.

Erika Nardini had graduated from Colby College in 1998 with a degree in sociology and philosophy. During her time at Colby, the fit brunette played goalie for the school's women's lacrosse team. If you've ever watched a lacrosse game, you know how tough and marginally crazy one has to be to play that position. Hard rubber balls being fired at you from just a few feet away—while wearing a very minimal amount of protection. No, thanks.

Nardini took that fearlessness with her into the corporate world. Only fresh out of college, as a Media Manager for Fidelity Investments in Boston, she was quickly put in charge of all digital media planning and purchasing for the company. No one at Fidelity really understood the internet, and Nardini was tasked with conquering that unknown.[1] She said:

> "Print was very glamorous and the internet was underground, wild, and nebulous. Nobody cared about the internet or wanted to work on it, but they gave me a lot of money

---

1   Nardini started in the legal department and moved over to the marketing side, taking a large pay cut to do this.

to go figure it out. What I saw was that the internet provided a space to create something, have someone react to that something and to be able to measure the audience's reaction. The almost-instant feedback was incredible. I saw the cause and effect of what we purchased."

This understanding allowed Nardini to excel in her next role at Arnold Worldwide, an ad agency, where she managed a team of 17 people creating and deploying content on the web. And over the following decade, she leveraged her experience on the internet into several high-profile jobs at Microsoft, Yahoo!, and AOL. But her ability to land jobs at different blue-chip orgs didn't necessarily mean she always found success in those roles: for instance, she served as Chief Marketing Officer for AOL for only two years.

"I failed a lot," Nardini admitted. "Not everything I tried worked. I worked at big companies, I would try startups [DigitasLBi, Modelinia]. They would fail. I would go back to a big company. I haven't had one of those careers that was very prescriptive, linear, or even logical."

That circuitous path led to a meeting with Jesse Jacobs of The Chernin Group in the summer of 2016. By then, she had become President and CRO of Backstage, a digital marketplace that connected musicians to fans, and the two were discussing Fullscreen, one of Chernin's portfolio companies that had a similar strategy to Nardini's. During the conversation, Jacobs happened to flippantly mention they were searching for someone to be CEO of a company Chernin had recently invested in, one she had probably never heard of: Barstool Sports.

Nardini froze. She had heard of them: in fact, the former jock was a massive fan. "I've always had a guy-ish sense of humor." Instead of discussing Backstage, for the rest of the meeting, she gushed about Portnoy and Barstool. During her time working in Boston, Nardini had been an avid reader of Dave's website, and she believed what he had built on the internet was extraordinary. "I loved the idea that Dave was out there like a Don Quixote pursuing his own path and he was on a quest, brick by brick, sharing a point of view, whether it was popular or unpopular, it was a point of view. I really admired that." She even owned one of Dave's infamous blue Roger Goodell clown shirts.

Sensing the moment, Nardini launched into a quasi-pitch: "I pulled out my phone and showed Jesse the Barstool app. I told him it sucked, but it didn't have to. Then I went on a rant about all the things I would do to improve the company." Even though she had joined Backstage only six months prior, Erika left the meeting wanting the Barstool CEO role. It would be an inherently risky move—she followed the company closely enough to know this—but her experience in digital, her admiration for Barstool and where it could go, her willingness to tackle the unknown (there would be plenty of that)—all of it lined up perfectly. "I knew in my heart that this was the job for me."

Nardini initially believed it would be a dream deferred, however, one that would shrivel up like a raisin in the sun. She didn't have an MBA, she didn't work in sports, she had never been a CEO, and last but not least, she was a woman. The job would to go to some white guy in his mid-40s, she thought. It was Barstool *Sports*, after all.

But like Portnoy, Nardini wasn't one to take her ball and go home: "I really, from that moment on, didn't think about much else other than how I could meet Dave Portnoy, and how I could get connected, and have a chance to have this opportunity." Being resourceful, she reached out to former CEO of *The Huffington Post* Betsy Morgan, who was a member of Nardini's "Women's Mafia," a group of successful professional women who networked together, and who knew Dave from the Nantucket social scene. Morgan brokered a rendezvous.[2]

---

2   Morgan had become an advisor to Barstool.

♣

Seated at a table inside Kubrick Coffee, a flowery café directly across from his new apartment in the West Village of Manhattan (Portnoy had relocated prior to the office move), the Barstool founder was introduced to Morgan's friend. It was a bit of a setup: Morgan hadn't told Portnoy that Nardini wanted to be the CEO of his company. Portnoy explained how he first met Erika:

"One day, Betsy Morgan was in my neck of the woods, New York, and she [asked], 'You want to meet for coffee?' and I [said] sure. So I walked over, and with her was Erika who was Betsy's friend. So Erika just happened to be there for the coffee, and we just started talking."

Although Portnoy wasn't there to conduct an interview, he immediately hit it off with Nardini. The pair discussed the strength of the Barstool brand and zeroed in on his e-commerce business. Nardini said, "When I was looking at Barstool, the diversification of the revenue model was one of the most attractive things to me. There's a question in media about independent publishers and small publishers and how they survive. I don't think you survive in this day and age on an ad-only model." It was a thesis that hit home with Portnoy, who hadn't designed this revenue model by accident; as far back as the nude photos of Tom Brady's son, the Barstool founder refused to bend the knee to advertisers and instead relied on the loyal Stoolies to buy his merch so Dave Portnoy could remain El Pres. Both Nardini and Portnoy understood it was a competitive advantage over other media companies who didn't have such freedom.

After speaking a bit more about Barstool's strategy, it became clear that Portnoy and Nardini were aligned on pretty much everything: "Everything that Erika said that she liked about Barstool and the business model, I was like, yes, that's what I think, yes, that's what I think," Portnoy explained. Aside from talking shop, Nardini also made it obvious to Portnoy that she was a fan: she knew about

Hankgate, Portnoy's 6-12-18-24 challenge,[3] and what it meant to be J-Mac'd on the internet.[4] Following the meetup, Dave walked away impressed. By now, through the efforts made by Chernin and an outside executive search firm, Portnoy had met with a total of 74 different CEO candidates—all male—and he didn't like any of them. Maybe it was because he was at the end of the line, or maybe the idea of a female running the company would be exactly what Barstool needed (although Portnoy claimed gender had nothing to do with Nardini's hiring, critics would call it a cover), but after that meeting Portnoy dialed Kerns and told him, "I think I found our CEO. Do you know Erika Nardini? She's awesome."

Kerns told Dave that The Chernin Group knew Erika and that he'd even overlapped with her for a bit at Yahoo!. She was, in fact, awesome, Kerns said. He would reach out to see if she was formally interested.

Portnoy and Nardini met again, this time on a pair of barstools. As she recalled, "Dave ordered this girly cocktail, I ordered a beer." Nardini could hang with the guys, which was mandatory if she were to lead a company like Barstool. And when she met with the rest of the team, Markovich told her something that may reveal the reason Dave made that call to Kerns: "You're the only one that didn't ask me about the girls. You're the only one that didn't ask or give an opinion that Barstool needed to shut down 'Smokeshow of the Day' or this that or the other thing. Or talk about how 'The skeletons and controversies in Barstool's past are innumerable.'"

As Nardini explained:

---

3   The 6-12-18-24 challenge was a combination of running, drinking, masturbating, and eating donuts. A participant could choose to apply any of those four acts to either 6, 12, 18, or 24 and have to complete the act that number of times in under 24 hours. Portnoy's was run 6 miles, drink 12 beers, masturbate 18 times, and eat 24 donuts. He failed to complete the challenge.

4   Being J-Mac'd on the internet meant falling for something that was fake. The name comes from the blogger J-Mac who was known for being tricked by the internet.

"The reason I didn't ask is because I think, at its core, Dave created a brand for consumers, and all he ever cared about was how they connected with their audience. And I felt what was most important was not to change the nucleus of that thing but to make that thing become and evolve into something much bigger and to frankly preserve the heart of the relationship between Barstool and its fans."

In laymen's terms, she was keeping the T&A.

Katz did have one question for Nardini during their meeting: "Why the fuck would you want this job?" Barstool was still a mess. Markovich, who would become the Editor in Chief of Barstool that year, hadn't actually spoken to Dave directly since 2014. Portnoy's guys were rejuvenated by the deal with Chernin, but they still weren't necessarily sure Barstool was going to be around in five years. Nardini seemed way too career-minded to join a venture as unstable as Barstool Sports.

It would be a question also asked by Nardini's peers. "People did have a lot to say, you know, that it was career suicide, that it was a horrible [idea]," Nardini explained. And her decision wouldn't come without collateral damage: the move cost her those relationships inside her Women's Mafia, which as a whole saw joining Barstool as a betrayal to female professionals. "After they heard I was going to Barstool, every single one of them dropped me like a bad habit." Nardini was even asked to step down from several boards she was on. But as she explained, "I think putting yourself out there is one of the best things you can do, and it hurts sometimes, and it's not comfortable, but it makes you stronger." She wanted the job.[5]

On July 19, 2016, Dave posted an Emergency Press Conference introducing his new hire. To the surprise of most Stoolies, when they looked at the video thumbnail of Portnoy—once again in Times

---

5   Nardini would also say there were people in her life who encouraged her to take the job.

Square, once again in a tux—there was a woman standing next to him, dressed in a Barstool Sports jacket. Although Dave would share equal power with Nardini as Chief of Content, fans would soon come to learn that Barstool now had a new leader, someone with actual business experience. But the title Nardini went by was one they wouldn't find on LinkedIn: Token CEO.

20

Barstool's new headquarters was literally nothing like the one in Milton. Located on the third floor of a skinny 11-story building in the NoMad neighborhood of New York City, the 5,909-square-foot office looked like exactly that: an office. The dentist sinks were replaced by rows of actual desks, which gave the illusion that a serious business was operating there, although the clutter and assortment of bizarre artifacts collected by Barstool employees would soon change that (such as Big Cat's "desk pile," where random paraphernalia would slowly build up around his desk to the point where it looked like he was working inside a small fortress of clothing and whatever else Barstool fans sent him).

Aside from the bays of cubicles, Barstool's new digs also had two legitimate media rooms, one for its radio show and one for podcasting, and a control center with switchboards and mics, where producers would work behind the glass to ensure each show ran smoothly (although they didn't). A complex and expensive lighting system hung from the ceiling in the main room, so viewers could actually make out the face of who was speaking to them. The setup was now a little more involved than one camera on a tripod in Portnoy's upstairs office.

There was one feature of the office, however, that might have led a visitor to believe something unusual was going on: at the center of the space sat a full wooden bar, with TVs and barstools, in front of which were three La-Z-Boys that Portnoy, Clancy, and Katz would sit in to host The Rundown. The arrangement had the Barstoolian feel—which Katz helped preserve by refusing to use the bathroom and instead relieving himself in the sink or off the fire escape, and Dave also helped maintain by purchasing a human-sized birdcage to put Nate in—a notion that was top of mind for Portnoy and Nardini when mapping out the new HQ. The co-leaders of The Stool—and the only two with their own offices—had recently negotiated a five-year lease with the real estate company that owned the building. Barstool would outgrow the space in less than 9 months.[1]

It was a testament to the value Chernin, and more specifically, Nardini brought to Portnoy's operation. (On her first day on the job, Nardini created Barstool's first ever P&L Statement.) As Dave said, "Erika is the best hire I made in 20 years doing Barstool." Almost immediately Nardini was able to boost revenues for Barstool, signing blue-chip advertising partnerships with H&R Block, Dunkin' Donuts, and DirecTV—which, if you recall, was once featured as an advertiser in Portnoy's paper, unbeknownst to the company itself. The fact that these companies weren't beer or gambling companies validated the Barstool brand and indicated that the climate inside advertising was changing. As Kerns explained at the time, "The younger folks within agencies and brands get Barstool and recognize the world is increasingly taking itself less seriously." Nardini was able to capitalize on this.

But the CEO's main emphasis for the company was exercising the ideal she had shared with Portnoy in their initial meeting: that Barstool shouldn't rely on an ad model alone. Instead, Nardini took what she describes as a "content into commerce" approach, hiring an outside consultant firm to assist with the strategy. "Our objective was to drive revenue from their online store," Tyler Prone, former VP of Paid Media at Hawke, explained. "They were sitting on a huge following stemming from their blog and greater digital community. Our goal was to meet their business goals by redirecting a lot of that

---

1   Barstool would take over the floor above them, which would be reserved for sales employees and other areas of the business.

traffic to the store." Search ads to the Barstool merch store now took priority over those directed towards ad-supported content.

Barstool also ran a telethon promo for Black Friday and Cyber Monday the first full year Nardini was there, which included employees answering phone calls from fans and stunts like Portnoy being buried alive in a coffin. "About to get buried alive to put food on Shea Clancy's table," Dave tweeted. The push registered 35,000 orders of Barstool merchandise, generating revenue in the millions.[2]

> "Cyber Monday ends at midnight. Thank you to everybody who bought stuff. The #1 thing that has allowed Barstool to be Barstool...and given us the freedom to not worry about our critics is our fans buying Merch. It's very much appreciated."
>
> —@stoolpresidente

In November 2017, Nardini continued to diversify the company's cash flow, buying the amateur boxing organization Rough N' Rowdy. By the third show in February 2018, with Portnoy, Katz, and others calling the fights, Barstool was able to sell more than 40,000 Pay-Per-Views, at anywhere from $9.99 to $15.99 based on when you signed up (it was the second acquisition made by Nardini, the first being southern media brand Old Row in August 2016). Broadcast from West Virginia, the event was perfectly Barstool, with attractive (and unattractive) ring girls gyrating in bikinis, and fighters, sometimes dressed in jeans, with names like *Shizzat Da Rizzat* and *Raccoon Boy*—who entered the ropes after being wheeled down the stage in a trashcan—wailing on each other until someone fell over. A few Barstool employees would also enter the ring to settle some workplace differences, which was always good for the PPV number.

---

2   Shea Clancy is Kevin Clancy's daughter and Portnoy's "arch nemesis." And Barstool actually did a Black Friday push the year before, which generated around 20,000 orders.

Nardini struck gold with her *"Saturdays Are for the Boys"* campaign. The slogan spawned from a random tweet by Feitelberg, who overheard this toast at a bar:

> "FRIDAYS ARE FOR THE MEN, SATURDAYS ARE FOR THE BOYS - some old guy just yelled that, it makes no sense, but I love it"
>
> —@FeitsBarstool

Feitelberg pushed the saying on social media, and Barstool began to merchandise it. The phrase eventually went viral, helping spread the word about Barstool as the company made millions on hats, flags, t-shirts, and anything else it could put the letters SAFTB on. Content into commerce.[3]

Following Nardini's hiring and the subsequent move to NYC, the number of visitors to Barstool's site grew, reaching 8M monthly uniques in 2017. That number would explode in the years that followed: by 2020, Barstool would boast 66M monthly unique visitors across all its social media platforms. Nardini helped turn Barstool into a digital media powerhouse.

One of the main reasons the CEO was able to pull this off was her ability to gel with the garage band that made up Barstool Sports. She was approachable and would joke around with the guys— Barstool personalities were comedians, after all—and they would reciprocate.[4]

> "God dammit Erika. If you tell me I can't pee off the fire escape anymore, I may have to quit."
>
> —@BarstooBigCat

---

3   Feitelberg didn't make much money off the viral marketing campaign, which he griped about.

4   Nardini would catch some flak for a response in a *NYT interview where she said she expected interviewees to text her back within three hours, and that she texts her employees at odd hours. It ended up being much ado about nothing.*

Her ability to co-exist seamlessly with Portnoy was also significant, if not paramount. Nardini was often asked what it was like working with Dave, as fans were curious how the Barstool founder was in a "corporate setting." Many pictured a bull in a China shop. They were half-right. Nardini explained, "Dave is actually quite humble and a great listener and intellectually very curious. What's great about him is that he has this rare quality where he knows a lot, but he doesn't pretend to know what he doesn't know. He doesn't have interest in owning things for the sake of owning things or control."[5] At the same time, when it came to things he did have interest in, "Dave could be the alpha," she said. "I didn't need to be the alpha. I didn't want to be the alpha. What I could do is say, 'Oh, you want to go do this? Then I'm going to build it.'"

As Head of Content, Portnoy was still guiding the overall direction of the company, all the while working side-by-side with Nardini; the last thing Portnoy did was take a step back. As Kerns explained, "Dave's doing all the content, but he's more involved in the business than people realize. Even though he says he doesn't want to do the business side, he's always doing the business side; he can't help himself."

For Portnoy, the move to NYC meant the Pats fan had to live in a city he wasn't a fan of, quite literally. "I hate it more than I thought I would," he said, laughing, when he answered a question in 2016 about his recent move to Manhattan. "It's too busy. There are people everywhere. Everything is just a hassle. Everything I thought I wouldn't like about living in Manhattan is probably 10x worse. People keep telling me it takes three years—three years!—to say, 'Yup, I like this city.' So, who knows? I am no closer to liking it." His opinion on the subject wouldn't change.

---

5   This quote is a combination of two separate quotes from Nardini. You will see in the back of the book that there are two different sources listed. You can copy-paste the link to see where each part came from.

Katz echoed Dave's feelings when walking around NYC a few months before the move: "Look at that. Trash everywhere. Disgusting. Get an alley, once. Put your trash in an alley like a normal person. Why would you want to live in a city where everyone is on top of each other when you could live anywhere else? Like a nice clean city like Chicago." Both, in their humility, continuously reminded Barstool fans of the sacrifice they were making on their behalf.

Working together under one roof was the other noteworthy change for the Barstool bloggers, but as Portnoy explained, "All the Boston guys were in an office together before, so they were used to the drill." Also, Katz and Clancy both had, in fact, worked in "the real world," so to them this wasn't a huge deal. However, the irony was not lost on Clancy, who had built his entire persona on making fun of corporate life. "I've officially gone full circle and I'm back in the cubes now," he would say.

And Portnoy turned out to be prophetic in his thinking about what the move would do to Barstool's content. Almost immediately, the in-person dynamic led to fresh entertainment, this time at Dave's expense. In the second week at the new office, the Barstool team *sans* Portnoy attended a Kanye West concert. When Dave found out he was the only one not invited, he took to Twitter.

"Where would 'Club Cool' be without me?" he commented on a picture of the crew in a suite at Madison Square Garden. Portnoy doctored the image as follows:

- ○ Clancy—Accountant
- ○ Katz—Real Estate
- ○ Markovich—Copy Editor
- ○ Feitelberg—Telemarketer
- ○ Hank—Museum of Science Ticket Taker

Portnoy spent the next week lambasting "Club Cool." When he set up a Facebook Live stream to admonish them, the Barstool employees gathered in the office and played "Portnoy Bingo" on camera, with the spaces on their cards consisting of phrases Dave would probably use in his rant: "Go Pres Go," "Brick by Brick," "Delivered Too Many Newspapers," "Big Brain," "Make Everybody Stars," "Lorne Michaels," "The Team, The Team, The Team," "Do I want to be? (doing something)," "Salt of The Earth," "Shea Clancy," "Accountant," and "Real Estate" were a few notable ones.[6]

The weekly in-office power rankings blog by Markovich was also a heavily read feature following the move. Markovich slotted Portnoy at #5 overall for the first full week's rankings:

"Power Rankings: 5) Coworker Dave

"Doesn't matter how tough the exterior is, deep down, Coworker Dave wants to be liked and maybe just maybe work his way into the Cool Club. Kicking off the week with Bagel Mondays was a great start. Consistently calling Clem "wide load" and Riggs "cross-eyed fuck" and Nate "creepy little freak" keeps him up at 5, but definitely a solid showing for the week regardless."

Portnoy had been tough on his employees during the Milton days; following the move, he leaned further into this dynamic. "I'm never comfortable around Dave," said Clancy, who was working alongside Portnoy for the first time in 2016.

"He keeps you on edge. It's an intentional thing he does," Feitelberg added. But as Portnoy explained:

---

6   In the infamous Club Cool photo, two other previously unmentioned employees also received titles: Caleb Pressley, a new hire and former QB at UNC, received the title of "Unemployed"; Lou Roberts aka Lightswitch Lou, who had worked under Gaz in sales at Milton before the move, was dubbed "Con Artist."

"I think there's an element of the office that wants to be kumbaya and hold hands. I like controversy, I like agitating, our best moments are like the Club Cool thing, if that's what people like; if we're holding hands and roasting marshmallows, we lose out on some of that content."

Following through with his grand plan to create an internet reality show, Portnoy installed cameras in the ceiling of the office. "It's fuckin' big brother in here," he would say. "So, we have the entire place wired. One good thing we've never been able to capture is real-time interactions with people. We miss so much shit. Not anymore. 24/7." The cameras caught unscripted happenings inside the office, including those created by people who didn't actually work at Barstool:[7]

"Annnnd We're Off, Random Dude Walks into the Office Un-Announced to Tell Us about His "Viral" Facebook Video"

But the biggest move towards this never-ending content model, where the footage from these cameras was usually placed, came with the installation of "Stool Scenes," a once-a-week behind-the-scenes show produced by a new hire from St. Louis named Ben Friedman, aka Young Pageviews (he earned the name from his viral YouTube rap video about Portnoy). Friedman would walk around the office with a camera glued to his shoulder. Like that scene in *The Departed* when Matt Damon is hired to find the mole in the Boston Police Department, at times this made Friedman an unpopular employee. Bloggers knew if they did something stupid, they'd end up on the site.

The segment peeled back the curtain—one that was already ajar—to the Barstool world, and fans got a continuous glimpse of the day-to-day life of working at the company. The show also usu-

---

7   They would eventually hire a security guard named Ebony.

ally featured drama on the Barstool website from a different, more in-the-weeds angle, and unsurprisingly, "Stool Scenes" became one of the most-watched vehicles on the site.

That's because there was a lot to film. The office of 20 or so employees became stars of Portnoy's fun factory. The heads of the different sites—Portnoy, Katz, Clancy, Nate, Smitty, and Markovich (Editor in Chief)—were joined by the likes of Tex, Spags, Riggs, Kelly Keegs, Coley, Tommy Smokes and others.[8] Trent, who ran Barstool Iowa, would later join the NYC office after winning a bet with Portnoy (some part-time contributors to the Barstool site weren't invited to relocate to the NYC office).

> "Yes, if Iowa beats Michigan, I'll bring @BarstoolTrent to NYC"
>
> —@stoolpresidente

Iowa football upset Michigan—they were 22-point underdogs—and Trent was off to New York. Glenny, a fat college student from Long Island, earned a job as an intern at the company in similar Barstool fashion. Another personality named Caleb Pressley brought him outside on the street and filmed him sprinting, which was funny enough to win him a meeting with Portnoy. His interview didn't go particularly well, but as Glenny was leaving, Dave asked him if he had any nicknames. "My friends call me 'Balls.'" He was hired.[9]

For Balls and others who joined the Stool, it was a dream job. Much like he did with Clancy when he first launched the NYC site, Portnoy allowed his employees to do pretty much whatever they wanted in terms of creating content inside the new office. The lati-

---

8   Tex was an intern named Dylan Stone. Kelly Keegs was another personality who remains with Barstool today. Riggs was a former Harvard grad who also remains with the company as of this writing. Tommy Smokes was an intern from Fordham. Posts were still designated by city on the website.

9   Glenny later made an appearance on Andy Cohen's talk show *Watch What Happens Live*.

tude he provided was unlike anywhere else in digital media. As Katz tweeted about this dynamic: "Barstool and Dave give me the freedom to have the best job on Earth. That's a fact." And although he's been described as "mercurial," the fact that Portnoy never fired anyone made working at Barstool that much more attractive. As Portnoy explained, "There's a degree of loyalty I have to the people—as long as I feel like you're working hard and giving an A+ effort here, I have pretty intense loyalty to our guys, the guys I hire. That's why nobody ever leaves, for the most part."

Thanks to the new post-Chernin setup, the content his employees created and Barstool in turn broadcast to the digital world took a more professional turn. Nardini helped the crew land its own channel on Sirius XM, which included a lineup of shows featuring Portnoy, Clancy, and an ensemble of other personalities, with Dave's reality TV thesis remaining the central focus.

"Dave *hates* segments," Clancy explained. *Top 5 Lists* or *Would You Rathers* were banned from the radio show. Clancy continued: "All that shit is shtick, Dave hates shtick. And anytime the producer would try to book a guest, he'd [say] 'Get this the fuck out of here.' ... But I think truly great radio doesn't need all that. I think he's right, in that sense." Portnoy instead favored pitting people against each other, which would often devolve into the hosts screaming at one another. Because Stool-Scenes was only once a week, Barstool Radio was where Stoolies went for their daily in-office drama; with Portnoy there, they got it: "I'm the straw that stirs the drink."

But Barstool also put together organized productions like Barstool Idol, where contestants competed to earn a spot working at the company; the winner of the inaugural series was a Harvard grad and comedian named Francis Ellis, whose persona included being a Harvard grad, and whose blogging actually had proper grammar and was delightfully bizarre.[10]

---

10   Tucker Carlson called Ellis his favorite writer on the site.

To assist in bringing Barstool up a digital notch, Portnoy hired an experienced producer named Sean Loughlin ("Loud Sean" to the Barstool fans). Sean would handle all production-related work for Barstool and unintentionally become part of the company's content, as he could not help but scream when he spoke. During their interview at a coffee shop, Portnoy says at least three people came over and tapped Sean on the shoulder to be quieter. "He cleared out that coffee shop twice." Loughlin still got the job.[11]

Loughlin was joined by another important behind-the-scenes-but-still-in-the-scenes guy named Pete Overmyer, or "All Business Pete." He was in charge of technology at Barstool, and like many others who would call Barstool home, Pete became a constant target of Portnoy. A few headlines from the blog:

- "Shout Out All Business Pete. At Least I Don't Have to Watch Michigan Get Destroyed on a Live Stream Because We Don't Have TVs that Work."

- "Fuck All Business Pete.

- "New episode is live from my summer location where All Biz Pete refused to get me wired Internet because he doesn't care about or respect my needs as the Chief of Content."

And Portnoy's Twitter followers often heard about the Barstool tech guy:

> "I also told @allbusinesspete I would spend any amount of money to guarantee I have flawless internet since you know I do run an internet company, and somehow I have zero internet"
>
> —@stoolpresidente

---

11   Loud Sean played another employee, Chris Spags, in an epic game of 1v1 basketball for content. It got personal.

The theme of Barstool being an internet company that constantly lost connection to the internet was what kept "The Barstool Difference" intact and continued to endear the company to its loyal Stoolies. Even when a video was presented as a well-budgeted, sleek production, there could often be something slightly wrong with the sound quality, lighting, or camera angle.

Still, the company was putting on a more serious front. The website received a major update: gone were the cheap-looking ads that littered the side columns of the page, and the black background that Portnoy's "Superblog" on top of was replaced by a clean white and blue base. At the top of the homepage, users could now browse through five or six featured stories, and a menu bar that featured "Videos, Podcasts, Popular" sections. Stoolies could smell Chernin's money as they scrolled.

The number of celebrities that walked through the office door also helped lend credibility to the company. A main reason why Portnoy had chosen NYC as his headquarters was because he believed, correctly, that it would be easier to get high-profile guests to visit the office for content, as opposed to the smaller city of Boston. Stars like Judd Apatow and Ice Cube added Barstool as a stop on their book tours: the company was now masquerading as a real media outlet.

It was an interesting time for Barstool Sports to become a more "mainstream" media outfit. In 2016, Trump had just been elected, and it seemed as if railing against PC culture suddenly was *en vogue*. Portnoy had about 13 years of practice in this arena, and the political climate at the time would lend one to believe Chernin's money wasn't the only reason Barstool started to become a household name (ironically, Portnoy's mantra since he started his company was "no politics.").

And as Barstool grew more popular, other media companies tried labeling what sort of phenomenon was occurring. A notable piece from Jay Caspian Kang of *The New York Times* provides a good example:

> "There exists a swarm of angry sports fans who maintain that they do not want to talk about Colin Kaepernick or the national anthem, and Barstool has cleared a space for them to gather and talk, mostly, about just how much they don't want to talk about politics. They claim to be an overlooked majority—the vast market inefficiency that will richly reward anyone who will let them watch their games, memes, and funny videos without having to feel bad about themselves. Barstool is their safe space."

Whether or not this is an accurate description of Portnoy's following is up for debate. But as 2017 arrived, there was no denying that Barstool was becoming one of the hottest media companies on the internet: suddenly, everyone wanted to work there. The number of applications the company received for any position skyrocketed. "ESPN was definitely on my mind when I got to college," Noah Ives, a Barstool employee, told Kang on why he decided to apply to Portnoy's company. "But Barstool is just a cooler brand that people my age just respect more. The takes are just much more relatable. It's like Pres says—Barstool is by the common man, for the common man."

Portnoy's vision for Barstool to become the next *SNL*, where up-and-coming comedians and entertainment folk would send their resume, was coming to fruition. The Chernin Group had done its part de-risking such a move, because those same people certainly weren't sending that resume to Milton. And thanks to Nardini, operationally Barstool was no longer considered a mess. That title would be reserved for Portnoy's not-so-personal life.

21

While the investment from Chernin didn't change El Presidente's renegade approach to digital media, fans began to notice that it had begun to change *Dave*. The Barstool founder was now a skinny—almost malnourished—Italian-designer-wearing 40-year-old. As he did with most things, Dave let his fans in on the secret to his transformation (besides having money to buy nice clothes):

> "I almost never eat breakfast, but when I do, my breakfast is coffee. Black. Like a man. With a side of cream and sugar. It's like a straight shot of adrenaline to the brain. No grease from breakfast foods to interfere or dull the effect. Maybe wash it down with an Adderall."[1]

The fat, dumpy Dave who inhaled a full Panera baguette in his upstairs office before eating lunch every day was nearly unrecognizable. Fans also began to notice something else about the founder: he now rarely, if ever, mentioned his wife Renee. A few comments from Stoolies on the Barstool Reddit page at the time:

> "Did Renee and Dave split?

> "I doubt it but it has been weird how out of the picture she's been. Now Dave is living alone, she doesn't tweet anymore, and she isn't mentioned at all. Realistically, she's off enjoying Dave's money but it is at the very least curious.

---

1   Portnoy was purportedly known to frequently take Adderall.

"Only thing that throws me off is that Dave isn't wearing his wedding ring anymore."

Barstool fans were able to piece together that something was up between Portnoy and his wife, which eventually led him to respond in a blog post about the situation:

"Okay, so right now people are freaking out about my personal life, so I want to clear some shit up. First things first. Yes, I'm separated right now from the First Lady."

Although to those followers, it appeared as if he had ditched his wife after getting "famous," Portnoy claimed otherwise:

"I didn't mention it out of respect to everybody involved, but it was mutual. I love her. I will always love her."

And Renee didn't hold a grudge against the man who specialized in doing just that: as she explained, "I'll always be Dave's biggest fan. I still am. And say what you want about him, but he is honest perhaps to a fault. He's also loyal, transparent, generous, and the funniest person to ever grace the internet." The split was amicable; it's what happened after that was Twitter-worthy.

Around the same time, Portnoy began dating a 24-year-old blonde woman named Jordyn Hamilton. It was the first in a series of moves that would become known to Barstool fans as the "Club Dave" era, an unwanted nickname given to him by his employees as they watched Portnoy attempt to enjoy the fruits of his labor, with Manhattan's nightlife as his vessel. (Dave claimed he hated going out, saying it was usually Hamilton's idea.) It didn't help that the founder had begun spending time in Miami, a city where rich middle-aged men head to live like they're in their 20s. Also, Club Dave was a slightly awkward sight: the designer pants he wore didn't really fit, and they became—along with his new title—a funny metaphor for his rising media mogul status. Katz commented on Portnoy watching a Patriots game:

"A big game calls for your finest black skinny jeans
#ClubDave"

—@BarstoolBigCat

Regardless of how little blood flow his legs were receiving, Dave was an adult; he could do what he pleased. The problem was Portnoy had built his entire company on transparency, with his personal life being one of if not the main reason that Barstool fans followed the company. So when Portnoy showed up to a Facebook Live stream to watch the Pats game one Sunday, slightly buzzed from brunch with Hamilton by his side, Barstool fans lost their collective minds. They couldn't believe Portnoy had swapped their beloved Renee for a twenty-something blonde, one who chatted about pretty much anything besides sports the entire time. Equally as baffling was that although the live stream was set up so fans could follow Dave's commentary on the Pats, the self-proclaimed defender of the Patriots wall barely paid any attention to the game.

Some labeled it a mid-life crisis—most did, actually. Others believed all those years blogging about young attractive girls had finally taken hold in a brainwashing of sorts. It was the first time Barstool fans would refer to the Milton days as "Old Dave."

The response from the Stoolies was loud enough that it forced Portnoy to acknowledge the criticism:

"So yes, I recently met a girl and we started dating. It sucks ass that every time you go out, people look at you like you're a scumbag because they know my personal life inside and out. But honestly, it was sort of a relief to get it off my chest. I probably got carried away with the newfound honesty and that led to the Facebook live event on Sunday. Hand up. I'm to blame for it. I also realize that by doing that, we now both open ourselves up for Stoolies to smash both of us. I'm actually fine with that. I understand the rules. I've built this company for 13 years by being brutally honest about my entire life and making fun of people."

But as he was prone to do, Dave also pushed back:

"But nobody and I mean nobody has sacrificed more on every single level to make this NY move happen than me. Seeing people say I'm ruining Barstool when there is no way this company happens or we move to NYC without me and I broke my balls to make it happen is fucking laughable. Why the hate? Because I'm dating a young chick and had her on Facebook live? It was stupid. Big fucking whoop. If you want to keep trashing me, that's your fucking right. I don't hate it. I love enemies. I thrive on it. The real Go Pres Go guys will rise to the top like they always do. That's the loyalty you get from 13 years of putting it on the line day in and day out. So I'm not going to apologize for 1 fucking bad Facebook live in a blowout game."

In a comical twist of fate, and what disgruntled fans would call foreseeable, a month later Hamilton reportedly cheated on Portnoy with a SoulCycle instructor. Portnoy tweeted the news to his followers:

> "Remember when I wrote the blog defending @ jhammmmmy when nobody else would. I take it all back. Tune in to @barstool-radio tomorrow."
>
> —@stoolpresidente

Portnoy turned the entire situation into original content, mostly because he was furious, and probably a little heartbroken. Still, this was his business model, and the Barstool founder leaned into the drama. Aside from Dave's Twitter posts telling people to tune into Barstool Radio the next day, Clancy wrote a blog the following morning describing March 10 as *Grudgement Day*, posting pictures of Barstool employees patiently waiting for Portnoy to walk through the door.

And he did, wearing a SoulCycle t-shirt. The founder went on his radio show that day and took shots at Hamilton but directed most of his anger towards the popular fitness brand—he had graduated from holding a grudge with a grilled-cheese company. "I wonder if SoulCycle is looking to hire instructors who are trying to fuck existing instructors who are already dating other instructors?" he asked. "From a business perspective, I'm not sure if it's good or bad for SoulCycle instructors to bang customers. Guys won't want girls to go."

During this drama, Portnoy also started a fight with another company—American Express—after it told him he wasn't able to cancel his card, which Hamilton was allegedly still using to take Ubers, without losing all of his points. (Dave spent two hours on hold with AmEx during an episode of Barstool Radio.)

As SoulCycle week went on at Barstool, Portnoy monetized the entire affair, printing up CuckCycle shirts to sell in the Barstool store, and the term "cucked" became popular in the Barstool world for the next several months. Some Barstool fans, however, thought the founder looked pathetic:

> "Honestly, this was just so embarrassing [for] Dave. The man is fucking 40 years old and acted like a 14-year-old with his first girlfriend"
>
> —@Ronaldo119

But a large number got behind Portnoy, who explained:

> "The Stoolies have been pounding (no pun intended but intended) SoulCycle's social media all day. To the point that both SoulCycle's Instagram and Twitter comments were

shut down. Nobody, and I mean nobody, mobilizes social media after their idiot leader has been cucked more than the Stoolies. God Bless."

Sports Illustrated's criticism of Barstool weaponizing social media wasn't completely off-base. In fact, it was pretty much exactly what happened in this instance. Hamilton had to make her Instagram and Twitter accounts private as well; she said of the entire situation, "It was really tough for me and my family, everything being put online." Also, aside from its Twitter account being heavily swarmed by Barstool fans, SoulCycle began to worry that Portnoy or someone at Barstool was going to harass one of its employees in person. SoulCycle issued a company-wide memo:

> "Dear NYC studios and soul managers. We've received notification that some employees from Barstool Sports are planning to walk into a NY studio this afternoon to ask questions regarding the personal life and alleged activity of one of our soul instructors. Should anyone arrive at the studio and make you or your team feel uncomfortable, threatened, or if you don't know how to handle the situation, please dial 911 immediately and call Gaby Cohen. Any additional questions can be directed to your area manager."[2]

Portnoy only fanned the flame:

> "Best way to avoid calling 911? Don't have your instructors fuck the girlfriend of head of major media company. #dailysoul @soulcycle"
>
> —@stoolpresidente

---

2 Portnoy would deny anyone from Barstool was planning on showing up to SoulCycle.

Eventually, however, like anyone who has been cheated on or dumped, Portnoy moved on. There wouldn't be any fallout from the ordeal, and Barstool fans took solace in the fact that while "Old Dave" was dead, "New Dave" could still hold a grudge. But towards the end of 2017, it would be something "Old Dave" had said that would torpedo a lucrative opportunity for Barstool, and more specifically, for Katz.

22

In 2017, Portnoy and Barstool were making a concerted effort to diversify their content distribution channels. Facebook Live was becoming a popular new way for media outlets to reach their audiences, having launched the year before. But Barstool's experience with the platform was up and down: according to Kerns, "Facebook has so many rules about third-party advertising. They are notorious for dangling the carrot, getting people to do things, then pulling it back and making it harder [to reach your audience with the same amount of spend]. They try to figure out a way for you to pay for distribution." Also, it didn't help that when Portnoy met with one of Facebook's top guys, he had gone through the Barstool website and found a blog where one of Dave's employees, Chris Spags, had written "Fuck Facebook." "He read it right in front of me," Portnoy explained with a smirk.

At the same time, Nardini had been making a push to get Barstool on television, pitching Barstool's *Rundown* show to networks in L.A. "The future of Barstool is operating as an omnichannel brand" she said of the effort, and in January 2017, as you know, the Stool landed a one-week special with Comedy Central. Shot live from Houston during the Super Bowl, it featured four 30-minute episodes of Portnoy, Katz, and Clancy doing the Barstool Rundown; although the move excited their fan base, the overall ratings of the midnight show were only OK at best. The program premiered with decent numbers, but those numbers subsequently decreased each day from Monday to Thursday, eventually landing in the same range as the *Futurama* reruns that had been in that time slot the week before.

While Barstool would spend several unsuccessful years attempting to break into television, it became clear that "The Barstool Difference" that had made the crew so popular with its fans wasn't made for the traditional airwaves. During this pitch for TV, the entire Barstool group met with United Talent Agency, where the president of UTA and other agents were all dressed to the nines in suits and ties. At one point during this meeting the UTA president was talking about TV strategy, and as Portnoy described, "He turned to 22-year-old Hank, who was wearing a t-shirt and shorts, and asked, 'And who's going to produce this? Not *this* guy.'" The disconnect between Barstool and Hollywood was too large a gap to bridge.

Still out in LA for these meetings, Portnoy & Co. gave The Chernin Group a taste of what it was really like working with Barstool. As Portnoy said, "Mike Kerns, at one point, was getting Stockholm Syndrome. He was with us three-four days straight. And you could see him almost start to become a Barstool person, which is bad because we needed him to be the smart one with us in the room."

"He was slowly becoming a child, like us," Katz said.

Clancy explained further: "We were aimlessly walking around the streets at one point looking for our next meeting, and nobody knew the address. And I [said] 'Kerns, this is your job. What's the address of the next place?' And he kind of mumbled to himself, 'I used to manage 2,000 people, and now I'm just walking around with these guys.' I think it was a few meetings later where he [said] 'Enough's enough! Here's how we're doing it. I've had enough of these fucking idiots!'"

In another meeting in Peter Chernin's office, the Chernin guys tried to untangle what exactly was happening inside the company they had poured millions into, particularly with the podcasts, which were all over the place. As Portnoy explained:

"They pulled up this flowchart with all of our podcasts. All the way from Kevin's, to my new one, to Dan's new one, to ones I had never even heard of. And you had myself, Dan, Kevin, and Hank on one side of this big table, and you had all the Chernin guys on the other side of the table, screaming at each other as this podcast chart was up, trying to figure out what the fuck was going on. We were all just sitting [and] giggling, and they were legitimately getting red in the face, yelling at each other."

However, unlike with TV, Barstool did have success with audio, and podcasting became a central focus of the company's strategy. Portnoy said, "We didn't do podcasts at all before Chernin. So that was something where we said, we should be doing this. It seems to be popular. I guess I had my head in the sand because we weren't doing it." It was a timely decision: by 2017, the number of Americans listening to at least one podcast a month had climbed to 21 million, up from about 9 million in 2008.

Podcasting was the perfect medium for Barstool: as Nardini explained, "We were able to take people who started as bloggers and wrote very funny commentary on sports and life and moved those to an audio form. It allows for authenticity, with a very low barrier to entry." It was a low-overhead, high-margin vehicle compared to video and television, and Barstool wasn't beholden to a powerful corporation's platform that could change the rules on them at any given moment. Although Barstool's podcasts were served up by Apple and Spotify (who operated as third-party hosts), the red tape that existed around audio was significantly less than video on YouTube or Facebook Live. And the intimate, casual delivery of the entertainment podcasts provided went hand in hand with Portnoy's "for the common man" approach to content. By the end of 2018, 35% of Barstool's revenue would come from its podcast business, earning significantly more advertising dollars—$15M—for the company, compared to its website.

In addition to the Barstool Radio show, *The Dave Portnoy Show* premiered weeks after the Chernin deal was announced and immediately became a must-listen for Barstool fans. This show featured Portnoy giving another behind-the-scenes look about what was happening at Barstool—and literally anything else that popped into his head. *Zero-Blog-Thirty* with Uncle Chaps, a former marine, was also a popular pod for the Stoolies at the time. And despite Portnoy's claim that Barstool didn't have podcasts before Chernin, there was the *KFC Radio* pod with Clancy, which had been around for several years. In fact, Clancy claimed he was the reason that Barstool went into podcasting, but Portnoy often refuted this with something along the lines of "You didn't *invent* podcasting."

As the company hired more talent, the number of shows began to grow. *Spittin' Chiclets* was an NHL-focused podcast with former players Ryan Whitney and Paul Bissonnette. *Call Her Daddy* was a raunchy show about sex hosted by Alex Cooper and Sofia Franklyn, and it emerged as an unlikely mega success for Barstool. (More about Cooper and Franklyn later.) *Fore Play*, a golf show with long-time Barstool employees Riggs, Frankie, and Trent also became a well-known pod that Barstool produced, as did the female lifestyle show *Chicks in the Office* with Francesca Mariano and Ria Ciuffo. Eventually, Barstool had more than 30 podcasts operating under its umbrella. But none would be as popular among Stoolies as Katz's *Pardon My Take*, a show he co-hosted with another talent named Eric Sollenberger.

Sollenberger, who sported long dirty-blonde hair and wore dark sunglasses inside to hide his identity while on camera, joined Barstool following the Chernin deal; Katz had convinced Portnoy to bring him on board, having met the internet personality via (predictably) the internet. "It's funny that the way we became friends was people would accuse Big Cat of stealing my takes, and then people would accuse me of stealing Big Cat's jokes because we have such similar senses of humor," Sollenberger said. "And so enough people on Twitter started tagging us in each other's posts that we both started following each other."

Sollenberger would keep his real name hidden until 2018, and instead was known to his fans as PFT Commenter, short for Pro Football Talk Commenter (Pro Football Talk was an NFL Insider website Sollenberger commented on with that username). The D.C.-area native had spent a few years writing at *SB Nation* and *Kissing Suzy Kolber* before joining Barstool. By that time, PFT had built up a solid following on Twitter thanks to his sharp sense of humor and somewhat strange commentary that often included intentionally misspelled words and poor grammar.

> "Before anyone ever cared where I blogged, I was just a kid from the ProFootballTalk comment secton. Its where I learned how to give barrel fire sports takes, where i learned about the loose change video, and where I honed my abilty to make broad sweeping generalizations without reading the actual artcle about what Anotonio Cromartes latest child means in regards to how much I would pay in taxes if I made more money. Its where I found my voice & my passion."

PFT's persona and his equally mysterious approach to writing delighted readers and befuddled industry peers. "I didn't know what to make of him," said Mike Florio, the founder of Pro Football Talk, "I wasn't sure whether I was in on the joke or the butt of it."

As Florio alluded to, Sollenberger's PFT character was a play on how seriously journalists took themselves; a metacritique. At the GOP debate in Cleveland in 2015, while covering the presidential election for SB Nation, PFT interviewed Ben Carson, a conservative neurosurgeon and strong anti-abortion candidate. Sollenberger put the doctor in a pretzel by asking "Would you go back in time and abort baby Hitler?" After Carson responded by saying he's strongly against abortion, PFT jokingly replied, "Ok, so pro-Hitler; got it." His ridiculous question and answer got picked up by major news outlets. "That actually gave me really good insight into what modern day journalism is about," PFT said. "Because maybe after 30 or 45 minutes of putting that out, there was an article on the front page of CNN.com saying 'Ben Carson would not abort Baby Hitler.' And I was like uh-oh we're fucked."[1]

When Katz and Sollenberger teamed up for *Pardon My Take* (after meeting for a beer in Chicago a year earlier), satirizing sports journalism became the theme that their show was built on. It turned out to be a profitable approach. After the pair recruited Hank to produce the pod and after several episodes of trial and error (they got rid of the air horn that blasted every 30 seconds), the show became an instant hit. By the end of its first week in existence, PMT was the number one sports podcast in the U.S.[2]

Pardon My Take pushed Barstool into another stratosphere. Only a few years later, thanks to Barstool's emphasis on podcasting and the duo of Katz and Sollenberger, Portnoy's company would become the No. 6 largest U.S. podcast producer, just ahead of ESPN.

---

[1]   At the same GOP debate, PFT also went viral for holding up a sign that said, "Is Joe Flaco a Elite Quarterback?"

[2]   One popular segment featured Larry the gambling goldfish, who made picks by swimming to one end of his tank.

23

John Skipper's southern accent stuck out in the hallways of his company's Bristol, CT headquarters. The President of ESPN was a rangy 61-year-old North Carolinian with grey hair and round spectacles who had spent the last 20 years working at the conglomerate. In 1997, Skipper joined to launch *ESPN The Magazine*, and its success helped him climb Disney's Rapunzel-like corporate ladder, where he eventually became head of the most influential sports media company on the planet.

Being from the south, Skipper retained a relatively easygoing demeanor for someone in his position of power; as he said: "None of this is life and death. It's the business of sports. And I generally manage to keep that in perspective, [given] how important, how profound ESPN's business is." Even when he did have to make tough decisions, such as suspending popular anchor Jemele Hill for her outspoken comments on President Trump, Skipper remained far from a tyrant among his employees. As Hill wrote of the days following the incident, "Before we even sat down to breakfast, [Skipper and I] hugged. He wanted me to know that despite the attacks from the White House, his belief in my ability remained unchanged. We laughed together. He suspended me from ESPN, but we're still friends."

Skipper's approach to leading was more personal and democratic: he had close relationships with his top executives, and he relied on their input, especially when it came to decision-making about ESPN's content. So when VP of Programming Burke Magnus and Content Chief Connor Schell[1] came to him in the beginning of the year with a pitch to do a show featuring Barstool's Dan Katz and Eric Sollenberger, Skipper was open to the idea—even though it seemed risky, given Barstool's reputation.

Magnus had heard about the pair's satirical sports podcast *Pardon My Take* from his teenage son, who was a fan of the show (like almost every other 18- to 34-year-old, it seemed). Katz and Sollenberger launched PMT, the number one sports pod on iTunes, in March 2016, and just a year later, they were boasting anywhere from 750,000 to 1.5M listeners per episode. To put that into context, ESPN's top-rated debate show, *Pardon the Interruption* averaged around 1M viewers across ESPN and ESPN2 combined.[2] At the same time, ESPN was grappling with the question of how to remain relevant in a disruptive media landscape—and, more important, how to connect with a younger generation that, as the Stool's intern Noah Ives mentioned, didn't think ESPN was *cool*. The fact that the average age of ESPN's audience was rising backed this up.[3]

After speaking with Magnus and Schell, John Skipper found himself in the same seat that WEEI's Jordan Wolfe had sat in six years earlier, when Wolfe took a risk on Portnoy only to be burned by a lewd blog about Tom Brady's son: Skipper wanted Barstool's audience. But Disney's brand was quite literally the opposite of the one Portnoy had built, and all three execs understood a partnership would require some finessing. Still, there was optimism that *Pardon My Take*'s content could exist on ESPN's airwaves: several of ESPN's personalities had already appeared on the show, and Katz and Sollenberger wanted to be on the network. As Katz said, "It was never something that we *have* to be on TV—it was something that

---

1   Schell had worked with Bill Simmons in 2007 to create the critically acclaimed *30 for 30 film series for ESPN.*

2   *Pardon My Take's crew would receive a cease-and-desist letter from ESPN, which also had a popular show called First Take.*

3   From a *Sports Business Journal study.*

was presented to us, and we thought it was going to be a really cool opportunity."

As John Ourand, writer for *Sports Business Journal* reported, "ESPN executives viewed Big Cat and PFT as potential stars, who traded on sophomoric humor that did not turn vile. Magnus and Schell both liked Big Cat and PFT's *Pardon My Take* podcast and listened to it frequently. But they saw Portnoy as a loose cannon. If the show was going to have a run on ESPN, Portnoy could not be part of it."

In an attempt to insulate ESPN's image from Portnoy's, the execs decided a solution would be to have it appear as if they were working solely with Katz and Sollenberger. When Magnus began negotiating a deal with the Barstool side, he pushed to have just the *Pardon My Take* branding, not Barstool's, in the title. At first, he was successful. But two weeks before the show was set to air, "The name change got suggested—from *Pardon My Take* to *Barstool Van Talk*," PFT explained. "I was against the name change. Dave felt otherwise."

"ESPN thought they were going to get Barstool without Barstool. How does that even work?" Portnoy asked later about the entire situation. Katz and Sollenberger were under contract with Barstool, and they were still going to operate as Barstool employees even if they did a show on ESPN's channel. Portnoy's company needed to gain something in the deal from a branding perspective.

The name change was a concession Skipper, Magnus, and Schell would have to make if they wanted the 18-34 demographic Barstool was offering, and they did. But after giving into this request, Magnus made it clear about the position they were taking on the show when he said this to *USA Today*: "We do not control the content of Barstool Sports. We are doing a show with Big Cat and PFT, and we do have final say on the content of that show." Eventually, both sides settled on a 20-week program, filmed with the PMT pair in the back of, ironically, an Astrovan, airing every Wednesday in the 1:00 a.m. time slot on ESPN2. With Katz and Sollenberger appearing on his channel, Skipper now had his younger generation.

It turned out to be a massive mistake. The day before the show was set to air, Sam Ponder, the stunning host of ESPN's *NFL Countdown* and top female anchor at the network, tweeted the following message:

> "Welcome to the ESPN family @BarstoolBigCat (& welcome to all your minions who will respond to this so kindly)"
>
> —@Sam_Ponder

Underneath the tweet were two screenshots of a blog Portnoy had written about Ponder in 2014, in response to her tweeting, "Blogs/websites that constantly disrespect women and objectify their bodies, then take a strong stance on the Ray Rice issue really confuse me."[4] Here's Portnoy's headline, in all caps:

"FUCK SAM PONDER THAT BIBLE THUMPING FREAK"

The blog also called her "a chick that has a job where the #1 requirement is to make men hard." Ponder subsequently referenced a video clip from later that year of Katz and Portnoy bashing her, with Portnoy saying:

> "No person watching GameDay wants to see a picture of her and her ugly kid. Nobody cares, Sam Ponder. We want to see you sex it up and be slutty and not see some prude fucking jerk who everybody hates. Sam Ponder, you fucking slut. I don't want you at these games talking about God and religion."

---

4   Ray Rice was an NFL player who assaulted his wife in an elevator. How long he should have been suspended for by the NFL was heavily debated.

Ponder had been waiting in the tall grass for Barstool, and after three years, the TV host made her move. "I almost respect her for it," Portnoy said later.

Back at ESPN, Skipper now had a mess on his hands. A very public one, with more prominent female personalities at ESPN speaking out publicly against the partnership:[5]

> "Saying you oppose misogyny is easy in the abstract. Actually opposing it in a way that's uncomfortable or inconveniences you is tougher."
>
> —@SarahSpain

> "Regardless of which person at Barstool wrote this, it's disturbing in so many ways. Stay strong @ sam_ponder."
>
> —@Sage_Steele

But after calling a late-night emergency meeting with Magnus and Schell, who both continued to advocate for the show, the President of ESPN decided to push forward with *Barstool Van Talk.*[6] The execs weren't completely blindsided by Ponder's post: according to Ourand, in the time leading up to the show's premiere date, Ponder's super-agent Nick Khan had sent them an email that contained the posts of Portnoy attacking his client. After the group looked over the materials, Stephanie Druley, SVP of events and studio production, informed Ponder the show was still going to air. The ESPN host had taken matters into her own hands.

Determined to reach new viewers, Magnus released a statement following Ponder's tweet:

---

5   Skipper actually met with Katz and Sollenberger and let them know he had their backs.
6   This was according to Ourand's article.

"The comments about Sam Ponder were offensive and inappropriate, and we understand her reaction. She is a valued colleague and doing a great job for us. As stated previously, we do not control the content of Barstool Sports."

He reiterated that ESPN had final cut on the show.[7]

On October 18, after 8 months of production, *Barstool Van Talk* premiered on ESPN2. The 30-minute show was unlike anything ever seen on ESPN, featuring primetime host Scott Van Pelt wedged between Katz and PFT in the backseat of their van, the pair feeding cheese to a rat in a small NYC park, and a dead octopus. The episode drew 88,000 viewers—a decent debut for that timeslot. Two thirds of that total was between ages 18-34, which was an 84% increase in that category compared to the previous four-week average for that time. Katz and PFT brought their audience.

But back in Bristol, Skipper's seat was getting hotter. In the days that followed the premiere, the execs at ESPN received major pushback from a growing number of female employees about continuing the partnership with Barstool. "I talked to Burke that Saturday night, and I asked Burke flat out, 'Do we have a problem?'" Nardini said, "And he [said], 'Look, there's a lot of pressure internally. But I think we're fine.'"

"From what we heard, there was a mini-uprising," was Portnoy's take. It was an unsurprising development given what was happening at the time. Two weeks before Ponder's tweet, on October 5, 2017, *The New York Times* published its first story detailing decades of allegations of sexual harassment against Harvey Weinstein. From there, the #metoo movement began, launching a global, survivor-led crusade against sexual misconduct. October 2017 simply wasn't a

---

7   Unfortunately, I can't tell you exactly why Skipper went forward with the show. I can only surmise all three execs believed the controversy would blow over, like previous ones involving Barstool had. And in this case, it seems Skipper's reliance on his execs' input would come back to bite him.

great time to be teaming up with a company that some viewed as misogynistic. And it was an even worse time to try to survive a bomb like the one Ponder dropped.

Skipper sat in his expansive Bristol office and mulled over the situation. The leader of ESPN then turned to his computer and typed www.barstoolsports.com into his browser. As he scrolled through the blogs on the main page, he came across a headline that took his breath away: "Is This Pumpkin Trying to Get the Pipe?" A Barstool blogger named Uncle Chaps had posted a picture of a pumpkin with holes in it that looked vaguely similar to a woman's private area.[8]

Though it was most likely the pushback from his employees that forced Skipper's hand, blogs such as the one Chaps published certainly didn't help. "They couldn't get over the association with Barstool," Nardini said. And how much due diligence Skipper and other execs had actually done on the company would be questioned heavily in the days following Ponder's tweet.

On Monday October 23, less than a week after the first episode aired, Skipper released the following statement:

> "Effective immediately, I am cancelling *Barstool Van Talk.* While we had approval on the content of the show, I erred in assuming we could distance our efforts from the Barstool site and its content. Apart from the decision, we appreciate the efforts of Big Cat and PFT Commenter. They delivered the show they promised."

The ESPN-Barstool marriage was never going to work, as their partnership featured two brands that were diametrically opposed. And during the fiasco, the TV network had managed to piss off both sides of the proverbial aisle: those who were against Barstool were

---

8   This is based off of Ourand's report that ESPN looked further into the Barstool website. Also, several Barstool employees had heard it was this particular blog that upset ESPN.

upset that ESPN had agreed to put them on air, and those who supported Barstool were angry that ESPN had kicked them off. It was an embarrassing blunder by the decision-makers in Bristol. And other media outlets came out of the woodwork to lambast Skipper's company, which now had its fair share of egg on its face:

"One-Episode Partnership Makes ESPN Look Bad"
—*The Boston Globe*

"ESPN's Barstool Sports Debacle Is the Sports Network's Reckoning"
—Salon.com

"ESPN Wanted Barstool Sports, But Without the Stench"
—Deadspin

"According to sources familiar with the situation, ESPN originally did not want the Barstool Sports name and logo associated with the new show, but caved after Barstool president Dave Portnoy insisted on the branding...It's laughably predictable that ESPN would give in on this point, intent as they are to seem cool, or subversive, or whatever it is the dang kids are into these days."

—Laura Wagner, Deadspin.

And just two months later on December 14, *The Boston Globe* released an extensive investigative report on sexual misconduct at ESPN:

"At ESPN, the Problems for Women Run Deep."

Four days after the article came out, John Skipper resigned as President of ESPN, in what can only be described as bizarre circumstances:

"Report: ESPN President John Skipper resigned over cocaine extortion plot."

"The former president of ESPN said he resigned from the sports network after an extortion plot by someone who sold him cocaine. He also said 'rumors and speculations' that mistreatment of women contributed to his resignation were untrue, and he denied having any inappropriate relationships or sexually harassing anyone."

—ESPN.com

24

Katz and Sollenberger were stars by the time ESPN came knocking in early 2017. And Portnoy wasn't oblivious to this fact. "I was always a little uncomfortable with the deal because I thought ESPN just wanted to test drive Dan and PFT." Dave was more than a little uncomfortable with it. Portnoy knew ESPN was trying to poach his talent, as Dave later told Barstool fans:

> "ESPN needed us more than we needed them. Everybody saying 'ESPN's not cool,' no one's paying attention to ESPN. They're all paying attention to the Barstools of the world. Why? Because we're authentic. They've got to cater to all the complaints and what the few say. We do not. We will not."

But Katz wanted to be on ESPN, which meant Portnoy had another Jenna Marbles situation developing. A homegrown star was beginning to outgrow the Barstool platform. Dave, who would tell people he knew he needed to let Katz spread his wings (a.k.a. keep him happy), eventually relented and agreed to the ESPN partnership.

Despite Portnoy's appeasement, the period surrounding the failed deal marked the most tumultuous time between the two faces of Barstool, Portnoy and Katz. Tensions had been running high since the Comedy Central Rundown earlier that year: "He [Katz] wanted no part of that. We would like plan the show," KFC said, and Portnoy cut him off: "Yeah, he [Katz] was not happy with us [Barstool]." Katz wouldn't comment on the rift.

Katz and Sollenberger had recently signed with Michael Klein, an agent at Maxx Sports. As Portnoy eloquently stated, "I fucking hate agents." But this was the new reality Portnoy was dealing with as head of a now-major digital media company; they weren't in Milton anymore. Portnoy admitted, "That's the one thing about my role that became very different. I'm a huge part of content, but then I was also thrown into this business world where I'm dealing with agents and I hate it. I fucking hate it." Referring to Katz and Sollenberger, he said:

> "I really fucking hate the guy who repped them. It was a big thing, I think Dan knows this, the agent was trying to get them on the same contract. The year length, PFT and Big Cat. And I [said] 'I will not do that.' Because they were already off-centered. There's no way in any world we're putting them on the same year so they can go to market together and be like 'We want 500 zillion dollars' and I'm like 'I'm not fucking [doing] it.' So, I think there was a lot of stuff going on with that."

Contract issues aside, in the initial days following Ponder's tweet missile, Katz was still hoping to salvage his show. Katz calmly responded on Twitter several times to the ESPN host, explaining where the video and blog she referenced had come from.

Portnoy took a different approach: he immediately initiated his Grudge Dave modus operandi and began pulling up old tweets from Ponder, introducing the ESPN host to the Barstool world with a simple caption, **"Welcome to the Mud."**

> "Watching the Lakers in the Finals is like watching the slutty girl win best looking in HS. She probably deserves it but eew."
>
> —@Sam_Ponder

> "If u ever want to learn about ur family, play a game called "say anything." Apparently my family is sexist, racist and a little redneck."
>
> —@Sam_Ponder

Portnoy also turned to his fans, asking in a blog post about Ponder calling him out:

"Should I retire for the good of Barstool?"

He immediately followed it up with one that read:

"Update—I Thought about It. I Ain't Leaving.

"People think this shit is gonna take me down? I've been through the wars. I've been dragged, redragged, shot, killed, and I'm still fucking here. What doesn't kill Barstool only makes us stronger. I like my guys. #TEAMPORTNOY is salt of the earth for a reason. We don't run from controversy. We embrace it and thrive off it."

Katz and Sollenberger didn't sound thrilled with the fact that Dave was fighting back. As PFT said (in a somewhat somber tone) on an episode of *Pardon My Take*, "On that Tuesday, that's when Dave looked back through Sam's tweets, started firing off some tweets at her, that reignited the controversy." (Note: Some Stoolies believed PFT wasn't a fan of Portnoy to begin with, due to his ties to others in media who opposed the Barstool founder.)[1] Thanks to Dave's outburst, Nardini received a phone call from Burke Magnus letting her know that if her company still wanted *Barstool Van Talk* to air, they would have to refrain from saying anything else publicly on this. Dave reluctantly bit his tongue. But the damage was done: Portnoy had fired his shots. It was a reflex for the Barstool founder at this point; there was a better chance of Portnoy joining ESPN himself than not responding to what Ponder dropped on him.

---

1   PFT knew Deadspin writer Drew Magary, who had helped him get a job in digital media years before.

And it didn't help that Dave was the one who was to blame for the original comments in 2014 that Ponder referenced. "The slut comment [by Portnoy] was wrong," Katz said, and PFT added this:

"The two or three people who fought so hard to keep us off the air. They chose to go with just a lazy, ignorant point of view about [our show]. And lump us in with something that somebody [Portnoy] said 3 years ago, in an out-of-bounds rant."

But Katz, who had been at the company since 2012, didn't completely distance himself from Ponder's attack:

"Here is the one thing I'll slightly disagree with you on. I deserve to be lumped in. Because guess what, my Twitter handle is @BarstoolBigCat. I've been working at Barstool for five years. I've helped build this company through blood sweat and tears. You lump me in because I am lumped in. What I think we've gotten to—like any other media company...Dave's voice and my voice are not the same. We disagree on things many times. I have been publicly chastised from inside these walls for disagreeing with Dave on Erin Andrews. Or sometimes people will harass people on Twitter in the name of Barstool, and I've said that's fucking bullshit, and it shouldn't happen. So just in summation, [it] sucks we got cancelled, but at the end of the day, it was politics out of our control."

After *Barstool Van Talk* was axed, both Katz and Sollenberger didn't show up to the Barstool office for several weeks, and Katz was visibly absent from his usual post as a host of The Rundown show. Followers of Barstool were convinced the star duo's days at the company were numbered, as these comments reveal:

"Big Cat and PFT have to leave Barstool soon. Portnoy's bullshit is now holding back their careers. Neither of these guys are representative of the bad parts of Barstool."

"PFT and Big Cat are not like the rest of the company. The show could've had a shot if Portnoy kept his fucking mouth shut."

"This is all Prez's doing."

Portnoy's fans were tuned in to see how the founder was going to get himself out of another self-made catastrophe. And the online commenters weren't the only ones concerned that *Pardon My Take* was leaving the company. The Chernin guys had been watching the entire saga unfold quietly from the sidelines, a position they were now quite familiar with.

As 2018 approached, Portnoy and Kerns had been discussing a new investment from Chernin's fund, thanks to the revenue growth driven by Nardini, and most important, the success of their podcasts. The sides had settled on Chernin providing Barstool with another $15M, at a whopping $100M valuation. This was way up from the original $12.5M price tag that The Chernin Group had placed on Barstool three years earlier. In fact, when Kerns and Portnoy first sat down to discuss their initial investment in 2015, a potential exit of $25M was a dream scenario. As Kerns said of those numbers, "The company has far exceeded our plans and all our models. There are a lot more areas we need to invest in."

The cash would give Dave's Milton guys some much-deserved spending money; it would also allow the company to splurge on new hires, technology, and merchandising ventures, such as Barstool-branded alcohol—the *Spittin' Chiclet*'s podcast's Pink Whitney New

Amsterdam vodka would make the company millions—and further down the road, Barstool-themed bars like the one the company would open in Scottsdale, AZ and Nashville, TN. As for the overall value of Portnoy's operation, the price someone theoretically would have to pay to own what started as an eight-page newspaper rag now had eight zeroes next to it.

But that was before the ESPN deal fell through. Now, The Chernin Group had begun discussing whether or not to follow through with its second investment. Kerns said, "We didn't know if Big Cat and PFT were going to go off the rails and leave the company. We didn't know whether they thought working at Barstool would hamper their careers. We were unsure of what was going to happen." So Kerns picked up the phone and dialed Portnoy.

"Dave, we need to take a step back here."

25

"Barstool Sports Is Now Valued at Over 100 Million Dollars (GASP)"

"So today was a big news day as we announced that Chernin has invested more money in Barstool at a valuation over 100 million dollars. Lots of people (me) are saying I'm super rich now. That's not really the case until we sell it again, but it's still pretty fucking surreal. Like this little ass company that I started basically in my basement is now worth 100 fucking million dollars. What the fuck? #BrickByBrick Indeed."

Katz and Sollenberger stayed at Barstool. As for The Chernin Group, once they realized *Pardon My Take* wasn't going anywhere, the investors came back to the table and got a deal done. And Kerns would apologize for his "let's take a step back here" comment to Dave. "I'll fall on that sword," he said. "I said the wrong thing at the wrong time." Kerns would later state that Chernin never had any intentions of abandoning ship.

But before the PMT crew was resolidified at his company, Portnoy reminded The Chernin Group who they were working with. "I flew to LA [after the phone call from Kerns] and met with Peter because my philosophy was once I have a deal, the numbers become almost irrelevant. It's like 'Nope, we had a deal.'" Portnoy, who was unsurprisingly pissed about them reconsidering the investment explained, "I said the two options are you honor the deal, or

I'm basically done." It was a repeat of two years earlier, when Portnoy almost walked following their disagreement over the lawyer fees. And while he did appease Katz with the ESPN partnership, Portnoy told Chernin he believed Barstool would survive even if Katz left. "I've known Big Cat forever so I wasn't as worried [that he would leave], but we had survived too much already not to. If Dan left, I was ready to step up and fill that void," Portnoy said.

He wouldn't have to. Aside from both Katz and Sollenberger being stuck in contracts with non-competes, things had cooled off in the weeks following the failed partnership. "It turned out to be the best thing that ever happened to us," Portnoy said. "Barstool was at an interesting point. If [after both of their contracts were up] ESPN made a big offer, we wouldn't have been able to match it. It drove Dan back to Barstool fully and it really kind of galvanized us vs. the world. It played to our advantage."

"As much as it sucked at the time, I'm very happy in the long term it didn't work out with ESPN," Katz said. Though we'll never know, it's unlikely Katz would be as popular as he is today—Big Cat has 1.6M followers on Twitter—if he had moved to ESPN. The humor that earned him this following would have undoubtably been curtailed by the powers that be over in Bristol. As he described of his (very) short time working there, "We did one episode and got half our jokes cut." Luckily for him and his fans (and Portnoy), Katz avoided becoming another watered-down blue checkmark.

Following the failed deal, Barstool leaned on its pirate ship ethos. "I don't think we change who are, what we stand for, or how we do it," Nardini said. "I'm really proud of those things."

"We live in the mud, we were born in the mud," Clancy explained. "Barstool is going to inherit the Earth because everyone is gonna have to go to the mud and we're already there."

Industry observers agreed with Portnoy's assessment that this was probably the best outcome for his company. "I think [Portnoy] sticking to his guns [during the ESPN drama], from the brand perspective, is probably the correct approach," said Tülin Erdem, a business professor at New York University and head of the school's marketing department. "Going more mainstream," she said, could "alienate their core [young male] group, which brought them here."

Apart from Katz staying and Barstool's hockey-stick growth over the last two years, Chernin followed through with its reinvestment in Portnoy's company, thanks to the legalization of sports gambling in 2018. That year, the U.S. Supreme Court struck down The Professional and Amateur Sports Protection Act (PASPA) of 1992, which effectively outlawed sports betting nationwide and opened the floodgates for companies like FanDuel and DraftKings to start taking over our television sets with their mind-bending number of advertisements. In June 2018, New Jersey became the first state to offer legal sports betting (outside Nevada and a few other select areas of the country), raking in a $16M total handle for that month. Five years later in November 2023, that number would increase by 100x, to $1.6B.

Barstool was in prime position to capitalize on the rise of sports betting. Remember that Portnoy had started his newspaper as a gambling and sports publication; he often spoke of his crippling gambling addiction, one that saw him go bankrupt in early 2004. It was a well-known habit of Portnoy, both among his fans and those who worked at his company. "Please stop gambling. It's just a genuine request from a loyal employee at this point," Clancy tweeted at him in 2014. Following the monumental court ruling, Portnoy and Barstool leaned further into gambling content, and that became probably the only time in the history of sports gambling that someone with such an addiction would be able to turn a long-term profit from betting on sports.

Barstool had already been producing shows centered around gambling; the College Pick Em' vehicle Portnoy and Katz hosted had been in existence since 2013. And in 2018, Portnoy & Co. added a spruced-up production centered around the degenerate pastime, called *Barstool Sports Advisors*. The show featured Portnoy, Katz, and a man in his late fifties named Stu Feiner, a legendary tout from Long Island who was louder than Loud Sean and spoke more about "eating ass" than he did about sports. The trio provided their weekly picks on the upcoming NFL games, along with random but oddly compelling banter. The production was the most sophisticated piece of content Barstool had developed to date, with comedically timed graphics and editing that made the show a hit among Stoolies.[1]

Following the premiere of *Sports Advisors*, gambling suddenly took centerstage at Portnoy's company. In their Manhattan office, Barstool employees would gather around the television to watch sports on a live stream to their fans, who followed along as the Barstool personalities lived and died with their bets. This setup would become known as the "Gambling Cave," and though it was basically just a bunch of out-of-shape sweaty dudes sitting on couches, screaming at a TV, Stoolies tuned in to watch.

Barstool's approach to sports gambling would be in line with how Portnoy operated. It was an authentic endeavor, in the sense that he (and Katz) gambled and (often) lost their own money. As others in media hopped on the sports betting gambling train, Portnoy called out the competition for not being real gamblers: "Jamie Foxx, he's the face of MGM gambling…are you kidding me, Jamie Foxx?" And when someone compared Jamie Foxx to Dave Portnoy in the gambling space, the founder's response was simple: "That is a beatdown." Portnoy advertised this as the main reason to follow Barstool's gambling content: it wasn't fake.

His father Mike Portnoy attested, "Your gambling issues, you know how your mother and I have felt about that. But I came to realize that it's so real with you, and if it wasn't real, Barstool wouldn't be what it is."

Sports gambling entertainment at Barstool was a full-blown venture financially supported by The Chernin Group, and Portnoy

---

1   *Barstool Sports Advisors appeared on TBG and WPIX NY MyPhilly and in Boston The CW before leaving TV and going fully digital.*

(though Chernin never bankrolled his actual bets) who stated, "The moment I knew legalization was happening I walked into Erika's office and said this is it, this is our time." On May 14, 2018, somewhat prophetically, Portnoy posted the following blog:

"I'm Pretty Sure These New Sports Gambling Laws Should Make Me Rich Beyond My Wildest Dreams But I Can't Figure Out How Yet

"So the big news of the day is that the Federal Ban on sports gambling has been lifted, paving the way for all states to decide individually whether they want to allow it or not. It's huge news that has been a long time coming. It should be especially huge news to everybody at Barstool and to myself and probably Dan in particular.

"Why? Because we are both degenerate gamblers with huge followings. I'd argue we are two of the most mainstream gamblers on the planet. And not the fake kind like Clay Travis and Bill Simmons who don't really bet, but pretend to. Me and Dan are the real deal, motherfuckers.

"Hell, Barstool Sports started strictly as a gambling blog. I flew out to Vegas before I started Barstool and tried to get a job out there. My first clients were Party Poker, The Greek, and Bet Jamaica. I know everything there is to know about sports gambling. I've easily lost mid-seven figures in my lifetime gambling (humble brag that makes me want to puke), but it should all be worth it now because Barstool and myself are primed to take advantage of this legislation."

Besides Portnoy and Katz (who posted a picture every Saturday of the donuts he acquired, along with the caption "Let's win our bets today"), there were others who realized the potential benefit of the dive into sports betting. As KFC said, "We are the first and only media company with the two biggest gambling personalities on the planet to get in at the ground floor of legalized gambling." Clancy, however, was the one main personality at Barstool who never ventured into the gambling world, despite the company-wide movement. "It was the one vice I didn't have." When asked why he never got into it, he said, "I didn't want it to be phony, and there were other people doing it (outside of Barstool), and you could tell that it was fake, and that's the worst." Instead, Clancy focused more on comedic content—a move the blogger would come to regret.

As for the company, the overall direction of Barstool was now clear, and CEO Nardini explained Barstool's new strategy: "The way we've talked about sports betting is to make it very conversational, and to really make sports betting an organic, authentic, and integrated part of what we do." Following legalization, advertising from gambling outfits poured in.

Although sports gambling became a main focus, in 2018, Barstool kept a good amount of its original programming untouched by the fad. Portnoy's 24/7 digital reality tv show was still on the air, and the first episode of that year featured a very public drama centered around Clancy:

> **"Barstool Sports star KFC's wife claims he's been cheating on her since pregnancy"**
>
> —*The New York Post*

On January 4, Barstool followers woke up to an Instagram post from Clancy's wife:

> "Last night after I put my 2-year-old daughter and 6-month son to bed, I caught my husband sending messages to his mistress, who he's apparently been seeing since I was 8

months pregnant. Days before I gave birth, he was at a hotel in Manhattan with her. Days after I gave birth, he was [there] too. The rug [has] been pulled out from underneath me."

Stoolies went bananas on Twitter, and Clancy eventually posted an apology video, with a caption that read "I'm sorry to my wife and kids and everybody I let down." In the video, he said, "I have ruined my marriage, my family, and my life because I acted selfishly, I acted like a coward, and I behaved like a boy when I should've behaved like a man."

Unfortunately for Clancy, the rules of Barstool dictated that this was going to be turned into content for Barstool fans. "I didn't want Barstool to be silent here," Portnoy said when addressing the situation that morning. "It sucks. I'll say what everybody else is probably thinking, KFC comes across as a scumbag here. But, again, we don't know anything. I'm sure he'll address when he sees the time is right."

Clancy followed the protocol and went on Barstool radio that day to face the music. "I'm not going to hide from the public," he said, "Because I always have been public, I have always talked about myself and talked about other people's personal relationships, so it would be disingenuous of me to not sit here and do the same when I'm the one going through the mud."

Ironically, Clancy had added "being the family man" to his persona after he got married in 2014. While Katz and Portnoy were single (Dave since 2016), Clancy played the role of the Barstool personality who griped about having real responsibilities. "You had this image," Portnoy said to Clancy on the radio that day, "which a lot of people say is of the everyday guy who's miserable, married, but not *really* miserable, and I think it just stunned people. I think that was a huge factor."[2]

---

2   When I say Portnoy and Katz were single, it refers to the fact that both were unmarried.

From a business perspective, Portnoy was unsure of how to handle the situation. In the minds of their sponsors, it would be tough to wheel out KFC on the Rundown and have him tell fans to buy one of their products when the entire internet "thought he was a scumbag." Later that day on the show, Portnoy, Katz, and a lifeless-looking Clancy sat in their patented Laz-E-Boy chairs in front of the Barstool Bar.

Portnoy began by saying, with a smirk, "I think you're gonna have to get a Rundown suspension, Kevin, we've gone back and forth on it, but the subjects are too light, too easy, and you're front-page news on *People* Magazine for all the wrong reasons, so we're gonna give you a two-week Rundown suspension."

"It's fair, I get it," a defeated Clancy replied, before getting out of his chair and walking off set. It was a fitting end to the day, one that Stoolies would often reference in the weeks and years going forward. Much like when Portnoy was going through his divorce, Clancy paid the price for being a main contestant on Barstool's reality show. But Portnoy didn't let the gravity of Clancy's actions stop him from getting in at least one shot at his radio rival, as he quipped to him on air: "I've been married, separated…by the way, you made me look good."

There were other controversies that Barstool's ringmaster leaned into during 2018:

- ○ Michael Rapaport, a B-list actor, was hired and then very publicly fired by Portnoy after tweeting, "If you call yourself a Stoolie, you've already lost in life."

- ○ An employee named Louis Roberts a.k.a. "Lightswitch Lou," who had worked under Gaz since 2011, was fired for starting his own canned wine company while working at the Stool. Portnoy accused him of stealing company resources:

"We had a snake who worked here," Portnoy openly told Barstool radio listeners, "A filthy snake, and he was doing things that directly harm every single person in this company. And it manifested itself over the last 24 hours. I am [now] catching wind of it," Dave said about Lou. Portnoy refused to call Lou by his real name going forward and instead referred to him and the few other employees who helped him as "The Bubbly Gang."

o Barstool also had a very public breakup with Pat McAfee, the former NFL Punter and popular media personality who had joined the Stool in 2017. McAfee, who was operating from a satellite office in Indianapolis, left Barstool after he allegedly believed the sales team wasn't prioritizing selling ads for his show. He tweeted about the situation, "The business side of things with me made it very difficult being 713 miles away. Financial decisions were being made for me by people I'd never met, deals were getting made AND PULLED without my knowledge."[3]

Following these internal dustups (which satisfied Stoolies' Barstool gossip fix), Portnoy continued to manufacture attention. In February 2019, he was escorted out of the Super Bowl wearing a mustache-and-dark-glasses disguise and a "I <3 Goodell" shirt. Here is the headline he posted after being released from the holding cell at Mercedes-Benz stadium:

"Emergency Press Conference—I Walked Right [out] of Jail to Find out the Pats Made History!"

---

3   McAfee didn't blame Portnoy or Nardini. But it didn't help that Portnoy learned McAfee was an investor in Louis Robert's wine company, though McAfee claims Roberts told him Portnoy knew about it and was also an investor (and of course, he wasn't). Regardless, Portnoy tweeted that he begged McAfee to stay. Roberts would work for McAfee after both left Barstool.

Portnoy's feud with the commissioner of the most valuable sports league in North America resulted in the NFL banning the Barstool founder from events like the one Portnoy attended incognito. But this played right into Barstool's hand: Portnoy & Co. mocked Roger Goodell for being overly serious and out of touch, and those two sentiments were on full display in the video of Dave being aggressively removed from the Super Bowl. After being discovered, the blogger intentionally went limp in the arms of the security guards, as they lugged what looked like a dead body to the exit of the stadium. Goodell's heavy hand on Portnoy went mega-viral: he had taken the bait.

By early 2019, this sort of chaos, their podcasts, and being on the frontier of sports gambling combined to make Barstool officially one of the most popular media companies in the U.S. On February 20, Nardini tweeted the following: "Turner, ESPN, and the no rights, no television Pirate Ship @barstoolsports." Beneath her tweet sat a graphic with the title "Top 10 U.S. Sports Media—January 2019: Based on Actions (reactions, comments, shares, retweets and likes)." Barstool ranked number three on this list, right behind the massive conglomerates Turner and ESPN and ahead of CBS Corp, 21st Century Fox, and NBC/Comcast. (Nardini's "no rights" comment was a reference to the other orgs having live rights to sporting events, which was a massive ratings driver.)

And although the entertainment was unlike anything else on the internet—the founder of Buzzfeed wasn't being dragged up the stairs at the Super Bowl—Barstool was now sitting alongside legitimate media outlets, and the company was operating more in that lane. The *"Local Smokeshow of the Day"* posts were banished from the website, so was the company's famous *"Guess That Ass"* and *"Wake Up With"* features. There were still attractive girls being posted on the site and features like Jerry Thornton's *"Grading the Newest Sex Scandal Teacher"* that kept Barstool somewhat risqué, but overall, the T&A had been largely toned down. And most notably, the separate-city model that Portnoy used to build his company in the mid-2010s was now completely deemphasized.

Thanks to the cash infusion from Chernin, and a move to a larger, more dynamic office in the middle of 2019, the 180 employees who now called Barstool home operated as a unified, well-oiled content machine. By the end of that year, Barstool took home nearly $100M in revenue. The company was growing faster than its digital media counterparts as well: Barstool saw 65% year-over-year revenue growth, compared to 13% for the rest of the digital media industry.

By this time, The Chernin Group, Nardini, and Portnoy had strategically leaned the company into sports gambling with the hopes of being acquired by a large gaming outfit like DraftKings or FanDuel, with the obvious idea that Barstool would promote the buyer's brand and bring its audience to their betting platform. "I'm biased because I own Barstool, but it would be the biggest no-brainer deal of all time," said Portnoy. "Fox is gonna spend how much with the NFL to advertise FoxBet? People care about what *we* say more than them. And we're not charging the same prices. You're gonna spend millions in a war to get advertising, to get clients, to get customers, or you could buy us, own the media, and we have this authentic group." To further his case, Barstool revealed that 62% of Stoolies already bet on sports.

The leaders of Portnoy's company all had a massive exit in sight, particularly with how much money was flooding into the gambling industry: DraftKings, Caesars, and FanDuel alone spent a combined $84M on advertising in 2019, $314M in 2020, and by 2021, the overall ad spend for the industry reached $1B. With Barstool's eye-popping growth numbers, it seemed as if a lucrative payday was on the horizon. But there was another company, one that would use the same tools Barstool had honed during its rise to the top of the digital media world, that would try its best to stop this from happening.

26

"What Fresh Hell Is Barstool Sports?

"I never saw Barstool Sports coming. I probably should have. I am the guy who founded Deadspin, after all, and during the years I actively ran the site—now more than a decade in the past—I was ostensibly in charge of figuring out what was coming next on the sports internet…I don't think I could have stopped Barstool had I tried—and I had absolutely no interest in trying. But when you look at the industry power they have accumulated (a $100 million valuation, sponsorships with major brands, an XM radio show that always seems to be spitting at me when I scroll by it on the dial), mostly by steering into the skid of the worst of what the internet has to offer—which has proven to be a rather lasting and successful business plan!—and at how they have used that power to relentlessly abuse women in the industry, I sure do wish I had fought harder."

—Will Leitch, Founding Editor at Deadspin

Founded by Nick Denton at Gawker Media in 2005 (Will Leitch joined as Deadspin's Editor soon after), Deadspin got its start around the same time as Barstool. Denton's publication, which was way more popular than Portnoy's in those early blogging days, was a go-to for internet users looking for a more conversational commentary on the state of sports in our country. Like Barstool, Deadspin also covered pop culture, with writing that was not as brazen as Portnoy's but still upset old media guys like Buzz Bissinger.

The beginning of the Barstool-Deadspin relationship was actually a friendly one: starting all the way back in December 2006 when Will Leitch gave credit to Barstool for posting a funny blooper video of Dan Marino pulling a Bill O'Reilly inside the broadcasting booth. *Fuck it, we'll do it live!* For the next several years, Deadspin provided links to different Barstool articles, which helped grow Portnoy's brand online, as Deadspin, unlike the Stool, had a national presence.

It wasn't until September 2012 that Deadspin posted the first negative article about Barstool on its website, where it listed Barstool as one of the "*67 Worst Twitter Accounts.*" Still, over the next several years, Deadspin refrained from going after Portnoy, even occasionally crediting Barstool for a story. But starting in 2017, two young twenty-something Deadspin writers, Samer Kalaf and Laura Wagner, took aim at Portnoy's online empire.

In May of that year, a blogger named Spags (one of Portnoy's post-Chernin hires) posted a blog calling Rihanna fat. Kalaf fired the first shot:[1]

"Barstool Sports Founder Comes Up with Dumbest Possible Reason to Delete Dumbest Possible Post"

—Samer Kalaf

"Barstool Sports, a blog for dipshits, by dipshits, caught hell Tuesday after senior director of editorial strategy and growth—this does not sound like a real job—Chris Spagnuolo wrote a blog about how Rihanna might be fat. Spagnuolo believed the criticism came because no one read past the headline, which was "Is Rihanna Going to Make Being Fat the Hot New Trend?"

---

1   Other writers at Deadspin also went after Barstool.

"After enduring vituperation for hours, the site deleted the tweet that linked to the story, and founder Dave Portnoy published a blog at 4:19 p.m. in which he announced that he would delete Spagnuolo's post, not because "feminists" hated it, but because it wasn't funny and Spagnuolo is a shitty writer."

A few months later, during the ESPN fiasco, Wagner joined her colleague in harpooning Portnoy's company (after taking a few shots at ESPN):

"ESPN Is Trying Anything"
—Laura Wagner

"It's not a shock that ESPN is willing to overlook *Pardon My Take*'s open antagonism, since ESPN is desperate to be seen as being in on the joke, but it is surprising that the network is willing to ally with Barstool Sports, which sells itself on poorly written blogs, guilt-free Jew jokes, and, generally, humor that might have been cutting in the time when every comedian was a guy in a leather jacket."

Kalaf and Wagner went on to lead Deadspin's anti-Barstool crusade.

- **"The Barstool Sports Gang Had a Blackface Whoopsie"** —Samer Kalaf

- **"Comedian Says Barstool Sports Stole Her Video, Tried to Bribe Her with $50 Gift Card"** —Samer Kalaf

- **"Barstool Sport's Dave Portnoy Actually Trembles While Being Asked about Harassing Women"** —Samer Kalaf

- ○ **"Barstool Sports Publishes Bizarre Blog on Missing Woman, Deletes It after Police Charge Suspect with Her Murder"** —Samer Kalaf

- ○ **"ESPN Wanted Barstool, But Without the Stench"** — Laura Wagner

- ○ **"Barstool Employee Unhappy about Being Filmed in the Shower by His Boss"** —Laura Wagner

- ○ **"The Bruins Don't Want to Talk about Getting into Bed with Barstool Sports"** —Laura Wagner

For Barstool fans, Deadspin became enemy number #1. And Portnoy zeroed in on the Deadspin duo:

"Worst Writer on the Internet—Samer Kalif of Univision Back at It"

"Samer Kalif is the worst writer on the internet. He's click-bait city. He's a kid who grew up popping his zits at UNH idolizing me and then threw a tantrum when he wasn't good enough to work here and has had an axe to grind ever since. He's a kid who grew up [in Boston] and hates the Pats. He's basically a loser who hates everything successful because he was never part of the in crowd and got picked on his entire life."

"Resident Worst Writer on the Internet Samer Paloof of Deadspin Lies about Whether South Carolina Coach Will Muschamp Talked to His Players about Voting"

"What a weird story, huh? I mean I know all the "writers" at Univision are minimum-wage hacks with no talent or integrity who only can get clicks with salacious headlines, but this is a new low even for Samka Panooka."

While Portnoy's purposeful misspelling of Samer Kalaf's name could be viewed as racially charged, it was his attack on Wagner that raised eyebrows. Wagner called the Barstool founder "a sniffly raisin" and a "short-tempered Adderall pill"; she also wrote an article that included more than 30 hateful, vulgar emails she had received from Stoolies, who were upset when she became the first to publish Sollenberger's—PFT's—real name. Here's how Portnoy responded:

> "@laurawags publishing a bunch of emails today was such a heel move I can't help but love her for it. Felt it in my plums. #dateme"
>
> —@stoolpresidente

> "I cannot quit this woman. I shouldn't say I love her but I love her...I love you Wags"
>
> —@stoolpresidente

> "Short-tempered Adderall pill will never not be funny which is exactly why I think Wags has the right stuff"
>
> —@stoolpresidente

> "Hey @laurawags I mean it. Somebody tell Laura Wagner that when she gets fired I'll hire her nasty little potty mouth in a heartbeat."
>
> —@stoolpresidente

"I Need Laura Wagner to Be my Valentine

"Another day and another hit piece by the indominable Laura Wager. I honestly think I love this fucking woman. She's just so potty mouthed and so vile and so vindictive. She's just so obsessed with hating Barstool, I can't get enough… she's been working at Deadspin for less than a year and she's written about us 100 times already. She goes to bed dreaming of Barstool. She wakes up dreaming of Barstool. Our demise is what keeps her going. It's her motivation to live. Seriously, I can't get enough of this cutie pie. I need her in my life. Laura Wagner, will you be my valentine?"

In a since-deleted blog post, Portnoy called Wagner a "total wildcat in the sack" in his headline and declared "I want to stick my tongue down her throat." On Barstool radio, he called in to explain how "I couldn't love her any harder...my only mistake is I'm tweeting love emojis at her again on Twitter because I can't restrain myself, and I hope I don't get banned for harassment, even though I just want to kiss her."

Dave's attack on Wagner had an undertone that many people, including Wagner herself, saw as sexual harassment. "Since I was writing about Eric Sollenberger's place at Barstool, I wanted to give him the opportunity to comment on his boss's sexual harassment of me," Wagner said.

Outsiders critical of Portnoy and his company often bemoaned how Barstool claimed to operate under the guise of comedy in these sorts of situations. And it was a claim Portnoy did, in fact, make. For example, after making a female employee cry by telling her she wouldn't be able to put her face in front of the camera in five years, Portnoy said of the backlash he received: "We're a comedy site, and people treat us like a news network. It's not fair." But unsurprisingly, others in media weren't laughing at Portnoy's "jokes" about kissing Wagner, as *Business Insider* noted at the time:

> "After a string of negative media stories accusing him of promoting a culture of sexual harassment and online trolling, Barstool Sports founder Dave Portnoy is defending his controversial site..."

While doing battle with Deadspin, in the middle of 2018, Portnoy also went somewhat off the rails on Sam Ponder, the ESPN host who had torpedoed the *Barstool Van Talk* show.[2] Ponder told her Instagram followers that she didn't have anything to do with Barstool's show getting cancelled, which Portnoy (and pretty much everyone else) thought was an egregious lie:

> "Right now, I feel like I'm slowly suffocating her, in an internet online war, and I'm excited, it's not ending, I will get #SamPonderLies trending, I said a free t-shirt to anybody who gets a Sam Ponder lies shirt on any telecast, any station, we are now back in this, and it's all her fault."

This comment didn't go unnoticed by Wagner:

"Sociopathic Barstool Founder Dave Portnoy Giddy about 'Suffocating' ESPN Host Sam Ponder in 'Online War'"

"As any woman in sports media who has drawn the ire of Barstool in the past can tell you, tweets and blog posts from the site's employees are a precursor to sustained harassment from the site's rabidly misogynistic fanbase. Portnoy understands this just as well as anyone else and spent yesterday encouraging Ponder's harassment…Portnoy then went on the radio to talk about his intent to 'slowly suffocate' Ponder in an 'internet online war.'"

While his 2018 attack on Ponder wasn't sexual in nature (though many believed his 2014 attack was), the fact that his target was a woman didn't help Portnoy's cause with those who claimed he was a misogynist. Clancy rebuked this sentiment, saying, "Dave responds to Ponder in the way Dave responds to everyone: men, women, old, young, fat, skinny, employees." Regardless of Clancy's defense,

---

2   Portnoy ran into Ponder in 2020 and had an intense exchange with the ESPN host.

one thing is certain: Portnoy wasn't telling Barstool nemesis Jamie O'Grady of *Sports Illustrated*, after O'Grady dropped his hit piece on Portnoy's company, that he wanted to stick his tongue down O'Grady's throat.

Although the rest of Barstool took a somewhat muted tact when Portnoy launched attacks like the one on Ponder or Wagner, a few employees did (somewhat) denounce their boss's actions. In his article on Barstool, *The Daily Beast*'s Robert Silverman wrote, "Reached via text message, Sollenberger claimed he'd asked Portnoy on-air 'to not go after Laura Wagner and implored the audience to do the same,' a request he reiterated in private." And eventually Sollenberger broke his PFT character—something he almost never did—to write the following post about Portnoy's attack on Ponder:

"Dave always says he goes after men online more frequently than women—that is absolutely true. Dave and everyone [here] at Barstool fight back when they feel they have been attacked regardless of sex/race/etc. I also think it is absolutely true that there are different things to consider when publicly calling out a female journalist on twitter…When someone on twitter wants to criticize them they frequently don't call them an "idiot" or a "moron," like they would a man- but rather they go straight to calling them a slut, or saying they're ugly, or that they slept their way to the top. That type of stuff actually does take a toll psychologically in a way that it wouldn't for a man… In other words- it's one thing to go after Roger Goodell or Michael Rapaport, and a different thing to attack Sam Ponder relentlessly. In that case we needed to defend ourselves against things that she said that were demonstrably false, but it's another thing to take it to a level that would constitute harassment… To be totally fair to Dave, sometimes stuff gets misconstrued…But there are other times when Dave asks the troops to swarm and it turns into a cycle of harassment, response, response to the harassment, and then it becomes part of the next critical article about us. And that is what I think we can do without. Dave's the one who put his life into building this company, and while I'm in a high position here at the company, Dave's still my boss and the best I can do is make him aware of my opinion and ask him to consider it."

Katz, for his part, leaned on his original stance that he was against any sort of harassment, saying, "I don't want to get #SamPonderLies trending; I don't want people to go after her, I don't want any of this. I just want to move on because I've moved on. I hate this shit. I want to make people laugh and I don't care about this stuff." Of course, both Katz and PFT had previous experience with Portnoy v. Ponder.

As for the perceived undertones of sexual harassment sent towards Wagner, Clancy, another leader at Barstool, had this exchange with Portnoy on Barstool radio; it followed Wagner's hit piece on Barstool claiming Portnoy was "giddy" about harassing Ponder and centered around whether Wagner wanted Portnoy sexually, a notion Clancy pushed back on:

Portnoy: You don't think she's playing like—this is a dance we're doing with each other right now?

Clancy: I think she's playing the internet dance, I think she loves the attention and the clicks and all that shit. I think she wants no part in having sex with you.

Portnoy: Oh I think she may. I think this is a dance—

Clancy: Here comes the sociopath.

Portnoy: But she keeps doing it! [writing about Barstool]

Clancy: The narcissism is out today. Ok genuinely, you think Laura Wagner wants to fuck you? Genuinely, truly?

Portnoy: I don't think she'd admit it yet, but [I think] there's a part of her that thinks about it. I really do.

While key personalities at Barstool spoke out about Portnoy's actions, The Chernin Group stayed silent. After the initial spotlight shined on them following their investment in 2016, the financiers had assumed their normal position, operating in the background of the chaos. When articles like the one Wagner wrote in 2018 or *The Daily Beast* hit piece appeared, Kerns (who was then-President of Digital for The Chernin Group) declined to comment. Dave saw this as a net positive: "Would I have liked Chernin once to [say] 'I support him' publicly? Yeah, but he never said 'I don't support him' really when things got hot, and that's hard. Not a lot of people would do that."

Outside of Katz, Clancy, or even The Chernin Group, most looked to Nardini when Portnoy went on the offensive against the likes of Ponder, Wagner, and others, for the obvious reason that she was a female leader of the company, a situation she often referenced when defending Barstool. "There are people who say I'm just here because I'm female—and I think that's the most sexist thing of all."

Nardini knew what she was getting into when she joined. Before any of these incidents occurred under her leadership, she told *The New York Times*, "Every time anyone mentions us in the media, they're always going to write that requisite paragraph." Her specific response to Portnoy's attacks were relatively diluted. She didn't comment publicly on Dave's crusade against SoulCycle; following the ESPN meltdown (when the 2014 video of Portnoy calling Ponder a slut surfaced) Nardini said on Twitter:

"[Barstool] isn't for everyone, but you don't have to watch it. In today's world, if people don't like something, they think it shouldn't exist. The good the bad the funny, it's all out there. We're a comedy brand that's been on the internet for 15 years and not for everyone. Barstool grew an undeniable audience because it was unafraid to have a hot take, an unpopular opinion or cross the line."

She also tweeted during that time in 2017, "We have a zero-tolerance harassment policy."

In September 2018, roughly two weeks after Portnoy's statement that he was "suffocating Ponder in an online war", which was also around the same time Portnoy said he "just wanted to kiss" Wagner, and "I want to stick my tongue down her throat" (and his Barstool radio appearance with Clancy discussing whether Wagner wanted Portnoy sexually) Nardini wrote the following blog:

"A Blog from the Token Female CEO of Barstool Sports

"This whole thing is complicated.

"I am a woman CEO. I am a woman CEO of a comedy brand dressed up as a sports media site. There aren't a lot of us (female CEOs or comedy brands couched in sports). We have a female CRO [Chief Revenue Officer], not a lot of those either. I've been in media for 20 years. I'd say 99% of my peers wouldn't choose this path.

"Am I glad I did? You bet.

"Would I do it again? Absolutely.

"Want to know what I find sexism to be?

"Telling a woman with 20+ years' experience at some of the biggest media companies in the world that she is only in charge of a company because she wears a skirt.

"If you are someone looking for that condemnation and judgement—you win. You will always win. Everything these guys have written and said for over a decade lives on the internet, in print, in audio, in video. Quotes can be pulled out of the context and presented as the real, serious opinions of their authors from now until eternity.

"We fuck up. We say the wrong thing sometimes...I love Barstool and the people here. I believe in us. But more than anything, I am proud of the integrity and character inside this company. I have found myself here and feel at home."

The Barstool CEO did not specifically address Portnoy's comments. A month later in October 2018, she told *The New York Post*, "There's a very strong PC culture [that believes] anything outside of it should be silenced and should not exist. My job as CEO isn't to contextualize 2014 Dave's words. I do think we've evolved big time." The problem for Nardini was that Portnoy's comments about Wagner weren't from 2014, but instead just weeks prior.[3]

Nardini's unwillingness to publicly criticize Portnoy might have stemmed from her close relationship with Barstool's founder. "At the heart of it, I joined Barstool to work with Dave. I liked Dave instantly and I trusted him," she said. "And I am protective of him to this day...I love him, I really do." But critics, like the ones in her former Women's Mafia, would say this "protection" was rooted in the fact that Portnoy was her ticket to a corporate windfall, and unsurprisingly, Deadspin called Nardini complicit.[4]

"In these press hits, Nardini shows herself to be a master of saying as little as possible. She trots out the same stories

---

3   Like Kerns, Nardini didn't provide a comment to *The Daily Beast* in its 2018 Barstool piece or Wagner's 2018 article about Ponder and Portnoy.

4   Nardini, in the same interview, while saying she was protective of Portnoy, also stated Dave didn't need protecting.

about growing up a Patriots fan and how her female friends abandoned her after she took the Barstool gig and says she's proud of what the company has accomplished. She likes to mention there were 74 other applicants for her job, all of whom were men. She tells obsequious interviewers that Barstool is successful because it "doesn't have an agenda," and on the rare cases in which she's asked about the chauvinism that is very much its agenda, she turns it into some meta-commentary.

"The reason Nardini does these interviews, of course, is not to say something interesting about the company she runs or about being a woman in the male-dominated field of sports media, but to launder Barstool's image. 'See,' she practically screams, 'Barstool can't be misogynistic, because I'm a woman! All those other women, the harpies constantly bitching about how they're relentlessly harassed by my employees and our readers, just need to lighten up and be cool like me!' The journalistic outlets that publish these interviews are simply being played."

—Megan Greenwell, Former Editor-In-Chief at Deadspin

Barstool's rivalry with Deadspin would become regular entertainment to Stoolies, and those who rooted for Portnoy to prevail were handsomely rewarded in the back half of 2019, when a Boston-based private equity firm named Great Hill Partners purchased Gizmodo Media—Deadspin's parent company—from Univision. In April of that year, Great Hill Partners hired a man named Jim Spanfeller as CEO to oversee their newest asset. Spanfeller's background included running Forbes.com from 2001-2009, and enlisting the 62-year-old was viewed as bringing on an executive with deep experience in digital media.[5]

But the start to his tenure overseeing Deadspin was rocky. Spanfeller immediately clashed with Deadspin's editorial team, and in August 2019, Laura Wagner posted an in-depth investigative report into her own parent company—and more specifically into the hiring practices of Spanfeller.

"This Is How Things Work Now at G/O Media

"When Jim Spanfeller and a private equity firm called Great Hill Partners took over G/O Media [Deadspin's parent company]—formerly Gizmodo Media Group—in April, their stated goal was to make the company profitable. It was a welcome refrain for employees all too aware of how the company had languished under Univision's doomed ownership. But as Spanfeller began to implement his vision, that hope was replaced by employee frustration and skepticism over his hiring practices and interference with the company's journalism."

In her piece, Wagner detailed how numerous female employees at her company were passed over for leadership roles following the transition that were instead given to former male colleagues of Spanfeller:

"These men, and others who now hold C-suite positions at the company, were each hired without a public recruitment process, and several were installed over high-ranking women who had been successfully performing those jobs at the company for years. In one case, sources say Spanfeller did offer to promote a woman to run human resources, but

---

5   Univision had purchased Gizmodo in 2016 following the Hulk Hogan scandal and Gawker's ensuing bankruptcy.

on the condition she fire another woman at the company as her first order of business. (Spanfeller denies this claim.)"

As you can imagine, Spanfeller was less than thrilled with this development, and Wagner highlighted his pushback in her story:[6]

"Over the last few weeks, during their attempts to hinder or prevent the publication of this story, Spanfeller invoked concerns about Deadspin's credibility in covering G/O Media."

It was this "interference with the company's journalism" that was becoming the largest point of contention between Spanfeller and his writers, and a few weeks after this article was published, Deadspin's Editor-in-Chief Megan Greenwell resigned from the company:

"'I have been repeatedly undermined, lied to, and gaslit in my job,' Megan Greenwell said in a brief phone call with *The Daily Beast* on Friday. Among the many grievances, Greenwell said, G/O leadership refused to guarantee editorial independence for Deadspin and asked for the site to 'stick to sports'—a long-running source of frustration for a staff that also covers media, politics, and culture beyond sports."

As the wheels began to come off his rival company, Portnoy danced on Greenwell's grave:

"Oh No!!! Hearing Megan Greenwell Is out at Deadspin! The Horror!!!!

"I guess when you make no money, trash your boss, constantly bitch and moan that everything is everybody else's fault, take no accountability, you quit on your own free will. (Wink, wink)."

---

6   Deadspin was unionized.

And just two months later, inside their NYC Headquarters, Deadspin revolted against the "stick to sports" edict issued by Spanfeller and G/O Media brass. As *The New York Times* reported on October 30:

> "On Monday, the journalists at the freewheeling website Deadspin were instructed by its owners (again) to stick to sports. On Tuesday, the site's interim editor-in-chief, Barry Petchesky, was fired for refusing to obey that order. On Wednesday many longtime staff members quit in protest, hurling Deadspin into chaos. Laura Wagner, a reporter, was among the six staff writers—out of 10—who quit."

The mass exodus at Deadspin coincided with an involuntary industry-wide one. In 2019, roughly 8,000 people lost their jobs in media (by comparison, that number totaled 5,000 from the years 2014-2017 combined); Buzzfeed alone cut 200 jobs in January of that year. Spanfeller's unpopular demand to specialize in sports coverage was, at its core, a private equity firm's attempt to find profit in a declining sector. But the Deadspin writers didn't care, and they walked.

Portnoy, who happened to be in charge of one of the few media companies that was actually growing (thanks to his loyal fanbase), again wasted no time celebrating Deadspin's apparent demise:[7]

"Dear All Deadspin Employees: I Will Post Any Blogs That Your Boss Keeps Deleting Without Your Permission If You Ask Me Nicely."

"Oh No. Laura Wags out at Deadspin."

"Are Samir Paloof and Drew Magary[8] the Two Biggest Cowards on the Planet [for Not Quitting]?"

---

7   Barstool was more profitable than Deadspin, and posted nearly $20M more in revenue for 2019.

8   Magary was another Deadspin *writer*

"So by now everybody knows that Deadspin has imploded. 90% of the staff has either been fired or quit. It's over. They are dead. I have destroyed them just like I have destroyed every single enemy who has ever dared cross my path. Megan Greenwell fired. Barry Petchevsky fired. Tom Ley quit. Laura Wags quit. On and on it goes."[9]

The Barstool founder reserved a special ritual for his fallen enemies, such as Laura Wagner. It was one that his fans tuned in for en masse. From the HBO Sports feature on Barstool in the summer of 2019:

Soledad O'Brien [narrating]: "Dave Portnoy is the kind of guy who keeps a list of his enemies. Literally. An engraved list, to be precise. As we saw in his office."

Portnoy: "These are champagne bottles for when my enemies fail. I have the names engraved on them, and then if something bad happens to them where I feel like we've defeated them, *professionally speaking*, I will sit on camera and pop the champagne and celebrate in their face."

Soledad O'Brien: "Isn't there something…sick, about that?"

Portnoy: "It's diabolical. It motivates me though. It's like my enemies motivate me. I know a lot of people say success is the best revenge. No, I need to succeed and see my enemies fail."

Pop.

---

9   Barry Petchevsky, Drew Magary, and Tom Ley were Deadspin employees upon whom Portnoy dug up dirt.

27

Dave Portnoy stood at a podium in front of his employees. It was the 2nd Annual Barstool Dunkin' Awards, and the company was handing out trophies in recognition of its most outstanding pieces of content, with categories like "Best Celebrity Guest Appearance" and "Best Rough & Rowdy" moment. The gathering was being filmed, of course, for content. And the event was not insignificant. The multinational coffee company was an important sponsor—a fact Portnoy reminded his employees of in an email prior to the show, writing, "Put in some effort and dress up for the occasion."

And though he was inside a Dunkin' Donuts, the Barstool founder was leading by example, wearing a sharp dark suit and purple tie that matched his neatly tucked-in pocket square. But as he looked around the room, Portnoy noticed not everyone was sporting such attire. And that was now a big problem.

"Alright, welcome ladies and gentlemen to the 2nd annual Dunkin' Donuts, the go-to awards, the Barstool awards, thanks for everybody coming," Portnoy opened, his blood beginning to boil. "Kmarko looks great, congratulations. Feitelberg, nice outfit. Liz, lovely. Young Pageviews, like you dressing up. KFC, you look like shit. Francis, you could use the less than 70 people that signed up for your comedy special to buy a nice outfit. We coulda done that. The people who didn't dress up, if it were up to me, we'd do a firing squad right now. But it's the Dunkin' Donuts awards, so we won't do that. But I'll tell you this right now, if you're not dressed up...bad, real bad."

♣

By the summer of 2019, Barstool had moved into a new 35,000-square-foot mega-office in the Chelsea neighborhood of Manhattan. The space comprised two floors: downstairs, there was a multitude of podcast rooms, offices, a green room for celebrities who visited, a green-screen room for Barstool content creators, the customary wrap-around bar, and most important, the Gambling Cave—a room whose wall was lined with TVs and black leather chairs that sported the red stool logo. Portnoy's company was still looking for a buyer, and this setup was an important part of that pitch.

The second floor, like the old office, was reserved for the business end of the company, and was mostly occupied by conference rooms, breakout rooms, and a modestly sized kitchen. In the lobby, visitors were greeted by an old blue *Barstool Sports* newspaper bin and a security guard named Ebony who manned the front desk. In a tour of the new space for his audience, Portnoy said:

> "It is surreal going from my parents' house—my parents' basement, basically—to a studio month by month in South End. My first apartment when I started Barstool, no joke, was probably the size of this [pointing to a phone-booth-sized room]—then where'd we go? To Renee's parents' house in Abington. Worked out of there. Then we got our first office in Milton, and we were there for [about] 8 years. Which again is tiny. I thought it was a huge deal when we went to New York in the middle. And now this place is like a real huge fucking office."

The office was big enough to fit the almost 200 employees that now made up Barstool Sports. Portnoy's digital circus had been progressively expanding since the first NYC move, with characters like Zvataida T. Chimedza, or "Zah," the self-proclaimed "Midget from Zimbabwe" who became a relied-upon producer for Portnoy's team. Zach Etkind, a/k/a "the Wonton Don" or "Donnie Does," was Barstool's travel correspondent and fellow Masshole who lived in China for several years and landed on Portnoy's radar when he snuck into the ring after a Manny Pacquiao fight overseas. Evan McDowell, or "Big Ev," a hefty 20-something who was hired after someone tricked him into thinking he had an interview at Barstool Sports: he showed up at the office after traveling across the country, only to walk in and was asked why he was there. And Brandon Walker, a sharp-tongued Mississippian who Portnoy hired during his feud with the gambling site MyBookie over its dubious payout policy. A struggling content creator, Walker was hosting a live show in his basement when thousands of Stoolies suddenly descended on the chat. His confusion and attempt to figure out what was going on (he knew nothing about Portnoy calling out his employer) turned out to be entertaining content, and because of this—and to spite MyBookie—Portnoy hired Walker.

But out of the growing cast of characters still with the company today, Portnoy's most impactful—and inspirational—hire was a man named Frank Fleming. Known as Frank the Tank, the 500-pound,[1] short, single, child-like, glasses-wearing New Jersey native was an overly pessimistic superfan of the Mets, Dolphins, and Devils. (Honestly, it is difficult to describe him.) Before Barstool, Fleming had worked in the local courthouse while managing his own blog called *The Sports E-cyclopedia*, which was essentially a custom Wikipedia on the history of sports.[2] The website hosted posts from Frank and features like "*On This Date*" in history, in which Fleming would provide random facts about sporting events that occurred on that day. Although it was rudimentary and probably read by only a

---

1   Now 350-pound.

2   If you recall, one of Portnoy's early writers, Jerry Thornton, also worked at the courthouse.

few people, Frank had been updating the site daily since 2001. The man lived for sports.

Portnoy hired Frank after he was featured in a local news story about commuters dealing with delays on NJ Transit. The report began in a serious tone, from the narrating journalist: "Cancellations made it nearly impossible to get around. For some, the frustration was overwhelming." The camera then cut to Frank inside the train station, who was wearing a Mets shirt, jacket, and hat, and was having a meltdown:

> "The Jersey Transit is the absolute WORST! [nearly hyperventilating]. I'm not going to get to my game now because they are INCOMPETENT! [his voice cracking]. INCOMPETENT! They tell us Track G, Track H, Track E, and then I get on Track H and they say, 'No, this train's not going—their announcement was…'"

Frank is still screaming when the narrator's voice is heard again, talking over his muted outburst: "This man was clearly irate about possibly missing the Mets opening day game."

The report was unintentionally hilarious and went viral, with this headline: **"Mets fan rages because he can't get to the game."**

After seeing the video, Portnoy put the wheels in motion to make an offer for Fleming to join Barstool Sports, and Fleming eventually became one of the most well-known personalities at Barstool (his genuine persona made him beloved by such celebrities as J.J. Watt). Following his 150-pound weight loss and unlikely rise to stardom, in his speech at the 2023 Barstool awards, Fleming reflected on what Portnoy's offer meant to him:

> "I worked as a court-clerk. I settled as a court clerk. I studied broadcasting in college and it took—I never gave up, though. And that's the lesson here. Never give up your dream! And

now I am working my dream job here at Barstool. Never give up your dream!"

Portnoy basically saved the man's life.[3]

In 2019, the size of Barstool's offices and headcount should have made Portnoy feel satisfied that he had officially "made it" as a legitimate player inside the digital media world. It didn't. Instead, Portnoy was becoming increasingly frustrated with those who *did* feel this way:

> "The problem with our office is that with [the] exception of probably 5-7 people, the rest haven't worked an honest day in their life and just waltzed into a Dream world and have no sense of reality, and we need to be their boss and parents."
>
> —@stoolpresidente

As the founder, Portnoy had created Barstool with his bare hands by literally handing out newspapers alone inside the dirty subway of downtown Boston (he often reminded pretty much everyone of this fact). But as the jobs at his company became more glamorized, and with newly hired content creators immediately benefitting from the Barstool bump, he was slowly realizing (as most founders do) that not everyone appreciated his company the same way he did:

> "I love when employees complain their jobs are too stressful and they work too hard and talk shit about

---

3   It was this type of hire where Portnoy exercised his superpower: knowing what his audience found funny. Frank's popularity exploded. In January 2024, *The New York Post published an article with the headline, "Barstool's Frank the Tank Fleming Lost Over 150 Pounds Since Peak of 500." Scott Van Pelt, Mike Francesa, and Saquon Barkley have all joined Frank on his walk.*

the entrepreneur who worked their ass off to build
the company and now want to work 1/10 as hard
as [the] founder who built [the] company on their
own blood, sweat, and tears, with zero pay."

—@stoolpresidente

By now, a large part of Portnoy's persona had morphed into
that of a boss constantly upset with his employees. "There's so many
people at this company with a silver spoon up their ass," he reiterated, and outbursts like the one seen during the Dunkin' Awards
were becoming a regular occurrence. When a group of Barstool
employees forgot to clean up their trash following a Yankees live
stream, Portnoy lambasted them on Twitter and his blog, dubbing
the incident "Slobgate," eviscerating them publicly for several weeks.
One employee in particular, Adam "Smitty" Smith, who was formerly head of Barstool's Philadelphia site, caught the brunt of the
founder's ire:

"By the way, @SmittyBarstool being lazy doesn't
benefit me or barstool. But let's call a spade a spade."

—@stoolpresidente

"Mantis [another Barstool employee] vs. Smitty for
least-productive employee of last 6 months is a dog
fight! Mantis hasn't worked here this year. Still a
dogfight."

—@stoolpresidente

"Apparently, they are now teaching how I'm a great
boss and Smitty is a horrible employee in business school."

—@stoolpresidente

Portnoy was genuinely upset with his employees in these moments, but he also knew what he was doing with these public lashings. Stoolies loved them. They often griped in the comment section about how easy Barstool employees had it: hanging out in a laid-back office and being filmed all day seemed like a breeze. It wasn't a "real job," like the ones they were miserably working. Although most of this criticism was rooted in jealousy, Portnoy still gave his readers their pound of flesh on a regular basis. As Markovich explained, "The follow-up from [a scolding] from Dave is the worst part. You can deal with Dave yelling at you to your face, but then he brings it to the Stoolies. And then rips you even worse, and lets them… it's open season on you."

But in August 2019, Portnoy's act landed him in actual trouble. Another digital media company, coincidentally Bill Simmons' *The Ringer* (the same Bill Simmons who had denied Portnoy an interview during his newspaper days) had recently announced its plans to unionize; times were getting tougher for writers at other companies like The Ringer. After hearing this news, Portnoy reposted an old blog about his thoughts on labor unions (spoiler alert: Barstool was not unionized):

> "BAHAHA! I hope and I pray that Barstool employees try to unionize. I can't tell you how much I want them to unionize. Just so I can smash their little union to smithereens."

A journalist named Rafi Letzter tweeted a response to Portnoy's blog, inviting readers to direct-message him if they worked for Barstool and wanted help unionizing. Portnoy replied to the journalist's tweet: "If you work for @barstoolsports and DM this man, I will fire you on the spot." To his fans, this threat was just Portnoy mocking the PC crowd that tries to ruin everyone's fun.

But well-known New York politician Alexandria Ocasio-Cortez wasn't in on the joke, tweeting, "If you're a boss tweeting firing threats to employees trying to unionize, you are likely breaking the law and can be sued, in your words, 'on the spot.'" Unfazed, Portnoy responded to AOC with a phrase he had used before:

"Welcome to the thunderdome @AOC"

—@stoolpresidente

Following this exchange, the Freelance Journalists Union filed a complaint with the National Labor Relations Board, which looked into the issue. Dealing with the NLRB was a little more serious than dealing with SoulCycle, and the founder eventually "informally settled" with the organization and removed his tweets. After the settlement, AOC did a victory lap on Twitter:

"Well, well, well: Remember when we put the CEO of Barstool Sports on notice about tweeting threats to intimidate his workers from unionizing? Looks like he just had to settle with the NLRB over his actions. Reminder: Threatening workers who want to unionize is illegal :)"

—@AOC

With that tweet, AOC became the only one who could actually say she silenced the mighty Portnoy on the internet, as he wisely didn't address the issue again.[4]

Portnoy clearly wasn't afraid to drag his company into the mud, but by 2019, the founder had become somewhat jaded by the dozens of hit pieces that had piled up over the years and wasn't willing to have conflict for conflict's sake. Apart from ripping people like Smitty for being lazy, he also took issue with those who weren't qualified to do battle on behalf of Barstool but who did so anyway. A few months after the AOC dustup, Portnoy went after Mike Geary,

---

4   Barstool remains ununionized.

an employee nicknamed "Blind Mike" (whose vision was legally impaired). On Barstool Radio, Portnoy erupted at Blind Mike for posting a blog on the Barstool site that criticized a "feminist" who ripped the Stool:

> "We have a long history, whether the person [the feminist] is crazy or whatever, right or wrong, people write articles about it. You're a nothing here...I don't want you leading Barstool into battles when you've been here for a fucking minute. How hard is that to see?!"

As Clancy would probably quip, for Blind Mike, this was, in fact, hard to see.

Although tenure was important in Portnoy's analysis of which employees were worth getting into the mud for, he also factored in a trait he valued above all others: loyalty. Dave wasn't going to do battle over someone he felt was just using Barstool to further their own careers, and he believed there were a number of those people in his company by now, people who weren't "Team Portnoy." He applied such thinking in the case of Barstool fan favorite Francis Ellis (around the same time as the AOC and Blind Mike quarrels), who posted a blog that brought Barstool some severely unwanted attention.

In the post, Ellis wrote about a missing University of Utah female student named Mackenzie Lueck, following *The New York Post*'s report that her Instagram account was recently active according to her friends. Operating under the assumption she was still alive, and in an effort to be funny—he was known for his dark comedy—Ellis referenced reports that claimed Lueck had been on "sugar daddy" websites; based on her Instagram profile, Ellis implied that Lueck was a fan of *Call Her Daddy*, the Barstool podcast. Sadly, shortly after the post, Lueck was found dead, and both Barstool and Ellis immediately received blowback from all corners of media, with headlines like the one published by the Daily Beast:

"Barstool Sports Slut-Shames Mackenzie Lueck, Murdered 23-Year-Old Female College Student."

Portnoy, who never fired anyone, fired Ellis, saying, "There're certain things I can't justify and can't stand by. I know he meant well with it, but it just doesn't matter." Portnoy viewed Ellis as someone who was more focused on pursuing his own stand-up comedy career than he was the overall success of Barstool:

> "If it had been someone who I felt was Barstool to the core, we probably would have kept him. I'm not blaming him, by the way, I've said we hire people and you should use Barstool as a stepping stone like Alex Cooper [who was the host of that immensely popular *Call Her Daddy* podcast) used it to benefit her career. She was never 'Die for Barstool.' But when there's a major fuck-up, it makes it easier for me to [say] 'Well, I'm not gonna let this drag us down, it's easier to just cut bait,' and I didn't lose sleep over that decision."

There was also the issue of Ellis's relationship with the sales team. As Dave explained when talking about the growing pains Barstool suffered from as a larger media company, "It's a fine line with the advertiser angle of it because we have to sell ads and we have to pay salaries, and then content [people like Ellis] is looking out for themselves, so they don't always want ads or reads because it can hurt views, it can hurt or perceive to hurt your content."

Ellis disputed Portnoy's claim that he heard he was the most difficult content creator to work with from a sales perspective: "That's just not true, I did a ton of ads… what happened was, I was getting these companies that would message me and say, 'Hey, we love your Instagram, would you be willing to do an ad for us on there?' and then I asked one day if I was allowed to do that because they were willing to pay me a couple thousand bucks or something, which would have been nice." But when he asked, Barstool told Ellis this was a workaround against the sales team and went against company policy, one that was employed as a result of creators like Ellis being able to monetize their own brand more directly. Ellis explained his side of the story further:

> "I said, 'ok, totally fine, that's fair.' But then the sales team hit me one day and [told me], 'We've sold ads on YOUR Instagram, and I [asked], 'Are you gonna give me any money?' I thought our personal social media handles and platforms were our own. So then I went to Dave, and Dave was like 'okay, yeah, I guess, ya know, you don't have to do it,' and to Dave's credit he [said], 'ya know, you should take one for the team.' And I should have."[5]

Being a team player meant you were on the short list of people Dave said could come with him when he went back to Milton and restarted Barstool Boston—a plan Portnoy often spoke of but never acted on. Ellis wasn't on that list.

Ellis's departure highlighted another issue Portnoy and Barstool management were dealing with: an editorial process that hadn't kept up with the growing number of employees who now posted content on the Barstool website. Nardini alluded to this in her farewell to Francis:

> "I loved working with @FrancisCEllis. He is a unique talent and so gifted - a one-man variety hour. That said, there are things that will never, ever, ever fly and this blog was one. There are things we need to fix here."
>
> —@Erika_

Markovich, Barstool's editor in chief, received heavy flak for allowing Ellis's blog to make it on the site. At the time, certain

---

5   Ellis returned to Barstool in 2022.

employees were given the freedom to post without editorial review. Following this debacle, that number shrank. Only a year later, Markovich was removed from his post as Editor in Chief, after a contentious run-in with Barstool's satellite Chicago office and Barstool personality Kirk Minihane.[6]

As the end of 2019 approached, Portnoy had gone from being upset with his employees, whom he continued to believe lacked appreciation for still having a job in a crumbling industry, to considering real alternatives: "I should just fuck these people and stay in Nantucket…let all these people fend for themselves." Much like in 2015 when Katz and Clancy convened to tell Portnoy they needed a change, this time it was Dave who wanted one.

The Chernin Group wasn't oblivious to this fact, as Kerns added, "There's been several times where Dave's been like 'I fuckin need to go to Nantucket more, I want to be less involved, I want more money,' and he deserved [that]… It was fair for him to [say], 'Look, I could go sit in my backyard in Nantucket and make millions of dollars and do a podcast a couple hours a week and sell some t-shirts on my own and not have to deal with this whole company and this whole brand.'"

Apart from dealing with his employees, Portnoy was feeling burnt out in general: "Essentially, I [wondered at that time] 'How am

---

6   The Chicago satellite office opened in 2019 by personalities Eddie, Chief, Carl, and WhiteSoxDave: it was basically a closet operating inside a State Farm office. The four clashed with Markovich over a blog post that he denied because it was somewhat critical of an advertising partner. In the case of Minihane, a brash Boston radio personality Portnoy hired that same year, Markovich allowed a guest blogger named "Zonker" to write a politically charged blog post critical of Minihane. "I yelled at him like he was an intern, which I've never done," Portnoy said. "I was very mad that thing got published." Zonker also owned the URL www.barstool.com and refused to sell it to Portnoy, instead often redirecting it to funny videos, including one of Jenna Marbles, who he begrudged.

I gonna get out of this thing?' I'm so tied in, I'm working so much. I've been fucking grinding at this thing for 17 years."[7]

Then, in January 2020, as first reported by *The Big Lead*:

"Barstool Engaged in Advanced Talks to Sell to Penn National Gaming"

---

7   This quote is a combination of two separate quotes from Portnoy. You will see in the back of the book that there are two different sources listed. You can copy-paste the link to see where each part came from.

28

Since the beginning of 2019, Portnoy & Co. had been shopping their company. It wasn't going well. The group had been meeting with large gambling outfits with the pitch that they would bring their audience to that buyer's platform. But as Portnoy said, "We met with everybody. FanDuel, DraftKings, nobody made an offer." It was the same paradox that Portnoy had to overcome when trying to find potential advertisers before Chernin came along: what made Barstool so popular—the controversies, the disregard for societal norms, and the founder himself—made potential buyers wary of Barstool. "They were scared of me and scared of the controversy," Portnoy stated.

But in the particular case of both FanDuel and DraftKings, Portnoy believed he would be able to overcome this obstacle. Barstool had worked closely with both sports betting firms: nearly a decade earlier, the DraftKings team had offered Portnoy equity in its company, which Dave declined. In 2015, Portnoy, who at the time had no idea just how much money he would make, wrote of the decision:

> "Hey, Pres, remember that time you turned down equity in DraftKings? You know, that company that is now valued at 1 billion dollars. Yup, no biggie, they just got a Unicorn valuation. Your stock would probably be worth a cool 12 million dollars or so now? Only worth more than you'll ever come close to making with Barstool. Don't sweat it, though. Your entire operation is worth 3 million internet dollars. Sweet decision, brah."

And if you recall it was a DraftKings ad deal that was the genesis of The Blackout Tour.

As for FanDuel, Portnoy had become close with its leadership team, saying, "I really like the FanDuel guys and was thinking if they made an offer that was competitive, [then I might say] 'Ok, we can win with these guys.'" Ironically, it was this close relationship that prevented a deal from happening. Both DraftKings and FanDuel had already spent a sizeable amount of money advertising on Portnoy's site: as Dave noted, "We had worked with them for a while, so I think they thought, 'Hey, we've gotten everything we can out of them. We've gotten their audience.'" While Barstool had positioned itself to cash in on the sports gambling craze, actually finding a buyer willing to fork over millions of dollars for Portnoy's operation was proving more difficult in practice…until Barstool's Head of Corporate Development David VanEgmond ("DVE") brokered a meeting between his company and Penn National Gaming's two SVPs, Chris Rogers and Jon Kaplowitz.[1]

Following the legalization of sports gambling in the U.S., Penn had begun looking into launching its own sportsbook app. The company (valued at $9B) held the largest number of gambling licenses in the U.S. and owned 41 properties across 19 different states. Being a brick-and-mortar operation, Penn was searching for the right digital partner to execute this strategy; as Penn Gaming's CEO Jay Snowden explained:

> "We had a great casino brand. What we were missing was a great sports betting brand. And the audience inside these casinos skews older, so we knew we needed a partner, and we

---

1   Portnoy would later say FanDuel could have gotten the company for much cheaper than Penn.

started meeting with all sorts of companies, big ones, FOX, NBC, CBS, Disney, regional sports networks, you name them, we met with them. We had probably met with 12 to 15 companies before we were introduced to Barstool."[2]

Initially, Snowden had no idea Barstool was looking for a potential buyer, but as a chiseled former Harvard quarterback, he read Portnoy's site frequently and was a fan. And when Rogers and Kaplowitz came back from their meeting with Barstool excited, "I was like, wow, Barstool, no way," Snowden said.

The following week, Snowden met with Dave and Erika. Seated in a bland conference room, both sides expanded on what they were looking for in a partner. From the Barstool side, apart from the obvious lucrative payout, they envisioned their next step in the gambling world as one that included a Barstool sportsbook, an app that allowed them to "activate their audience." As Portnoy has admitted, Barstool would have never been able to build a sports betting app on its own. Barstool was an internet company that often didn't have a working internet connection, and its own Barstool app had been a journey fraught with failure. When someone thought of Barstool, they didn't think technology ("The Barstool Difference" is still alive and well).

Barstool was also interested in the retail locations Penn owned: opening a Barstool bar and physical sportsbook was always something Portnoy and Erika had envisioned. Both wanted a space where Barstool could host events—a space that wasn't a Dunkin' Donuts. But most important, this move would bring Barstool Sports, which had started as a sports-gambling publication following Portnoy's 2003 trip to Vegas, full circle: as he explained, "This is what I always wanted to do with my life, to be honest. I wanted to be involved in shaping [in a way] the gambling industry."

---

2   Penn first partnered with William Hill to launch its sportsbook app in Pennsylvania and also worked with DraftKings but then shifted to Barstool.

As for Penn, aside from acquiring Portnoy's audience and turning them into betting customers, Penn saw Portnoy's company serving as the official media and marketing arm of its sports-betting operation; Barstool wasn't just going to be a small part of Penn. "That had Dave grinning ear to ear," Snowden recalled. The Penn CEO believed Barstool could help distinguish his company inside an increasingly competitive space; as Snowden said: "A huge part of it was the people behind Barstool, and for users to be able to go on our app and interact with Big Cat and El Pres and others who are passionate about sports betting was a really big deal. If you were to go on our app, it's not just transactional."

That meant Snowden needed to ensure the Barstool personalities were invested in the partnership; as he explained: "The last big thing for me was all around structure. We wanted to structure [a deal] in a way where [the Barstool guys] didn't quote-unquote 'cash out' and were rich and onto the next thing." The potential plan was for Portnoy and Nardini to receive roughly half of their compensation in the form of Penn Stock that vested over the next five years; although a lump sum payment in cash would have been nicer, the reality was there wasn't anyone else at the table.[3]

Despite being the CEO of a $9B company, Snowden was comfortable with Barstool's past—and more specifically, Portnoy's. As he said, "Much of the media criticism about David Portnoy attempts to paint him as a misogynist or racist. If Dave were those things, I can assure you, Penn would never have partnered with him."

Partnering with Barstool did not come without any risk; in fact, quite the opposite. Sports gambling is a *highly* regulated industry. After repealing PASPA[4] in 2018, the Supreme Court left it up to the states to determine how to enact sports betting inside their dis-

---

3   The stock agreement was a little more complicated than that, but I use the term vesting to show they were committed to Penn for five years.

4   The Professional and Amateur Sports Protection Act was a 1992 federal law that restricted all except for a few states from legalizing sports gambling.

tricts, which meant Penn had to endure scrutiny from each state's respective gaming commissions if it wanted to earn a license and legally operate there. However, Snowden believed that Barstool, with the proper guidance (including avoiding jokes about problem gambling)[5] would be able to successfully navigate this process. In an interview, CNBC's Jim Cramer asked Snowden, Portnoy, and Nardini about this conviction:

> *Cramer:* "Erika, let me ask you. Some of these casino commissions can be conservative, I don't think you guys are radical, but some people think you're radical. Are you worried at all that some of these organizations would say, 'Ya know, I don't know think Barstool's the right fit?'"

> *Erika:* "We thought a lot about that from the onset of what this partnership would look like. If you give us the boundaries, we'll play within the boundaries, so it will create changes within our company from behind the scenes how we understand what the rules are, making sure we have the right infrastructure to make content that fits."

> *Cramer:* "And Jay, you're comfortable with the idea—you're a conservative company—you know that these guys are a different culture?"

> *Snowden:* "No question. Dave and I have had a lot of conversations, and I feel like they understand what those guardrails are. We're all very comfortable we can pull this

---

5   Under the new partnership, Portnoy would avoid describing himself as a "degenerate gambler," and would be restricted from posting tweets like the one in 2019 where he urged his followers to "bet your house, kids, and family on the Kansas City Chiefs." Problem gambling would become a topic that was off-limits for content, with addiction hotlines appearing in every ad following any sort of betting promotion on Barstool. Also, employees would be required to undergo numerous trainings on the subject.

off. Barstool can be Barstool. It's such an amazing company and they're so engaged with their fans; it's so entertaining, they can still be all of that but be responsible around topics like gambling."

Cramer: "So you won't be reined in? I still get my El Pres?"

Portnoy: "Yeah, I would never do a deal—it wouldn't work for anybody—where I thought we couldn't be us. We're still going to be funny, irreverent, but like Erika said, there's guardrails which we totally understand, and throughout the 17-year history, we've morphed. We understand we live in different times, there's different jokes you can make, so we'll play with them, and we'll be just as funny, if not funnier, than we've ever been."

Besides having to appease the gaming commissions, Penn was a publicly traded company, which meant it also had to answer to its shareholders. Snowden (who happened to be the son of a poker dealer), was placing a big bet that Barstool would now play by the rules, and more significant, that these third parties would condone the actions of Dave Portnoy.

Following this initial meeting, the acquisition process sped up quickly. As Snowden said, "It didn't take us four or five meetings to figure it out."

Portnoy confirmed this: "We named our price. And Penn was like, yup, that's it."

Penn would acquire 36% of Barstool for $163M at a $450M valuation. Following Snowden's request, Portnoy and Barstool agreed to take their compensation packages with a split of 45% cash and 55% Penn stock. The terms of the agreement also required Penn National to increase its ownership to 50% on the third anniversary, with the option to buy the remaining 50%. It was a two-part deal, which further incentivized the Barstool side; Penn had this luxury because again, there wasn't anyone else at the table.

But after spending a year looking for a buyer, Portnoy would finally be getting his payday. More important for Barstool fans, the founder was remotivated:

> "If I'm telling the whole story of Barstool, I think we're maybe at the halfway point, if that. This is a whole next step. I am fully convinced that we are going to be the biggest gambling company, Penn will be, in the United States. That's how confident I am in the DNA and the brains of Barstool, and what we know about social media, and the internet. And the combo with sports gambling being legalized, I think we are going to destroy our competition."

Portnoy was going to sign the deal, become laughably rich, and take Penn to the moon. At least, that was the plan.

29

Mike Kerns was pacing in his driveway. It was a cathartic exercise, because the Chernin liaison was listening to the man whom he had worked alongside for the last four years scream at him so loudly he had to pull the phone away from his ear. As Kerns described it, "Dave was calling me a bunch of names I had literally never heard before. And I'm just sitting there wearing everything he's saying to me. Just…trying to be as calm as I possibly can."

Prior to the transaction going through, Portnoy called Kerns. The founder wasn't satisfied with the compensation for Katz. As Dave explained, "I was not fighting on my behalf. Dan deserved it, and we were getting this big payday, and it's gambling we're doing, so he's fucking key. I wanted him to be psyched."

Though he knew no one besides Penn had made an offer, after his request for a change was met with hesitation, Portnoy erupted, telling Kerns he would walk away from the deal. Kerns explained, "I remember I was in my driveway, and I came inside to my wife and [said] 'That was the worst conversation I've ever had in my life, professionally. Like ever.'"

Portnoy, smiling, said of the phone call, "I don't remember it being *that* bad."

After Portnoy's alleged screaming, Chernin agreed to work out a new compensation package for Katz.[1] "We got past it," Kerns said of Portnoy's third time threatening to leave him at the altar.

---

1   As part of the Katz Compensation Agreement, Katz would be issued 141,669 shares of Barstool, worth approximately $7M, prior to the sale to Penn, to be bought in cash. This was on top of the equity he most likely already owned.

At the time of the sale, The Chernin Group owned 60% of Barstool and would be taking its compensation entirely in cash. Dave explained Chernin's decision to not invest in any Penn stock (besides cash being king): "Chernin bought Barstool with the intent purpose to resell it, that was always why they did it." Although he continued to have a good relationship with Kerns, the founder viewed The Chernin Group as mercenaries.

"Dave hasn't made any bones about it," Kerns said. "He's said, 'I've made Chernin hundreds of millions of dollars,' and the truth of the matter is, he has." The Chernin Group was passing the baton to Snowden's company, and although The Chernin Group would never say anything publicly on the matter, it had been a fruitful, but *long* four years, and there was no public thank-you from Peter Chernin.[2]

"I don't know that Chernin's given me anything," Portnoy said. "Not even maybe a thank-you card. A couple nice emails maybe. I like those guys, but they haven't [given me anything]."

As for the other stakeholders, Nardini, though she wouldn't make nearly as much as Portnoy, still made millions immediately upon the sale (as did Katz).[3] Clancy, however, wasn't listed as a Key Employee in the transaction, despite being part of the original "Big Three" of Barstool. Only Portnoy, Katz, and Nardini were designated Key Employees status. That meant despite grinding for more than a decade, due to the terms of the two-part Penn deal, Clancy had to wait several more years for his respective payout—one that would have come sooner and would have been larger if he had been into

2   Once Penn acquired Barstool, Chernin would become fully divested on the third anniversary of the deal.

3   This is an assumption based on her position, how long she had been there and the size of the deal. Thornton, who started working for Barstool in 2004, wouldn't get any sort of payday. He left Barstool for WEEI in 2014, and returned after the Chernin investment in 2016. Gaz however, would make millions (again, this is a mere fact-based assumption but it's been alluded to several times by Portnoy and others).

gambling. As Clancy admitted, "There were times I [thought], 'Fuck, I wish I gambled'; it ended up biting me in the ass."[4]

Although Clancy griped publicly about this, Portnoy told him to stop complaining: "[Clancy is] going to be making so much more money than he ever dreamed of when he got into this thing." And as for any other issues from anyone else about the deal, he said, "I was doing this ten years almost before they [Clancy and Katz] came on. So that's the element of where it's like 'yeah, I made a shit ton of money,' but that's what I get as the one who started it."

The Barstool founder actually offered Clancy a loan following the initial sale to Penn, with zero interest, until Clancy was set to be paid. Clancy turned it down, saying, "I would literally go to the poor house before I took a loan from Dave Portnoy." And although he regretted not being involved more with gambling, he also blamed his relationship with Portnoy as a reason why he may have been left out of that part of the deal:

> "I didn't have to be part of the deal, but I would have liked to have been part of the process, to be in on some of those meetings and represent the non-gambling side. But I do wonder sometimes if Dave and I were on better terms if he would have [said] 'We have to get my boy Kevin in here to talk about things or be in the conversation.'"

All that screaming at Portnoy on Barstool Radio may have cost Clancy some money, though without a foil in Clancy and the entertainment his battle against Portnoy brought the Stoolies, one could argue Barstool would have never made it to that point. But at the end of the day, Clancy (who eventually became a multi-millionaire) said, "If I had the choice between not being bought by Penn and continu-

---

4   This quote is a combination of two separate quotes from Clancy. You will see in the back of the book that there are two different sources listed. You can copy-paste the link to see where each part came from.

ing what we were doing or the deal, I'm taking the deal a hundred out of a hundred times."

On January 29, 2020, Portnoy posted a video entitled:

"Emergency Press Conference—All Aboard the Barstool Sports Rocket Ship."

Dressed in a black suit and standing in front of his patented Milton-days water jug podium, Portnoy began by saying:

"Music! 17 years ago, I started a little gambling rag in my parents' basement called Barstool Sports. I had no idea, nobody could predict, the wild ride that would set my life on. It took me to New York City, where 4 years ago, I stood in Times Square, I told the world I sold half the company to Chernin Group. That I had ambition, bigger than the New York skyline. That I wanted to own the moon, that I thought we were better, funnier, and smarter than everybody else on the internet. Guess what, for the second time in 17 years, I'm here to tell you, we've taken another strategic investor in Barstool Sports. Penn National Gaming. Penn is a publicly traded company. So, you at home can buy the stock and become part of this journey. I'm locked in, Dan's locked in, Erika's locked in. Key people aren't going anywhere. Get on board the rocket ship, cuz the next stop is literally the moon. Music!"

At the end of the video, Mike Portnoy, the lawyer who had handed his son Dave the $25,000 check that began it all, read a *Star Wars*–style scrolling financial disclaimer. More skeptical onlookers might opine that, in true Barstool fashion, Dave may have broken some sort of SEC rule in his announcement.

Either way, Portnoy was now rich beyond his wildest Swampscott imaginations. "We now estimate Dave Portnoy's net worth to be

$200M" read the headline of a Celebrity Net Worth tweet. Although Portnoy refused to say whether this was accurate, in 2016, following the first Chernin investment, Portnoy had ended his announcement by stating, "P.S. I'm kinda rich now." In 2020, he used a different line:

"I've got unlimited money."

30

"Ok, Emergency Press Conference time. Well, it took 'em long enough, cancel culture finally coming after Barstool. I mean, they've come after Jimmy Kimmel, Joe Rogan, Bill Simmons; now it's our turn, you knew it was gonna happen. To be honest, they've been coming after me for 17 fucking years."

—Dave Portnoy

By all accounts Dave Portnoy was now a media mogul. Private jets? *Check.* Dating an Instagram Model? *Check.*[1] Ill-advised real estate investments? *Check.*

"Rate this piece of art I bought for my new Miami house, which will never be finished ever. @jojoanavim"

—@stoolpresidente

"I'm in my Miami house, which honestly you could tell me I spent $10M or $50M on, and I wouldn't know because I just keep paying fucking bills to get the construction done."

—@stoolpresidente

---

[1]   Portnoy actually started dating Silvana Mojica in 2021.

"I may need throw this house out and buy a new one."

—@stoolpresidente

Dave's new post-Penn deal setup certainly seemed glamorous: his $14M home in Miami was, in fact, awesome, even if it did take forever to finish.[2] And he did make one prudent real estate investment following this payout: Dave bought his parents a new waterfront condo near their old home. He said in all the milestones Barstool achieved, that was the only time his mom cried. Dave also let his sister know she didn't have to worry about paying for her kids' college education. He made sure the people who supported him were covered (he also bought property for Renee), though when Mike Portnoy heard his son was telling fans about the condo, he tweeted:

"Happy that my son could afford our condo. Not for nothing, we paid for a few things before he became El Presidente: food, clothing, etc., Michigan education. Just didn't feel right to brag about it. Different strokes for different folks, I guess."

—@TheCousinMike

All joking aside, the older Portnoy was extremely proud of his son's $450M accomplishment, telling Dave, "It's surreal. I can't think of another word. Your mother and I are both numb. What can you say, how could you ever expect this is where you'd be?"

Dave's explained his own reaction to the megadeal:

"It's really hard to fathom. I've had an unbelievable string with Barstool of things coming along at the exact right time.

---

2   Regarding Portnoy's wealth, I say in the prologue an acquisition by Penn would vault his net worth past the $200M. I am making this speculation based on the fact that he wouldn't confirm or deny the Celebrity Net Worth tweet about being worth $200M around the time of the deal, and then a year later, $PENN peaked at 3x the price of when that tweet occurred, before dropping back down.

Like Mike Kerns decided to call me with Chernin at the exact right time. It was what we needed to get everybody back in and excited. Meeting Erika, I met her by accident. The Chernin Group put together maybe 100 people with recruiters for me to hire a CEO, and I met Erika through a mutual acquittance [*sic*]. Without Erika, this does not happen. And then four years, I was getting a little burnt out, I'd been doing this for fifteen. Now I'm so excited for this opportunity, I want us to be the biggest gambling company in the country."

As for what it was like to have sports betting being the reason this opportunity existed, Portnoy said, "Dan and I talked about it. We're the only two people who beat the book. I mean literally, like in gambling, we won. Nobody wins. *We* won. It's crazy."

Unsurprisingly, the Stoolies were just as excited about the deal as Portnoy. On the first episode of Barstool Radio following the Penn announcement, callers rang in:

> "Longtime stoolie here, 2012, and I got to say what you've built [is] incredible. Just with us Stoolies, whenever I see someone wear a Barstool shirt, immediately we have something in common. All the stuff that we've gone through, I would even say together because people that hate Barstool hate us Stoolies. Reading this news today was the biggest 'fuck you' to them; congratulations, to the moon, and I can't wait to see what's next."
>
> —Kevin

> "Hey Pres, congrats, Boston transplant to Chicago here, I remember the days of you riding the Red

Line, brother; you've come a long way, you deserve every freakin' penny."

—Ryan

"Hey, Dave, congrats on the big deal. Incredible what you've done, turning this company in your basement into a $450M giant."

—Josh

Dave let them know he appreciated the congratulations and that Barstool wasn't really changing much from an organizational perspective, saying, "Nobody should be worried about their job here except Pete [Barstool's tech guy]. He's had us by the short hairs for a long time, in that it was 'Well, if Pete's not gonna do it, we have nobody else who can.'" In response, Overmyer (who stayed with the company) tweeted the following:

"I wonder if Penn has their own IT people? Probably not, right…"

—@allbusinesspete

More important, Dave let the Stoolies know that just like with the Chernin deal, Barstool's content wasn't going to drastically change—although they weren't allowed to joke about anything involving problem gambling. And Barstool fans were still going to get their El Pres, as seen during that same episode of Barstool Radio when he called out HBO's Bryant Gumbel; two years earlier, Gumbel had publicly questioned whether Barstool was really worth what it was being valued at (at the time):

"Fuck you, Bryant Gumbel, I'd buy and sell you [now], dude. I may find out where he is and just shower him with money. I may have to be one of those Sheikhs; that's my new move: people I don't like, I just shower them with hundreds."

Portnoy's financial situation became just another vehicle for entertainment: on one of his podcasts, he told his fans, "This is my dad 101. I was so sold on this deal, I wanted to buy more Penn stock. So I ask my dad, 'is this insider trading if I buy more stock?' and he [said], 'Of course you can buy more stock.' I then called Jim Cramer [who said] 'They will arrest you so fast if you do that; who gave you that advice?' and I said 'Oh, my dad; he's an attorney.'"

"I knew you'd get that in there," Mike said.

Aside from understanding how to manage it all, another aspect of having this kind of money that Portnoy hadn't fully thought out pertained to his horse-betting partnership with Elio. Over the years, the pair had been going to the track as a tandem, pooling their money together and splitting whatever they won. As Dave remembered, "We had a long talk about, if this went final, how it would affect the future of our horse relationship. What we decided is I will bet enough where it hurts me still, which will be a lot, he bets what hurts him, and we still split the total. So, he *really* benefits from this."

Portnoy's bankroll was certainly bigger now, and he was spending and betting accordingly. But the timing of his newfound wealth wouldn't be ideal (if that's even possible). After the Penn transaction was completed, Portnoy's team went to ring the bell at the New York Stock Exchange, and in very Barstoolian fashion, that day turned out to be one of the worst days in stock market history.[3] This was thanks to the arrival of Covid-19. Just as Portnoy secured his new lifestyle, he was going to be restricted from fully relishing it.

And by the summer of 2020, Coronavirus had wholly wrapped its arms around the country, at which point people were either getting sick or losing their minds. In May, George Floyd's death lit the fuse of a nation that was stuck inside, with too much time on its

---

3   In 2017, following the SoulCycle drama, Portnoy predicted he would do this, saying, "I can't wait for five years from now when she [Jordyn] is still trying to fuck these guys that ride bikes and I'm ringing the bell at the stock exchange."

hands, just waiting to erupt. And it did: by June, the cancel culture movement was underway:

> **"'Cancel culture' seems to have started as an internet joke. Now it's anything but."**
>
> —*CBS*

> **"Americans tune in to 'cancel culture'—and don't like what they see."**
>
> —*Politico*

> **"Why brands need to pay attention to cancel culture."**
>
> —*Forbes*

As far as qualified targets, Barstool was a ripe candidate, if not one of the ripest. A few weeks after Floyd's death, a Twitter account called @RzstProgramming posted a Barstool Rundown clip from 2016, when the drama surrounding NFL QB Colin Kaepernick kneeling for the national anthem was unfolding. In the video, Portnoy explained his initial thoughts after seeing Kaepernick take a knee: "So, I'm going to say something racist. When I first heard the story [about him not standing], I was like 'Oh, he's an ISIS guy.'" Portnoy went on to state that he thought Kaepernick was Arabic, mostly because of his beard. "Throw a head wrap on this guy, and he's a terrorist…I guess he's Black. Ok, I didn't know that; I thought he was Arabic. When I think of an Arabic person not standing for the national anthem, I go terrorist right away. This can't be held against me; that's just how my brain works."

In the *Rundown*, Katz laughed along, but at the same time, he questioned Portnoy's thinking. As did Clancy. Portnoy also posted a tweet with Kaepernick's face photoshopped with a turban on, side by side with the actual picture of Osama bin Laden, saying "Anybody who disagrees with me saying Kaepernick looks like he's related to bin Laden is a moron."

After ESPN personality Jemele Hill tweeted out the video with the caption, "This is terrible. But then again, consider the source," the video went viral. Portnoy, as he was prone to do, went to Twitter to issue a strong rebuke: "I'm uncancelable. You don't cancel me, I cancel you!" And much like he did with Sam Ponder, Portnoy (or someone taking orders from him) dug up a transphobic tweet from Hill that she had made 11 years earlier about Red Sox player Manny Ramirez, writing "My FB friends are calling him 'Manny the Tranny'...so inappropriate and hilarious." Hill apologized for the tweet after Barstool fans followed the Portnoy playbook and were able to get the hashtag #CancelJemele trending on Twitter.

But when Portnoy responded later that night to Hill's original tweet with a video that he believed showed his comments were taken out of context, @RzstProgramming immediately replied with two more videos, both of which featured Portnoy using the N-word. "This you?" asked @RsztProgramming. And with that, it became clear this situation wasn't going anywhere.[4]

The following day, while Clancy and Katz issued something close to an apology for the Kaepernick rundown, and while other media outlets picked up the story, Portnoy remained defiant:

> "I'm not gonna apologize, I'm not gonna bend the knee. The thing people are coming at me now [for], the Kaepernick, it's literally a joke from *The Office*—which, by the way, Steve Carell has said would never exist nowadays because people would cancel it in two seconds, yet the cancel peo-

4   It was actually another account, Expose Barstool, that tweeted it and @ RzstProgramming retweeted it.

ple probably fucking love that show. They just fuckin' hate me. So alright, keep trying to cancel us, we'll keep growing stronger."

In this message posted to his Twitter account, Portnoy didn't address the two videos using the N-word—the first was Portnoy singing along to a rap song, the second was the Barstool founder quoting a rant from EDP, a popular Philadelphia Eagles superfan. Regardless, Stoolies flooded the comment section and the Barstool reddit page r/barstoolsports as well, with support for Portnoy. The most upvoted comment of the former was this:

"Awesome blog. Sadly, a good percentage of Barstool blogs the last month have been celebrating cancel culture though...Dave is the only one who tells it like it is. If he ever leaves, it's deadspin 2.0."

But while this sort of "Grudge Dave" move might have flown without any repercussions in 2016 (and definitely earlier), by June 2020, the company had added several African-Americans and other minorities as employees. After the videos surfaced, several people sat down for a podcast to discuss what it was like being a minority working at Barstool, particularly after what just transpired: the group included former NFL player Willie Colon; former Notre Dame football player Brandon Newman; other content personalities Tyler "Trill" Withers, Liz Gonzales, and Shaun Latham; Barstool producer Zah; and Ebony, Barstool's security guard.

It's not as if this group didn't know what they were getting into when they joined the company: Barstool was historically white and male, as was its audience, and the company's history unfortunately included moments like the one Portnoy was now answering for, as well as other insensitive decisions.[5] In 2018, a photo appeared online

---

5   Barstool has no female African-American content creators.

of Gaz wearing Blackface to a Halloween party, which led to Gaz writing on the Barstool website, "In hindsight, I wish I didn't dress in blackface to be [basketball player] Kevin Garnett a decade ago for Halloween with my two best friends who are African American." In another incident, KFC joked about a hypothetical situation ending slavery, saying, "Hey black people, I could have saved you, but I wanted to make you sweat a little bit first." And there were others.

But the Kaepernick incident came from the leader of the company, their boss, which put the group in a difficult position, particularly because Portnoy didn't apologize. As Withers stated bluntly about Dave, "He stands by what he says, that's how he feels." The fact that the videos leaked around the same time the Black Lives Matter protests became prevalent only compounded the situation. Colon explained, "We had a lot to say about George Floyd…now here it is, your boss is saying inflammatory things and [people are saying] you guys are being quiet. People are shooting at us, saying 'I guess you guys really don't care.'"

As for the specific comments, Withers said, "When [Dave] says, 'I know I'm about to say something racist,' [he] should probably stop right there….that's just a general rule of thumb. If you have the presence of mind to make that statement, then you probably know you shouldn't say what you're about to say." Liz and Zah said that after working closely with Dave, they believed he wasn't racist; no one in the group outwardly called Portnoy one. But Withers said this:

> "If you have to keep saying, 'well, I'm not a racist,' but then I don't think you can be surprised when people mistake you for that. It goes with [what] Liz and Zah were saying: they know Dave probably a little bit better than I do, and it's ok for all you who do know him, perhaps [you don't think he's a racist], but for us who don't know him, I can't say 'Well, I know him; I know he's not a racist.' I just can't say that. All I

have to go on is clip after clip where he's saying racist things. So, I'm not sure what else to go off of."

Colon added, "If it looks like a duck and it walks like a duck, it's a mother-fuckin' duck," and Withers responded, "Forgive me for thinking it's a duck."

In their conversation, Colon mentioned that Erika had texted him, telling him not to post anything on social media before speaking with the Barstool founder. Reflecting on his talk with Dave, Colon said:

> "I had a long conversation with Dave about it. Dave never apologized; he explained why he was wrong in some instances, but he never apologized. Dave said [he] understood what [he] was saying was racist, and as I was sitting there, I [thought], *Bro, this is kind of shady.* And [Dave asked me], 'Willie, after 9/11, did you not think when you saw someone with a turban on, you didn't think of a terrorist, [that] person could do something?' I said, 'Dave, I'm from New York; I went to school with Muslims. Plus, I'm black, 6'3" with dreads, I put a hood on, I'm not different from a terrorist or whatever, so it's pretty much racial profiling.' He went on to say, 'I get that point, but still,' and I was like, 'Ugh, where do we go from here?'

> "And I [asked] Dave, what about the Ja-Rule thing?[6] And he goes, 'well, ya know they're singing it in the song.' And I said, 'would you say it if you were in the car with a bunch of black guys.' He said, 'well, if I knew them well enough, I would say it.' And I was like, 'Well, that's a problem in itself.'"

Ebony (the security guard) added some context to the Ja-Rule song video:

---

6   Portnoy rapping the N-word.

"I was there actually when Dave shot the video, the Ja Rule video, and he asked me if I was offended. And I [said], "Personally, you're not quoting me—you know the N word—but I don't think you should say it." That was my take on it; he still did it anyway. [Afterwards] the office was dead silent. It was awkward, it was real weird. I remember it like it was yesterday."

The group's reflection was shockingly honest, and the surprises for Portnoy didn't end there. After their discussion on Colon and Newman's podcast, the episode appeared on Barstool's website the next day with a six-letter acronym as its title, one that caused Barstool fans to do a collective double take. In the subtitle below it, there was a short explanation for what the acronym stood for:

"Now It's Gonna Get Extremely Real."

31

Following the post on Barstool's website, news outlets like *Variety* and *The New York Post* wrote stories about the podcast episode.

> **"Barstool Sports uses N-Word in 'Extremely Real' podcast title."**
> —*The New York Post*

Stoolies lost their collective minds on Twitter, mostly criticizing Colon and Newman for the inflammatory title, and though no-one in the group who sat down for the podcast episode (besides Colon and Newman) knew they were going to call it that, it was clear Portnoy now had some sort of mutiny on his hands.

The next day, Eric Sollenberger broke his PFT character (again) with a blog discussing Colon's initial point on the position he and other minorities at the company found themselves in, with those from the black community calling them complicit for not quitting:

> **"It's Insanely Unfair that We've Put Our Black Employees in this Situation**
>
> "When I saw that clip of ignorant and racist comments from the 2016 Colin Kaepernick rundown, I, like a lot of my colleagues, was mad and embarrassed…. Dave won't apologize because in his eyes, it means giving in to the outrage mob—so now our black colleagues are being held to account for something that had nothing to do with any mistakes they've made whatsoever… To put it bluntly, it's especially

fucked-up that our black coworkers have been unfairly put in the position of choosing to either a) accept racist remarks, or b) publicly fight with their boss. If Dave doesn't truly feel sorry, then he shouldn't apologize. But understand that the consequences of that will mean that our black coworkers will have to suffer blame, shame, and embarrassment that they don't deserve, and that's fucked-up."

For the first time in 17 years, the "outrage mob" Portnoy was accustomed to battling worked for him. And after the minority-led podcast episode and PFT's blog, Portnoy issued a second statement in less than a week:

"Ok, Emergency Press Conference time. So, two days ago, I did another Emergency Press Conference. It was basically on cancellation culture. I did a very poor job in that first video, making it clear who I believed I was responding to, which is just pure Barstool haters. Here's what's happened. Unbeknownst to me, and something I didn't plan on doing, I alienated a lot of the people who work for me now. And one of the great things that Barstool has done over the years, more minorities, more women, and we have a bunch of African-American employees now, and all their followers are like 'how the fuck can you work for this guy? This guy won't even admit he did anything wrong. He's a racist asshole.'

"And listening to these guys, I didn't realize how much it affected them. Me doing that rant. Because it hung them out to dry a little bit. And that's not what I want to do. I want to have everybody's back who works for me. I want them to use the platform I built to help fuckin' say whatever you want to say, get your message across; what other place actually does that from the top down? I sent an email three days ago, [saying] 'hey, if you disagree with me, you can say, do, write whatever you want.' But it's not enough. I have to have their backs.

"And I shoulda had their back from the beginning and be like, 'Yup, I wish I didn't fuckin' say that shit. I'm sorry I said it, I'm sorry it offended people, I was just tryin to be fuckin' funny.' I can't apologize for my existence, but I can be better. And I'm gonna be better for those guys. And to those guys, I want this to be a place that you can be fuckin' proud of, and if you're not this second, we'll get there. We'll fucking get there because that's who I fuckin' am, and that's what Barstool Sports should fuckin' be."[1]

Whether Portnoy actually wanted to issue an apology—one Barstool fans would have mixed reactions to—the company simply wasn't going to be able to move forward if he didn't address their comments made in that podcast, which included what to do from here. Colon commented further:

"I want Barstool to get to the point where we can't lash out at people who feel offended. And I want to open the door to young black writers, comedians, producers, and content creators and let them know that there's a home here for you. We all have different walks of life, and if those who we want to bring in here to diverse [sic] and to solidify and set a foundation for Barstool feel like the light's not on for them,

---

1   This Emergency Press Conference has been edited for clarity. You can watch the actual EPC if you copy-paste the link from the notes section in the back of this book. Also, the hosts of Barstool's *Million Dollaz Worth of Game podcast,* Wallo and Gillie, said in one of their episodes that they believed it's ok to use the N-word in a rap song, and Portnoy referenced this in his defense.

then that's up to us to make sure we keep the light on. If it's not us, then who?"

Newman, who went by "Black Brandon" at Barstool, echoed this attitude:

"Going forward, I think we have to be comfortable with being uncomfortable. I talk about race a lot just because by design—because of home dynamics—it's just been a part of my life. I've had to assimilate into white culture just to get in front of you guys right now. Recognizing that everyone doesn't live in the same world and addressing that and being that martyr is kind of like the cross that I bear. NPR has plenty of podcasts about race; why can't Barstool?"

Unfortunately for Newman and the rest of the group discussing this kind of change, most of Barstool's audience didn't come to the site for topics like race. It was a notion Liz acknowledged in the sit-down podcast: "It goes back to the point of a lot of our audience isn't really interested in listening to that [stuff]. And I understand that, so I don't know what to do."

This was something Maurice Peebles understood back in 2011, when he was the only black blogger for Barstool: "Most of my writing was not about racial stuff. The vast majority of my writing was not about racial stuff." Obviously, being an African American writing for Barstool back then meant Peebles couldn't fully avoid the issue of race. "I did get called the N-word a lot [in the comment section]. I got to learn a lot about what people in America actually think. And in 2016, I wasn't as shocked as a lot of people were [when Trump was elected]." Eventually, Peebles left the company on good terms, however, saying, "I'm forever grateful and appreciative of Dave and everyone at Barstool for making me a tougher person, giving me thicker skin, making me a hard worker. Still love the guys, still want to keep in touch."

A decade after Peebles began writing, Barstool was still some form of escapism. "We just want to make people laugh" is a phrase Portnoy said until he was blue in the face. And although the people who sat down for that podcast with the shocking title looked different from those who sat in the old Milton office, the audience did not. To Liz's point, what does a media company that wants to diversify and change do, if its fans, for the most part, don't want it to? Both Portnoy and the podcast group would agree that bringing in a new audience would be a net positive, but finding the balance between diversity and losing your core demo was difficult. In the next several days, Barstool followers would see what Portnoy thought of a seemingly more radical approach to change, one that was being pushed by Newman.

A day after Portnoy released that second Emergency Press Conference, an employee named Muj Fricke, a former producer at Barstool, released the following statement via Twitter:

"I am no longer affiliated with Barstool."

"What has happened and been happening at Barstool in no way reflects my beliefs or what I stand for. I want no association with the Barstool brand, effective immediately. As a white man, I could easily stand by, say nothing, and continue collecting a check from this company. But as someone who was raised Muslim, by a Puerto Rican mother, in a diverse community and attended Morgan State, an HBCU, how pathetic would I be if I continued to support and work for those whose beliefs so staunchly oppose my own?"

Brandon Newman then tweeted the following above Muj's tweet:

"Muj is irreplaceable. One of the few people who I felt had my back during my first couple of months. He told me his vision then executed with @stool-holiganz [his E-sports team he created at Barstool]. I'm honestly shook. Happy for him; sad for us."

—@BrotherBrandon

Portnoy, who obviously didn't love what Muj wrote in his good-bye (and had never been a fan of him) responded sarcastically to this tweet from Brandon that called Muj "irreplaceable."

"Finally, Brandon made me laugh! Now that's how you do comedy!

—@stoolpresidente

Brandon responded to this with the following tweet:

"Aye!!! I made Dave laugh w/o saying the N-word! Happy Independence Day"

—@BrotherBrandon

Portnoy responded to this rebuttal:

"The beauty of this country is that I was able to work my ass off for 2 decades and built this platform to give others like you an opportunity. I can't delete my history like Muj did with all his racist, homophobic, sexist tweets. If you truly think I'm racist, you should quit."

—@stoolpresidente

Brandon followed up with his final tweet:

> "If I quit, how do I help you and everyone at @ barstoolsports change the company from the inside? Unless that's not what you're looking for…I choose to believe your words during your second Emergency Press Conference. But now you're suggesting I jump ship?"
>
> —@BrotherBrandon

Portnoy answered with his last post:

> "You've been here for 38 seconds. The office has been closed for 37 seconds of that time. If you were here longer than a cup of coffee, your words would carry more weight. We want to make people laugh. You stink at that. If you think I'm racist, go quit and find another opportunity."
>
> —@stoolpresidente

Portnoy, who was mostly operating from Miami (the Barstool office would be closed during Covid into October 2020), then called into his company's radio show and elaborated on whether he needed Brandon to "change" Barstool:

> "We're trying to get better, and [more] diverse, and capture a new audience. [We're not trying to take] a different tone. When Brandon Newman says, 'How am I going to change Barstool?' Ya know, we gotta be better at diversifying and being more inclusive to more audiences, finding more ways to reach everybody, but … Brandon Newman isn't here to fucking change me. You've been here for two fucking seconds. And for most of those seconds, the office has been closed."

Dave also went on to explain why he had hired Brandon in the first place, which came across as box-checking:

"The reason we're hiring Brandon Newman is because we want to diversify. Like, no offense, but if he's white, he's not fucking hired. Not in a million fucking years. Because nine gazillion people want to work here, who are white, and in my view, more talented. And we don't hire them. Because we're trying to diversify. And then he turns around and basically says I'm fucking racist."

If Dave said that because he simply wasn't a fan of Brandon Newman, it nevertheless sounded as if he wanted diversity for diversity's sake, which wasn't an acceptable strategy to employ, let alone say out loud.

The situation between Newman and Portnoy was, unsurprisingly, starting to bring the company some bad press, with headlines like this:

"Barstool's racism is finally catching up to it"

—*The New York Daily News*

Samer Kalaf, Portnoy's former Deadspin foe, pointed out Portnoy's attack on Newman as running contrary to his earlier statement made in his second Emergency Press Conference:

"It hasn't been a full two days since Portnoy talked about how his employees are free to disagree with him, and now he's telling one of them to leave if they aren't happy with his apology"

—@Samer

But those around Portnoy said the Barstool founder didn't care whether someone was black, white, purple, male, female: if they made him money, he'd put them front and center at the Stool. Barstool's overly sexual and off-putting talk show *Call Her Daddy* was a prime example of this. The two female cohosts and their fast-growing fanbase couldn't be further from Barstool's core audience, but Portnoy championed the money-making duo frequently. Although *Call Her Daddy* got its fair share of eyerolls (and of course, comments) from the Stoolies, they fell on the right side of that balance between growing a new audience and pissing off his old one, mostly because they avoided being political. In Dave's mind, as a comedy brand, there was a negative correlation between his employees speaking on political and racial topics, and making money.

As Peebles explained, "Dave's about his dollar. And I respect him for it. I've always respected that Dave wasn't super political. He cares more about green than he does red or blue."[2]

Despite some of the negative press the saga brought the company, following their respective "Welcome to Barstool" moment, Penn National Gaming chose to support Portnoy. Snowden spoke at the SBC Digital Summit North America conference on July 14, 2020 (only two weeks after the old racially charged videos of Portnoy hit the internet), where he said this about the controversy:

> "They've been at it for 17 years and everything he has said is on video for those last 17 years. I talk[ed] to Dave extensively about it, and he's said this publicly that times change. And he looks back at some of the things that he did or said in 2008 or 2011 or 2013 that if it were today, he probably wouldn't have said. But the vast majority of the content they [have] created is entertaining: they're entertainers and comedians. I've yet to meet or listen to an entertainer or

---

2   Barstool had actually tried to get into politics around 2016 with a podcast called *Hard Factor. It failed.*

a comedian that thinks everything they said or did hit the mark when they did it."[3]

Snowden wasn't necessarily inclined to publicly chastise the man he had recently invested in, considering Penn's stock price remained up 12% since the acquisition. Also, in July 2020, Penn had only just begun applying for sports-betting licenses, a highly scrutinized process that wouldn't heat up for at least another year.[4] For now, Snowden was sticking with Portnoy.

---

3   Nardini also issued a broader statement with phrases like "We have and will continue to evolve" and "Change doesn't come from cancellation" without specifically mentioning Portnoy.

4   Penn received its first license in its home state of Pennsylvania, which was a layup, in September.

32

Portnoy's hair was slicked back and shining, even *glistening* wet. It was a look that would have made Gordon Gekko spit out his coffee and he wasn't even drinking any. Wearing a light blue suit and tie, the Barstool founder was appearing on Tucker Carlson's primetime show, *Tucker Carlson Tonight*. The Fox News host began:

> *Tucker:* You have the most fervent haters of anyone I've ever met.
>
> *Portnoy:* We have fervent, fervent haters.
>
> *Tucker* (laughing): They're *all in* on hating you.
>
> *Portnoy:* They are quite devoted to it.

While Dave preached to his staff to avoid politics and race when producing content at Barstool, the company had been thrown into cancel culture's vortex in part because of his own actions inside the political sphere. The founder had begun making appearances on different Fox News programs, and the timing of Portnoy's appearances coincided with the @RzstProgramming Twitter account's release of those old damning videos: a quick scan of the account's page will tell you it's a left-leaning account. You can connect the dots.

By now, Portnoy should have known more than anyone that his actions were tied tightly to the company he started. Portnoy was Barstool, and vice versa. It was as simple as when people saw him go on Fox News: they associated Barstool with that side of the aisle. "I know we used to say Barstool doesn't do politics, and now we are obviously towing a hypocritical line with that," Clancy said of Portnoy's recent moves, ones Portnoy defended as free marketing for the company. Portnoy claimed that Fox News was essentially the only political network that would invite him on, stating he'd go on any network anytime and that "I don't really talk politics when I go on." Unlike Clay Travis, another sports media personality whom Portnoy claimed sold out to the right wing (and copied Dave's shtick), Dave felt he wasn't positioning himself in that arena.

However, Portnoy wasn't naïve: "When I go on Fox News, that's certainly viewed as political." It was clear the founder had different rules for himself than for his employees. But while the conservative side of the aisle began to claim him as his own, Portnoy defined himself as a moderate, often tweeting statements like this:

> "95% of people in this country are normal. The extreme right sucks and extreme left sucks. Both sides filled with lunatics, crazies, and morons. And almost all politicians are hypocrites who manipulate these idiots for personal gain."
>
> —@stoolpresidente

Still, these tweets didn't preclude many from labeling Portnoy and the Barstool phenomenon as being part of a new-generation conservative movement. Some in academia went even further. In the *Society of Sport Journal*, University of Rhode Island professors Kyle Kusz and Matthew Hodler likened Barstool's ideology to that of "White nationalist post-racialism" and the Proud Boys' "Western chauvinism." The pair believed Barstool created "a safe space for young white men" where they "feel free to do whatever the f—they want without guilt, constraint, apology, or penalty," which they likened to the Proud Boys' effort to protect white men from "social justice warriors" and "woke mobs." They also wrote that Barstool's use of humor as part of this effort paralleled the Proud Boys, "who use ironic and satirical humor to draw aggrieved whites to their projects."

Portnoy's association with the right increased in July 2020, when the Barstool founder received an invitation from Donald Trump, Jr. to interview his father. Dave liked Trump Sr. (though his father, Mike, notoriously hated him). As Dave described the sitting president: "I don't care if he's a joke. I don't care if he's racist. I don't care if he's sexist ... I love the fact he says shit nobody else will say." After Trump Jr. and Portnoy exchanged DMs, and with only a couple of days to prepare, Dave found himself in the Rose Garden interviewing the president of the United States. The interview began:

Portnoy: Your son is a big fan of our website.

Trump: He's a big fan of you.

Portnoy: Even before this started, I was trying to get a retweet out of him for about six months.

Trump: We'll do that.

Portnoy: Well, you got me one on one, but he'd DM me, and I'd [say], "Okay, get the old man to get a retweet. Get the numbers up, then we'll talk business."

Trump: Well, you're doing pretty well on that.

Portnoy: Yeah. Well, so are you.

Trump: Yeah, we are. We have good numbers.[1]

---

1   Note: If you've seen *MacGruber*, the above exchange starting with "Well, you're doing pretty well" should remind you of "You and your dick jokes, it's fun to say them, it's fun to hear them...."

Portnoy: I consider myself, believe it or not, apolitical. I don't consider myself wildly Republican, Democrat, caught down in the middle. In fact, this is my first interview I've ever done, so I started at the top.

Trump: You started very well, that's good.

Although he brought up the Kaepernick kneeling situation (which was bold, considering the previous month's debacle), Portnoy refrained from asking Trump any tough questions; on a topic that pertained more to Portnoy's world, the Barstool founder asked Trump about Twitter:

Portnoy: Do you love doing Twitter?

Trump: There are times when I love it, too much sometimes, right?

Portnoy: Yeah. I follow you on Twitter, and I know I do this, but I'm not the Presi—, well my nickname is El Pres. Do you ever tweet out and wake up like, "Oh man, I wish I didn't send that one out."

Trump: Too often.

Dave also used the opportunity to ask Trump if he could exercise his presidential power against NFL Commissioner Roger Goodell, after he had publicly eluded Portnoy:

Portnoy: So, you may not know this, but during the NFL draft, [Goodell] said, "I'm going to do a charity auction, and somebody can sit in my basement, watch *Monday Night Football* with me, and the charity will go to Covid." Well, I bid. And won, I spent $250,000 to win that. I won it fair and square; he rejected it.

Trump: Well, he wanted no part of you, obviously.

Portnoy: I know. I don't know if you can arrest the guy for that.

Trump: No, but I think it was a wise move.

Portnoy: Yeah, by him.

Dave ended the interview by FaceTiming with his father Mike, whom Dave intended to surprise, but Mike had been tipped off earlier that day:

Dave Portnoy: My dad's not the biggest fan of yours; what I want to do is kind of a prank...I want to call him, FaceTime him, and just he'd die if he saw that I was with you.

Trump: Go ahead. Oh, he doesn't [like me], that's bad. That's too bad.

Mike Portnoy: I knew something was going on, and I'm not shocked, although I didn't expect to see your [Trump's] face just now.

Trump: It's great to see you.

Mike Portnoy: I was wondering why you were pinning me down. Mr. President, he never calls me.

If you told someone who had received a copy of the newspaper from Dave in a dirty Boston subway station about the interview, they'd probably chalk it up as fake news. But there he was, sitting in the Rose Garden, El Presidente interviewing The President (and people drew parallels between the two). It was a surreal moment for

Portnoy, who would be the first sort-of internet personality to interview Trump.[2] Portnoy announced the video with the following tweet:

> "I did not expect to interview Donald Trump at the White House yesterday but here we are."
>
> —@stoolpresidente

It was also another "Do as I say, not as I do" moment for Dave, and probably the largest in the history of the company, considering it came only a few weeks after those old videos were released and the ensuing entanglement with his employees, where he advised them to avoid politics. But for Portnoy, the costs of pissing some people off, including and especially those who worked for him, didn't outweigh the benefit of that kind of exposure, regardless of the timing. "If the sitting president asks me to go interview him, I'm gonna do it," he explained. "People might not agree, but I really think it's good for the brand to do that. Because the audience is fucking huge. It exposes us to people who may not be exposed."

He was right: people did not agree. Katz, in particular, took exception to this move. He knew Portnoy had been on Fox News, but this was different. This was Trump. Although he had never expressed his political leanings (and many speculated he leaned to the left), Katz went on Barstool radio the next day to vent about Portnoy's interview with the president:

> "This fucking sucks because I do not want to talk about politics. But if you're gonna interview the president, you have to be ready. It can't be softball questions. I've seen [the interview], it's softball questions. [Before you do the interview, you have to ask yourself] is it going to be a softball interview that's going to be used to make someone likeable? I don't think it's a coincidence that the President's office

---

2   Later, President Trump did interviews with other groups, such as The Nelk Boys.

reached out to Barstool four months before the election when he's polling at his worst spot. And that bothers me because it feels like we're being used in a political race. And from day one, I've always thought that what we do here is make people laugh and we don't get into politics. But you can't pretend now. You can't say we don't do politics. When you interview the president in an election year, four months before an election, you can't then say 'we don't do politics.'"

More significant, even though Katz had been with the company since 2012 and was just as important in building Barstool to that point as Portnoy himself, Katz hadn't been made aware that Portnoy planned on doing the Trump interview. That rankled Katz further:

"The part that is killing me to my core this morning was that I found out via Twitter and text message just like everyone else. And you may say to yourself 'that's not a big deal,' but I'll give you a little backstory on why it hurts. Because in December 2019, I sat down with Dave, Erika, [and] Jay Snowden, and they told me 'You are a key part of the deal.' They looked me in the eye and said, 'you are a key part of this.'"

Katz explained how when Dave found out, the day before the interview, that he had the opportunity to talk to Trump, Dave spoke with Erika, The Chernin Group, and Jay, but not him:

"So, Dave just blatantly said, 'I do not care what Dan thinks about this.'... And it hurts, man. It fucking hurts. It feels like something that I didn't expect because Dave and I have worked together for a very long time. We have a very close relationship. And I just didn't...I thought he thought more of me. I thought he would at least give me a phone call. Just give me a heads up. Let me just weigh in. And if Dave didn't agree with [my opinion], that's fine. But not even getting a chance to weigh in, it says a lot. It says a lot about what he thinks of me, it says a lot about what Erika thinks of me, and unfortunately, it's put me in a real pretzel mentally, because I don't really know where that leaves me."

Portnoy said the first thing he did following the Trump interview was to reach out to Biden's camp and offer to do the same, but Biden declined. Dave also said he didn't regret doing the Trump interview, although he did acknowledge Katz's frustration:

"He [Katz] was definitely upset about that. And I get that. That's a tough situation, because again, it goes for Barstool, which he kind of rightfully felt, people view him as Barstool, they certainly view me. So, …if I'm interviewing Trump, he [Katz] has to answer for what I'm doing."

However, Portnoy also said this:

"I feel differently about that. Part of me, a little bit [feels], if I ask Dan, and he's gonna say no, maybe it helps him, but I [think], 'Well, what am I gonna just not interview the President?' I knew I was doing it."

Most Stoolies took Portnoy's side in this. The top upvoted comments below Katz's discussion on the interview were as follows:

"The Interview overall benefits the company. Dave has been great at bringing attention to his company, negative or positive. It's all about page views. That's how it should be viewed, imo."

"So you think Dave should have asked President Trump hard-hitting questions [or] talked about serious issues, but at the same time, [you] think Barstool should not engage in anything political?"

As for how Portnoy's actions affected other significant members at Barstool, Chernin, Nardini, and Snowden didn't comment publicly on the interview. Clancy did comment, but he didn't feel as strongly as Katz did about having to answer for Dave, saying:

> "I feel like we have gotten to a point where Barstool has gotten big enough and our own individual platforms grew large enough...everybody kind of stays separate. I don't think anybody should have to run their content by me. Dave got an opportunity to talk to the President and he took it. I do think it was very bad timing, and I think that the implications of it after everything that's gone on is not good, but I also have never been offered to talk to the President, so... [Dave is] gonna do his thing; I'm gonna do mine. And I definitely don't want to speak on it and get involved in it because it's just a mess, man."[3]

Clancy was right. On the one hand, Dave's employees wanted to get political; on the other hand, the faces of the company (which included Katz and Clancy) wanted to avoid talking politics. At the same time, Dave seemed to be doing both. Inside Barstool, the confusion over what the platform should be used for was clouding the future of Portnoy's company.

Eventually, Portnoy hired minority content creators whose content wasn't political. This would be the blueprint Barstool used to attract a more diversified audience. (Also, much like what happened following the ESPN deal, Katz stayed with the company.) In August, Dave hired Deion Sanders, a former NFL star and prominent African-American football coach, whose YouTube reality show *Coach Prime* followed his journey coaching his son's high-school football team.

---

3   Dr. Fauci later appeared on *Pardon My Take, which Katz co-hosted.*

Also around that time, Dave hired two African-American personalities, "Gillie Da Kid" (born Nasir Fard) and "Wallo" (Wallace Peeples), putting their popular podcast *Million Dollaz Worth of Game* under the Barstool umbrella. Sanders and the *Million Dollaz Worth of Game* duo produced content that wasn't political or racially charged. "Entertainment is Gillie's top priority" read the caption on a clip posted to the *Million Dollaz Worth of Game* YouTube page from March 18, 2023. The rapper and podcast host explained if you're making music, you need to focus on making a hit over politics. And the same applied to making content. "All of this shit is entertainment," said Gillie. They weren't trying to "change" Barstool; they were reaching a new audience for the company without upsetting the apple cart.

It was a different angle than the one pushed by Brandon Newman. And those who didn't jive with it would eventually leave. Two weeks after Muj's very public departure, Tyler Withers, who was one of the more outspoken members in the discussion following those old videos of Portnoy, also quit. A couple months later, following his spar with Portnoy and Dave's interview with Trump, Brandon Newman left the company, announcing on the radio, "This will be my last week at Barstool. Next Monday. Walking away. Everything that happened on Twitter with Dave, it really feels like there's not much coming back from that." The following year, NFL player and host Willie Colon also left.

The cancel culture movement died down, and Portnoy's company stuck to jokes; Barstool's website remains free of any NPR-like podcasts discussing race.[4] Out of the seven minority employees who sat down for the infamous podcast with the N-word title, only two are still with the company today: Zah (the producer) and Ebony (the security guard).

---

4   Portnoy still makes occasional appearances on Fox News.

33

By 2021, Dave Portnoy had become an A-list celebrity. The Barstool founder, who remained working remotely from Miami and Nantucket while his employees returned to the office, appeared on the cover of the May 2021 issue of Nantucket's *N Magazine*. But when the publication apologized for the profile on Portnoy following backlash from its wealthy community, Dave was again pitted against yet another media outlet, this one hitting close to home. Dave said:

> "It's unfortunate that the powers that be at *Nantucket Magazine* are spineless jellyfish who are held hostage by the whims of the vocal minority. If you took a poll on Nantucket of people who like me and hate me, I'd bet 99 percent like me. Everyone who doesn't can go fuck themselves."

Although he wasn't accepted by the old-money crowd (and his lashing out may suggest he wanted to be), there was no denying Portnoy's fame. The Barstool founder was now being comped at exclusive restaurants in Miami, and he received custom gift baskets (pizza-themed ones were popular) at seemingly every hotel he stayed. "You know what's crazy, the more money you have, the more it's like…if I go out to a club, people will *give* me a table instead of me paying for it." Eventually, Portnoy acquired an invite to Michael Rubin's celebrity-packed White Party in the Hamptons, which was a bit more star-studded than the White Party Portnoy had thrown in Boston back in 2004. Kraft had been joking in 2016 when he said, "It's Brady, Belichick, and Portnoy," but now, when naming the current icons to come out of Boston, that might have actually been the list.

This was partly because while Portnoy was being assaulted by cancel culture at the time, something opportune also happened during Covid: Barstool took over the internet. As Nardini explained, "Barstool blew up over Covid because one, the content was good. And two, because everybody we competed with couldn't figure out how to work with just an iPhone and a computer or was too busy unionizing or ignoring their business." Thanks to the creative freedom Barstool gave its employees, the company as a whole was able to adapt quickly to the crisis, coming up with unique ways to entertain a country stuck indoors. Content like *The Dozen Trivia*, a skype-based game show produced by an employee named Jeff D. Lowe, became popular during early Covid and eventually became a staple of Barstool's programming. (The show is played in-person today, with the finals filmed in front of a live audience.) Other programs that kept Barstool viewers coming back to the site included the toy horse races that Katz broadcast from his living room, as well as his attempts at winning a college football video game championship with a fictional coach named Coach Duggs. (As I'm typing this, I realize how ridiculous these seem, but that shows how little was going on during those first few brutal months of Covid.)

Portnoy led by example with his *Unboxing* series of videos, where he opened (live, on camera) packages sent by fans, and these became strangely fascinating to watch. Portnoy filmed these on his iPhone, showing him surrounded by brown boxes stacked to the ceiling; his apartment looked like a UPS warehouse. During the *Unboxing*, Dave was seen opening anything a Barstool fan thought to send: custom artwork; large loaves of finely baked Italian bread; a live goldfish he named Randolph; a Samurai sword he used to slice open the next round of boxes. A Stoolie who got dumped sent Portnoy all of his ex-girlfriend's stuff. There was even a cocaine scare—though it turned out to be baby powder.

Looking back on it now, the segment was probably dangerous: by this time, Portnoy did have a growing list of enemies. Dave was

HOW THE JESTER BECAME KING

aware of this fact, so he had an assistant scan the items pre-opening for anything that might be nefarious (usually just checking for glitter-bombs). Still, that didn't mean the segment wasn't hazardous. During one show, Portnoy was opening a box that contained a small but very sharp arrow-shaped pocketknife. "I think I just sliced my hand," he said, then paused and looked down. "And I did, wide open. Ahhhhhhh!" After fans listened to him yell expletives off-camera for a short while, Portnoy left for the emergency room. But Dave came back to finish the episode. With blood on his shirt and a large bandage on his hand, Portnoy reappeared on his Instagram Live stream: "Am I gonna cry about it? Yeah, I'm gonna cry about it."

Portnoy also unboxed the world of financial trading. *Davey Day Trader Global* (DDTG, for short) became a daily show featuring the Barstool founder sitting at his desk, trading stocks using $3M he had dumped in an E-trade account, mostly questioning how everything worked. "I don't like the way this whole stock market system is set up," Dave tweeted. Portnoy, whose motto became "Stocks only go up!" was eventually enthralled in the world, which he found out was really no different from sports gambling. And much like he had in media, Portnoy became a character who exposed the big boys for being nothing more than Brooks Brothers customers with salon-quality haircuts:

> "That's the Suits' entire game. Pretend they know more than you. Call you stupid. Make you scared. Make you sell. Then they buy the dip and get rich off you. I won't allow it. I know their moves before they do." #ddtg

> "The blue check marks and pinstripes don't know what to do. I'm up 400k overall."

Although he was rich, the founder-turned-retail-investor positioned himself as the little guy, the common man:

313

"The only time CNBC and the Suits care about protection is when it's the establishment getting their teeth kicked in. As long as the big banks are winning, the stock market is great. The second retail takes the wheel, it's all unfair."

This was an angle Dave employed to call out what he viewed as bad actors in the space, which happened frequently when it came to crypto, an opaque area of an already mysterious finance industry. Dave said this about FTX and Sam Bankman-Fried:

"This guy is one of the great pieces of shit of all time. How is this guy—I can't breathe without people criticizing it—and this fucking guy is living in an apartment with the entire company on the top floor, just running a fuck fest, like Bang Bros, running FTX, just stealing people's money. Fuck this guy, get this guy outta there, drag him through the streets!"[1]

Portnoy's foray into finance exposed him to a new audience, which he called Fintwits—people who spent much of their time tweeting about finance and perusing Reddit's r/wallstreetbets. This group watched Portnoy interview RobinHood CEO Vlad Tenev after the company halted trading of GameStop's stock during the wild Reddit shorting saga—a move that many people believed was a way to protect large investors while screwing over retail ones. (It's worth noting that Portnoy lost $700,000 in the move.) CNBC billed it as

---

[1]   Portnoy had his own issues with crypto. He promoted SafeMoon, a currency that became worthless and was eventually investigated by the SEC. He was not named in the SEC's complaint against SafeMoon. Portnoy was sued by investors of SafeMoon, but they eventually filed for his dismissal from the lawsuit. Also, VanEck agreed to pay a $1.75M civil penalty over BUZZ, its failed ETF. According to the SEC, VanEck failed to disclose its relationship with an online influencer that it paid to promote BUZZ. Portnoy was promoting the launch of BUZZ in March of 2021. He was not named in the SEC's complaint against VanEck.

"*Portnoy vs. Tenev: Barstool Founder Grills Robinhood CEO.*" Here's an excerpt:

> *Vlad:* I'm proud of the way the team handled the crisis. We are able to protect the firm and were able to prevent customers from having bigger issues.
>
> *Portnoy:* That line you just said: 'proud of how we handled it.' How can that be possible? You guys are billed as a firm to retail traders (hence the name Robinhood), and you screwed them over.

The interview—which for Portnoy's standards was actually fairly tame—garnered heavy commentary from the Fintwits, who were mostly split on what they thought of Dave:

- ○ "I realize a lot of people here don't like Portnoy, but I laughed multiple times at how bad he destroyed Vlad."
- ○ "I think he's okay, don't fully understand the hate."
- ○ "Imagine asking a question so bad that Vlad doesn't thank you for your question."

Dave wasn't the next Warren Buffett, but he acted like it. As Robert Silverman of *The Daily Beast* wrote, "Everything Barstool does is drenched in a thick coat of kayfabe." And like anyone else who ever tried their luck at day-trading, Portnoy lost money. On one noteworthy occasion, he admitted, "I lost one million today in the stock market. Am I worried? Nope. I'm just gonna do what I always do. Put some fucking hats on sale."

Moves like Portnoy's jump into the world of finance kept his company afloat during Covid and propelled him to the front page of the internet. There were also other less-calculated ones that had the same effect, such as Dave's very public dispute with the *Call Her Daddy* hosts over their contract.

Alex Cooper and Sofia Franklyn, two good-looking NYC roommates in their mid-20s, were discovered by Portnoy on Instagram after Dave came across a series of clips from their podcast. It was unlike anything he'd seen on the internet, with the pair talking very, *very* openly about their sex lives, using language that made *Portnoy* blush. "*You're Just a Hole*" was the title of one of the show's episodes (you can figure out on your own what they meant by that). But in some sense, the show was just a female version of how Portnoy spoke: it was authentic. And after Dave hired the duo in 2018, they exploded.

By May 2020, *Call Her Daddy* was bringing in millions for Barstool and had become the number one podcast at the company. (In 2020, *CHD* ranked #15 on the top 50 most-listened-to podcast list, according to Edison Research.) Portnoy had created a monster. And once again, he found himself dealing with homegrown stars who had eclipsed the platform he built for them. Just one year into their three-year deal with Barstool, the pair wanted to renegotiate, given their newfound status. They even cryptically referred to being held prisoner in their episodes around this time, and eventually, they halted their release altogether. At the same time, unbeknownst to Portnoy, Franklyn's boyfriend was Peter Nelson, a powerful HBO Sports executive (whom Franklyn called "Suitman" on her podcast), and Nelson had allegedly begun shopping the *Call Her Daddy* podcast behind Portnoy's back. When he found out, Portnoy said, "If you guys take *Call Her Daddy* and go somewhere else, we're going to sue the fuck out of you...you're under a three-year contract."

In an attempt to avoid this outcome, Portnoy eventually held a meeting with Cooper and Franklyn on his rooftop, where he offered them $500,000 salaries, six months off their contract so they could hit the market sooner, and all IP-rights to *Call Her Daddy*. From

Dave's perspective, this was a generous proposal: it was way more than their previous guaranteed salaries of $75,000, and companies don't usually give hosts the rights to the intellectual property of their show. This was all under the notion that, according to Dave, he had the right to let things remain status quo since they were legally under contract with Barstool for three years.

Cooper wanted the deal, allegedly, Franklyn did not. This led to the pair fighting and ultimately splitting up. "I never spoke to her again after that," said Cooper. As this split was happening, *Call Her Daddy* fans were officially introduced to Portnoy after he hijacked the podcast and released an episode with himself as the host. Portnoy explained the situation between the two hosts to the listeners: "Sofia said no [to my offer]. She said it was 'Because my boyfriend has stuck his neck out and has gotten us a deal at Wondery, and he's gonna look like an asshole if we pull out.' And they got in a fight about that. And now it's a he-said-she-said."

As the drama unfolded, Barstool started selling merchandise with the phrase "Cancel Suitman," and Stoolies, once again, were able to get the directive trending on Twitter. The entire Suitman Saga brought more eyeballs to the company, as it pulled an eclectic assortment of media players into the Barstool world, including HBO, which had to issue a denial of Portnoy's claim that Nelson most likely 'greenlight[ed] a hit piece on me."

Much like the Soul Cycle incident, this one eventually ended, and Cooper stayed at Barstool before signing a massive three-year, $60M contract with Spotify in 2021. Franklyn, who no longer dates the HBO exec, did not return to Barstool and did not get such a deal (she hosts a podcast called *Sofia with an F*, presented by her own company, *Sloot* Media).

As for Peter Nelson, Portnoy predictably popped one of his custom champagne bottles when Nelson left HBO in August of 2020, right as HBO's parent company AT&T began widespread layoffs across its media brands. "It's almost like Suitman thought Grudge

Dave was just an urban legend or a fairytale. That he didn't exist in real life...Suitman was dead fucking two months ago, when I knew he was a problem. It was just, when was I going to kill him?"

There were other Barstool happenings during Covid—such as Dave starting a podcast called *BFFs* with two 20-year-olds named Josh Richards and Bri LaPaglia, aimed towards the Gen Z audience— that launched the founder toward top-tier celebrity status. However, none were more significant than his creation of The Barstool Fund. From the very beginning of social distancing, Portnoy had been an outspoken critic of the lockdown, eventually becoming a face of those frustrated by the day-to-day restrictions handed down by the government. For instance, Dave wrote "FUCK THAT MIDGET ANTHONY FAUCHI" [*sic*] on the whiteboard behind where he sat during his *Davey Day Trader Global* streams. On December 11, 2020, after the New York mayor re-closed indoor dining in the city, Portnoy posted a video on his Twitter titled "**Politicians Are Stealing the Basic Right to Earn a Living,**"[2] which went on to say:

> "The Bar and Restaurant is getting squeezed and squeezed.
> They've tried everything. They've been creative as possible
> to save their livelihoods. How do you expect these people to
> survive? It's insanity."

Portnoy's rant would go mega viral, racking up millions of views, thousands of comments, and more than 120,000 likes on Twitter (that is a very, very large number for a Twitter post). One of the comments caught Portnoy's eye: it came from Marcus Lemonis, the celebrity host of CNBC's *The Profit*, a popular show about building small businesses:

---

2   Portnoy was criticized for saying, in response to Covid, "I don't care about people dying, I don't care about a lot of things...I care about my wallet."

"Hey @stoolpresidente put your money where your mouth is...I'll put up 500k if you match it to create a relief fund for NYC area restaurants"

—@marcuslemonis

A week later, Portnoy posted a video with the following caption:

"Introducing The Barstool Fund. If you are a small business that needs help staying in business because of Covid, email us your story to barstoolfund@barstoolsports.com. We will try to help as many people as we can."

Although Lemonis started his own initiative instead of teaming up with Barstool, Portnoy did have some experience helping small businesses: his *"One-Bite Pizza Review"* videos usually drove waves of customers to the pizzerias he judged—so much so that whatever place he reviewed often ran out of pizza the day after the video was released.[3]

Dave's plan for enacting The Barstool Fund initiative was inspired by the cameraman in those reviews, Frankie Borelli, whose father owned a restaurant on Long Island. As Dave stated in his announcement:

"Borelli's is the perfect example of the business we're trying to save." Throughout this pandemic I've [asked], 'Hey Frankie, how's Borelli's doing? How's your dad doing?' And every month, it gets a little bleaker. He hasn't shut off his payroll. He's like 'I'm going down with the ship...I can't fathom not paying these people.' So that's the rule, to qualify for money from us, you have to be still paying your employees, your payroll has to be on."

---

3   Portnoy later launched his One Bite Pizza App, where you could see all the places he reviewed, and Walmart sells his frozen One Bite pizza

The initiative began with $500,000 from Portnoy (and Borelli's received the first official donation); in its first two weeks, the Barstool Fund raised more than $8M from Stoolies. In total, Barstool raised $41M, for 443 businesses, from more than 231,407 donors, including Tom Brady, Elon Musk, Guy Fieri, Aaron Rodgers, and Kid Rock. Moreover, throughout the campaign, glowing headlines about Portnoy and Barstool rolled in (in place of the usual derogatory ones):

"Dave Portnoy Launches Barstool Fund to Raise Money for Small Businesses Hurt by Pandemic Shutdown"
—Yahoo Finance

"Chicago Restaurant Owner Gets Helping Hand from Dave Portnoy of Barstool Sports"
—NBC Chicago

"Barstool Fund Help 'a Miracle,' New York Restaurant Owner Says"
—Fox News

Thanks to the grassroots effort and the powerful vignettes of restaurant owners crying after Portnoy FaceTimed them to let them know they were being selected, Portnoy's profile had never been higher. And while he truly wanted to help small business, the timing of the effort was undoubtably beneficial. Because Barstool was now owned by a publicly traded company, one that also had to deal with hawkeyed regulators, controversy wasn't nearly as welcome anymore. Sure, benign disputes like the one with *Call Her Daddy* were good for business, but old racist videos leading to a mass exodus of minority employees at Barstool? Not so much. But now, those videos were forgotten. Instead, Barstool was being hailed as a beacon for small business in the dark times of Covid.

Following the goodwill the company earned from the Barstool Fund, Penn Gaming donated around $4.6 million to the charity. Snowden's public endorsement of Portnoy during the cancel culture movement looked as if it were paying off. And for the most part, it remained that way, until the spring of 2021.

34

APRIL 2021

Barstool employees gathered around a computer tucked into the corner of the office. They were watching something you're not supposed to watch at work, although technically, it was work-related. Also, by now, pretty much everyone had seen it: *The New York Post* had run this story hours earlier:

"Barstool's Dave Portnoy Shrugs at Sex Tape as Penn Stock Slides"

In early April, a video leaked of Portnoy and a young woman having sex. It wasn't your run-of-the-mill, boring celebrity sex tape, however. This was *graphic*; let's just say a collar and leash made an appearance, and Portnoy didn't own a poodle. As the video made its rounds on the internet—Portnoy has said he doesn't know how it got out—Penn's stock began to fall. Following the release, the Barstool founder issued a statement via Twitter, "A stock is down because somebody has consensual sex? Are you fucking kidding me? I would jump on this dip and fuck it, no pun intended."

Portnoy's somewhat cavalier response was partly due to the fact that he already had two other sex tapes hit the internet. The first dropped in December of 2019, right as Barstool was negotiating the sale to Penn. That tape was not nearly as graphic as the April 2021 tape, and in typical Barstool fashion, it was turned into content: during an episode of "Stool Scenes" (the behind-the-scenes Barstool show), Barstool employees were filmed making jokes about their boss resembling the batting stance of baseball player Jeff Bagwell.

With a grin on his face, Ben Friedman explained the office's reaction: "I tell ya, working at Barstool, you never know what to expect, and today we woke up and our boss is laying pipe on video." Portnoy responded with a now-infamous tweet inside the Barstool world: "Breaking: Dave Portnoy fucks."

While Penn and Snowden remained silent on all three videos featuring the face of their sports-betting venture, this time around (in April 2021), there weren't any funny *Stool Scenes* episodes being released; this last video looked different. It looked *rough*.

Also, in what is certainly not a coincidence, that same month, a reporter from *Business Insider* named Julia Black began digging around Portnoy's private life, to which Dave responded:

> "Hard hitting research from @BusinessInsider dm'ing girls who follow me on insta asking if they've Dm'd with me."
>
> —@stoolpresidente

Below his tweet was a snapshot of the reporter's message to the girl:

> "Hi [name redacted], Thanks for accepting my follow/sorry to reach out like this! I'm a reporter for *Business Insider* and I'm working on a story about Dave Portnoy. I saw a TikTok you posted about Dave, and I'd love to ask you a few questions about it. Namely: Is that a real DM?"

For the next six months, Portnoy had people reaching out to him giving him a heads-up that a reporter was asking for dirt on him. "Everybody who likes me didn't comment," he explained, "Except Elio [Imbornone]." Dave's longtime friend Elio was a genuinely nice guy. As a father of three, Elio's chosen path in life was a stark contradiction to his famous friend's. The restaurant owner also wasn't the smartest chef in his kitchen. Portnoy posted his text exchange with Elio:

> *Elio:* Just did a 20 min interview about you for *Business Insider*. Send the check in the mail.

> *Portnoy:* It's a hit piece you idiot. We're all ignoring it.

While this did make Stoolies laugh—by this point, the Barstool audience knew some sort of article was coming—Portnoy was growing more unnerved about the impending "hit piece." For a while, he wasn't sure exactly what angle *Business Insider* was taking. By now, he had pretty much seen it all—from the angry Boston callers about his Tom Brady blog, all the way up until the recent unearthing of those old problematic videos, everything under the sun had been said about Portnoy and Barstool. The tropes calling them racist, sexist, etc. had all been played.

But this was starting to feel as if it wasn't going to fall into any of those categories: the approach was focused not so much on that sort of commentary but instead on Dave's personal life, and particularly, his sex life. As he learned more about how many people Julia Black was speaking with and how many of them were women much younger than him that he knew, and what kind of questions she was asking them, and others, he began to truly worry. "That article's coming," he told fans on his DDTG stream, "I just found out that [someone] went on the record...a former employee, who was here for a cup of coffee...who knows what he said...it's not fucking good." It turned out to be worse than that.

35

"'I was literally screaming in pain': Young women say they met Barstool Sports founder Dave Portnoy for sex and it turned violent and humiliating."

—Julia Black, *Business Insider*

On Thursday, November 4, 2021, *Business Insider* published its article, which included claims by three young women, with two of the three providing detailed accounts of their interactions with Portnoy. *Business Insider* gave the pair pseudonyms Allison and Madison:

"...*Insider* spoke with more than two dozen people with direct experience with Portnoy and Barstool, including eight current or former employees. Some women, as young as 19 who had no professional connection to Portnoy, recounted having sexually explicit online exchanges with him. Three of these women said they had sex with Portnoy, now 44, and that the encounters turned into frightening and humiliating experiences that have taken a toll on their mental health. Two, including Madison, said Portnoy both choked and filmed them without advance permission; another, who has had depression, said she was suicidal after the two had sex. And all three were afraid to speak out, fearing retaliation from the media mogul and his rabid fan base."

In her piece, Julia Black relayed jarring accusations from both women, starting with Madison. (A third woman, who is unnamed, allegedly told Black that Portnoy had choked and filmed her without consent, but as previously mentioned her account was not detailed in the article.) Black reported that Madison met Portnoy on Instagram; after reaching out to him via DM, Portnoy flew Madison to meet him at his house in Nantucket:

> "...After dinner, they started kissing. Madison, a 20-year-old college student at the time, said she first became uncomfortable when Portnoy pulled out his phone and started filming her—without asking permission—as she performed oral sex on him. 'I never said anything. I was scared. He was just so mean,' she said.

> "From there, things escalated until, as Madison put it, 'I felt like I was just a human sex doll.'

> "Two days later, Madison texted a close friend. 'It was so rough I felt like I was being raped. He videotaped me and spit in my mouth and choked me so hard I couldn't breathe,' she wrote in messages viewed by *Insider*. 'And it hurt and I was literally screaming in pain.'

> "She recalled crying and shouting, 'Too much! Too much!' and 'It hurts!'

> "'It was so painful,' Madison said. 'I kept trying to get away and he was like, 'Stop running away from me. Stop running away from me.'

> "But Portnoy, she said, 'just went harder.'

> "Madison's flight home wasn't until two days later, so she slept on Portnoy's couch both nights. They did not have sex again."

Julia Black then detailed Allison's account: Allison had also reached out to Portnoy on Instagram; her parents owned a house on Nantucket, so she was able to meet him on her own:

"'...He leaned in and started kissing me, and I didn't know what to do at that point. And we went upstairs, and he was really aggressive, and I didn't know what to do and we had sex, and that was it and he kicked me out.'

"Allison said her memories were fuzzy because of her emotional distress surrounding the event, but, like Madison, she said Portnoy choked her. 'He kept spitting in my mouth, which was really gross,' Allison said. 'I was kind of scared. I didn't want to disappoint him.'

"A little over an hour later, Allison's friends picked her up. One of the young women who was in the car told *Insider* that Allison was uncharacteristically quiet. 'She was clearly almost in shock,' she said.

"'She basically couldn't talk the next day,' Allison's mother told *Insider*.

"Allison does not describe what happened to her as sexual assault but said she was still deeply disturbed by the experience. 'I just felt very preyed on,' she said.

"Soon after Allison's encounter with Portnoy, two photos—a selfie Allison had taken with Portnoy and a photo her friend took of her leaving his house—began to circulate the island. Both were posted on private Snapchats by Allison's friends but were then screenshotted and shared widely. Before long, it felt as though the entire island knew what had transpired between Allison and Portnoy, Olivia [Allison's sister] said.

"Allison, who has had depression, said she felt stressed and overwhelmed following her sexual encounter with Portnoy and the subsequent attention it got. 'I guess it was kind of my breaking point,' Allison said.

"Three nights after having sex with Portnoy, Allison was suicidal and was hospitalized. While she was in the hospital, her mother began going through [Allison's] phone, trying to understand what had happened. After finding Portnoy's messages, Allison's mother called the Nantucket Police Department. She told the police, 'Go put somebody outside his door because you're going to see every day there's some young girl being dropped off.' *Insider* viewed police documents confirming this call. Her mother wanted to pursue some sort of legal action against Portnoy, but Allison refused.

"'I knew he would drag me through the mud,' Allison said."

Portnoy was stunned by the article. Though he had sensed something dark might be coming, never in his life had he expected to read anything like that. After it dropped, he released a 12-minute video filmed in his apartment using his iPhone, in which he vehemently denied the allegations:[1]

"Ok, so *Business Insider* finally published the hit piece on me that's been eight months in the making. Not the normal hit piece, not the normal stuff about jokes we've made, videos we've made, things we've done at Barstool. This is [*sic*] far more serious allegations, portraying me really as

---

[1] Portnoy realized eventually that this wasn't going to be a normal hit piece: "I could tell it was taking a pretty dark turn by what—girls were calling me, leaking the—they were taping the conversations with the reporter, so I could hear the line of questioning and what they were saying." Also, Another reporter named Kat Tenbarge contributed to the report.

a sexual deviant…I've never done anything remotely non-consensual…The first girl, Madison, flew to my Nantucket house last July. At no point was it not consensual, at no point did she tell me to stop. There was no weirdness after, totally fine, normal interaction. It was 100% consensual.

"…incident number two was a girl on Nantucket. She DM'd me, she asked to come over. She came over. We hung out by the pool. Starting hooking up. Had sex. And then it says she went home, she took a selfie with me, got super depressed when the selfie circulated. And three days later was in the hospital with depression. The mother apparently called the Nantucket cops, I've never been contacted by the authorities because I've never done anything that's remotely not consensual. This is 11 minutes of me pouring my soul out, I didn't know how else to do it. But it sucks to be attacked like this. [After] 8 months, [I have] 24 hours to respond: that's what the reporter said. Give me a fucking break."

Portnoy addressed only the two accusers whose stories were detailed, and he did not identify them. "I don't want to identify them because I don't know what that will do to them."

After sending Julia Black's report to Barstool, *Business Insider* did in fact tell Portnoy he had only 24 hours to review what was in the article. Before posting his denial video, Portnoy immediately convened with his lawyers, The Chernin Group, Nardini, and Penn to discuss how he was going to respond to these accusations, ones he let the group know he whole-heartedly denied.[2]

At first, following the advice of his lawyers, Portnoy made a video saying he didn't know the girls and it was impossible to defend himself against anonymous accusations. After sleeping on it, he deleted

---

2   *Business Insider* ended up giving Portnoy an extra day to respond after Portnoy's lawyer said they needed more time.

it and went with his unfiltered 12-minute response, addressing the two girls' specific allegations because he knew who they were. As Portnoy explained:

"I got to the point where I didn't trust anybody but myself. We're dealing with big companies, whether it's Chernin or Penn, everybody's gotta watch their ass a little bit. I was on a call, and the Chernin guys [asked me], 'Have the Chernin lawyers looked at this?' [his 12- minute response video], and I [said] 'no.' And they [asked], 'Are you gonna let them?' and I [said] 'no. This is me. You guys do what you're gonna do, this is *my* character that's been assassinated. I'm gonna respond how I think is best.'"

A week later, Portnoy announced to his fans that he was holding an Emergency Press Conference, in which he would provide evidence he believed exonerated him: "2 P.M. EST. I WILL BE DOING A LIVE EMERGENCY PRESS CONFERENCE EXPOSING *BUSINESS INSIDER.* TICK TOCK, JULIA BLACK, TICK, TOCK HENRY BLODGET [*Business Insider*'s CEO]." Portnoy got the hashtag #2PMPortnoy trending, and he explained in a follow-up tweet:

"#portnoy2pm Also this is not a quick presentation. This is a comprehensive review of this entire hit piece with nothing but facts and proof. Clear your calendar."

Standing in front of his water-jug podium, in a blue suit and glasses, Portnoy began his press conference like he usually did: complaining about the setup, telling the crew behind the cameras, "Can we turn one of these lights off? I feel like I'm in an interrogation chamber." Eventually, Portnoy got to why he was holding this presser:

"I've said this from the beginning. If anybody looked at the details of this case, details of this article, my reaction to it, the facts of it, you'd realize that there's nothing there. Julia

Black, *Business Insider*, even though they say they never accused me of raping a girl, they describe rape. They accuse me of rape. Period. They say they didn't, there's no actual allegations, but if you read it, it's like 'Girls running away, Dave won't stop.' That's rape. I've said this from the top, I don't care how many times a girl says 'yes, yes, yes' before, if at any point she's like 'no, stop' and you don't stop, that's rape. That's what they say I did; I never did that. Let's go through the details because everything happened fast and there's a lot more details backing me up. *Business Insider* as of this time, has not corrected, added, nothing in that original article. Even though there are facts that have come out, they've added nothing. So, let's start."

The article from *Business Insider* was unique in the sense that it implied sexual assault but did not outwardly accuse Portnoy of such a crime. In fact, he was never charged with one. It fell into the dreaded gray area, which Portnoy said was strategic: they didn't want to open an official investigation, which Dave claimed would prove his innocence. So, Dave took it upon himself to highlight evidence that he believed would clear his name. In the video, he referred to the following key points and opinions, with emails, DMs (some explicit), and other items displayed while he spoke about them:

○ Julia Black covered her bases, emailing Dave at first in a friendly tone and deleting 4,000 tweets before the article dropped, attempting to hide bias.

○ *Business Insider* was reaching out to Barstool advertisers as soon as they published the piece, asking for comment, which was a scare tactic.

○ Allison was DM'ing with him, wanting to meet up again even though she would claim to have severe trauma after they had sex, and *Business Insider* intentionally didn't include the police report because it was bogus and "read like *The Onion*."

○ Madison, whom *Business Insider* claimed didn't want to be identified, identified herself by creating a video where she reacted to Portnoy's 12-minute denial post, and in the comment section she stated, "Nobody said he was a rapist" and "The article never said the sex wasn't consensual." Dave also included her anti-Trump posts.

○ Portnoy posted a video of Ava Louise, the only woman (who had an experience with Portnoy) to be identified in the article. The video shows Louise on *Dr. Phil*, admitting to lying for attention. Louise and Portnoy exchanged DMs, but never met up.

Portnoy said this about filming without these women's permission: "I did not film without advanced permission. Total, total, total lie." He addressed the third unnamed woman, who allegedly told *Business Insider* that she was filmed and choked without consent, as follows:

"There were two major accusations, two girls, an Allison and a Madison. There's a third that they'll say that—there's no context, no proof, no nothing. It basically just says Dave had sex with a girl and was aggressive. Nothing, no date, anything, you could have said that a hundred times."

In his denial press conference, Portnoy also said Allison's claims that he "kept spitting in my mouth," were "a bald-faced lie." (In the graphic sex tape released in April, which did not involve either of these two women, Portnoy is seen spitting on the woman's face at least one time). He did not address Madison's claim that "he spit in my mouth."

Dave concluded the speech with a video of Henry Blodget, the CEO of *Business Insider*, being introduced by Matt Lauer (yes, there's some irony there) as a former stock trader who was permanently banned from the financial services industry by the SEC after being charged with securities fraud, claims he settled for $4M without admitting guilt. "This is my new arch enemy," Portnoy said, ending the video. "If this is a baseball game, we're in the top of the second. People keep saying 'Why are you getting so mad?' I got accused of rape, arguably the most horrific thing you can be accused of. With 0.0 evidence. And they fucking knew it. Music."

In trying to figure out why *Business Insider* did this, Portnoy began to believe that Julia Black was just a pawn, "a patsy." This went above the lowly freelance writer. Dave said that Blodget was friends with Steve Cohen, well-known hedge-fund billionaire and owner of the New York Mets. Cohen's company had put nearly a billion dollars into Melvin Capital, the fund that had been famously shorting GameStop stock during the grassroots Reddit drama; another hedge fund, Citadel, was also an investor in Melvin Capital. So when Robinhood CEO Vlad Tenev suspended trading of GameStop's stock on its platform, many saw it as following orders from Citadel, one of Robinhood's largest customers, to protect its investment in Melvin Capital and investors like Steve Cohen.

Portnoy was highly critical of the move, as seen in his CNBC interview with Robinhood's CEO and on his DDTG streams. Portnoy believed that *this* was why someone like Cohen would reach out to Blodget and have him put the wheels of a "hit piece" in motion. It didn't help that Portnoy was often highly critical of the larger financial players in general; Portnoy openly mocked them whenever his portfolio went up:

"The reason the establishment doesn't like me is they don't want you knowing a regular guy can do what I do #DDTG."

In an interview on his Dave Portnoy show on November 9, 2021, host Barstool Eddie asked Dave about this, as well as Blodget's connection to Cohen:

Portnoy: "I heard the GameStop shit, after I went after Cohen and Vlad and Citadel, they're gonna get me."

Eddie: "Does your gut tell you DDTG was a big cause of this?"

Portnoy: "Yes."

Eddie: "So, you think this is a higher-level thing going on?"

Portnoy: "Yes. I think Blodget's involved. I think someone told him to do this. His finance background, who he's connected with. And he just hands it off. It's perfect. They have the perfect willing people who fucking hate me. The article is from the same group, the 'Deadspin' (for lack of a better word) crew. But there was something far more sinister at play here. Yes, I do believe that. Can I ever prove it? No. I'd love to know, like on my death bed—weirdly, part of me is like 'I tip my cap to fuckin' Cohen, like, you're the real deal, man. You really fuckin' did it.'"

Whether Portnoy was actually in a real-life episode of *Billions*[3] was never proven, but the timing of the article was curious. November 4th was the day the article dropped; it was also the day Penn announced Q3 earnings. Portnoy's accusations, along with disappointing financials, caused the stock to fall off a cliff: $Penn was down 21% at the day's close, wiping away $2.5 billion in market value. But other gambling companies' earnings were somewhat

---

3   The TV show was based on Cohen.

similar to Penn's, and they did not suffer anywhere close to the same fall.

Portnoy highlighted something else that was odd, saying, "There was a wild shorting of the stock the day before the hit piece dropped." The Twitter account "Unusual Whales" (the account followed the investment activity of high-profile figures inside the stock market and has 1.2M followers) tweeted a response to Portnoy's first denial video, which included a graph with $Penn's trading activity from the day before:

> "@stoolpresidente—it seems someone was frontloading it [Penn's stock], too, buying large put positions. Someone was seemingly planning the dip."

Madakat Capital's Twitter account chimed in:

> "@stoolpresidente someone knew about the story and leveraged up short against $Penn."

Also, in the months leading up to the article hitting the internet, the short interest on $Penn had begun to increase at a faster clip relative to other sports-betting stocks, beginning in the month of April, the same time Julia Black began digging around. Although Nardini confirmed she had heard rumors about the article weeks before from a hedge fund manager, Portnoy continued to publicly question whether Blodget's inner circle had financially benefitted from Black's reporting.

Follow the money.
—Deep Throat

36

This wasn't Deadspin Portnoy was allegedly dealing with. When it comes to the world of high finance, guys like Steven Cohen know how to fuck people. Portnoy acknowledged their alleged tactics as the last arrow in the anti-Barstool quiver: "The only thing that can move the needle that they haven't done to me is these sex crimes. Everything else, people have heard before, but you put that salacious headline, which they did, forget about it." For the first time in 18 years, Portnoy was truly rattled:

> "That was the only time I've been *down*. It was something that really elevated what I am usually accused of. Which is a joke that went sideways, like singing a lyric I shouldn't have five years ago, I can live with that. I make mistakes, or wouldn't do it again. But that, 'girl running away from Dave,' that was tough to see."

In the weeks following the article, Dave remained on edge. *Business Insider*'s model for this sort of piece more often than not included a follow-up, and Julia Black's Twitter account said as much. Pinned to her profile was the ominous statement, "If you have any additional tips you'd like to share about Portnoy or Barstool, please shoot me a note at…"

Portnoy admitted, "I'm walking around waiting for a piano to drop on my head. Just sitting here waiting for these fucking people to do it again. I can't stop people from making accusation."

If it's not obvious by now, Dave felt like the victim. While *Business Insider* had portrayed him as preying on younger girls, Dave explained that, in fact, this sort of thing went in the opposite direction: "Go through my DMs. I get pursued *aggressively*." In response to people saying it's morally wrong for him to be going after these 19- or 20-year-olds, Portnoy replied, "I don't go after them, they go after *me*. These girls, I'm not sliding into their DMs, they're aggressively sliding into my DMs." Portnoy continued to explain, "After I made that 'How to DM' video [he refers to it as a funny video, in which he tells girls in order to get noticed with a DM, say 'I fuck'], I had a zillion girls [DM'ing me] 'I fuck, I fuck, I fuck.'"

Gaz corroborated this: "Being out in Miami with him, I know how many girls are messaging him. I know when I'm in Nantucket how many people want to hang out, I know how much he doesn't want to have parties at his place. I'd stand up for him on that 100% at all times."

Portnoy continued in this vein, saying "I'm being heavily pursued. I'm not doing anything creepy. Now you can argue 'hey, just by ever hooking up with a 19- or 20-year-old in your life, you're creepy at … 40, you can argue that…. If you have a moral problem with it, that's fine, change the laws of the country." He also explained, with a hint of anger:

> "[But] if you're gonna say it's wrong for me to accept [these advances], then I'd say 75 to 80 percent of well-known single people 45 and under are all going to jail. I go out in Miami, it's guys in their 30s, 40s [and girls in their] young 20s, no one blinks an eye. Also, I would call bullshit on a lot of fucking guys out there who are sitting on their fucking couches, with their fucking beer bellies and drinking, when a fucking gorgeous 20-year-old [says] 'hey, I'm really into you, can we hang out?' and they're like 'No no,' get the fuck out of here. And I love our audience, but all you losers at home who aren't rich, famous, and single have no idea the amount of pussy that is being thrown at me."

Portnoy had supposedly fallen prey to the trappings of fame:

"I don't realize—this is gonna sound cocky—how big I've gotten. To me, I'm me. I'm still kind of [back in Milton] eating the baguette. Am I going to be far more careful going forward? Yeah, of course. But it never crossed my mind because I wasn't doing anything wrong."[1]

Portnoy also said he'd never videotape sex again, and he lamented the fact that *Business Insider*, as well as that leaked tape, had made him seem sex-crazed. He said that the dog collar used in that video was pretty much the only time he had ever done that.

For a young woman living in 2021, reaching someone famous was as simple as a click of a button. In Nardini's response to the article, she commented on this notion: "What you're seeing in this case is there are a lot of women who are approaching Dave of all different ages [from] all different places who are looking for a variety of things, they're finding them and then they're talking about them. And I think it raises a lot of questions about sex culture and celebrity." The Barstool CEO continued by stating she has a zero-tolerance policy on anything criminal, and she explained her own role in this:

"My purview, our purview is to maintain a workplace that is strong and has good standards and that is a safe place for people to work and where issues that make people uncomfortable or that put people in difficult positions are able to be resolved confidentially and with positive resolution. I don't think it's an employer's job to manage someone's private life."

---

1   This quote is a combination of two separate quotes from Portnoy. You will see in the back of this book that there are two different sources listed. You can copy-paste the link to see where each part came from.

When viewed through the lens of a CEO, one could argue this was a rational approach. No charges were filed, and Portnoy wasn't pulling a John Lasseter at Pixar; Barstool had never had anything public come out about alleged harassment inside its walls.[2]

But Nardini wouldn't intervene, mostly because she believed Portnoy, saying:

> "The thing that's most important to me is that the piece has kind of fallen apart in the aftermath in terms of the facts weren't well constructed. In fact, they've been pretty directly refuted. Two, the piece matched a narrative by a reporter with a lack of oversight from her editors and was used to fuel a subscription machine known as *Business Insider*... Dave Portnoy is the most honest, forthright person I have ever met and 100% to a fault. I believe him and what the facts are showing is that what Dave is saying is true...and I've been through a whole gamut of emotions, I know Dave has been through the whole gamut himself, it was hard to see someone I work so closely with [go through that], who I have so much respect for, who I have a deep friendship and partnership with, who I care about immensely. And it rocked us, it just...rocked us."

Following the release of Julia Black's article, *The Daily Beast* reporter Zachary Petrizzo tweeted:

> "Barstool Sports employees are currently 'on edge,' according to a person inside the company. 'Everyone's kind of on eggshells at the moment.'"
>
> —@ZTPetrizzo

---

2   John Lasseter, head of Pixar and the creative mind behind *Toy Story and other Pixar classics was removed from the company in 2019 following accusations of sexual misconduct in the workplace.*

Despite Petrizzo's reporting and Nardini's comments saying they were rocked by the story, Portnoy received overall support from his employees, via email or in person. Portnoy had sent them an email right before the article came out, stating that it wasn't true, and if they had any questions, they could speak with him about it. As the boss, however, it was sometimes difficult for Portnoy to determine just how sincere their backing was. Following his hour-long press conference, when asked what his employees thought of his performance, Dave said, "I'm not going to get a real answer from these people; they'll say I deserve an Oscar." However, one thing was certain: while those first few moments after the story dropped might have been tenser than usual inside the Barstool office, unlike during the cancel-culture saga, no one left the company. Portnoy also said he appreciated the notes he received from Barstool employees.

Two people whose opinions he did trust were Clancy and Katz, since both had been with him for more than a decade. In a video posted on YouTube addressing the situation, Clancy echoed Nardini's opinion that the supposed facts inside the piece were poorly constructed, and he drew on his own experience with this sort of situation:

> "I can speak from going through my own scandal, where I had personal details and salacious details of my sex life put out there, that when you write an article about someone, you use certain words, you use certain quotes, you use certain details that are like the illicit details and the salacious parts of everything, you can paint a picture where everyone who reads it [is] gonna just draw the conclusion that this person looks like a scumbag. I firmly believe that writing this kind of shit about people's personal lives, when you don't know the details, when a lot of it is 'he said/she said' or an incomplete picture, it's not a fair thing to put somebody

through. That's why painting this as some sort of investigative journalism is fucking crazy."

Katz's public comment on the situation came in the form of a
retweet of Portnoy's first response video: "If you read the *BI* article,
please also watch this video." As for Portnoy's inner circle, he had
told his parents in advance that the *Business Insider* article was coming, and they stood by him:

> "People who love Barstool will continue to love it;
> haters will continue to hate it. This is the world we
> live in. By the way, I love my son."
>
> —@TheCousinMike

As did his girlfriend, Instagram model Silvana Mojica, whom
he had started dating earlier that year, and his ex-wife Renee, who
tweeted that November that she would always support Portnoy.
Still, the entire situation was undoubtably difficult for Dave, as he
explained:

> "I may have this [tough] exterior, but it sucks. There's no
> other way to say it. To be accused of these things sucks. And
> the relationship with Silvana has been super hard. Like bru-
> tal. She's been super supportive; it's just stressful. No par-
> ents, no [significant other] is meant to see the shit that's
> being put out there."

But the support was there. In an unexpected turn of events,
Jordyn Hamilton of the SoulCycle drama even reached out to
Portnoy with words of encouragement. And Stoolies, as they always
had, rallied around Dave after his hour-long DM-filled denial. Some
more seriously than others:

> ○ "This is a future blueprint for everyone to know how to deal
>   with untrue allegations, Dave is blazing trails. Bravo."

- ○ "I wish more celebrities that were falsely accused would do this…if there really is no evidence, then defend yourself publicly."
- ○ "*I have craved fill from you.*' Sounds Eastern bloc."

With respect to their thoughts on *Business Insider*'s journalistic integrity, the Barstool fanbase collectively blasted *BI*'s decision to place the article behind a paywall (partly because they didn't want to pay for it) as a shady exploitation of sexual assault victims and a revelation of its true motivation for writing the piece. But what rallied them further—evidenced by the fact that the next Black Friday event raked in the most dollars in the history of the company—was Portnoy's defiance. Although he may have shown a more vulnerable side on his *Dave Portnoy Show* podcast, if his response video wasn't clear enough, Portnoy let fans know where he stood on the matter the day after the story hit the internet:

> "Imagine not buying the $penn dip today. I'm not
> a financial advisor. I'm also not going anywhere."
>
> —@stoolpresidente

Portnoy headed to Tucker Carlson to defend himself, with the Fox News host framing his segment by stating, "The question is, can *Business Insider* succeed in killing Dave Portnoy? That's a question anybody interested in free speech should care about." Portnoy didn't avoid talking politics on this particular appearance. The Barstool founder believed because he had interviewed Trump, this attack was somewhat politically motivated, as he told tell Tucker: "I'm being treated like a politician, and politics is the dirtiest game there is."

His fans also watched him pull a vintage "Grudge Dave" move when tech journalist Kara Swisher hosted a Twitter Spaces (basically a public conference call).[3] When Portnoy noticed Blodget was on the call, he hopped in and ambushed the *Business Insider* CEO: "So, I saw that piece of shit Henry Blodget's on this call. My first question is why would a piece of shit who's banned from the SEC for talking about stocks be on there?" As Swisher tried to stop Portnoy, "Alright, Dave alright," he continued talking over her: "My second question is, hey Henry, you fucking coward, you know everything you wrote about me was bullshit; why don't you ever sit down with me, you fucking piece of shit coward?" Blodget's mic remained on mute.

Following his weeks-long defense, Portnoy told his fans he believed he had dominated the PR melee against *Business Insider*. "I feel like I've won the public opinion battle. I feel like I have come across far better than *Business Insider*. I don't think anybody who has willingly looked at the facts of that article can ever be like, Dave did anything illegal."[4] Again, Portnoy was never charged with a crime. And in some sense, his public defense and willingness to fight the charges head on (despite his lawyers telling him to remain quiet) was enough to clear him in some people's minds. If *they* were innocent, they'd scream it from the mountain tops, or so the thinking usually goes.

But it has been pointed out that Portnoy had made jokes about sexual assault. And if his most graphic jokes lined up with the description of what happened in the *Business Insider* article, the PR battle might have tilted in a different direction.

> *Business Insider* 2021: "She arrived at Portnoy's four-bed-room home about 3 p.m... 'It was so painful,' Madison said. 'I kept trying to get away and he was like, 'Stop running

---

3   Swisher was the same journalist that The Chernin Group was supposed to send its Barstool investment announcement to, back in 2016.

4   This quote is a combination of two separate quotes from Portnoy. You will see in the back of the book that there are two different sources listed. You can copy-paste the link to see where each part came from.

away from me. Stop running away from me." But Portnoy, she said, 'just went harder.'

Portnoy's blog 2011: "The bigger issue is, why was she getting changed in the CEO's house? Like if you're this hot and you work for me, and you enter my home, you better believe you're getting a dick or at the very least a tongue rammed down your face. Seriously, what did she think was gonna happen here?"

Portnoy claimed these statements were simply him trolling the feminists in 2011-2012, around the time of the rise of the "Knockout Barstool" movement. But in this particular example about a hypothetical employee getting changed at his house, Portnoy hit on a specific critique in the *Business Insider* article, which painted him as a Harvey Weinstein apologist:

"Take a 2017 episode of the podcast *Barstool Radio*, during which Portnoy seemed to defend a hypothetical casting-couch scenario in which Harvey Weinstein says to a struggling actress, 'Hey, if you sleep with me, I'm going to put you in a starring role.'

"'No force, just a question,' the Barstool founder said. 'Do you have a problem with that trade?'"

Dave disputed this claim as taken out of context:

"It's such a preposterous lie. They quoted something I never said. The actual clip from Barstool radio was when we were talking when the Harvey Weinstein case first broke, it was myself, Kevin Clancy, Fran, and Tommy. I was talking to Fran: it was like a woman in the conversation and the thing starts with Kevin [saying] 'he's a monster, he's the worst' and the discussion just turned into more [about] should prostitution be legal."

However, even before that 2017 Barstool Radio episode and the 2011 blog, Portnoy had been making other jokes on this topic:

○ 2008: "So if you're interested in this high-paying, high-profile, high-stress job, send me an email to portnoy@barstoolsports.com. Hot chicks who love giving BJs in the front seat of Astrovan get preference."

○ 2009: "Blah, blah, blah. Listen, I know a thing or two about hiring sluts, and I can promise you this much: nobody in the smut business gives a rat's ass [how] a chick [speaks]. It's all about how good you look and how good you are at sucking cock."

Portnoy wrote about sexual assault and the power dynamics of a young woman and an older male boss. He called them jokes, simply words on a page. But a decade later, these jokes manifested themselves into accusations he had to answer for. If the Barstool founder had listened to those young college students who rallied against him at Northeastern, he might have avoided this entire situation. But if he had, would Barstool be as popular as it is today? I think you know the answer to that by now. And that is where the issue becomes larger than just one man behind a keyboard.

As for the impact *Business Insider*'s article had on Barstool's business, advertisers stuck with the company, for the most part. Snickers reportedly backed out of an ad deal it was negotiating with Barstool, but there was no reported mass exodus from Barstool's corporate partners. It was similar to the outcome that had occurred a year earlier, during the cancel culture movement, when ad purchasers at Macy's department store reportedly stopped working with the company, but almost everyone else continued to work with Portnoy.

(NASCAR put a pause on its partnership with Barstool during Covid, but it resumed working with the company in 2021.) Even if there had been a mass exodus of sponsors, Nardini, as she set out to when she took the job, hedged Barstool against something like that happening. By that time, almost half of the company's revenue came from merchandising and licensing agreements.

Still, Portnoy would bemoan the fact that *Business Insider* was putting his business—and more specifically, his employees—at least somewhat at risk:

> "If another hit piece comes out, does it matter if it's true or not? At some point, is an advertiser [thinking] how many times [will this happen?] That's where they [*Business Insider*] get you. People don't understand: I always think about the company. I'm always going to be fine. But they are so bloodthirsty for me, they don't think about the people they're affecting."

Portnoy said that if his name were taken off the allegations, there wasn't a person who wouldn't believe the subject of *Business Insider*'s article was innocent. He believed the hatred for him alone was why this supposed witch hunt was occurring. In an interview, when asked "Do you think in a world where you did leave, do you think those people would stop going after Barstool?" Portnoy bluntly replied, "Yes, I do." But the Barstool founder had signed a five-year deal, and as he tweeted, he wasn't going anywhere.

37

The most significant reaction to the allegations was to come from the company Portnoy had signed that deal with. Barstool's future hung in the balance: the acquisition by Penn Gaming was a two-part deal for this very reason. If Penn wanted to, it could back out of fully buying Barstool. But as he did during the cancel culture movement, Snowden stuck behind Portnoy. From his article in New York Magazine, Reeves Wiedeman reported:

> "The day after Portnoy's 'Emergency Press Conference,' Jay Snowden, the CEO of Penn, hosted a conference call with non-Barstool employees at Penn. More than 300 people were on the Microsoft Teams call at 4 p.m. on Friday, November 12. According to multiple people on the call, Snowden more or less defended Portnoy, dismissing the *Business Insider* story as sensational and suggesting that other media companies like to take shots at Portnoy because they are jealous of his success. The furthest he went to acknowledge the severity of the allegations was to say that the story had been 'emotional' to read, and he encouraged his employees to watch Portnoy's press-conference response. Penn's head of HR asked Snowden a few questions, and the meeting ended. During the call, Snowden wore a Barstool quarter-zip sweatshirt. (Penn did not respond to a request for comment.)"

Meanwhile, Penn attempted to cover its bases, sending an email to gambling regulators the morning of the article's publication, with the subject reading "Confidential—David Portnoy Article." In this email, Penn's chief compliance officer, Chris Soriano, wrote, "We wanted to reach out to let you know that we have seen the article, understand the serious nature of these allegations, and are reviewing it carefully." By that point, Penn had successfully earned licenses in three more states (following the first in Pennsylvania)—Michigan, Illinois, and Virginia—and was in the process of applying for more, including New York, the highest-populated state with legalized gambling. Whether or not Portnoy had jeopardized Penn's chances for a NY license, Snowden said in his defense of Barstool and Portnoy, "Barstool has delivered on what they said they would do." The company had increased its revenue by 150% since joining Penn, and "they're profitable," Snowden added, "which is rare for a lot of digital media businesses."

But in the weeks following Penn's vote of confidence, Portnoy's fear of another exposé was mounting; "I'm hearing rumors that they are going to hit me again," he told his fans. And his premonition was correct. On January 20, a little over two months after *Business Insider*'s publication, the Barstool founder took to Twitter:

"Julia Black and *Business Insider* Are Preparing to Drop Another Make-Believe Hit Piece on Me Today:

"Ok, Emergency Press Conference time. My old friend, that scumbag Julia Black, is back up to her old tricks. I got an email yesterday like 'Hey Dave, here's a billion new allegations about you being a sexual deviant and some sort of pervert and you should be in jail. You gotta respond in 24 hours or we're printing it'...I have distinct evidence that what they're saying and what they felt about me is not true. This time, we sent it to Julia Black."

Portnoy had an insider at *Business Insider*. "We had a mole," he told his fans later. Someone working at the Axel Springer-owned company sent Portnoy the exact copy of what Julia Black was planning on publishing (*Business Insider* would conduct an internal investigation to find out who sent him the article, but it's unclear if anyone was ever found) and unlike last time, Portnoy responded to her 24-hour deadline email with a detailed rebuttal, which included his correspondence with the accusers that he said contradicted *Business Insider*'s accounts:

> "She fucking has [the evidence]. So, she knows what she is about to print is garbage, not the truth, defame, you name it, she knows it now…I debated publishing the charges before them, with the evidence [which proves] that they're full of shit, but this is a game of cat and mouse at this point; I want to sue the fuck out of Julia Black and *Business Insider*, so I want them to publish it *knowing* that they have the evidence. And my lawyers said if I publish it first then they can be like 'we didn't do damage he already did it.'"

In the tweet, Portnoy included the letter sent to *Business Insider* by his lawyer, whose firm also sent one of the subjects of the article a notice demanding she retract her statements. He ended the video with this declaration:

> "Your move, Julia…you know you're setting me up again, you know that none of this shit is true. These girls *want* to hang out with me. They solicited sex with me, they *wanted* to be there. And I have the proof. If you drop this article like you say you are, then I'll drop my evidence instantly. They're just trying to be like, look there's 6 girls, 8 girls, where there's smoke, there's fire. No, there's not. I've debunked every single one of them; there's no truth to any of this shit. Again, your move Julia, your move *Business Insider*…let's see whose got the big balls now."

Despite Portnoy's threat of litigation, *Business Insider* published the story. On February 2, two weeks after its initial email to Portnoy requesting comment, the article hit the internet:

"3 more women say Barstool Sports founder Dave Portnoy filmed them without asking during sex" —Julia Black and Melkorka Licea

"...Three more young women have told *Insider* that Portnoy filmed them during sex without asking for permission. They ranged in age from 18 to mid-20s at the time. One of these women, given the pseudonym Kayla by *Insider*, says Portnoy broke one of her ribs during an encounter that he filmed. A physician diagnosed the injury as an 'assumed fracture'....In total, five women have now told *Insider* that Portnoy filmed them during sex without seeking permission. Four of them said the sex that was recorded started consensually but then turned violent and frightening beyond what they would have agreed to had they been asked.

"One of these five women had a different experience. She said the sex with Portnoy was rough, but consensual throughout. However, she told *Insider* that she never consented to Portnoy filming her during sex."

This time, Portnoy did not host an hour-long press conference. Instead, he opted for a short video denying the accusations that sat above a detailed written defense. Portnoy included the following points and opinions in this blog:

- A review and further denial of the three previous women's allegations. He included the fact that Madison created an OnlyFans account the day after the first hit piece was published. He also provided a video of her admitting to lying to manipulate people.

○ The fact that Muj followed Madison on Twitter (Muj was the employee who had publicly denounced Barstool and quit during the cancel-culture movement). And he mentioned that Madison also followed Sofia Franklyn on social media, who he claims was digging up dirt on him during their contract dispute.

○ DMs (some explicit) that showed the only girl *Business Insider* named in the new article—Black gave her the pseudonym Kayla—continued to correspond with Portnoy three years after her encounter, and these DMs contradicted some of her statements in the article. As for the rib injury, he wrote, 'I remember her joking about her rib injury even though she says she never told me about it. Once again, I have proof we joked about it and she's lying." He provided a DM with her joking about it.[1]

○ The original excerpt Julia Black was going to publish of a detailed account from a second woman (not Kayla) before Portnoy's lawyer responded with his email containing Portnoy's correspondence with her. He alluded to the fact that this woman was mad that he began dating his girlfriend (instead of her) and included DMs that showed her as recently as three weeks before the article was published, telling him she did not speak badly about him to *Business Insider* (and included texts from her friend, warning Portnoy that the woman was turning on him). Julia Black mentioned her in the story, saying she stopped cooperating once Portnoy made his lawyer's letter public.

---

1   *Business Insider* acknowledged that Portnoy disputed her statement that she didn't tell him about the rib injury through his lawyer Andrew Brettler. Brettler represented other high-profile clients such as Prince Andrews and Armie Hammer.

Portnoy did not address claims from the third unnamed woman in the article, who claimed the sex was consensual but the filming was not. Instead, he addressed the claims of videotaping with the women's permission by stating in his video, "I've never filmed anyone without their consent" and wrote the following in his blog:

"One of the main themes in the *Business Insider* article is that I video girls without their consent. This is absolutely not true. I have never done that once in my life, and I never will. I'm so scarred, I'll probably never video again anyway. But it doesn't even make sense the way they claim it happens. Like these girls say I video them without consent and I'm too rough for them, and then they come back over a week later and we have sex again and I video them without consent again, and then they come back over a week later and I video them again without consent. All the while, we are actively texting and DM'ing each other without them saying a word to me that they are upset."

In addition to claiming Portnoy filmed without permission, the article also stated:

"A total of four women have now told *Insider* that Portnoy has sent them at least 19 unsolicited videos of what appears to be him having sex with other women…'He would text me or message me and be like 'Hey I thought you'd like this,'" [Kayla] said. 'First of all, no I don't like it. Second of all, I doubt that girl knows that you're sending that degrading video to other girls'… Annie Seifullah, an attorney at C.A. Goldberg PLLC, a national law firm that represents victims of privacy violations and sexual abuse, explained that in New York under a 2019 law, 'Even if a person consents to having an intimate image being taken in the first place, it is still a violation of the law for someone to distribute that image without their consent' if there's intent to harass, annoy, or alarm."[2]

In his response blog, Portnoy did not deny sending videos of him having sex with other women, but dismissed the idea that this sort of content was unwelcomed, stating, "I would never just keep sending girls explicit material if they weren't responding positively towards it." On this notion, *Business Insider* wrote:

"Brettler [Portnoy's lawyer] wrote that she [Kayla] also responded to a sexually explicit video Portnoy had sent her in which she wrote 'fucking hot . . . miss that dick.' [this DM exchange is posted in his denial blog] Kayla told Insider she didn't recall writing these messages but usually answered sexually explicit videos he sent her with short replies meant to end the conversation quickly."

After Portnoy's second denial, *Business Insider* released an Editor's Note. Here is an excerpt from that:

"...We published our stories on Dave Portnoy because we consider them to be in the public interest and newsworthy.

"When a rich, famous, and powerful person uses their power in a way that is harmful to other people, it is newsworthy. When such a person faces such accusations from credible sources and denies them—and then more accusers make new, credible accusations that corroborate and add detail to the alleged pattern of behavior, it is newsworthy.

---

2   The notion of Portnoy allegedly sending unsolicited explicit content was not mentioned in the first *Business Insider* article. BI said it reviewed several of these videos. Another woman is quoted in the article as saying they were "so awful" and she "just stopped responding to him."

"It is wrong to take a sexual encounter that began consensually and turn it violent without first asking one's sexual partner for permission. Five young women have now told *Insider* they experienced sex with Portnoy that began consensually but turned more violent and degrading than they would have agreed to.

"It is wrong to film someone during sex without asking. This article and *Insider*'s November report have credible allegations from five women who say Portnoy did that.

"They say realizing he was recording them was humiliating and made them feel powerless and at risk during and after their encounters with him. They say knowing he may still have videos and photos of them on his phone makes them feel fearful to this day."[3]

Portnoy, again, wasn't charged with a crime. However, unlike the previous article published in November, the public response from Nardini and the other leaders of Barstool was much quieter, if not nonexistent. (The Chernin Group did not issue a public statement following either article.) But Snowden again supported Portnoy. The Penn CEO explained to shareholders on Penn's Q4 call, "The allegations are from anonymous sources made about Dave in his personal life and Dave has responded publicly—many of you have probably seen that—just as he did last time." He then asked them to compare Dave's response with the accusations before making a verdict on the Barstool founder. Snowden was also more defensive about the *timing*

---

3   *Business Insider* added a fifth woman to the claims that "sex with Portnoy began consensually but turned more violent and degrading than they would have agreed to" by the time they issued this note. One of the women also accused Portnoy of sending the video he recorded of her to a friend, which is illegal to do without her consent. Both *Business Insider* articles detailed in this book are excerpts, as is the Editor's Note.

of the second article, which was published the day before this earn-ings call "from the same paywall, subscription-based publisher as the last article and which also happened to be on the same day as our earnings call exactly three months ago."

Business Insider denied the timing of both articles being pub-lished right as Penn released its financials to the public was coor-dinated, saying, "Of course, we did not time our story around their earnings," a spokesperson told *The New York Post*. A few days after the second article was released, Penn's stock fell to $45, down 40% from the day before the first article was published.[4]

The title of the long blog Portnoy posted detailing his defense after the second article dropped read as follows: **"I Am Officially Suing Julia Black and *Business Insider*."** Portnoy stayed true to his word, filing a lawsuit for defamation and invasion of privacy against CEO Henry Blodget, editor-in-chief Nicholas Carlson, and reporters Julia Black and Melkorka Licea.

In the lawsuit, Portnoy claimed *Business Insider* caused "signifi-cant and irreparable damage" to his reputation and business, stating by that point, Barstool Sports had lost at least $12 million in adver-tiser revenue since the first article was published. Almost ten months later, in November 2022, Chief U.S. District Judge F. Dennis Saylor of Massachusetts dismissed the case, stating Portnoy did not "clear [the] high bar" of proving *Business Insider* acted with actual malice when publishing both articles.[5] They remain on its site today.

---

4   Penn reported disappointing earnings again.
5   In the Judge's written opinion dismissing the case, he added a footnote saying that "the article does not reasonably suggest that plaintiff had an intent to secretly record her, as the crime of surreptitious recording would require. See Mass. Gen. Laws ch. 272, § 105(b)."

38

In the summer of 2023, Barstool was preparing to head west—or at least some of the company was. Katz had made it clear for several years now that his goal was to move back home to Chicago to raise his kids: the former editor of *The Hot Glove* blog was now married with three young children. "I've made some money, I have a family, I want to live in the city I want to live in. If you told me for the next ten years, I had to live in New York, I'd seriously contemplate, you know, do I want to do that? Do I want to find another job? But I don't want to find another job, I only want to work for Barstool. I'm getting older. Fucking sucks."

A few months earlier, in April, *Crain's Chicago* reported that Barstool had leased a warehouse at near Fulton Market in the city's West Loop neighborhood. The two-floor, 40,000-square-foot space featured a basketball court in the center of the complex, AstroTurf, a golf-simulator, an industrial kitchen for cooking content, multiple studios for recording podcasts (*Pardon My Take*, *The Dogwalk*, *The Yak*, *A New Untold Story*, to name a few) a green room, a green-screen room, a gambling cave, two fully-stocked bars (a staple of The Stool) and last but not least, actual offices.

The fantasy-factory setup was something Katz and others at Barstool had pictured as a vehicle to newer, more entertaining content; besides Katz wanting to go back home to Chicago, this sort of space just wasn't realistic in Manhattan. However, even including the midwestern discount, the effort cost Penn a cool $20M. When Portnoy was asked if he would have made this move if it were his money, he replied, "Yes, I think I would have, because Dan is so critically important to everything we do. He wanted to move back there; he's bringing a lot of the company. I think there will be return on that."

By August, half of the company's content creators had moved to Chicago, while the other half remained in New York. The move left Barstool fragmented. From the Stoolie's point of view, if you were a Barstool talent, the Chicago office was where you wanted to go. And some employees in New York agreed. "They [Chicago] are the A team, they are the focus of the company," Francis Ellis said on an episode of *Barstool Radio*.[1] "I think the truth of the matter is that there's a sense of loss ever since those guys went to Chicago...there's a major inferiority complex running around here."

"The [NY] office is just a place for resources now," Clancy said. "It's not really a house of content anymore. I used to finish up in the studio, then walk back over to the blogger bullpen to get on *Stool Scenes* or stir the pot, talk some shit. Now people just come here and use the studios, it's not really an atmosphere of content."

Kelly Keegs, another host of NY's *Barstool Radio* show, elaborated on this after a caller highlighted the fact that the quality of entertainment coming out of the New York office had taken a nosedive since the move. "I think there is a void of leadership in the NY office. Dan himself is a force, people orbit him and do whatever he says. We don't have that same element now. A lot of people were affected by this split in content people, and we just need to kind of figure it out. You hope that someone would step up to lead by example because that's what Big Cat does."

Katz may have felt a tinge of guilt: him wanting to be back in Chicago affected pretty much the entire company. Barstool had signed a ten-year lease at its current NYC office, which meant some people had to stay behind, and the Chicago native took back with him mostly those with whom he created content. Of course, there

---

1   Ellis had been rehired by Barstool after being fired for his blog on the missing University of Utah student.

were also some who simply couldn't uproot their lives and leave the east coast. But to those who questioned his move, Katz responded, "I remember when we first opened the Chicago office, I [felt] this has been a decade of my work. And I don't want to say I deserve it, but I've worked very hard for this, so anyone who [thinks] 'Oh, this is bullshit,' no it's not."

Stoolies attempted to drum up a rivalry between the new offices, just like the old days, but Katz downplayed this notion: "Barstool is my life; I'll work here for the rest of my life. If New York died, that'd be a very big blow to the company. So [with respect to the rivalry thing] I don't want you [NY content people] guys to fail; I want you guys to succeed even better than everyone so I can retire someday."

With Katz gone, the absence of Portnoy became glaring: for example, Dave used to stand in front of the elevator and interrogate every employee who walked in late (to the amusement of the Stoolies). Keegs said, "It's Dave we're missing. Dave is not here all the time; he's been here this week, and we've had the best week. We love Dave here: it puts everybody on edge in a good way." Borrowing his line, Keegs called Portnoy "The straw that stirs the drink."

By 2023, Dave had taken a step back from content. This development had nothing to do with the *Business Insider* accusations or the subsequent failed lawsuit, which Portnoy knew he would probably lose: "a famous person can't win this case" he admitted to his fans, after telling them he went against the advice of his lawyers and sued anyway. Portnoy also wrote, "The reason *Business Insider* gets away with the shit they do is because they bank on guys like me who are not willing to go through the hassle of a lawsuit. Who don't want to spend tons of money and potentially years of their lives inside a courtroom. This is where they fucked up with me." It was a bold effort. It didn't work. Although Portnoy would probably argue the lawsuit was just a means to an end, which was to prove he would fight *Business Insider* until he legally couldn't (though he eventually dropped his appeal).

Following this saga, the founder retained his usual bombastic online presence, tweeting an updated *"Hate List"* with the *Business Insider* crew now slotted at the top, just ahead of Roger Goodell and John Skipper. Towards the end of 2023, Dave celebrated with his patented champagne bottle when Henry Blodget was "fired" from *Business Insider*; he stepped down from the CEO role and became chairman. Here's Dave's response to this:

> "The guy who tried to run me out of town, that guy's gone. Out. Now, I have a champagne bottle, ready for him, engraved with his name on it, but I think it's in my Nantucket house. Wait, is it in my Saratoga house? Is it in my Miami house? No, I'm here. Oh, it's in my Montauk house. I got so many houses, I can't remember what wine cellar it's in. It's in the Montauk house. So, when I go back there for the summer, I'll get the bottle, and I'll pop it rightfully. But for now, Henry you piece of shit, kicked upstairs. They have this thing 'Oh, he's on the board,' you're not the board, he got fucking outed. So, here's to you, Henry, you piece of shit. Another one bites the dust."

Portnoy's popularity didn't wane following the *Business Insider* articles; quite the opposite. Just a couple of months later, the Barstool founder shared his experience meeting a certain celebrity, who turned out to be a fan. "Wayne Gretzky came up to me and [said], 'Sorry to bother you, do you mind if we get a picture together?'" It seemed the Barstool founder was in fact "uncancelable."

Portnoy's decreased day-to-day role at Barstool actually had begun during Covid, when he left New York for Miami and never permanently returned (for tax purposes, he was required to spend more than half the year in Florida, where he declared his residency). Portnoy explained this decision at the time:

"As I've been working remote, I've come to believe I can work remote full time. If I have to come to New York I'll come to New York. But I can do so much stuff in Miami, I'm there anyways. And for taxes, at the end of like five years, I'll either have the same amount of money in NY, or I'll have the same amount of money in Miami except I'll have a place I own. So if you can do it, it's really stupid financially not to do it."

Still under contract with Penn, he continued to host several podcasts, travel with the crew to do the *College Football Show* and Penn-sponsored events (related to Penn's opening of several Barstool-themed sportsbooks at its casino locations) and appeared on the Monday rundowns with Clancy and Katz. However, not being in the office everyday naturally limited the amount of Portnoy's exposure on Barstool's site. Clancy explained what that meant for Barstool, and more specifically the New York office: "With Dave, it was never 'I'm leaving the office'; it was just 'I'll be in Miami, I'll be here, whatever,' and I wonder if he had [said] 'I'm leaving, a new era needs to start,' if it [had been] announced like that, would it have been different [here]?"

When asked on *The Dave Portnoy Show* about his absence affecting the company, Portnoy said bluntly, "It is what it is." Despite this development, in some ways Barstool had come full circle: Katz was back in Chicago, Clancy was in New York, and Portnoy was off in his own office, though this one wasn't based in Milton and happened to be squirrel-free. The Barstool founder operated remotely from either South Beach, Nantucket, or Montauk.

It was an arrangement Penn National Gaming seemed comfortable with. In February, a year after the second *Business Insider* article was released about Portnoy, Snowden's company completed its acquisition of Barstool Sports, doling out another several hundred million dollars to buy the remaining stake of Portnoy's website, making Portnoy & Co. even richer. In total, Penn National spent $550M on the Barstool acquisition. "We are extremely pleased to welcome Barstool Sports fully into the PENN Entertainment family," Snowden said in an official press release announcing the deal. PENN provided a checklist of milestones Barstool had achieved in the first three years of its partnership, which included:

- o   Grew its audience 194% and recorded total podcast downloads of 1.6B.

- o   Increased ad sales by 160%.

- o   Sold more than 5 million units, including apparel, licensed products, and accessories.

But in terms of converting its audience to betting customers—which was the number one reason for the acquisition—the results for Barstool were mixed. According to industry research firm Eilers & Krejcik Gaming, the Barstool betting app ranked seventh by revenue in 2023 compared to other apps in the U.S, and it owned only 3% of market share, which was half of what analysts had expected. But in its defense of Barstool's business, Penn said that the newly built Barstool Sportsbooks enticed younger bettors to visit their casinos, and these patrons usually became repeat visitors who spent money gambling, eating, and drinking. On an earnings call in late 2022, Snowden told analysts that 20% of Penn's revenue now came from customers between the ages of 21 and 44, which doubled what that percentage had been only several years earlier. Snowden also said, "Barstool and Mr. Portnoy have been amazing partners for us."

However, even if its numbers began to skew younger, after considering how things had been going with the gambling regulators, Penn's Barstool takeover became a head-scratching move.

39

Following the release of *Business Insider*'s first article about Portnoy, in November 2021, Penn had been denied a sports-betting license in the largest U.S. state with legalized sports gambling: New York. A few months later, in March 2022, after the second article dropped, both Nevada and Indiana's gaming commissions began investigations into Portnoy, according to *The Wall Street Journal*:

> "...In a statement, the board chairman, Brin Gibson, said the [Nevada] board's obligation 'is to protect the reputation of the state and the reputation of the state's gaming industry.' In a public board meeting in December, Mr. Gibson said he had requested information from Penn because he was concerned about Barstool.

> "The Barstool sports-betting app doesn't operate in Nevada. Gambling regulators in Indiana, where Barstool's app does operate, said they are conducting a review of Penn and Barstool related to the recent news articles about Mr. Portnoy."

Indiana's gaming commission let Penn's lawyers know they deemed the accusations as "very serious, requiring prompt communication regarding Penn's planned course of action." In Illinois, the assistant general counsel to the state's gaming commission sent a note to fellow employees stating Portnoy was "a creep who has questionable sexual encounters with much younger [women]."[1]

---

1   Penn paid a $17,000 fine in Illinois for a TikTok video posted by an employee who joked about gambling losses.

It wasn't only the *Business Insider* blowback that Penn was dealing with. Later that year, it was reported that the state of Ohio Casino Control Commission contacted Penn, informing the company that Barstool Sports was facing a potential fine of up to $250,000 for "allegedly targeting underage bettors" at the University of Toledo.[2] Towards the end of 2022, Penn endured a long, drawn-out application process in Massachusetts (Barstool's hometown state), where the state's gaming commission was critical of Barstool's push to attract a younger demographic.

During one hearing, Massachusetts Gaming Commissioner Eileen O'Brien stated,

> "I'm concerned about some of the historical marketing associated with Barstool. And I had that concern historically on what that brand is and reaching out to a demographic that was helpful to your company. It is also a group that is particularly vulnerable to addiction, albeit it over the age of 21 for the most part. This is not simply an article or a conversation about David Portnoy's conduct. This goes to the brand itself."

In the end, Massachusetts granted Penn a Category 3 (temporary) license to operate inside the state, with conditions attached: Penn was required to cooperate with an investigation into Barstool Sports by the IEB (the Investigations and Enforcement Bureau of The Massachusetts Gaming Commission); restrict anyone under the age of 21 from attending *Barstool College Football Show* events; and provide the Commission with workforce diversity goals and information on supplier spend.

---

2 Barstool Sportsbook agreed to pay $250,000 in fines after entering a settlement with the Ohio Casino Control Commission. Penn admitted that an advertisement for their sportsbook that was read during Barstool's College Football Show at the University of Toledo violated Ohio law. Penn's Chief Compliance Officer Chris Soriano said, "In this matter we fell short of the mark. We accept responsibility for that."

In November 2022, around the same time as the comments from the Mass Gaming Commission, *The New York Times* published an article about Penn and Portnoy, titled *"Desperate for Growth, Aging Casino Company Embraced 'Degenerate Gambler.'* The piece was written by Emily Steel, an experienced journalist who won a Pulitzer in 2018 for undercovering the numerous settlements made by Fox News executives over instances of sexual harassment. In her writing, Steel highlighted Portnoy's past admissions of "degeneracy" related to sports betting, and she was the first to report that the Barstool founder had declared bankruptcy in his mid-20s partly due to his gambling addiction.

Of course, she also didn't gloss over the *Business Insider* accusations, and Portnoy claimed that originally Steel had sought to write another exposé in line with those types of articles: "For a year, I'm waiting for *The New York Times* to drop another similar hit piece. They didn't get anything, so they switched to 'Dave's a degenerate gambler.'" Still, the article packed a punch. Having the face of your sports-betting operation be someone who had openly admitted to having problem-gambling issues and who had filed bankruptcy as a (partial) result wasn't the best PR for Penn National Gaming. In her article, Steel quoted Keith Whyte, executive director of the National Council on Problem Gambling, who expressed regret about Portnoy being the face of Penn's sports betting venture, saying, "Portnoy is normalizing sports betting in ways that frankly often come off as irresponsible." Steel also harped on the fact that Barstool's audience was younger, and as O'Brien had said, more susceptible to problem gambling. At a broader level, it was a critique of Snowden's motives for partnering with Barstool: although the goal of angling towards a younger customer base would be viewed as strategic and applauded in other industries, that goal wasn't being received with a warm welcome inside the more hazardous world of sports gambling.

After Steel served up Portnoy on a silver platter to state regulators, the headaches for Snowden & Co. continued. A few months later, in March 2023, the Massachusetts Gaming Commission opened an investigation into Penn after being notified of its *"Can't Lose Parlay"* promo on Barstool Sportsbook. The offering was a satirical reference to Katz's betting record, which was abysmal, and anyone who followed Barstool or bet frequently knew that the odds of the promo hitting were long. (Unlike a straight bet, a parlay is more difficult to win because it requires a bettor to win multiple bets, and if one loses, then the entire parlay loses.)

The MGC didn't find it funny. Instead, the MGC was concerned with first-time gamblers also not getting the joke and believing that the "Can't Lose" promo meant they weren't actually going to lose money, that it was a "risk-free" bet (phrasing that was not allowed on such apps), which was obviously not the case; 90% of users who played the "Can't Lose Parlay" lost their first bet. As Jordan Maynard of the MGC stated, "I'm worried about the one person who doesn't understand the irony and doesn't know about Barstool Big Cat." Penn's argument was that a reasonable consumer would understand the "Can't Lose Parlay" *can* in fact lose, because it was a parlay. But O'Brien countered, "You can't say 'free' or 'risk free'. . . and maybe you can't say 'can't lose.' I don't accept your representation that just knowing bets have risk [is enough]." Ironically, the specific "Can't Lose Parlay" that sparked the investigation ended up winning.[3]

Straight out of a scene from *"My Cousin Vinny,"* Penn's lawyers argued that consumers know the popular cereal product Crunch Berries doesn't actually contain real berries, or that "There's no buffalo in Buffalo Wild Wings, and people understand that." The argument made the ridiculous two-hour hearing even more ridiculous. "This is a fascinating thread on @BarstoolBigCat Can't Lose Parlay (which we stopped doing) under investigation by Ma Gambling Commission," Portnoy tweeted to his fans. Cap'n Crunch and all, the absurdity of the entire two-hour meeting made it painfully obvious

---

3   The Massachusetts Gaming Commission didn't hold the hearing until June.

just how out of touch the gaming commission was with the world Barstool operated in.[4]

After three years navigating the regulatory arena with Barstool at the helm, one might have been inclined to ask Jay Snowden, "Besides all that, Mrs. Lincoln, how did you like the show?" According to a report, before buying Barstool, Penn had spoken with regulators who assured the company that because Barstool was simply Penn's marketing arm, and because technically Barstool wasn't the company being licensed, Portnoy and his company wouldn't undergo a thorough review from state gaming commissions. Obviously, that didn't happen. And as Portnoy had said seven years earlier, following Chernin's initial investment in his company, "You can't get in bed with us without our stink getting all over you." But Penn specially designed its acquisition of Barstool as a two-part deal, to protect against this very happening, which makes Penn's decision to complete the acquisition even more puzzling.

MAY 2023

Although the recent Chicago move had splintered Barstool employees, from a creative standpoint, the last three years under Penn had been fairly smooth. Like Chernin, Penn didn't overly police what sort of entertainment Barstool produced, as long as it wasn't related to problem-gambling. Still, those working at the company knew they had to answer to a corporate owner whenever they hit *publish*, and they were reminded of that fact in the spring of that year.

On May 3, Barstool employee Ben Mintz (known as "Mintzy" to the Stoolies) was hosting his *Wake Up Mintzy* show, a morning program that was recorded live to the Barstool site. Whether or not it was shtick, Mintzy's persona was being a dumb, lovable southern boy who skated by without working hard but still provided entertainment to Stoolies because Portnoy often reamed him out for it.

---

4   Penn had been licensed in 15 states by that time.

During the recording that day, Mintzy was singing along to a rap song while reading the lyrics from his phone, when he accidentally uttered the N-word aloud. Yes, it happened again.

The political climate at the time wasn't nearly as racially charged as when Portnoy's old video had surfaced, but this was still a major screwup (and Mintzy wasn't the boss). Under direction from Penn, Portnoy was forced to fire Mintzy, something he would not have done otherwise, saying:

> "Bad news: this sucks. So today we had to fire Ben Mintz. It stems from his *Wake Up Mintzy*…When it happened, he was immediately horrified and apologized. Not in my wildest dreams did I think we would [have] …to fire Ben Mintz. Penn felt differently. And I'm stunned by it, and I've been fighting tooth and nail, as has Erika, as has Dan, to keep Ben and say this is the wrong decision. But Penn operates in a world that we don't operate in."

Portnoy explained how his parent company was highly regulated by the government, and its all-important state gambling licenses could be taken away just as easily as they were issued. He continued:

> "Penn's a multibillion-dollar company, without their licenses, they are a zero-dollar company. Investors, families, employees, thousands of people, they feel it's their job to protect all of this. And the only answer is to fire Ben Mintz. I *still* disagreed with it. And maybe I'm naïve. I [believe] there is no way anybody can look at that clip and think the punishment fits the crime. It makes my skin crawl thinking a guy would lose their job on an innocent mistake… but from Penn's perspective, it's better than risking the entire livelihood of the company on a fuckup from Ben Mintz.

"And if you don't think Emily Steel is already frothing at the mouth to write about this and send it to the regulators and [ask], 'What are you gonna do about it?' you're not paying attention. So, it is what it is, and hopefully I don't have to make a press conference like this ever again, and it really, really, really sucks. That's all I got."

Portnoy, who was genuinely upset by having to fire Mintz, also worried publicly that the decision might alienate his fanbase:

> "By the way, for everybody saying Barstool is dead to them, I knew this would happen. I said it's so against everything we stand for that it could be a death blow. Penn understood this. They still did it. That's how frightened they were of regulators who operate with no impunity."
>
> —@stoolpresidente

Dave eventually employed a workaround by hiring Mintzy to be a salesman for his new watch company, Brick Watches. (Unfortunately, the company struggled: Stoolies weren't willing to fork over $3,000 for a watch pitched by Portnoy, who was never a watch guy until he started selling them.) But it was clear the Mintzy firing was eating at the founder, who had started Barstool so he could avoid this exact situation. And while he did his best to ignore the noise, Portnoy responded to the Stoolies:

> "So, I got every Tom, Dick, and Harry since this Mintzy thing [saying] 'Pres, you're a sellout; you're a sellout; hey Pres, you sold out.' This decision sucks, I hate it, it makes me want to puke, but guess what? When I 'sold out,' these decisions became no longer mine."

As the 20th anniversary of Barstool approached, Portnoy found himself making decisions that were "everything I've stood against for 20 years." He also didn't love being labeled as the reason Penn's stock price dropped or the fact that, as he admitted, "Penn got denied licenses because of me." The world Penn operated in wasn't one he particularly enjoyed: as he said, "Anybody who has followed, any of the states and Penn trying to get legalized and things like that, one thing is clear, they [the regulators] fucking *hate* me." Portnoy said he knew there were "investors, families, employees, thousands of people" affected by the decisions involving his parent company, and as he told *The New York Post* about being the reason regulators rejected Penn: "It was painful on a human level."

40

Whether Portnoy was actually at some sort of crossroads in the summer of 2023 didn't matter. Penn had seen enough. In late July, Snowden called Portnoy and let him know that Penn had signed a sports-betting deal with ESPN; Barstool was out. "It became clear we were an unnatural owner," Snowden told CNBC's Jim Cramer, the same host to whom he had gushed about the deal only three years earlier. "Barstool is not a company and a brand—I think we all came to this conclusion—that should be owned by a publicly traded, highly regulated licensed gaming company." Snowden ended his interview about Barstool with something WEEI and ESPN mostly likely would have advised PENN about after its failed partnerships with Portnoy's company: "There's probably long-term only one natural owner of Barstool Sports, and that's Dave Portnoy."

"It all happened very fast," Dave said on an episode of Barstool's *Stool Scenes*. Penn had been in talks with ESPN for a little while before letting Portnoy know of their plans. In the end, Snowden's company paid $1.5B to the world-wide leader for a ten-year partnership agreement, with ESPN's branding replacing Barstool's on its sportsbook app.[1] When he learned about Penn's deal, Portnoy admitted, "I was shocked." Snowden gave the Barstool founder two options: he could buy Barstool from Penn for the grand total of $1, with certain non-compete stipulations attached, or he could walk away and they would dissolve the company.[2]

---

1   Penn also provided ESPN with another $500M in warrants to buy Penn stock that was to vest over the same time period.

2   Snowden wouldn't publicly say he was going to dissolve the company; this is based on Portnoy's implication that this would happen.

By now, Barstool had around 430 employees. As he pondered the decision Snowden had forced on him, the humble leader selflessly thought of those people. "I care about, I wish I didn't, our idiots out there who would have no future, no lives, no nothing if they didn't work here." It wouldn't be an easy takeover, however; recently under Penn, Barstool had been bleeding money, to the tune of $16M in the first half of 2023 alone. But Portnoy was confident in his ability to turn that around, saying, "When I owned it myself, we always made money." After sleeping on it, Dave decided he wasn't finished with the company he had spent two decades building.

Portnoy spun the transaction as a major victory, and he was eventually hailed in the press for looking like a genius: who else has sold their company for half a billion dollars and bought it back for nothing? Penn, however, wasn't able to hide behind such numbers. After having spent three years dealing with cancel-culture backlash, *Business Insider*, *The New York Times*, and obtuse state regulators, the company wrote down an $800M loss on the Barstool deal. Despite the Barstool transaction costing his company almost $1B, Snowden remains the CEO of Penn Entertainment at the time of this writing.[3]

Portnoy's first move after Penn's departure (aside from having Nardini remain CEO) was to rehire Mintzy, who, staying true to his character, missed the phone call from Dave letting him know he was back with Barstool. When he did finally answer from his car, he almost veered off the road, exclaiming, "Holy shit, I'm floating down the interstate right now!" Soon after this, Portnoy let everyone who worked at Barstool know the news in an all-hands meeting. "Ok,

---

3   Penn lifted the restrictions on the stock owned by the Barstool employees. Also, Penn was entitled to 50% of any future sale of Barstool, and Portnoy agreed to a non-compete that forbade him from entering any sort of contract with another gambling company until after the 2024 NFL football season. Minutes after the Super Bowl in 2024, Portnoy announced a multi-year advertising partnership with DraftKings.

announcement time. Kind of a big one, shocker I'd say. So as of this moment, we are no longer a Penn company. We've gone our separate ways. I've bought back Barstool, so I own all of it now. I have no plans, ever, to sell Barstool again." The large group of employees seated around Portnoy gave an apropos applause. Although Portnoy eventually (and uncharacteristically) laid off 25% of the Barstool staff in order to get closer to profitability, Portnoy still saved the jobs of 300+ workers. And for a while, the founder had been somewhat absent from the company, one which was in need of direction. Portnoy assured his employees that he would be back in the mix. "Just when I think I'm out, they pull me back in."[4]

But as Portnoy regained control, the landscape he and his employees found themselves in looked quite different from the one twenty years earlier. As Clancy said:

> "We helped set this whole industry, and now people can just come in and shoot to the top. I feel like we grinded so much and set the tone for internet content in general that when I see someone else from the outside pop off quickly and have a millionaire career immediately, it infuriates me. One TikTok account and one podcast, and you're worth more than I've ever been worth in a year."

In this vein, Clancy asked Portnoy in a recent interview if he felt that Barstool was in danger of being passed up by up-and-coming talent, to which Dave replied: "No, definitely not. If you're talented, and you look at our track record and look at what we've done, it's kind of a no-brainer joining us if you think long term, because [joining Barstool] is still like taking steroids or rocket fuel, in two to three years you're going to go from normal to huge."

Portnoy also told Clancy he didn't worry about another competitor platform coming in and taking Barstool's place, saying, "You

---

4   There were plans to make the NYC office the "Comedy Office" via partnering with established comedians, but this plan was shut down once Penn sold Barstool.

couldn't restart Barstool now." Clancy added, "I don't think it'll ever happen again." Dave explained why he felt this way:

> "When we started, [the rules were] first you had to be on a TV network or radio to get your name out there, and then the internet leveled the playing field, so to speak. And we were the new network that could launch people, which we did. Whether it be Jenna [Marbles] or Alex Cooper. Now people can launch themselves, but I still think that is a harder value prop."

Clancy countered him by asking, "Do you think the same way we looked at big newspapers and ESPN and TV channels like 'you're fucking dinosaurs,' do you think the TikTok generation looks at us like that?"

"I don't," Portnoy responded. "The biggest compliment I get is that Barstool has been culturally relevant for almost two decades. If enough people don't like you or think you're edgy, like the Goodell thing or all the stuff people say about us, it keeps that counterculture vibe."

There had been *a lot* of people who hated Barstool over the years, and although the detractors certainly were a reason for the company's popularity, Clancy asked Portnoy, "If you could snap your fingers, would you go back in time and not have Knockout Barstool happen (who you have to give credit to because they are the ones that stuck that tag on us [and] made us the renegades) and instead stayed the funny sports guy?"

At first, Portnoy answered yes. But then he pondered the decision further, and Clancy pressed him, asking, "If all the *Business Insider* shit went away, but the money was significantly less, what would you do?"

"I'd still take the money."

♣

Dave ended his speech to the Barstool employees on the most important note: "Penn had an opportunity with ESPN, it ended up being really good for us and probably a spot we want to be in anyway. Where we can go back to just being ourselves, we don't have to worry about what we say, what we do."

For the first time in almost a decade, Portnoy had no one to answer to, which wasn't great news for those who landed on his Hate List. "I've got my voice back, I'm naming names," the Barstool founder said. And in his Emergency Press Conference to the loyal Stoolies later that day, Portnoy declared:

> "I'm not going anywhere. Barstool Sports. The pirate ship. The cannons. They will plunder now and for the next hundred years."

NOTES

*The quotes in the prologue are derived from Portnoy and Kern's conversation on: "Dave Portnoy Breaks Down the Chernin Group Deal that Changed Barstool History," *The Dave Portnoy Show*, Barstool Sports; https://www.youtube.com/watch?v=tMjt5jmpkek

CHAPTER 1

Pg. 9, "I don't understand what this money is for" —"The Story of Dave Portnoy Starting Barstool Sports," Barstool Documentary Series, Barstool Sports; https://www.youtube.com/watch?v=J-_6gDCFQGw&list=PLq62m2d0BarrFV3Sxt39ItIg-Ca7ilWN0G&index=2&t=1s

Pg. 11, "Before we started Barstool Sports…" —*Barstool Sports*, November 12, 2003; https://web.archive.org/web/20040701001542/http://www.barstoolsports.com/issues/volume1_issue12_first.pdf

Pg. 11, "The traditional media fed off…" —blog post, barstoolsports.com, January 29, 2020; https://www.barstoolsports.com/blog/1749253/from-the-astrovan-to-a-dollar450-million-moon-rocket-a-heros-journey

Pg. 12, "Dave is hellbent on…" —Jason Ankeny, "The Man Behind the 'Bible of Bro Culture,'" *NBC News*, December 13, 2013; https://www.nbcnews.com/id/wbna53821689

Pg. 12, "Liked to get a little banged up…" —Video posted by Dave Portnoy on his Instagram account, March 18, 2022; http://www.instagram.com/tv/CbPuD9WjtDC/?isgh=MWJ3czdqaHEzaXRhNQ==

Pg. 12, "My son did pretty well on the…." —tweet from Mike Portnoy, April 1, 2022; https://x.com/TheCousinMike/status/1510049471731838978?s=20

Pg. 13, "I really started Barstool just…"; "Yeah, that's for sure" —"Bonus Episode: Dave Discusses Massive Investment from Penn National," Barstool Radio podcast; https://podcasts.apple.com/ie/podcast/bonus-episode-dave-discusses-massive-investment-from/id1085919903?i=1000464021432

Pg. 13, "Dave always had something to say" —"Dave Portnoy Origin Story: Promise Big, Deliver Big," Barstool Documentary Series, Barstool Sports; https://www.youtube.com/watch?v=Qyx641z2dxg&t=460s

CHAPTER 2

Pg. 15, "My dad's an idiot…" —tweet from Mike Portnoy, May 14, 2018; https://x.com/TheCousinMike/status/996190647697727490?s=20

Pg. 15, "Congratulations to my son…" —tweet from Mike Portnoy, August 18, 2022; https://x.com/TheCousinMike/status/1560320875362222083?s=20

Pg. 16, "Funny and loyal…" —Reeves Wiedeman, "The Dave Portnoy Playbook: Staring down the sports-gambling gold rush—and amid sexual misconduct allegations—Barstool's founder bets on the culture war," New York Magazine, November 23, 2021; https://nymag.com/intelligencer/article/dave-portnoy-barstool-sports.html

Pg. 16, "The big thing about him…" —Julia Black, "'I was literally screaming in pain': Young women say they met Barstool Founder Dave Portnoy for sex and it turned violent and humiliating," Business Insider, November 4, 2021; https://www.businessinsider.com/barstool-sports-dave-portnoy-sex-choking-violent-stoolies

Pg. 16, "Waking up early to teach…" —"Dave Portnoy Origin Story: Promise Big, Deliver Big," Barstool Documentary Series, Barstool Sports; https://www.youtube.com/watch?v=Qyx641z2dxg

Pg. 17, "I've been a degenerate gambler my whole life…" —"Dave Portnoy Origin Story: Promise Big, Deliver Big," Barstool Documentary Series, Barstool Sports; https://www.youtube.com/watch?v=Qyx641z2dxg&t=654s

Pg. 17, "I was in my [early] 20s…." —David Meltzer, "Dave Portnoy: Building Barstool Sports: The Playbook Ep #26," https://www.youtube.com/watch?v=ant5txDUuWo

Pg. 18, "I knew I wanted to be in that field…" —Jason Ankeny, "The Man Behind the 'Bible of Bro Culture,'" NBC News, December 13, 2013; https://www.nbcnews.com/id/wbna53821689

Pg. 19, "What a great URL…" —"Dave Portnoy Origin Story: Promise Big, Deliver Big," Barstool Documentary Series, Barstool Sports; https://www.youtube.com/watch?v=Qyx641z2dxg&t=5s

Pg. 19, "They said, 'Don't do a website…" —Jason Ankeny, "The Man Behind the 'Bible of Bro Culture,'" NBC News, December 13, 2013; https://www.nbcnews.com/id/wbna53821689

CHAPTER 3

Pg. 20, "It might as well have been…" —blog post, barstoolsports.com, June 13, 2007; https://web.archive.org/web/20070617143834/http://www.barstoolsports.com/randomthoughts/2007/06/13/#stokke_show_dating_loser

Pg. 21, "When we upgraded from…" —"The Story of Dave Portnoy Starting Barstool Sports," Barstool Documentary Series, Barstool Sports; https://www.youtube.com/watch?v=J-_6gDCFQGw&list=PLq62m2d0BarrFV3Sxt39ItIgCa7ilWN0G&index=2

Pg. 21, "Let's just say…" —Barstool Sports, September 3, 2003; https://issuu.com/barstoolsports/docs/september_3__2003

Pg. 21, "Chaotic and nearly disastrous" —Barstool Sports, September 3, 2003; https://issuu.com/barstoolsports/docs/september_3__2003

Pg. 22, "I really only thought it would last…" —"The Story of Dave Portnoy Starting Barstool Sports," Barstool Documentary Series, Barstool Sports; https://www.youtube.com/watch?v=J-_6gDCFQGw&list=PLq62m2d0BarrFV3Sxt39ItIgCa7ilWN0G&index=2

Pg. 22, "When I pick up Barstool Sports from our…." —Barstool Sports, December 15, 2004; https://web.archive.org/web/20041217040456/http://www.barstoolsports.com/issues/volume2_issue34.pdf

Pg. 22, "I had bins at T-stops…" —"The Story of Dave Portnoy Starting Barstool Sports," Barstool Documentary Series, Barstool Sports; https://www.youtube.com/watch?v=J-_6gDCFQGw&t=330s

Pg. 23, "It was always a good reception when…" —"Dave Portnoy on the Business of Sports Media," Masters in Business Podcast with Barry Ritholtz; https://ritholtz.com/2020/10/transcript-dave-portnoy/

Pg. 23, "Welcome to the world of Barstool Sports…" —First official issue of Barstool Sports, August 27, 2003; https://web.archive.org/web/20040319122457/http://www.barstoolsports.com/, Google Image Search "First issue of Barstool Sports"

Pg. 24, "I haven't slept since Sunday…" —Barstool Sports, September 3, 2003; https://issuu.com/barstoolsports/docs/september_3__2003

Pg. 25, "The holiday season tends to…" —Barstool Sports, December 3, 2003; https://issuu.com/barstoolsports/docs/december_3__2003

Pg. 25, "1. Excuse Guy. Excuse guy is…" —Pre Website Hall of Fame Articles; https://web.archive.org/web/20040330223638/http://barstoolsports.com/halloffame/seven_faces_of_no.pdf

Pg. 26, "A few weeks ago, I mentioned…" —Barstool Sports, November 12, 2003; https://web.archive.org/web/20040319122457/http://www.barstoolsports.com/issues/volume1_issue12_first.pdf

Pg. 27, "I know I'm biased and…" —Barstool Sports, December 10, 2003; https://web.archive.org/web/20040331001544/http://barstoolsports.com/issues/volume1_issue16.pdf

CHAPTER 4

Pg. 29, "The bottom-line is…" —Barstool Sports, March 23, 2005; https://web.archive.org/web/20050513230637/http://www.barstoolsports.com/issues/volume3_issue9.pdf

Pg. 30, "I legitimately thought he was…" —"The Story of Dave Portnoy Starting Barstool Sports," Barstool Documentary Series, Barstool Sports; https://www.youtube.com/watch?v=J-_6gDCFQGw

Pg. 30, "Anybody who thinks my son…" —Emily Steel, "Desperate For Growth, Aging Casino Company Embraced 'Degenerate Gambler,'" The New York Times, November 20, 2022; https://www.nytimes.com/2022/11/20/business/barstool-sports-betting-david-portnoy.html

Pg. 31, "Well, I guess that explains…" —blog post, barstoolsports.com; November 20, 2013; https://www.barstoolsports.com/blog/170944/science-proves-once-and-for-all-that-men-objectifying-women-has-no-impact-on-chicks-self-image-at-all

Pg. 31, "Why do most male sports writers…" —Barstool Sports, December 24, 2003; https://web.archive.org/web/20040331012911/http://barstoolsports.com/issues/volume1_issue18.pdf

Pg. 32, "[I] received maybe the biggest compliment…" —Barstool Sports, October 19, 2005; https://web.archive.org/web/20051027001415/http://www.barstoolsports.com/article/Random_Thoughts/510/

Pg. 32 "Speaking of hounding people…" —Barstool Sports, November 19, 2003; https://web.archive.org/web/20040319122457/http://www.barstoolsports.com/issues/volume1_issue12.pdf

Pg. 33, "Weren't interested in marketing that way…" —Barstool Sports, January 7, 2004; https://web.archive.org/web/20040330225904/http://barstoolsports.com/issues/volume2_issue1.pdf

Pg. 33, "Bill Simmons, a.k.a. Boston Sports…" —Barstool Sports, December 17, 2003; https://web.archive.org/web/20040330212528/http://barstoolsports.com/issues/volume1_issue17.pdf

Pg. 34, "Yup, for the 2nd…" —blog post on www.barstoolsports.com, March 30, 2007; https://web.archive.org/web/20070408012838/http://www.barstoolsports.com/randomthoughts/2007/03/30/

Pg. 34, "Tonight's show was just tedious…" —Barstool Sports, June 30, 2004; https://web.archive.org/web/20040701001542/http://www.barstoolsports.com/issues/volume2_issue14.pdf

Pg. 35, "I figured I should have a website…" —Amy J. Downey, "Is This Really Boston's Next Media Mogul?" Boston Magazine, November 23, 2010; https://www.bostonmagazine.com/2010/11/23/david-portnoy-profile-is-this-really-bostons-next-media-mogul/4/

Pg. 35, "Join Barstool Sports on Friday…" —Barstool Sports, February 25, 2004; https://web.archive.org/web/20040319122457/http://www.barstoolsports.com/issues/volume2_issue5.pdf

Pg. 36, "We know that the concept for Barstool…" —State of the Union Address, March 23, 2005; https://www.barstoolsports.com/blog/647385/barstool-2005-state-of-the-union

Pg. 37, "It was the darkest day of my life." —State of the Union Address, March 23, 2005; https://www.barstoolsports.com/blog/647385/barstool-2005-state-of-the-union

CHAPTER 5

Pg. 38, "I don't know who the fuck you are…" —John Dennis Threatening Voicemail to Ryen Russillo, devoidzer01; https://www.youtube.com/watch?v=RSWYZqntNhk

Pg. 38, "You're going around telling people…" —John Dennis Threatening Voicemail to Ryen Russillo, devoidzer01; https://www.youtube.com/watch?v=RSWYZqntNhk

Pg. 40, "Simply the best cake on the planet…" —Barstool Sports, May 5, 2004; https://web.archive.org/web/20040604014950/http://barstoolsports.com/issues/volume2_issue10.pdf

Pg. 40, "Our best shot to convince advertisers…" —Barstool Sports, December 10, 2003; https://web.archive.org/web/20040319122457/http://www.barstoolsports.com/issues/volume1_issue16.pdf

Pg. 41, "Once we did that, advertising opened up…" —"The Story of Dave Portnoy Starting Barstool Sports," Barstool Documentary Series, Barstool Sports; https://www.youtube.com/watch?v=J-_6gDCFQGw&t=146s

Pg. 41, "I honestly can't believe how many girls…" —Barstool Sports, November 15, 2006; https://issuu.com/barstoolsports/docs/20170329095622

Pg. 42, "I used to read you guys all the time…" —Ian White email to Dave; https://www.barstoolsports.com/video/1406846/the-barstool-documentary-series-episode-3-blogging-before-blogging-was-blogging

Pg. 44, "Another outcome…" —Random Thoughts, barstoolsports.com, September 21, 2005; https://web.archive.org/web/20050930193709/http://www.barstoolsports.com/article/Random_Thoughts/438/

Pg. 44, "Let's start this week with the big announcement…" —Random Thoughts, barstoolsports.com, March 27, 2006; https://web.archive.org/web/20060331053703/http://www.barstoolsports.com/randomthoughts/827/

Pg. 45, "Founding father of personal blogging…" —Jeffrey Rosen, "Your Blog or Mine?" December 19, 2004; https://www.nytimes.com/2004/12/19/magazine/your-blog-or-mine.html

Pg. 46, "The thing that makes El Pres…" —Random Thoughts, barstoolsports.com, July 12, 2006; https://web.archive.org/web/20070227015345/http://www.barstoolsports.com/article/random_thoughts/951/

Pg. 46, "As a professional blogger there is…" —Random Thoughts, barstoolsports.com, July 11, 2007; https://web.archive.org/web/20090107134336/http://www.barstoolsports.com/article/random_thoughts/1470/

Pg. 46, "Is Jessica Biel too jacked…" —Random Thoughts, barstoolsports.com, December 27, 2006; https://web.archive.org/web/20070103102740/http://barstoolsports.com/randomthoughts/2006/12/27/

Pg. 47, "It looks like Bridget Moynahan's plan…" —Random Thoughts, barstoolsports.com, February 22, 2007; https://web.archive.org/web/20070227142911/http://barstoolsports.com/randomthoughts/2007/02/22/

Pg. 47, "This is a different voice…" —Craig Fehrman, "Leitch vs. Bissinger on HBO"; https://www.youtube.com/watch?v=tQrrcwMMKl4

Pg. 47, "Is there anything more hilarious…" —Random Thoughts, barstoolsports.com, April 20, 2008; https://web.archive.org/web/20080505122806/http://www.barstoolsports.com/randomthoughts/2008/04/30/

Pg. 48, "The head honchos here at…" —"El Presidente's New Years Resolutions," barstoolsports.com, December 26, 2006; https://web.archive.org/web/20090107135010/http://www.barstoolsports.com/article/presidentes_new_years_resolutions/1139/

Pg. 49, "It's that time of the week folks…" —Random Thoughts, barstoolsports.com, May 2, 2006; https://web.archive.org/web/20060502193936/http://barstoolsports.com/

Pg. 49, "Five seconds after something…" —"Dave Portnoy Screams at Nate after Being Forced to Layoff Employees," Barstool Radio Podcast Episode, https://podcasts.apple.com/us/podcast/barstool-radio/id1085919903?i=1000626111503

Pg. 50, "Our website has been growing…" —Random Thoughts, barstoolsports.com, December 9, 2005; https://web.archive.org/web/20051218074517/http://www.barstoolsports.com/randomthoughts/615/

Pg. 50, "Did Dana Bible or Don Jeans…" —Random Thoughts, barstoolsports.com, May 19, 2008; https://web.archive.org/web/20080520085729/http://www.barstoolsports.com/

Pg. 51, "This next random thought…" —Random Thoughts, barstoolsports.com, November 1, 2005; https://web.archive.org/web/20060217174323/http://www.barstoolsports.com/randomthoughts/522/

Pg. 51, "First off congrats…" —Random Thoughts, barstoolsports.com, March 20, 2006; https://web.archive.org/web/20060504100357/http://www.barstoolsports.com/randomthoughts/802/

Pg. 52, "In case you've been living…" —Random Thoughts, barstoolsports.com, August 11, 2006; https://web.archive.org/web/20060812080857/http://www.barstoolsports.com/

Pg. 53, "They handed me…", "I will never forget" —blog post, barstoolsports.com, March 26, 2020; https://www.barstoolsports.com/playlist/59/the-history-of-barstool-sports-59?video=1406859

Pg. 53, "The Stool was profitable this year…" —"El Presidente's New Years Resolutions," barstoolsports.com, December 26, 2006; https://web.archive.org/web/20090107135010/http://www.barstoolsports.com/article/presidentes_new_years_resolutions/1139/

Pg. 53, "From that point on it became clear…" —Chris Spargo, "Saturdays are for the boys: How Barstool Sports grew from a local Boston paper into a media empire," Daily Mail, November 23, 2016, https://www.dailymail.co.uk/news/article-3960576/Saturdays-boys-Barstool-Sports-grew-local-Boston-paper-media-empire.html

CHAPTER 6

Pg. 54, "Where the fuck is Dave Portnoy?…" —Random Thoughts, barstoolsports.com, April 16, 2008; https://web.archive.org/web/20080430025600/http://www.barstoolsports.com/article/random_thoughts/2231/ and see footnote on page 46

Pg. 54, "He's my daughter's boyfriend…" —Random Thoughts, barstoolsports.com, April 16, 2008; https://web.archive.org/web/20080430025600/http://www.barstoolsports.com/article/random_thoughts/2231/ and see footnote on page 46

Pg. 55, "I always thought he was really funny…" —"The Story of Dave Portnoy Starting Barstool Sports," Barstool Documentary Series, Barstool Sports; https://www.youtube.com/watch?v=J-_6gDCFQGw&list=PL1m2jOREUTBWxIQqa-oO6GhKNK8doeRGWv&index=2

Pg. 56, "Chalk up another milestone for the Stool…" —Random Thoughts, barstoolsports.com, April 16, 2008; https://web.archive.org/web/20080430025600/http://www.barstoolsports.com/article/random_thoughts/2231/

Pg. 57, "No one has ever been as good at their job…" —blog post, barstoolsports.com, March 27, 2020; https://www.barstoolsports.com/video/1406846/the-barstool-documentary-series-episode-3-blogging-before-blogging-was-blogging

Pg. 58, "Since the addition of Uncle Buck…" —Random Thoughts, barstoolsports.com, January 24, 2007; https://web.archive.org/web/20070204085205/http://www.barstoolsports.com/article/random_thoughts/1174/

Pg. 59, "It was hard for…" —Ben Strauss, "At Deadspin, can the cool kids of the sports Internet become its moral authority?" The Washington Post, February 25, 2019; https://www.washingtonpost.com/sports/at-deadspin-can-the-cool-kids-of-the-sports-internet-become-its-moral-authority/2019/02/25/c6045556-1368-11e9-b6ad-9cfd62dbb0a8_story.html

Pg. 59, "Ideally you want…" —Barstool Sports, August 27, 2007; https://issuu.com/barstoolsports/docs/20170407090955_cce3f012101172

Pg. 59, "Bottom line is that chicks…" —Barstool Sports, October 3 2007; https://issuu.com/barstoolsports/docs/20170424092755

Pg. 59, "I know everybody thinks I hate…" —blog post, barstoolsports.com, November 21, 2011; https://web.archive.org/web/20111122191618/http://www.barstoolsports.com/boston/super-page/how-is-it-possible-that-chris-brown-performed-at-the-amas/

Pg. 59, "Eva Longoria is a little slut bag…" —Random Thoughts, barstoolsports.com, April 19, 2007; https://web.archive.org/web/20070501180028/http://www.barstoolsports.com/randomthoughts/2007/04/19/#this_top_this_sportscenter

Pg. 59, "Paulina is on the right…" —blog post, barstoolsports.com, August 17, 2012; https://web.archive.org/web/20120818003450/http://www.barstoolsports.com/

Pg. 60, "I did gay jokes, I did rape jokes…" —Ben Strauss, "At Deadspin, can the cool kids of the sports Internet become its moral authority?" The Washington Post, February 25, 2019; https://www.washingtonpost.com/sports/at-deadspin-can-the-cool-kids-of-the-sports-internet-become-its-moral-authority/2019/02/25/c6045556-1368-11e9-b6ad-9cfd62dbb0a8_story.html

Pg. 60, "It's not rape, it's surprise sex…" —blog post, barstoolsports.com, September 26, 2018; https://www.barstoolsports.com/blog/1100855/the-hypocrites-at-deadspin-in-full-spin-zone-mode-as-many-of-their-staffers-sexist-and-homophobic-comments-come-to-light

Pg. 60, "To whom it may concern…" —Random Thoughts, barstoolsports.com, July 18, 2018; https://web.archive.org/web/20080721053608/http://www.barstoolsports.com/randomthoughts/2008/07/18/

Pg. 60, "Dear Webmaster at Barstoolsports…" —Random Thoughts, barstoolsports.com, October 19, 2007; https://web.archive.org/web/20100526010538/http://barstoolsports.com/randomthoughts/2007/10/19/

Pg. 61, "Does anybody know who this…." —Random Thoughts, barstoolsports.com, May 19, 2008; https://web.archive.org/web/20080520085729/http://www.barstoolsports.com/

Pg. 61, "This is Amanda Marsh…" —Random Thoughts, barstoolsports.com, May 5, 2008; https://web.archive.org/web/20080513135016/http://www.barstoolsports.com/randomthoughts/2008/05/05/

Pg. 63, "Just another day in the life…" —Random Thoughts, barstoolsports.com, May 5, 2008; https://web.archive.org/web/20080513135016/http://www.barstoolsports.com/randomthoughts/2008/05/05/

CHAPTER 7

Pg. 64, "April Fools' Day in the Cubes…Tread Lightly" —blog post, barstoolsports.com, April 1, 2015; https://www.barstoolsports.com/blog/249882/april-fools-day-in-the-cubes-tread-lightly

Pg. 65, "Bigger and better things…" —blog post, forsurenot.com, August 14, 2009; https://web.archive.org/web/20100411034822/http://forsurenot.com/

Pg. 66, "Blogging for El Pres seemed like it would be way more fun…" —Amy J. Downey, "Is This Really Boston's Next Media Mogul?" Boston Magazine, November 23, 2010; https://www.bostonmagazine.com/2010/11/23/david-portnoy-profile-is-this-really-bostons-next-media-mogul/4/

CHAPTER 8

Pg. 68, "The college tour was one of the…" —Jason Ankeny, "The Man Behind the 'Bible of Bro Culture,'" NBC News, December 13, 2013; https://www.nbcnews.com/id/wbna53821689

Pg. 68, "The cops told us…" —"The Concert that Almost Bankrupted Barstool Sports," Barstool Documentary Series, Barstool Sports; https://www.youtube.com/watch?v=kia_8g0xRRA&t=964s

Pg. 68, "Police arrested 15 UMass students…" —blog post, barstoolsports.com, May 3, 2010; https://web.archive.org/web/20100504000427/http://boston.barstoolsports.com/page/2/

Pg. 69, "The Milton working conditions…" —"Dave Portnoy Breaks Down 'Milton Tough,'" YouTube, Barstool Sports; https://www.youtube.com/watch?v=ODV7lvxVh3Q&t=116s

Pg. 70, "Stoolapalooza Ticket Update…" —blog post, barstoolsports.com, April 12, 2010; https://web.archive.org/web/20100414043545/http://boston.barstoolsports.com/page/3/

Pg. 70, "[The first show] was fucking bonkers…" —blog post, barstoolsports.com, April 17, 2010; https://web.archive.org/web/20100419014953/http://boston.barstoolsports.com/

Pg. 71, "I [now] just have a mishmash of bills…" —El Presidente's New Year's Resolutions, barstoolsports.com, December 26, 2006; https://web.archive.org/web/20090107135010/http://www.barstoolsports.com/article/presidentes_new_years_resolutions/1139/

Pg. 72, "El Pres is a character…" —Jason Ankeny, "The Man Behind the 'Bible of Bro Culture,'" NBC News, December 13, 2013; https://www.nbcnews.com/id/wbna53821689

Pg. 72, "There are times when…" —"Ask the Original BLK Blogger (feat. Mo) Ep. 5," 2Biggs podcast; https://www.podchaser.com/podcasts/2biggs-1142674/episodes/recent

Pg. 72, "I would get emails…" —"Dave Portnoy Breaks Down 'Milton Tough,'" YouTube, Barstool Sports; https://www.youtube.com/watch?v=ODV7lvxVh3Q&t=116s

Pg. 73, "It takes me 45 minutes…" —Amy J. Downey, "Is This Really Boston's Next Media Mogul?" Boston Magazine, November 23, 2010; https://www.bostonmagazine.com/2010/11/23/david-portnoy-profile-is-this-really-bostons-next-media-mogul/4/

Pg. 73, "I always looked…" —Amy J. Downey, "Is This Really Boston's Next Media Mogul?" Boston Magazine, November 23, 2010; https://www.bostonmagazine.com/2010/11/23/david-portnoy-profile-is-this-really-bostons-next-media-mogul/4/

Pg. 73, "The things that…" —Timothy Burroughs, "The President of Bros," The Michigan Daily, November 20, 2013; https://www.michigandaily.com/uncategorized/11timothy-burroughs-barstool-sports21/

Pg. 74, "Worked in a fucking tanning salon…" —"El Pres Confronts Jenna Marbles in New York," Barstool Sports; https://www.youtube.com/watch?v=SJimEymOnN0

Pg. 74, "Well Stoolies, it's been real…" —blog post, barstoolsports.com, August 11, 2010; https://web.archive.org/web/20100812170659/http://boston.barstoolsports.com/page/3/

Pg. 76, "So me and Prezzy…" —blog post, stoollala.com, April 5, 2011; https://web.archive.org/web/20110408234836/http://www.stoollala.com:80/

Pg. 76, "Per Jenna's blog trashing…" —blog post, stoollala.com, April 6, 2011; https://web.archive.org/web/20110408234836/http://www.stoollala.com:80/

Pg. 77, "This whole Jenna Marbles thing…" —blog post, barstoolsports.com, December 5, 2013; https://web.archive.org/web/20131207214055/http://www.barstoolsports.com/boston/super-page/is-it-possible-i-feel-bad-for-jenna-marbles-now

Pg. 77, "I went to high school with Renee…" —"How Gaz Became Barstool's first employee," LinkedIn Video; https://www.linkedin.com/posts/barstool-sports_how-gaz-became-barstools-first-employee-activity-6666020686173089792-0ydN/

Pg. 77, "This is our sales guy, but he hasn't sold…" —blog post, barstool-sports.com, May 9, 2019; https://www.barstoolsports.com/blog/1311728/comparing-the-milton-office-tour-vs-the-new-nyc-office-tour-is-bananaland

Pg. 78, "I work hard so [Gaz] can enjoy his life…" —tweet from Dave Portnoy, January 10, 2015; https://x.com/stoolpresidente/status/554023809876238338

Pg. 78, "Paul came in and was like…" —"Bonus Episode: Dave Discusses Massive Investment from Penn National," Barstool Radio Podcast; https://podcasts.apple.com/ie/podcast/bonus-episode-dave-discusses-massive-investment-from/id1085919903?i=1000464021432

Pg. 78, "Sales went well, comparably…" —"How Gaz became Barstool's first employee," LinkedIn Video; https://www.linkedin.com/posts/barstool-sports_how-gaz-became-barstools-first-employee-activity-6666020686173089792-0ydN/

Pg. 78, "There are almost no…" —Jason Ankeny, "The Man Behind the 'Bible of Bro Culture,'" NBC News, December 13, 2013; https://www.nbcnews.com/id/wbna53821689

Pg. 79, "I met with NY guy…" —blog post, barstoolsports.com, August 4, 2010; https://web.archive.org/web/20100806121055/http://boston.barstoolsports.com/page/4/

Pg. 79, "Wait, what? The Big Lead just sold…" —blog post, barstoolsports.com, June 2, 2010; https://web.archive.org/web/20100603084044/http://boston.barstoolsports.com/page/2

CHAPTER 9

Pg. 81, "It was the golden years of blogging…" —"The Return of Mailtime and the Best Barstool Moments of the Decade," The Kevin Clancy Show podcast; https://podcasts.apple.com/us/podcast/the-return-of-mailtime-and-the/id1492939892?i=1000461338500

Pg. 81, "You have gotta be…" —tweet from Kevin Clancy, April 25, 2018; https://x.com/KFCBarstool/status/989338211792146432?s=20

Pg. 81, "Only way that asshole gremlin…" —tweet from Kevin Clancy, February 17, 2017; https://x.com/KFCBarstool/status/832771394509234178?s=20

Pg. 82, "Don't mean to make this…" —tweet from Dave Portnoy, October 28, 2015; https://x.com/stoolpresidente/status/659558987256475648?s=20

Pg. 82, "@KFCBarstool and I get the hate…" —tweet from Dave Portnoy, January 16, 2022; https://x.com/stoolpresidente/status/1482763097060229122?s=20

Pg. 82, "I hated Kevin…" —"Talking the history of Barstool with KFC," The Dave Portnoy Show with Eddie & Co.; https://www.youtube.com/watch?v=d1yuzhNe9hg&t=2833s

Pg. 83, "So where are you two at..." —"Talking the history of Barstool with KFC," The Dave Portnoy Show, https://www.youtube.com/watch?v=d1yuzhNe9hg&t=2833s

Pg. 83, "If I was Jewish I'd…" —deleted tweet from Kevin Clancy; https://deadspin.com/idiots-hold-idiot-summit-1797659081

Pg. 83, "Why I love Barstool…" —deleted tweet from Kevin Clancy; https://deadspin.com/idiots-hold-idiot-summit-1797659081

Pg. 84, "We lost to Honduras…" —tweet from Kevin Clancy, February 6, 2013; https://x.com/KFCBarstool/status/299299704888508416?s=20

Pg. 84, "So the US Soccer team…" —tweet from Kevin Clancy, February 7, 2013; https://www.barstoolsports.com/blog/121259/us-soccer-loses-to-honduras-honduras-not-happy-with-me

Pg. 84, "Here's a completely misspelled sentence…" —blog post, barstoolsports.com, July 26, 2010; https://www.barstoolsports.com/blog/260615/the-blind-community-is-not-happy-with-your-boy-kfc

Pg. 84, "The Blindos blog set the tone…" —blog post, barstoolsports.com, March 27, 2020; https://www.barstoolsports.com/video/1406846/the-barstool-documentary-series-episode-3-blogging-before-blogging-was-blogging

Pg. 85, "Jersey City Pedophile Loses…" —Chris Fry, "Man Claims Sports Blog Defamed Him," Courthouse News, December 19, 2011; https://www.courthousenews.com/man-claims-sports-blog-defamed-him/

Pg. 85, "I wrote a blog about…" —Chris Fry, "Man Claims Sports Blog Defamed Him," Courthouse News, December 19, 2011; https://www.courthousenews.com/man-claims-sports-blog-defamed-him/

CHAPTER 10

Pg. 87, "I have a gambling…," "I think we had to put…," "I yelled at him more…" —"The Concert that Almost Bankrupted Barstool Sports," Barstool Documentary Series, Barstool Sports; https://www.youtube.com/watch?v=kia_8g0xRRA&t=964s

Pg. 88, "So 'Back to Stool' sucked…" —blog post, barstoolsports.com, October 8, 2010; https://www.barstoolsports.com/blog/899352/chiddy-bang-misses-concert-last-night-blames-it-on-me-like-yellow-belly-cowards

Pg. 88, "He was hitting that refresh…" —"The Concert that Almost Bankrupted Barstool Sports," Barstool Documentary Series, Barstool Sports; https://www.youtube.com/watch?v=kia_8g0xRRA&t=964s

Pg. 88, "We got fucking wiped out…" —Theo Von, "Dave Portnoy: This Past Weekend with Theo Von," podcast; https://www.youtube.com/watch?v=n_PKFg0yme4

Pg. 88, "You're not the fucking Beatles…" —blog post, barstoolsports.com, October 8, 2010; https://www.barstoolsports.com/blog/899352/chiddy-bang-misses-concert-last-night-blames-it-on-me-like-yellow-belly-cowards

Pg. 89, "If you don't like hearing…" —blog post, barstoolsports.com, October 8, 2010; https://www.barstoolsports.com/blog/899352/chiddy-bang-misses-concert-last-night-blames-it-on-me-like-yellow-belly-cowards

Pg. 89, "There were definitely times…" —"The Concert that Almost Bankrupted Barstool Sports," Barstool Documentary Series, Barstool Sports; https://www.youtube.com/watch?v=kia_8g0xRRA&t=964s

Pg. 89, "Dave would like walk into…" —"The Concert that Almost Bankrupted Barstool Sports," Barstool Documentary Series, Barstool Sports; https://www.youtube.com/watch?v=kia_8g0xRRA&t=964s

Pg. 89, "About every 3 months…" —blog post, barstoolsports.com, February 29, 2012; https://web.archive.org/web/20120301081402/http://www.barstoolsports.com/nyc/super-page/i-had-a-kfc-mental-breakdown-and-ive-learned-there-are-no-answers-to-fix-it/

Pg. 90, "One day, I got a job…" —"Dave Portnoy went on his first lunch break at his sales job and never came back, the rest is history," Spittin' Chiclets podcast; https://www.youtube.com/watch?v=ILeH1QmC1gc

Pg. 90, "At the end of the day…," "I realized then that…" —"The Concert that Almost Bankrupted Barstool Sports," Barstool Documentary Series, Barstool Sports; https://www.youtube.com/watch?v=kia_8g0xRRA&t=964s

CHAPTER 11

Pg. 91, "Check Out the Howitzer…" —"The Dave Portnoy 'Howitzergate' Controversy at Barstool Sports," Barstool Documentary Series, Barstool Sports; https://www.youtube.com/watch?v=2HmJKvwH41w

Pg. 94, "I stand by Brady blog…" —tweet from Dave Portnoy, August 11, 2011; https://x.com/stoolpresidente/status/101784031921836033?s=20

Pg. 94, "For those of you…" —tweet from Jason Wolfe, August 12, 2011; https://x.com/jasonlwolfe/status/101989186097262592?s=20

Pg. 95, "Now again, I repeat…", "BULLSHIT…" —"The Dave Portnoy 'Howitzergate' Controversy at Barstool Sports," Barstool Documentary Series, Barstool Sports; https://www.youtube.com/watch?v=2HmJKvwH41w

Pg. 95, "State police, open up!" —"Blogger removes naked photos of Brady's son," NBC Sports Boston, August 16, 2011; https://www.nbcsportsboston.com/nfl/new-england-patriots/blogger-removes-naked-photos-of-bradys-son/345066/ and O'Ryan Johnson, "Blogger caves, pulls nude pics of Tom Brady's son," The Boston Herald, August 16, 2011; https://www.bostonherald.com/2011/08/16/blogger-caves-pulls-nude-pics-of-tom-bradys-son/ and see footnote on page 79

Pg. 95, "We need to speak to…" —"Blogger removes naked photos of Brady's son," NBC Sports Boston, August 16, 2011; https://www.nbcsportsboston.com/nfl/new-england-patriots/blogger-removes-naked-photos-of-bradys-son/345066/ and O'Ryan Johnson, "Blogger caves, pulls nude pics of Tom Brady's son," The Boston Herald, August 16, 2011; https://www.bostonherald.com/2011/08/16/blogger-caves-pulls-nude-pics-of-tom-bradys-son/ and see footnote on page 79

Pg. 96, "The police just said they…" —"Blogger removes naked photos of Brady's son," *NBC Sports Boston*, August 16, 2011; https://www.nbcsportsboston.com/nfl/new-england-patriots/blogger-removes-naked-photos-of-bradys-son/345066/ and O'Ryan Johnson, "Blogger caves, pulls nude pics of Tom Brady's son," *The Boston Herald*, August 16, 2011; https://www.bostonherald.com/2011/08/16/blogger-caves-pulls-nude-pics-of-tom-bradys-son/

Pg. 96, "Are you happy now" —"The Dave Portnoy 'Howitzergate' Controversy at Barstool Sports," Barstool Documentary Series, Barstool Sports; https://www.youtube.com/watch?v=2HmJKvwH41w

Pg. 97, "So the question is…" —"Local Blogger Defends Posting Naked Photos of Tom Brady's Son," *CBS News*, August 12, 2011; https://www.cbsnews.com/boston/news/barstool-founder-defends-posting-naked-photos-of-tom-bradys-son/

Pg. 97, "I said he had a…" —"Local Blogger Defends Posting Naked Photos of Tom Brady's Son," *CBS News*, August 12, 2011; https://www.cbsnews.com/boston/news/barstool-founder-defends-posting-naked-photos-of-tom-bradys-son/

Pg. 98, "Going into the Stern…" —tweet from Dave Portnoy, August 16, 2011; https://twitter.com/search?q=stern%2020%25%20(from%3Astoolpresidente)&src=typed_query&f=top

Pg. 98, "We now have Dave Portnoy…" —"David Portnoy takes down Tom Brady's child's pictures after Howard Stern tells him it was wrong," batmanmmv; https://www.youtube.com/watch?v=nF7EtjI9iTY

Pg. 99, "Nope…what if something funny…" —"The Dave Portnoy 'Howitzergate' Controversy at Barstool Sports," Barstool Documentary Series, Barstool Sports; https://www.youtube.com/watch?v=2HmJKvwH41w

Pg. 99, "Dave has an unbelievable…" —"The Concert that Almost Bankrupted Barstool Sports," Barstool Documentary Series, Barstool Sports; https://www.youtube.com/watch?v=kia_8g0xRRA&t=964s

Pg. 99, "Dave just kept going…" —"The Return of Mailtime and the Best Barstool Moments of the Decade," *The Kevin Clancy Show podcast*; https://podcasts.apple.com/us/podcast/the-return-of-mailtime-and-the/id1492939892?i=1000461338500

Pg. 100, "He was relentless…" —"The Concert that Almost Bankrupted Barstool Sports," Barstool Documentary Series, Barstool Sports; https://www.youtube.com/watch?v=kia_8g0xRRA&t=964s

Pg. 101, "I ate too much popcorn" —TikTok video from Bffspod account https://www.tiktok.com/@bffspod/video/7333647474210409771?lang=en

CHAPTER 12

Pg. 102, "A Huntington, Long Island…" —Greg Cergol, "9 Hospitalized After L.I. Party Promoting 'Blackout' Alcohol Consumption," *NBC New York*, March 6, 2012; https://www.nbcnewyork.com/news/local/party-gone-wild-raises-questions-about-party-planner/2095904/

Pg. 102, "Thousands of young…." —"Cops Shut Down 'Barstool Blackout' Show In Montclair, N.J.; Tour Moves To NYC Friday," *CBS*

News, March 30, 2012; https://www.cbsnews.com/newyork/news/
police-shut-down-barstool-blackout-tour-show-in-montclair/

Pg. 102, "A destructive, roving dance…" —Lorena Mongelli, "Destructive 'Barstool
Blackout' set to hit NYC Tonight," *The New York Post*, March 30, 2012; https://
nypost.com/2012/03/30/destructive-barstool-blackout-set-to-hit-nyc-tonight/

Pg. 103, "Usually I'm not into techno…" —blog post, barstoolsports.com, April
4, 2011; https://web.archive.org/web/20110404172205/http://boston.barstool-
sports.com/

Pg. 103, "So, we said [to the fraternities] why don't we…" —"Planet Bri with Special
Guest Dave Portnoy," *PlanBri* podcast; https://app.podscribe.ai/episode/89208084

Pg. 103, "It was a party you did in your house…" —"The History of the Barstool
Blackout Tour," Barstool Documentary Series, Barstool Sports; https://www.you-
tube.com/watch?v=lI3CqxPH6ss&t=2s

Pg. 104, "I remember [thinking] this is a terrible idea…" —"Behind the Blackout
Tour," *KFC Radio* podcast; https://www.barstoolsports.com/podcast/979436/
behind-the-blackout-tour

Pg. 104, "One day Dave just said…," "We had one…" —"The History of the Barstool
Blackout Tour," Barstool Documentary Series, Barstool Sports; https://www.you-
tube.com/watch?v=lI3CqxPH6ss&t=2s

Pg. 105, "They [the group working with Avicii] were having trouble selling tickets…" —"Behind the Blackout Tour," *KFC Radio* podcast; https://www.barstool-
sports.com/podcast/979436/behind-the-blackout-tour

Pg. 105, "We rolled into Iowa…" —"Behind the Blackout Tour," *KFC Radio* podcast;
https://www.barstoolsports.com/podcast/979436/behind-the-blackout-tour

Pg. 105, "I can't explain how…it was incredibly dangerous…" —"The History
of the Barstool Blackout Tour," Barstool Sports; https://www.youtube.com/
watch?v=lI3CqxPH6ss&t=2s

Pg. 106, "At the beginning we…" —"Behind the Blackout Tour," *KFC Radio* podcast;
https://www.barstoolsports.com/podcast/979436/behind-the-blackout-tour

Pg. 106, "It was a big deal if…" —"Behind the Blackout Tour," *KFC Radio* podcast;
https://www.barstoolsports.com/podcast/979436/behind-the-blackout-tour

Pg. 106, "If Paul (Gaz) wanted to see…" —"The History of the Barstool Blackout
Tour," Barstool Documentary Series, Barstool Sports; https://www.youtube.com/
watch?v=lI3CqxPH6ss&t=2s

Pg. 107, "I remember pulling down…" —"The History of the Barstool Blackout
Tour," Barstool Documentary Series, Barstool Sports; https://www.youtube.com/
watch?v=lI3CqxPH6ss&t=2s

Pg. 107, "Every morning, you'd get in the car…" —"Behind the Blackout
Tour," *KFC Radio* podcast; https://www.barstoolsports.com/podcast/979436/
behind-the-blackout-tour

Pg. 107, "It's something that could exist only…," "We went from a couple…."
—"The History of the Barstool Blackout Tour," Barstool Documentary Series,
Barstool Sports; https://www.youtube.com/watch?v=lI3CqxPH6ss&t=2s

Pg. 108, "I remember Zollo walking up to me…" —"Behind the Blackout Tour," *KFC Radio* podcast; https://www.barstoolsports.com/podcast/979436/behind-the-blackout-tour

Pg. 109, "The more the media portrayed it…" —"The History of the Barstool Blackout Tour," Barstool Documentary Series, Barstool Sports; https://www.youtube.com/watch?v=lI3CqxPH6ss&t=2s

Pg. 109, "We became the face of EDM…" —"Behind the Blackout Tour," *KFC Radio* podcast; https://www.barstoolsports.com/podcast/979436/behind-the-blackout-tour;

Pg. 109, "There should have been, like, multiple deaths…" —"Behind the Blackout Tour," *KFC Radio* podcast; https://www.barstoolsports.com/podcast/979436/behind-the-blackout-tour

CHAPTER 13

Pg. 110, "I don't know what to expect right now"; "University Health and…"; "Dave is that you?"; "I just want you all…"; "We don't condone…"; "Let him talk!"; "Are you going to let me talk?"; "I hope you have a horrible night!"; "We don't condone…"; "You think I like doing this?"; "You can fuck off!"; "Fuck off! Fuck off…" —"KO Barstool vs. Barstool Blackout Tour," Barstool Sports; https://www.youtube.com/watch?v=kDK0ZMYIXvU

Pg. 112, "Just to make friends…" —*Knockout Barstool!* Tumblr, February 1, 2012; https://knockoutbarstoolsports-blog.tumblr.com/page/4

Pg. 112, "Even though I never condone…" —*Knockout Barstool!* Tumblr, January 25, 2012; https://knockoutbarstoolsports-blog.tumblr.com/page/8

Pg. 113, "Barstool Sports has perpetuated…" —*Knockout Barstool!* Tumblr, January 24, 2012; http://knockoutbarstoolsports-blog.tumblr.com/page/8

Pg. 113, "I would love to…" —*Knockout Barstool!* Tumblr, January 31, 2012; https://knockoutbarstoolsports-blog.tumblr.com/page/4

Pg. 113, "I'm a recent Northeastern grad…" —*Knockout Barstool!* Tumblr, February 1, 2012; https://knockoutbarstoolsports-blog.tumblr.com/page/4

Pg. 113, "Totally support what…" —*Knockout Barstool!* Tumblr, January 26, 2012; https://knockoutbarstoolsports-blog.tumblr.com/page/7

Pg. 114, "What is the ultimate goal…"; "Originally, we wanted Northeastern…"; "How do you think…"; "Joking about rape normalizes…" —Ingrid Adamow, "Knockout Barstool: Fighting The Trivialization of Rape," *The Quad, BU's Independent Online Magazine*, February 13, 2012; https://www.buquad.com/2012/02/13/knocking-out-blackout-a-word-from-el-pres-and-the-girls-of-knockout-barstool/#:~:text=A%3A%20Originally%20we%20wanted%20Northeastern,of%20rape%20on%20college%20campuses.%20%E2%80%A6

Pg. 115, "Do I play it straight…" —tweet from Dave Portnoy, April 6, 2012; https://x.com/stoolpresidente/status/188259960365400066?s=20

Pg. 115, "Lisa Guerrero just…" —tweet from Dave Portnoy, April 6 2012; https://x.com/stoolpresidente/status/188369296194416640?s=20

Pg. 115, "You posted the following…no I obviously don't." —*Inside Edition*, Purple Starfish YouTube page; https://www.youtube.com/watch?v=B7QTahhIBqI

Pg. 116, "You people are fucking pathetic…" —*Knockout Barstool!* Tumblr, January 26, 2012; https://knockoutbarstoolsports-blog.tumblr.com/page/7

Pg. 116, "'We don't condone…" —*Knockout Barstool!* Tumblr, January 26, 2012; https://knockoutbarstoolsports-blog.tumblr.com/page/6

Pg. 116, "When will KO Barstool…"; "KO Barstool…"; "I'm sorry, Anna Siembor…" —blog post, barstoolsports.com, February 9, 2012; https://web.archive.org/web/20120210231802/http://www.barstoolsports.com/boston/super-page/crazy-bitches-at-ko-barstool-now-protesting-blackout-parties-because-they-promote-drinking/

Pg. 118, "Hey, hey! Ho, ho….Thank you, Northeastern. Fuck KO Barstool!" —"KO Barstool vs. Barstool Blackout Tour," Barstool Sports; https://www.youtube.com/watch?v=kDK0ZMYIXvU

CHAPTER 14

Pg. 120, "God I love you Hot Glove…" —tweet from Devlin D'Zmura, June 26, 2012; https://x.com/TitansMayoMan/status/216798060410441728?s=20

Pg. 121, "Robby Lange Will Not…" —blog post, thehotglove.com, March 8, 2012; https://web.archive.org/web/20120327204510/http://www.thehotglove.com/page/2

Pg. 122, "Well, this is it…" —blog post, the hotglove.com, March 9, 2012; https://web.archive.org/web/20120327114239/http://www.thehotglove.com/

Pg. 123, "How about I'll just write a few Cubs blogs…" —"*Inaugural Guest* Big Cat from Barstool Sports," *If You Don't Grind podcast*; https://podcasts.apple.com/us/podcast/inaugural-guest-big-cat-from-barstool-sports/id1497913158?i=1000465115565

CHAPTER 15

Pg. 124, "We will get to the bottom of this…" —"President Obama Speaks on the Explosions in Boston," www.obamawhitehouse.gov, April 15, 2013; https://obamawhitehouse.archives.gov/blog/2013/04/15/president-obama-speaks-explosions-boston

Pg. 125, "What the fuck is going on…" —tweet from Dave Portnoy, April 15, 2013; https://x.com/stoolpresidente/status/323875661204819968?s=20

Pg. 125, "Current situation. Guy on boat is…" —tweet from Dave Portnoy, April 19, 2013; https://x.com/stoolpresidente/status/325390887301566464?s=20

Pg. 125, "All units stand by…" —tweet from Dave Portnoy, April 19, 2013; https://x.com/stoolpresidente/status/325395386338512897?s=20

Pg. 125, "Police say he is…" —tweet from Dan Katz, April 19, 2013; https://x.com/BarstoolBigCat/status/325396823877505024?s=20

Pg. 126, "Anybody who reports…" —tweet from Dave Portnoy, April 19, 2013; https://x.com/stoolpresidente/status/325394149664768000?s=20

Pg. 126, "The boom that the TV stations…" —tweet from Dave Portnoy, April 19, 2013; https://x.com/stoolpresidente/status/325396030566842368?s=20

Pg. 126, "Head lifting. He's alive…" —tweet from Dan Katz, April 19, 2013; https://x.com/BarstoolBigCat/status/325390337768054785?s=20

Pg. 126, "I hate how when my wife…" —tweet from Dave Portnoy, April 18, 2013; https://x.com/stoolpresidente/status/325032740397412353?s=20

Pg. 126, "Holy shit: is it back…" —tweet from Dan Katz, April 19, 2013; https://x.com/BarstoolBigCat/status/325383470559928321?s=20

Pg. 127, "Completely aside, House Boats…" —tweet from Dan Katz, April 19, 2013; https://x.com/BarstoolBigCat/status/325392985992871936?s=20

Pg. 128, "Are you kidding me…as much as I'd like" —"Barstool Interview with Marc Fucarile," Barstool Sports; https://www.youtube.com/watch?v=3RcNbgGGGDg

Pg. 128, "Obviously on a day like today…" —blog post, barstoolsports.com, August 22, 2023; https://www.barstoolsports.com/blog/191083/back-to-what-matters-barstool-interview-with-marc-fucarile

Pg. 129, "As much as we make fun…" —blog post, barstoolsports.com, August 15, 2008; https://web.archive.org/web/20080816092354/http://barstoolsports.com/

Pg. 130, "I read 'em a decent amount…" —"I Am Dave Portnoy, Owner and Founder of BarstoolSports.com," 2013 Reddit AMA; https://www.reddit.com/r/IAmA/comments/169yz5/i_am_dave_portnoy_owner_and_founder_of/

Pg. 132, "Viva La Stool from Ghana to the Great Wall of China to the Holy Land to the Jets Locker Room and Beyond…" —blog post, barstoolsports.com, April 10, 2011; https://web.archive.org/web/20110411135453/http://boston.barstoolsports.com/random-thoughts/viva-la-stool-from-ghana-to-the-great-wall-of-china-to-the-holy-land-to-the-jets-locker-room-and-beyond/

Pg. 132, "Soldier from Brockton…" —blog post, barstoolsports.com, December 23, 2013; https://www.barstoosports.com/search?query=viva%20la%20stool%20from%20&page=1&configure%5BhitsPerPage%5D=25&configure%5Bfilters%5D=site_barstoolsports%3D1&indices%5Bshopify_products_blog%5D%5Bconfigure%5D%5BhitsPerPage%5D=4&indices%5Bshopify_products_blog%5D%5Bconfigure%5D%5Bfilters%5D=&indices%5Bshopify_products_blog%5D%5Bconfigure%5D%5Bdistinct%5D=1&indices%5Bshopify_products_blog%5D%5Bpage%5D=1&indices%5BBarstoolSports%5D%5Bpage%5D=4

Pg. 132, "The moment I realized…" —Daniel Bernstein, "PMH alum Kevin Clancy turned social media into a career with Barstool Sports," Pelham Examiner, July 15, 2019; https://pelhamexaminer.com/15961/showcase/pmhs-alum-kevin-clancy-turned-social-media-into-a-career-with-barstool-sports/

Pg. 134, "We're like Pat Hill…" —"I Am Dave Portnoy, Owner and Founder of BarstoolSports.com," 2013 Reddit AMA; https://www.reddit.com/r/IAmA/comments/169yz5/i_am_dave_portnoy_owner_and_founder_of/

Pg. 134, "A lot of people have been asking…" "Emergency Press Conference Barstool LA (Part 1)," www.barstoolsports.com, November 8, 2013; https://www.barstoolsports.com/video/1100513/emergency-press-conference-barstool-la

Pg. 135, "This will be a brief press conference…" —"Emergency Press Conference, Barstool LA (Part 2)," www.barstoolsports.com, December 2, 2013; https://www.barstoolsports.com/video/1100592/emergency-press-conference-barstool-la-part-2

Pg. 135, "I remember walking…" —"*Inaugural Guest* Big Cat from Barstool Sports," *If You Don't Grind podcast*, https://podcasts.apple.com/us/podcast/inaugural-guest-big-cat-from-barstool-sports/id1497913158?i=1000465115565

Pg. 136, "Big Cat was the most interesting…" —"Ask the Original BLK Blogger (feat. Mo) Ep. 5," *2Biggs* podcast; https://www.podchaser.com/podcasts/2biggs-1142674/episodes/recent

Pg. 136, "Dan doesn't really love controversy…" —blog post, barstoolsports.com, April 1, 2020; https://www.barstoolsports.com/video/1406740/the-barstool-documentary-series-chapter-7-kneel-for-neil

Pg. 136, "Dan is much easier to advertise around…" —"Live with Dave Portnoy," *The Kirk Minihane Show*; https://www.youtube.com/watch?v=NJqooSc8Q3Q and blog post, barstoolsports.com, April 1, 2020; https://www.barstoolsports.com/video/1406740/the-barstool-documentary-series-chapter-7-kneel-for-neil

Pg. 136, "He could open doors…" —"The Story of Big Cat and Barstool Chicago," Barstool Documentary Series, Barstool Sports; https://www.youtube.com/watch?v=QqUE15-SkLo&t=5s

Pg. 137, "The story of *me*…" —"The Return of Mailtime and the Best Barstool Moments of the Decade," *The Kevin Clancy Show* podcast; https://podcasts.apple.com/us/podcast/the-return-of-mailtime-and-the/id1492939892?i=1000461338500

Pg. 137, "El Pres and Big Cat's Burrito/Pizza Challenge…" —blog post, barstoolsports.com, March 11, 2013; https://www.barstoolsports.com/blog/33064/el-pres-and-big-cats-burritopizza-challenge-official-rules-and-updated-odds

Pg. 139, "Dave is a motherfucker…" —"The Return of Mailtime and the Best Barstool Moments of the Decade," *The Kevin Clancy Show* podcast; https://podcasts.apple.com/us/podcast/the-return-of-mailtime-and-the/id1492939892?i=1000461338500

Pg. 139, "It was the first time I had real money…" —Justin Gordon, "The Brazen Ambition of Dave Portnoy: Building Barstool Sports Into a $600+ Million Media Empire," *Just Go Grind*, August 20, 2023; https://www.justgogrind.com/p/dave-portnoy

CHAPTER 16

Pg. 140, "Name another mogul who has…" —blog post, barstoolsports.com, September 4, 2014; https://www.barstoolsports.com/blog/207615/i-finally-met-my-office-roommate-aka-the-squirrel-who-live-in-the-wall

Pg. 140, "Her last two presents…" —"I Am Dave Portnoy, Owner and Founder of BarstoolSports.com," 2013 Reddit AMA; https://www.reddit.com/r/IAmA/comments/169yz5/i_am_dave_portnoy_owner_and_founder_of/

Pg. 140, "Everyone was in tight quarters" —"Dave Portnoy Breaks Down 'Milton Tough,'" Barstool Sports; https://www.youtube.com/watch?v=ODV7lvxVh3Q&t=117s

Pg. 141, "I was terrified to…" —"Dave Portnoy Breaks Down 'Milton Tough,'" https://www.youtube.com/watch?v=ODV7lvxVh3Q&t=117s

Pg. 141, "I never really had a long conversation with him." —"KFC Breaks Down Relationship with Dave Portnoy and Discusses Inside Barstool," KFC Radio; https://www.youtube.com/watch?v=b4EicGoLYd4

Pg. 141, "You are essentially…" —"Dave Portnoy Breaks Down 'Milton Tough,'" https://www.youtube.com/watch?v=ODV7lvxVh3Q&t=117s and Ben Axelrod, "Dave Portnoy says he wasn't caught off guard by Barstool CEO's exit," *Awful Announcing*, January 18, 2024; https://awfulannouncing.com/barstool/dave-portnoy-not-caught-off-gaurd-ceo-exit.html and see footnote on page 117.

Pg. 141, "As time went on…" —"Ask the Original BLK Blogger (feat. Mo) Ep. 5," *2Biggs* podcast; https://www.podchaser.com/podcasts/2biggs-1142674/episodes/recent

Pg. 141, "In hindsight he was probably just…"; "What it takes to turn…"; "Milton is something…" —"Dave Portnoy Breaks Down 'Milton Tough,'" Barstool Sports; https://www.youtube.com/watch?v=ODV7lvxVh3Q&t=117s

Pg. 142, "Dave, you're an asshole. Happy birthday…" —"Happy 40th Dave!" video on Barstool Sports Facebook page; https://www.facebook.com/watch/?v=10155213054802502

Pg. 142, "I used to torture Hank…" —"Handsome Hank's mom was not a fan of the 'Church of Dave Portnoy' in the early days of Barstool," *Spittin Chiclets* podcast; https://www.youtube.com/watch?v=dCXgFWaIMoI

Pg. 143, "Odds Hank ever figures…" —tweet from Dave Portnoy, September 1, 2014; https://x.com/stoolpresidente/status/506587602397720576?s=20

Pg. 143, "After 10 minutes… —tweet from Dave Portnoy, January 9, 2014; https://x.com/stoolpresidente/status/421334704525434880

Pg. 143, "I gotta say…" —tweet from Dave Portnoy, September 1, 2014; https://x.com/stoolpresidente/status/506588344302964736

Pg. 143, "There is nobody on earth…" —tweet from Dave Portnoy, October 8 2015; https://x.com/stoolpresidente/status/652151121708888066?s=20

Pg. 143, "Henry was never a lover of…" —Matt DiPesa, "Success After Scituate: Henry Lockwood's Story," *The Scituation*, May 31, 2017; https://www.scituation.net/features/2017/05/31/success-after-scituate-henry-lockwoods-story/

Pg. 143, "I told you not to trust that Dave Portnoy…" —"Handsome Hank's mom was not a fan of the 'Church of Dave Portnoy' in the early days of Barstool," *Spittin Chiclets* podcast; https://www.youtube.com/watch?v=dCXgFWaIMoI

Pg. 144, "Most of the time…" —"Dave Portnoy Breaks Down 'Milton Tough,'" YouTube, Barstool Sports; https://www.youtube.com/watch?v=ODV7lvxVh3Q&t=116s

Pg. 144, "The Most Mindblowing Fact…" —blog post, barstoolsports.com, June 16, 2014; https://amp.barstoolsports.com/blog/198490/the-most-mindblowing-fact-i-found-out-about-handsome-hank-this-past-weekend-is-that-he-used-to-trash-me-in-the-comment-section-while-working-here-update-i-just-fired-hank-no-joke

Pg. 145, "I turned Hank into…" —blog post, barstoolsports.com, March 31, 2020; https://www.barstoolsports.com/video/1406761/the-barstool-documentary-series-chapter-6-weird-brains

Pg. 145, "No one gave me direction…" —"Dave Portnoy Breaks Down 'Milton Tough,'" YouTube, Barstool Sports; https://www.youtube.com/watch?v=ODV7lvxVh3Q&t=116s

Pg. 146, "I've always thought…" —"The History of Barstool Sports with Dave Portnoy," *Spittin' Chiclets*; https://www.youtube.com/watch?v=Ezx1dbKkYm4

Pg. 146, "I just wrote that blog…" —Mayoral Pres Conference, Barstool Sports; https://www.youtube.com/watch?v=SZAezfSYFiY

Pg. 147, "I'd Die For Belichick…" –blog post, barstoolsports.com, January 21, 2015; https://www.barstoolsports.com/blog/225675/live-look-at-belichick-before-he-went-to-bed-for-20-minutes-last-night

Pg. 149, "It's Brady, Belichick, Portnoy…" —"It's Brady, Belichick, Portnoy," vivalastool TikTok; https://www.tiktok.com/@vivalastool/video/7322938011744734510

Pg. 149, "Cheeseboy is a…" —tweet from Dave Portnoy, May 31, 2011; https://x.com/stoolpresidente/status/75712630991495168?s=20

Pg. 149, "I appreciate it…" —tweet from Dave Portnoy, January 17, 2013; https://x.com/stoolpresidente/status/292038538596347905?s=20

Pg. 149, "Fuck you cheeseboy…" —tweet from Dave Portnoy, June 10, 2011; https://x.com/stoolpresidente/status/79252401382625281?s=20

Pg. 150, "It's The Bro Show Yo…" —blog post, barstoolsports.com, May 17, 2013; https://web.archive.org/web/20130607092322/http://www.barstoolsports.com/boston/super-page/its-the-bro-show-yo-recapping-the-week-at-barstool

Pg. 151, "Just rewatched the rundown…" —tweet from Dan Katz, January 25, 2016; https://x.com/BarstoolBigCat/status/691771495962509312?s=20

Pg. 151, "I legitimately thought…" —tweet from Kevin Clancy, April 6 2016; https://x.com/KFCBarstool/status/717854113506131969?s=20

Pg. 151, "When he turned around and started…" —blog post, barstool-sports.com, April 1, 2020; https://www.barstoolsports.com/video/1406740/the-barstool-documentary-series-chapter-7-kneel-for-neil

Pg. 153, "125 percent growth suckers!" —blog post, barstoolsports.com, September 23, 2015; https://www.barstoolsports.com/blog/375192/according-to-adweek-barstool-sports-saw-the-highest-growth-of-any-publisher-in-the-history-of-the-world-in-august-at-125-percent

Pg. 153, "I'd be home at…" —"*Inaugural Guest* Big Cat from Barstool Sports," *If You Don't Grind* podcast; https://podcasts.apple.com/us/podcast/inaugural-guest-big-cat-from-barstool-sports/id1497913158?i=1000465115565

Pg. 153, "I remember [thinking]…" —"The Return of Mailtime and the Best Barstool Moments of the Decade," *The Kevin Clancy Show* podcast;

https://podcasts.apple.com/us/podcast/the-return-of-mailtime-and-the/id1492939892?i=1000461338500

Pg. 154, "We were all separate…" —"*Inaugural Guest* Big Cat from Barstool Sports," *If You Don't Grind* podcast; https://podcasts.apple.com/us/podcast/inaugural-guest-big-cat-from-barstool-sports/id1497913158?i=1000465115565

Pg. 154, "It was just all stubborn…" —Emily Jane Fox, "Dave Portnoy Bought Barstool Back. Can Erika Ayers Badan Keep His Pirate Ship on Course?" *Vanity Fair*, August 14, 2023; https://www.vanityfair.com/news/2023/08/after-the-espn-penn-deal-barstool-just-wants-to-be-itself-which-was-the-problem

Pg. 154, "We were at a breaking point…" —"Dave Portnoy Breaks Down the Chernin Group Deal that Changed Barstool History," *The Dave Portnoy Show*, Barstool Sports; https://www.youtube.com/watch?v=tMjt5jmpkek

CHAPTER 17

Pg. 157, "The world didn't need…" —"Episode 1, Mike Kerns of Chernin Digital," *The Dave Portnoy Show* podcast; https://www.poorstuart.com/podcast-episode/Dave-Portnoy-Show/The-Dave-Portnoy-Show-Episode-1-Mike-Kerns-of-Cher/45348/

Pg. 158, "The interaction was analogous…Jesse's also a big sports fan" —Dan Primack, "The Story of How Barstool Sports Got Sold," *Fortune*, January 7, 2016; https://fortune.com/2016/01/07/the-story-of-how-barstool-sports-got-sold/

Pg. 159, "You go to sports talk…" —"The Barstool Sports, Dave Portnoy, Peter Chernin Deal," Barstool Documentary Series, Barstool Sports; https://www.youtube.com/watch?v=6Nod9rfYjOw&list=PL1m2jOREUTBWxIQqaoO6GhKNK-8doeRGWv&index=14&t=952s

Pg. 159, "Peter is a big believer…" —"Episode 1, Mike Kerns of Chernin Digital," *The Dave Portnoy Show podcast*; https://www.poorstuart.com/podcast-episode/Dave-Portnoy-Show/The-Dave-Portnoy-Show-Episode-1-Mike-Kerns-of-Cher/45348/

Pg. 159, "They knew about [things like] Babygate…" —Jay Caspian Kang, "Spurned by ESPN, Barstool Sports is Staying on Offense," *The New York Times*, November 14, 2017; https://www.nytimes.com/2017/11/14/magazine/spurned-by-espn-barstool-sports-is-staying-on-offense.html

Pg. 159, "We certainly understood…" —Dan Primack, "The Story of How Barstool Sports Got Sold," *Fortune*, January 7, 2016; https://fortune.com/2016/01/07/the-story-of-how-barstool-sports-got-sold/

Pg. 159, "This is America! You can't…" —tweet from Dave Portnoy, May 10, 2020; https://x.com/stoolpresidente/status/1259666105292947465

Pg. 159, "Barstool was a comedy site…" —"Episode 1, Mike Kerns of Chernin Digital," *The Dave Portnoy Show* podcast; https://www.poorstuart.com/podcast-episode/Dave-Portnoy-Show/The-Dave-Portnoy-Show-Episode-1-Mike-Kerns-of-Cher/45348/

Pg. 160, "I was really impressed by..." —"The Barstool Sports, Dave Portnoy, Peter Chernin Deal," Barstool Documentary Series, Barstool Sports; https://www.youtube.com/watch?v=6Nod9rfYjOw&t=777s

Pg. 160, "I called Jared..." —"Episode 1, Mike Kerns of Chernin Digital," *The Dave Portnoy Show* podcast; https://www.poorstuart.com/podcast-episode/Dave-Portnoy-Show/The-Dave-Portnoy-Show-Episode-1-Mike-Kerns-of-Cher/45348/

Pg. 160, "I wasn't desperate for an investment..." —Dan Primack, "The Story of How Barstool Sports Got Sold," *Fortune*, January 7, 2016; https://fortune.com/2016/01/07/the-story-of-how-barstool-sports-got-sold/

Pg. 161, "It wouldn't have even been close..." —"Dave Portnoy Breaks Down the Chernin Group Deal that Changed Barstool History," *The Dave Portnoy Show*, Barstool Sports; https://www.youtube.com/watch?v=tMjt5jmpkek

Pg. 161, "We would have never been able to..." —blog post, barstoolsports.com, April 13, 2020; https://www.barstoolsports.com/video/2257814/the-barstool-documentary-series-or-chapter-15-new-york-new-york

Pg. 161, "I can always tell..." —"Episode 1, Mike Kerns of Chernin Digital," *The Dave Portnoy Show* podcast; https://www.poorstuart.com/podcast-episode/Dave-Portnoy-Show/The-Dave-Portnoy-Show-Episode-1-Mike-Kerns-of-Cher/45348/

Pg. 161, "I wanted to see what kind of...," "Part of the thing for me...." —"Episode 1, Mike Kerns of Chernin Digital," *The Dave Portnoy Show* podcast; https://www.poorstuart.com/podcast-episode/Dave-Portnoy-Show/The-Dave-Portnoy-Show-Episode-1-Mike-Kerns-of-Cher/45348/

Pg. 162, "Dave was direct and professional..." —"Dave Portnoy Breaks Down the Chernin Group Deal that Changed Barstool History," *The Dave Portnoy Show*, Barstool Sports; https://www.youtube.com/watch?v=tMjt5jmpkek

Pg. 162, "The fundamental reason..." —"Episode 1, Mike Kerns of Chernin Digital," *The Dave Portnoy Show* podcast; https://www.poorstuart.com/podcast-episode/Dave-Portnoy-Show/The-Dave-Portnoy-Show-Episode-1-Mike-Kerns-of-Cher/45348/

Pg. 162, "Not only were we..." —Reeves Wiedeman, "The Dave Portnoy Playbook: Staring down the sports-gambling gold rush —and amid sexual misconduct allegations —Barstool's founder bets on the culture war," *New York Magazine*, November 23, 2021; https://nymag.com/intelligencer/article/dave-portnoy-barstool-sports.html

Pg. 163, "I didn't fight all that hard at giving up..."; "There are some things..."; "For all I know advertisers..."; "It was a miracle..." —"Episode 1, Mike Kerns of Chernin Digital," *The Dave Portnoy Show* podcast; https://www.poorstuart.com/podcast-episode/Dave-Portnoy-Show/The-Dave-Portnoy-Show-Episode-1-Mike-Kerns-of-Cher/45348/

Pg. 163, "I'd pay everyone their salary..." —"Dave Portnoy Breaks Down the Chernin Group Deal that Changed Barstool History," *The Dave Portnoy Show*, Barstool Sports; https://www.youtube.com/watch?v=tMjt5jmpkek

Pg. 164, "I didn't want the horses..." —"Episode 1, Mike Kerns of Chernin Digital," *The Dave Portnoy Show* podcast; https://www.poorstuart.com/podcast-episode/Dave-Portnoy-Show/The-Dave-Portnoy-Show-Episode-1-Mike-Kerns-of-Cher/45348/

Pg. 164, "Someone to capitalize on all the commercial..." —Dan Primack, "The Story of How Barstool Sports Got Sold," *Fortune*, January 7, 2016; https://fortune.com/2016/01/07/the-story-of-how-barstool-sports-got-sold/

Pg. 164, "They would see me as this crazy..." —"The Barstool Sports, Dave Portnoy, Peter Chernin Deal," Barstool Documentary Series, Barstool Sports; https://www.youtube.com/watch?v=6Nod9rfYjOw&t=6s

Pg. 164, "Dave is brilliant..." —"Episode 1, Mike Kerns of Chernin Digital," *The Dave Portnoy Show* podcast; https://www.poorstuart.com/podcast-episode/Dave-Portnoy-Show/The-Dave-Portnoy-Show-Episode-1-Mike-Kerns-of-Cher/45348/

CHAPTER 18

Pg. 165, "I think I got around $5M..." —"Planet Bri with Special Guest Dave Portnoy," *PlanBri* podcast; https://app.podscribe.ai/episode/89208084

Pg. 165, "I wanted to take Barstool..." —"Barstool Sports Emergency Press Conference —New York, New York," Barstool Sports; https://youtube.com/watch?v=V2VxODsf8Rk

Pg. 165, "I wasn't a business guy..." —"Dave Portnoy Breaks Down the Chernin Group Deal that Changed Barstool History," *The Dave Portnoy Show*, Barstool Sports; https://www.youtube.com/watch?v=tMjt5jmpkek

Pg. 165, "I thought the offer..."; "What I would have done differently..."; "The ad growth..." —"Episode 1, Mike Kerns of Chernin Digital," *The Dave Portnoy Show* podcast; https://www.poorstuart.com/podcast-episode/Dave-Portnoy-Show/The-Dave-Portnoy-Show-Episode-1-Mike-Kerns-of-Cher/45348/

Pg. 166, "Maybe the #1 request I get..." —blog post, barstoolsports.com, July 9, 2010; https://web.archive.org/web/20100711111630/http://boston.barstoolsports.com/page/2

Pg. 167, "This was above and beyond...we were in it together...." —"Dave Portnoy Breaks Down the Chernin Group Deal that Changed Barstool History," *The Dave Portnoy Show*, Barstool Sports; https://www.youtube.com/watch?v=tMjt5jmpkek and "Episode 1, Mike Kerns of Chernin Digital," *The Dave Portnoy Show* podcast; https://www.poorstuart.com/podcast-episode/Dave-Portnoy-Show/The-Dave-Portnoy-Show-Episode-1-Mike-Kerns-of-Cher/45348/

Pg. 168, "Uh, no, I don't..."; "We can cover..."; "Kamal, I don't...."; "You're going to..." —"Episode 1, Mike Kerns of Chernin Digital," *The Dave Portnoy Show* podcast; https://www.poorstuart.com/podcast-episode/Dave-Portnoy-Show/The-Dave-Portnoy-Show-Episode-1-Mike-Kerns-of-Cher/45348/

Pg. 170, "I hate this guy so fucking…"; "It was the most Barstool moment…" —Barstool Rundown, January 7, 2016; https://www.facebook.com/watch/?v=10153908859932502

Pg. 170, "Al Jazeera = Al Qaeda in…."; "Man who tweets…"; "@jenmacramos Lose some…"; "@jenmacramos do you mean…"; "@KFCBarstool @jenmacramos with that…"; "Not surprisingly, Barstool sports never…" —Nick Stellini, "How Barstool Sports Uses Social Media as a Weapon," *The Cauldron*; https://the-cauldron.com/how-barstool-sports-uses-social-media-as-a-weapon-7d440ab5f9e5

Pg. 172, "See, I understand that the…" —blog post, barstoolsports.com, September 14, 2012; https://web.archive.org/web/20120918011740/http://www.barstoolsports.com/boston/super-page/reader-email-hey-pres-how-do-you-put-up-with-the-delu-sional-losers-in-the-comment-section/

Pg. 172, "So I've noticed the comment section…" —blog post, barstoolsports.com, January 11, 2019; https://www.barstoolsports.com/blog/1192235/ive-made-the-ex-ecutive-decision-to-shut-down-the-comment-section-until-further-notice

Pg. 173, "He said we never condemn…" —Barstool Rundown, Section 10, January 7, 2016; https://www.youtube.com/watch?v=8Hlg7FOUPqM&list=PLD22d-YhH-Pbn4q1T94zI4QkggZCWDvqC2&index=4&t=554s

Pg. 173, "I don't like this philosophy…"; "I don't care…" —Barstool Rundown, Section 10, January 7, 2016; https://www.youtube.com/watch?v=8Hlg-7FOUPqM&list=PLD22d-YhHPbn4q1T94zI4QkggZCWDvqC2&index=4&t=554s

Pg. 174, "You think I like…" —tweet from Kara Swisher, January 7, 2016; https://x.com/karaswisher/status/685158991966556164?s=20

Pg. 174, "Kevin Clancy had just called me…."; "I'm not fucking doing…"; "Sounds good…"; "Everyone, including the press…" —"Episode 1, Mike Kerns of Chernin Digital," *The Dave Portnoy Show* podcast; https://www.poorstuart.com/podcast-episode/Dave-Portnoy-Show/The-Dave-Portnoy-Show-Episode-1-Mike-Kerns-of-Cher/45348/

Pg. 175, "Barstool Emergency Press…P.S. I'm kinda rich now…" —blog post, barstoolsports.com, January 7, 2016; https://www.barstoolsports.com/blog/450602/barstool-emergency-press-conference-new-york-new-york

CHAPTER 19

Pg. 177, "A sports blogger with…" —Kif Leswing, "A sports blogger with 250,000 followers barged into Twitter headquarters demanding to be veri-fied," *Business Insider*, February 2, 2016; https://www.businessinsider.com/dave-portenoy-crashes-twitter-hq-demands-verification-2016-2

Pg. 177, "There was just no explanation…"; "I said well my…" —"Episode 9, Peter Chernin," *The Dave Portnoy Show* podcast; https://podcasts.apple.com/us/podcast/barstool-radio/id1085919903?i=1000367254169

Pg. 177, "That's when I realized..." —"Rich Franklin, 10 Years at Barstool, and One Fetish Too Far," KFC Radio; https://www.dailymotion.com/video/x7sxsld

Pg. 178, "Every other word...you can't get into..." —"Episode 1, Mike Kerns of Chernin Digital," *The Dave Portnoy Show* podcast; https://www.poorstuart.com/podcast-episode/Dave-Portnoy-Show/The-Dave-Portnoy-Show-Episode-1-Mike-Kerns-of-Cher/45348/

Pg. 178, "I can't decide what's..." —Michael McCarthy, "No defending caveman Chernin's investment in Barstool Sports," *Sporting News*, January 11, 2016; https://www.sportingnews.com/us/more/news/chernin-group-barstool-sports-sold-boston-david-portnoy/1otp0rlsx96kg1drijp2yhndjz

Pg. 178, "I liked the caveman suit..." —"Episode 9, Peter Chernin," *The Dave Portnoy Show* podcast; https://podcasts.apple.com/us/podcast/barstool-radio/id1085919903?i=1000367254169

Pg. 178, "For the Chernin guys..." —"Dave Portnoy Breaks Down the Chernin Group Deal that Changed Barstool History," *The Dave Portnoy Show*, Barstool Sports; https://www.youtube.com/watch?v=tMjt5jmpkek

Pg. 178, "I thought that was..." —blog post, barstoolsports.com, April 13, 2020; https://www.barstoolsports.com/video/2257814/the-barstool-documentary-series-or-chapter-15-new-york-new-york

Pg. 179, "Print was very glamorous..."; "I failed a lot..." —Cecelia Townes, "Barstool Sports CEO Erika Nardini's Path of Nonconformity Has Translated into Success," *Forbes*, May 17, 2021; https://www.forbes.com/sites/cecelia-townes/2021/05/17/erika-nardini-ceo-of-barstool-sports-and-professional-nonconformist/?sh=4fcca5b963c1

Pg. 180, "I've always had..."; "I loved the idea..." —Anna Mazarakis and Alyson Shontell, "How the CEO of Barstool Sports beat out 74 men to land her dream job, and lost lots of friends in the process," *Business Insider*, January 19, 2018; https://www.businessinsider.com/erika-nardini-ceo-barstool-sports-interview-2018-1

Pg. 181, "I pulled out my phone...." —Anna Mazarakis and Alyson Shontell, "How the CEO of Barstool Sports beat out 74 men to land her dream job, and lost lots of friends in the process," *Business Insider*, January 19, 2018; https://www.businessinsider.com/erika-nardini-ceo-barstool-sports-interview-2018-1

Pg. 181, "I knew in my heart..." —"5 years at Barstool Sports," *Token CEO* podcast; https://youtu.be/qGNs0-cv3Bc?si=Kx_3FY-HLM6mWhqi

Pg. 181, "I really, from that moment..." —"5 years at Barstool Sports," *Token CEO* podcast; https://youtu.be/qGNs0-cv3Bc?si=Kx_3FY-HLM6mWhqi

Pg. 182, "One day, Betsy Morgan..." —"Masters in Business with Barry Ritholtz," *Bloomberg Radio*; https://ritholtz.com/2020/10/transcript-dave-portnoy/

Pg. 182, "When I was looking at Barstool..." —"Barstool Sports CEO Erika Nardini: 'I don't think you survive on an ad model,'" *Digiday*, February 8, 2017; https://digiday.com/media/barstool-sports-ceo-erika-nardini-digiday-podcast/#:~:text=When%20I%20was%20looking%20at,age%20on%20an%20ad%20model.%E2%80%9D

Pg. 182, "Everything that Erika said…" —"Masters in Business with Barry Ritholtz," *Bloomberg Radio*; https://ritholtz.com/2020/10/transcript-dave-portnoy/

Pg. 183, "I think I found our CEO. Do you know Erika…" —"Dave Portnoy Breaks Down the Chernin Group Deal that Changed Barstool History," *The Dave Portnoy Show*, Barstool Sports; https://www.youtube.com/watch?v=tMjt5jmpkek

Pg. 183, "Dave ordered this girly cocktail…" —"5 years at Barstool Sports," *Token CEO* podcast; https://youtu.be/qGNs0-cv3Bc?si=Kx_3FY-HLM6mWhqi

Pg. 183, "You're the only one…"; "The reason I didn't ask…." —Anna Mazarakis and Alyson Shontell, "How the CEO of Barstool Sports beat out 74 men to land her dream job, and lost lots of friends in the process," *Business Insider*, January 19, 2018; https://www.businessinsider.com/erika-nardini-ceo-barstool-sports-interview-2018-1

Pg. 184, "People did have…" —*#NoLimits Podcast with Rebecca Jarvis*; https://www.linkedin.com/pulse/im-here-build-great-brand-i-believe-company-erika-nardini-jarvis/

Pg. 184, "After they heard…" —Jay Caspian Kang, "Spurned by ESPN, Barstool Sports Is Staying on Offense," *The New York Times*, November 14, 2017; https://www.nytimes.com/2017/11/14/magazine/spurned-by-espn-barstool-sports-is-staying-on-offense.html

Pg. 184, "I think putting yourself…" —Anna Mazarakis and Alyson Shontell, "How the CEO of Barstool Sports beat out 74 men to land her dream job, and lost lots of friends in the process," *Business Insider*, January 19, 2018; https://www.businessinsider.com/erika-nardini-ceo-barstool-sports-interview-2018-1

CHAPTER 20

Pg. 187, "Erika is the best hire…" —Annie Goldsmith, "Erika Nardini Isn't Here to Apologize," theinformation.com, September 16, 2022; https://www.theinformation.com/articles/erika-nardini-isnt-here-to-apologize

Pg. 187, "The younger folks within agencies…" —Jay Caspian Kang, "Spurned by ESPN, Barstool Sports Is Staying on Offense," *The New York Times*, November 14, 2017; https://www.nytimes.com/2017/11/14/magazine/spurned-by-espn-barstool-sports-is-staying-on-offense.html

Pg. 187, "They were sitting on…" —"Marketing Masters: Barstool Sports Taps into Consumer Intent to Monetize Massive Following," *Hawke Media*, November 4, 2020; https://hawkemedia.com/insights/barstool-sports-sem-monitize-following/

Pg. 188, "About to get buried…" —tweet from Dave Portnoy, November 27, 2017; https://x.com/stoolpresidente/status/935276553717649408?s=20

Pg. 188, "Cyber Monday ends at…" —tweet from Dave Portnoy, November 30, 2020; https://x.com/stoolpresidente/status/1333598107976814594?s=20

Pg. 189, "FRIDAYS ARE FOR…" —tweet from John Feitelberg, June 11, 2016; https://x.com/FeitsBarstool/status/741482680907407360?s=20

Pg. 190, "Dave is actually quite humble…" —Anna Mazarakis and Alyson Shontell, "How the CEO of Barstool Sports beat out 74 men to land her dream job, and lost lots of friends in the process," *Business Insider*, January 19, 2018; https://www.businessinsider.com/erika-nardini-ceo-barstool-sports-interview-2018-1 and Podcast No. 99: Erika Nardini, Barstool Sports CEO, on Authenticity and Tuning Out Critics, *WHOOP* podcast; https://www.whoop.com/us/en/thelocker/podcast-99-erika-nardini-barstool-sports-ceo/

Pg. 190, "Dave could be the alpha…" —Emily Jane Fox, "Dave Portnoy Bought Barstool Back. Can Erika Ayers Badan Keep His Pirate Ship on Course?" *Vanity Fair*, August 14, 2023; https://www.vanityfair.com/news/2023/08/after-the-espn-penn-deal-barstool-just-wants-to-be-itself-which-was-the-problem

Pg. 190, "Dave's doing all the content…" —"Dave Portnoy Breaks Down the Chernin Group Deal that Changed Barstool History," *The Dave Portnoy Show*, Barstool Sports; https://www.youtube.com/watch?v=tMjt5jmpkek

Pg. 190, "I hate it more than…" —Brian Fitzsimmons, "Inside the unconventional and wildly successful world of Dave Portnoy and the Barstool Sports empire," *AOL*, September 26, 2016; https://www.aol.com/article/sports/2016/09/21/inside-the-unconventional-and-wildly-successful-world-of-dave-po/21476540/

Pg. 191, "Look at that. Trash everywhere…" —tweet from Dan Katz, January 7, 2016; https://x.com/BarstoolBigCat/status/685176939905167364?s=20

Pg. 191, "All the Boston guys…" —Brian Fitzsimmons, "Inside the unconventional and wildly successful world of Dave Portnoy and the Barstool Sports empire," *AOL*, September 26, 2016; https://www.aol.com/article/sports/2016/09/21/inside-the-unconventional-and-wildly-successful-world-of-dave-po/21476540/

Pg. 191, "I've officially gone full circle…" —tweet from Kevin Clancy, December 9, 2019; https://x.com/KFCBarstool/status/1204079018401812481?s=20

Pg. 191, "Where would 'Club Cool'…" —tweet from Dave Portnoy, September 6, 2016; https://x.com/stoolpresidente/status/773335949455585281?s=20

Pg. 192, "Power Rankings: 5) Coworker Dave…" —blog post, barstoolsports.com; October 7, 2016; https://www.barstoolsports.com/blog/639758/barstool-office-power-rankings-week-5

Pg. 192, "I'm never comfortable around…he keeps you on edge…" —"KFC Breaks Down Relationship with Dave Portnoy and Discusses Inside Barstool," KFC Radio; https://www.youtube.com/watch?v=b4EicGoLYd4

Pg. 193, "I think there's an element of the office…" —"Episode 31: Blogger Power Rankings," *The Dave Portnoy Show* podcast; https://podcasts.apple.com/us/podcast/barstool-radio/id1085919903?i=1000375671821

Pg. 193, "It's fuckin' big brother…" —blog post, barstoolsports.com, September 7, 2016; https://www.barstoolsports.com/video/620294/barstool-rundown-september-7-2016

Pg. 193, "Annnnd We're Off…" —blog post, barstoolsports.com, September 9, 2016; https://www.barstoolsports.com/video/621704/annnnd-were-off-random-dude-walks-into-the-office-un-announced-to-tell-us-about-his-viral-facebook-video

Pg. 194, "Yes, if Iowa…" —tweet from Dave Portnoy, November 12, 2016; https://x.com/stoolpresidente/status/797627719991300096?s=20

Pg. 194, "My friends call me 'Balls'…" —Dave Portnoy, "Caleb Pressley Tries out Glenny Balls for Dave Portnoy," YouTube; https://www.youtube.com/watch?v=7o3I0gJrq7Q

Pg. 195, "Barstool and Dave…" —tweet from Dan Katz, August 28, 2017; https://x.com/BarstoolBigCat/status/902167543321829376?s=20

Pg. 195, "There's a degree of loyalty…" —"Bonus Episode: Dave Discusses Massive Investment from Penn National," *Barstool Radio* podcast; https://podcasts.apple.com/ie/podcast/bonus-episode-dave-discusses-massive-investment-from/id1085919903?i=1000464021432

Pg. 195, "Dave *hates* segments…" —"KFC Breaks Down Relationship with Dave Portnoy and Discusses Inside Barstool," KFC Radio; https://www.youtube.com/watch?v=b4EicGoLYd4

Pg. 195, "I'm the straw that…" —blog post, barstoolsports.com, December 29, 2018; https://www.barstoolsports.com/blog/1094126/its-come-to-my-attention-that-some-nobody-robert-silverman-of-the-daily-beast-is-writing-a-hit-piece-on-me-5-years-in-the-making

Pg. 196, "He cleared out that…" —"Dave Portnoy Meets Stunning Look-Alike," *The Dave Portnoy Show*, Barstool Sports; https://www.youtube.com/watch?v=E6caSygkrsU

Pg. 196, "Shout Out All Business…" —blog post, barstoolsports.com, November 30, 2019; https://www.barstoolsports.com/blog/1553950/shout-out-all-business-pete-at-least-i-dont-have-to-watch-michigan-get-destroyed-on-a-live-stream-because-we-dont-have-tvs-that-work

Pg. 196, "Fuck All Business Pete…" —blog post, barstoolsports.com, March 21, 2019; https://www.barstoolsports.com/blog/1264333/fuck-all-business-pete

Pg. 196, "New episode is live…" —blog post, barstoolsports.com, May 31, 2022; https://www.barstoolsports.com/blog/3419553/maybe-one-day-all-business-pete-will-actually-respect-me

Pg. 196, "I also told @allbusinesspete…" —tweet from Dave Portnoy, June 15, 2022; https://x.com/stoolpresidente/status/1537136189416808448?s=20

Pg. 198, "There exists a swarm…"; "ESPN was definitely on my mind…." —Jay Caspian Kang, "Spurned by ESPN, Barstool Sports is Staying on Offense," *The New York Times*, November 14, 2017; https://www.nytimes.com/2017/11/14/magazine/spurned-by-espn-barstool-sports-is-staying-on-offense.html

CHAPTER 21

Pg. 199, "I almost never eat…" —blog post, barstoolsports.com, October 12, 2016; https://www.barstoolsports.com/blog/644090/i-disagree-with-this-list-of-the-5-most-crucial-things-successful-people-do-in-the-first-hour-of-their-day

Pg. 200, "Okay so right now…"; "I didn't mention it…" —blog post, barstool-sports.com, January 24, 2017; https://www.barstoolsports.com/blog/708564/ el-pres-state-of-the-union

Pg. 200, "I'll always be Dave's…" —tweet from Renee Portnoy, November 4, 2021; https://x.com/Renee_Portnoy/status/1456384753356189701?s=20

Pg. 201, "A big game calls…" —tweet from Dan Katz, January 22, 2017; https://x.com/BarstoolBigCat/status/823313863957417984?s=20

Pg. 201, "So yes, I recently met…"; "But nobody and I mean…" —blog post, barstoolsports.com, January 24, 2017; https://www.barstoolsports.com/blog/708564/ el-pres-state-of-the-union

Pg. 202, "Remember when I wrote the…" —tweet from Dave Portnoy, March 9, 2017; https://x.com/stoolpresidente/status/840033038411145216?s=20

Pg. 203, "I wonder if SoulCycle…" —tweet from Dave Portnoy, March 10, 2017; https://x.com/stoolpresidente/status/840084305615314945?s=20

Pg. 203, "From a business perspective…" —tweet from Dave Portnoy, March 10, 2017; https://x.com/stoolpresidente/status/840313850280964097?s=20

Pg. 203, "The Stoolies have been…" —blog post, barstoolsports.com, March 11, 2017; https://www.barstoolsports.com/blog/738646/reader-email-soulcycle-has-911-on-speed-dial-in-case-barstool-sports-shows-up-and-starts-making-people-uncomfortable

Pg. 204, "Dear NYC studios and soul managers…" —blog post, barstoolsports.com, March 11, 2017; https://www.barstoolsports.com/blog/738646/reader-email-soul-cycle-has-911-on-speed-dial-in-case-barstool-sports-shows-up-and-starts-making-people-uncomfortable

Pg. 204, "Best way to avoid…" —tweet from Dave Portnoy, March 10, 2017; https://x.com/stoolpresidente/status/840411730413015041?s=20

CHAPTER 22

Pg. 206, "Facebook has so many rules…"; "Fuck Facebook…" —"Episode 14: The Return of Mike Kerns," *The Dave Portnoy Show* podcast, https://www.poorstuart.com/podcast-episode/Dave-Portnoy-Show/ Episode-14-The-Return-of-Mike-Kerns/71787/

Pg. 206, "The future of Barstool is…" —"The future of Barstool Sports as Envisioned by Erika Nardini," *Cheddar News*; https://www.facebook.com/ watch/?v=1811818752472188

Pg. 207, "He turned to 22-year-old…"; "Mike Kerns, at one point…"; "He was slowly becoming…"; "They pulled up this…" —:Episode 3: Kevin Clancy, Dan Katz," *The Dave Portnoy Show* podcast https://podcasts.apple.com/us/podcast/barstool-radio/ id1085919903?i=1000364577706

Pg. 208, "We didn't do podcasts…" —Brian Fitzsimmons, "Inside the uncon-ventional and wildly successful world of Dave Portnoy and the Barstool Sports empire," *AOL*, September 26, 2016; https://www.aol.com/article/sports/2016/09/21/inside-the-unconventional-and-wildly-successful-world-of-dave-po/21476540/

Pg. 208, "We were able to take..." —Todd Spangler, "For Barstool Sports, Podcasts Are Now Around One-Third of Revenue," *Variety*, August 20, 2019; https://variety.com/2019/digital/news/barstool-sports-podcast-revenue-1203305912/

Pg. 209, "It's funny that the way we became friends..." —Jim Weber, "How *Pardon My Take* took over sports podcasting," *Awful Announcing*, June 12, 2017; https://awfulannouncing.com/online-outlets/pardon-take-took-sports-podcasting.html

Pg. 210, "Before anyone ever cared..." —blog post, barstoolsports.com, December 26, 2016; https://www.barstoolsports.com/blog/692762/50-introducing-barstools-newest-employee-uncle-chapspft-commenter-im-joining-barstool

Pg. 210, "I didn't know what to..." —Rick Maese, "PFT Commenter rose from an Internet 'cesspool' to podcasting glory. And no one knows who he is." *The Washington Post*, May 22, 2018; https://www.washingtonpost.com/sports/pft-commenter-rose-from-an-internet-cesspool-to-podcasting-glory-and-no-one-knows-who-he-is/2018/05/21/16077f24-5910-11e8-b656-a5f8c2a9295d_story.html

Pg. 211, "Would you go back in..." —PFT commenter, "Ben Carson would not abort Baby Hitler," *SB Nation*, November 11, 2015; https://www.sbnation.com/2015/11/11/9709934/gop-debate-is-ben-carson-pro-hitler

Pg. 211, "That actually gave..." —Jim Weber, "Mystery Man: The Legend of PFT Commenter," *Awful Announcing*, June 19, 2017; http://amp.awfulannouncing.com/online-outlets/mystery-man-legend-pft-commenter.html

CHAPTER 23

Pg. 212, "None of this is life or death...before we even sat down..." —Jemele Hill, "He Suspended Me from ESPN, But We're Still Friends," *The Atlantic*, November 29, 2018; https://www.theatlantic.com/ideas/archive/2018/11/john-skipper-suspended-me-espn-i-understand/576943/

Pg. 213, "It was never something..." —Jimmy Traina, "Barstool's Big Cat and PFT Wish ESPN Canceled Show Before First Episode," *Sports Illustrated*, October 25, 2017; https://www.si.com/extra-mustard/2017/10/25/pardon-my-take-big-cat-pft-espn-barstool-van-talk

Pg. 214, "ESPN executives viewed Big Cat..." —John Ourand, "How ESPN went from confident to queasy on Barstool Sports," *Sports Business Journal*, October 30, 2017; https://www.sportsbusinessjournal.com/Journal/Issues/2017/10/30/Media/Sports-Media.aspx

Pg. 214, "The name change got..." —Jimmy Traina, "Barstool's Big Cat and PFT Wish ESPN Canceled Show Before First Episode," *Sports Illustrated*, October 25, 2017; https://www.si.com/extra-mustard/2017/10/25/pardon-my-take-big-cat-pft-espn-barstool-van-talk

Pg. 214, "ESPN thought they were..." —Jay Caspian Kang, "Spurned by ESPN, Barstool Sports Is Staying on Offense," *The New York Times*, November 14, 2017;

https://www.nytimes.com/2017/11/14/magazine/spurned-by-espn-barstool-sports-is-staying-on-offense.html

Pg. 214, "We do not control…" —Richard Deitsch and Chris Chavez, "ESPN Abruptly Cancels Barstool Van Talk after One Episode," *Sports Illustrated*, October 23, 2017; https://www.si.com/media/2017/10/23/espn-cancels-barstool-van-talk-pft-commentator-big-cat-pardon-my-take#:~:text=As%20stated%20previously%2C%20we%20do,her%20the%20partnership%20was%20over.

Pg. 215, "Welcome to the ESPN family…" —tweet from Sam Ponder, October 16, 2017; https://x.com/samponder/status/920056799759339521?s=20

Pg. 215, "Blogs/websites that…" —tweet from Sam Ponder, July 24, 2014; https://x.com/samponder/status/492482810590949377

Pg. 215, "FUCK SAM PONDER…" —tweet from Sam Ponder, October 16, 2017; https://x.com/samponder/status/920056799759339521?s=20

Pg. 215, "No person watching…" —Luke Kerr-Dineen, "Barstool founder to Sam Ponder in 2014: Stop showing pictures of your 'ugly kid,' 'sex it up and be slutty,'" *USA TODAY*, October 17, 2017; https://ftw.usatoday.com/2017/10/christian-ponder-wife-sam-ponder-espn-barstool-sports-audio-rundown

Pg. 216, "I almost respect her for it…" —Andrew Bucholtz, "After Barstool Van Talk Cancellation…" *Awful Announcing*, October 23, 2017; https://awfulannouncing.com/espn/barstool-van-talk-portnoy-espn-played-right-into-our-hands.html

Pg. 216, "Saying you oppose…" —tweet from Sarah Spain, October 17, 2017; https://x.com/SarahSpain/status/920326688193511424?s=20

Pg. 216, "Regardless of which person…" —tweet from Sage Steele, October 16, 2017; https://x.com/sagesteele/status/920099974997610497

Pg. 217, "The comments about…" —Andrew Joseph, "Sam Ponder calls out Barstool Sports' offensive past ahead of its ESPN debut," *USA TODAY*, October 16, 2017; https://ftw.usatoday.com/2017/10/sam-ponder-barstool-sports-tweets-dan-katz-barstoolbigcat-espn-show#:~:text=ESPN%20EVP%20of%20programming%20and,the%20content%20of%20Barstool%20Sports. https://x.com/sagesteele/status/920099974997610497?s=20.

Pg. 217, "I talked to Burke…" —blog post, barstoolsports.com, May 10, 2023; https://www.barstoolsports.com/blog/3466696/watch-the-moment-big-cat-and-pft-commenter-found-out-espn-canceled-barstool-van-talk-back-in-2017

Pg. 217, "From what we heard…" —Andrew Bucholtz, "After Barstool Van Talk Cancellation…" *Awful Announcing*, October 23, 2017; https://awfulannouncing.com/espn/barstool-van-talk-portnoy-espn-played-right-into-our-hands.html

Pg. 218, "They couldn't get over…" —blog post, barstoolsports.com, May 10, 2023; https://www.barstoolsports.com/blog/3466696/watch-the-moment-big-cat-and-pft-commenter-found-out-espn-canceled-barstool-van-talk-back-in-2017

Pg. 218, "Effective immediately I am…" —Richard Deitsch and Chris Chavez, "ESPN Abruptly Cancels Barstool Van Talk after One Episode," *Sports Illustrated*, October 23, 2017; https://www.si.com/media/2017/10/23/espn-cancels-barstool-van-talk-pft-commentator-big-cat-pardon-my-take#:~:text=As%20stated%20 previously%2C%20we%20do,her%20the%20partnership%20was%20over.

Pg. 219, "One-Episode Partnership Makes…" —Chad Finn, "One Episode Partnership with Barstool Makes ESPN Look Bad," *The Boston Globe*, October 27, 2017; https://www.boston.com/sports/media/2017/10/27/ one-episode-partnership-with-barstool-makes-espn-look-bad/

Pg. 219, "ESPN's Barstool Sports…" —Taylor Link, "ESPN's Barstool Sports debacle is the sports network's reckoning," *Salon*, October 28, 2017; https://www.salon. com/2017/10/28/espns-barstool-sports-canceled/

Pg. 219, "ESPN Wanted Barstool…" —Laura Wagner, "ESPN Wanted Barstool Sports, But Without the Stench," *Deadspin*, October 19, 2017; https://deadspin.com/ espn-wanted-barstool-sports-but-without-the-stench-1819664413

Pg. 219, "According to sources…" —Laura Wagner, "ESPN Wanted Barstool Sports, But Without the Stench," *Deadspin*, October 19, 2017; https://deadspin.com/ espn-wanted-barstool-sports-but-without-the-stench-1819664413

Pg. 219, "At ESPN, the Problems…" —Jenna Abelson, "At ESPN, the Problems for Women Run Deep," *The Boston Globe*, December 14, 2017; https://www.boston.com/sports/media/2017/12/14/ women-whove-worked-at-espn-say-its-problems-go-far-beyond-barstool-sports/

Pg. 220, "Report: ESPN President…" —Associated Press, "Report: ESPN president John Skipper resigned over cocaine extortion plot," *ESPN*, March 15, 2018; https://www.espn.com/espn/story/_/id/22779033/ espn-president-john-skipper-resigned-cocaine-extortion-plot

CHAPTER 24

Pg. 221, "I was always a little…" —Ricky Keeler, "Dave Portnoy: ESPN Rejection Shaped Future of Barstool," *Barrett Media*, June 1, 2021; https://barrettsportsmedia. com/2021/06/01/dave-portnoy/

Pg. 221, "ESPN needed us…" —Hannah Withiam, "Barstool Sports fires back: 'ESPN needed us more,'" *The New York Post*, October 23, 2017; https://nypost. com/2017/10/23/barstool-sports-fires-back-espn-needed-us-more/

Pg. 221, "He [Katz] wanted no…"; "Yeah he was not happy…"; "I fucking hate agents"; "That's the one thing about…" —"Dave Portnoy Predicts the Future of Barstool Sports after the Full Penn Acquisition," *KFC Radio*; https://www.youtube. com/watch?v=lwUQtsmfsW0

Pg. 222, "Welcome to the mud…"; "Watching the Lakers…"; "if u ever want…" — Steve DelVecchio, "Sam Ponder admits she has been 'immature' after uncovering of old tweets," *Larry Brown Sports*, October 18, 2017; https://larrybrownsports.com/ media/sam-ponder-admits-she-has-been-immature-old-tweets/403187

Pg. 223, "Should I retire for the good…" —blog post, barstoolsports. com, October 17, 2017; https://www.barstoolsports.com/blog/864175/ should-i-retire-for-the-good-of-barstool

Pg. 223, "Update —I thought about it…" —blog post, barstoolsports.
com, October 17, 2017; https://www.barstoolsports.com/blog/864249/
update-i-thought-about-it-i-aint-leaving

Pg. 223, "On that Tuesday…"; "The slut comment…" —Jimmy Traina, "Barstool's
Big Cat and PFT Wish ESPN Canceled Show Before First Episode," *Sports
Illustrated*, October 25, 2017; https://www.si.com/extra-mustard/2017/10/25/
pardon-my-take-big-cat-pft-espn-barstool-van-talk

Pg. 224, "The two or three…"; "Here's the one thing," —Dan Patrick, *Pardon My
Take* podcast; https://www.poorstuart.com/podcast-episode/Pardon-My-Take/
Dan-Patrick/220058/

Pg. 225, "The company has far…" —"Barstool Sports Gets $15M Influx from
Chernin Group; Plans New Properties, More Hiring," *Sports Business Journal*,
January 24, 2018; https://www.sportsbusinessjournal.com/Daily/Issues/2018/01/24/
Finance/Barstool.aspx

Pg. 226, "We didn't know…"; "Dave, we need to…" —"Dave Portnoy Breaks Down
the Chernin Group Deal that Changed Barstool History," *The Dave Portnoy Show*,
Barstool Sports; https://www.youtube.com/watch?v=tMjt5jmpkek

CHAPTER 25

Pg. 227, "Barstool Sports is now…" —blog post, barstoolsports.com,
December 13, 2018; https://www.barstoolsports.com/blog/920528/
barstool-sports-is-now-valued-at-over-100-million-dollars-gasp

Pg. 227, "I'll fall on that sword"; "I flew to LA…" —"Dave Portnoy Breaks Down
the Chernin Group Deal that Changed Barstool History," *The Dave Portnoy Show*,
Barstool Sports; https://www.youtube.com/watch?v=tMjt5jmpkek

Pg. 228, "It turned out to be…" —Ricky Keeler, "Dave Portnoy: ESPN Rejection
Shaped Future of Barstool," *Barrett Media*, June 1, 2021; https://barrettsportsmedia.
com/2021/06/01/dave-portnoy/

Pg. 228, "As much as it sucked…" —tweet from Dan Katz, October 13, 2022;
https://x.com/BarstoolBigCat/status/1580670762653913090?s=20

Pg. 228, "We did one episode…" —Barstool Yak TikTok; https://www.tiktok.com/@
barstoolyak/video/7234338487820930346

Pg. 228, "I don't think we change…" —"Barstool Sports Sticking with Signature
Content Aimed at Young Male Demo," *Sports Business Journal*, November 8,
2017; https://www.sportsbusinessjournal.com/Daily/Issues/2017/11/08/Media/
Barstool.aspx

Pg. 228, "We live in the mud…" —Barstool Rundown, Barstool Sports, October 24,
2017; https://www.youtube.com/watch?v=2capkgGn1hs

Pg. 228, "I think [Portnoy] sticking to his…" —Travis Anderson, "Barstool Sports
Saying It's not Going to Change," *The Boston Globe*, November 7, 2017; https://
www.bostonglobe.com/metro/2017/11/07/amid-controversy-barstool-sports-
standing-its-brand/OLPbaEZaQOMH977o3kCR9O/story.html?event=event12

Pg. 229, "Please stop gambling…" —tweet from Kevin Clancy, August 4, 2014; https://x.com/KFCBarstool/status/496398925465944066?s=20

Pg. 230, "Jamie Foxx, he's…"; "That is a beatdown…" —Brad Allen, "Did FanDuel Pass on Barstool Sportsbook Before Penn National Deal?" *Legal Sports Report*, September 29, 2020; https://www.legalsportsreport.com/44576/fanduel-barstool-sportsbook-deal/

Pg. 230, "Your gambling issues…"; "The moment I knew…" —"Bonus Episode: Dave Discusses Massive Investment from Penn National," *Barstool Radio* podcast; https://podcasts.apple.com/ie/podcast/bonus-episode-dave-discusses-massive-investment-from/id1085919903?i=1000464021432

Pg. 231, "I'm Pretty Sure These…" —www.barstoolsports.com, May 14, 2018; https://www.barstoolsports.com/blog/994958/im-pretty-sure-these-new-sports-gambling-laws-should-make-rich-beyond-my-wildest-dreams-but-i-cant-figure-out-how-yet

Pg. 231, "We are the first…" —tweet from Kevin Clancy, September 18, 2020; https://x.com/KFCBarstool/status/1306950729077325827?s=20

Pg. 232, "It was the one vice…" —"Dave Portnoy Predicts the Future of Barstool Sports after the Full Penn Acquisition," *KFC Radio*; https://www.youtube.com/watch?v=lwUQtsmfsW0

Pg. 232, "I didn't want it to…" —"Talking the History of Barstool with KFC," *The Dave Portnoy Show*, Barstool Sports; https://www.youtube.com/watch?v=d1yuzhNe9hg&t=1201s

Pg. 232, "The way we've talked…" —Paolo Confino, "Dave Portnoy Buys…," *Fortune*, August 9, 2023; https://fortune.com/2023/08/09/penn-barstool-espn-dave-portnoy-sports-betting/

Pg. 232, "Barstool Sports star KFC's wife…" —"Barstool Sports star KFC's wife claims he's been cheating on her since pregnancy," *Fox News*, January 6, 2018; https://www.foxnews.com/entertainment/barstool-sports-star-kfcs-wife-claims-hes-been-cheating-on-her-since-pregnancy

Pg. 232, "Last night after I…" —Nicholas Parco, "Barstool Blogger Kevin Clancy…," *NY Daily News*, January 6, 2018; https://www.nydailynews.com/2018/01/06/barstool-sports-blogger-kevin-clancys-wife-claims-he-cheated-on-her-while-she-was-pregnant/#:~:text=%E2%80%9CLast%20night%20after%20I%20put,their%20wedding%20day%20in%202014.

Pg. 233, "I'm sorry to my wife…" —Jenny Stanton, "'I have ruined my marriage…," *Daily Mail*, January 7, 2018; https://www.dailymail.co.uk/news/article-5243183/Barstool-Sports-host-admits-cheating-pregnant-wife.html

Pg. 233, "I didn't want Barstool…" —Dana Rose Falcone, "Barstool Sports' Kevin Clancy Issues Public Apology after Wife's Accuses Him of Infidelity," *People*, January 7, 2018; https://people.com/sports/barstool-sports-kevin-clancy-apology-video-infidelity-allegations/

Pg. 233, "I'm not going to…."; "You had this image…"; "Alright it is January 7th…"; "it's fair, I get it…" —*Stool Scenes Episode 47 Part 1*, Barstool Sports; https://www.youtube.com/watch?v=wJPzr4pDYkc

Pg. 234, "If you call yourself…" —Michael Kaplan, "Michael Rapaport on his famous feuds with Kevin Durant, Barstool Sports & more," *The New York Post*, April 17, 2021; https://nypost.com/2021/04/17/michael-rapaport-on-his-famous-feuds-with-kevin-durant-barstool-more/

Pg. 235, "We had a snake who…" —"Snakes on a Domain," *Stool Scenes Episode 89*, Barstool Sports; https://www.youtube.com/watch?v=wHHbqdhQtUo

Pg. 235, "The business side of things…" —tweet from Pat McAfee, August 31, 2018; https://x.com/PatMcAfeeShow/status/1035595152323174400?s=20

Pg. 235, "Emergency Press Conference…" —blog post, barstoolsports.com, February 3, 2019; https://amp.barstoolsports.com/blog/1217559/emergency-press-conference-i-walked-right-of-jail-to-find-out-the-pats-made-history-stillhere

Pg. 236, "Turner, ESPN, and the no…" —tweet from Erika Nardini, February 20, 2019; https://x.com/erika_/status/1098250353890508800?s=20

Pg. 237, "I'm biased because I own…" —"Bonus Episode: Dave Discusses Massive Investment from Penn National," *Barstool Radio* podcast; https://podcasts.apple.com/ie/podcast/bonus-episode-dave-discusses-massive-investment-from/id1085919903?i=1000464021432

CHAPTER 26

Pg. 238, "What Fresh Hell Is Barstool Sports?" —Will Leitch, "What Fresh Hell Is Barstool Sports?" *New York Magazine*, September 25, 2018; https://nymag.com/intelligencer/2018/09/what-fresh-kind-of-hell-is-barstool-sports.html

Pg. 239, "Barstool Sports Founder…" —Samer Kalaf, "Barstool Sports Founder Comes up with Dumbest Possible Reason to Delete Dumbest Possible Post," *Deadspin*, May 31, 2017; https://deadspin.com/barstool-sports-founder-comes-up-with-dumbest-possible-1795677627

Pg. 240, "ESPN Is Trying Anything…" —Laura Wagner, "ESPN Is Trying Anything," *Deadspin*, October 5, 2017; https://deadspin.com/espn-is-trying-anything-1819177716

Pg. 240, "The Barstool Sports Gang…" —Samer Kalaf, "The Barstool Sports Gang Had a Blackface Whoopsie," *Deadspin*, December 12, 2018; https://deadspin.com/the-barstool-sports-gang-had-a-blackface-whoopsie-1831047100

Pg. 240, "Comedian Says Barstool…" —Samer Kalaf, "Comedian Says Barstool Sports Stole Her Video, Tried to Bribe Her with $50 Gift Card," *Deadspin*, March 5, 2019; https://deadspin.com/comedian-says-barstool-sports-stole-her-video-tried-to-1833048577

Pg. 240, "Barstool Sport's Dave Portnoy…" —Samer Kalaf, "Barstool Sports' Dave Portnoy Actually Trembles while Being Asked about

Harassing Women," *Deadspin*, June 26, 2018; https://deadspin.com/
barstool-sports-dave-portnoy-actually-trembles-while-be-1835883094

Pg. 241, "Barstool Sports Publishes…" —Samer Kalaf, "Barstool Sports
Publishes Bizarre Blog on Missing Woman, Deletes It after Police Charge
Suspect with Murder," *Deadspin*, June 28, 2019; https://deadspin.com/
barstool-sports-publishes-bizarre-blog-on-missing-woman-1835954257

Pg. 241, "ESPN Wanted Barstool…" —Laura Wagner, "ESPN Wanted Barstool
Sports, But Without the Stench," *Deadspin*, October 19, 2017; https://deadspin.com/
espn-wanted-barstool-sports-but-without-the-stench-1819664413

Pg. 241, "Barstool Employee Unhappy…" —Laura Wagner, "Barstool Employee
Unhappy about Being Filmed in the Shower By His Boss," *Deadspin*, February 6,
2018; https://deadspin.com/barstool-employee-unhappy-about-being-filmed-in-
the-sho-1822776835#:~:text=On%20Saturday%2C%20Barstool%20Sports%20
president,dick%20being%20on%20the%20internet.%E2%80%9D

Pg. 241, "The Bruins Don't…" —Laura Wagner, "The Bruins Don't Want to Talk
about Getting into Bed with Barstool Sports," *Deadspin*, May 29, 2019; https://
deadspin.com/the-bruins-dont-want-to-talk-about-getting-into-bed-wit-
1835100650#:~:text=NHL-,The%20Bruins%20Don't%20Want%20To%20Talk%20
About,Into%20Bed%20With%20Barstool%20Sports&text=The%20Boston%20
Bruins%20were%20happy,to%20talk%20about%20the%20partnership.

Pg. 241, "Worst Writer on…" —blog post, barstoolsports.com,
May 31, 2017; https://www.barstoolsports.com/blog/787105/
worst-writer-on-the-internet-samer-kalif-of-univision-back-at-it

Pg. 241, "Resident Worst Writer…" —blog post, barstoolsports.com, November 8,
2018; https://www.barstoolsports.com/blog/1143259/resident-worst-writer-on-the-
internet-samer-paloof-of-deadspin-lies-about-whether-south-carolina-coach-will-
muschamp-talked-to-his-players-about-voting

Pg. 242, "@laurawags publishing a bunch…" —tweet from Dave Portnoy, May 24,
2018; https://x.com/stoolpresidente/status/999771742162825216?s=20

Pg. 242, "I cannot quit…" —tweet from Dave Portnoy, May 29, 2019; https://x.com/
stoolpresidente/status/1133867569138556928?s=20

Pg. 242, "Short-tempered Adderall…" —tweet from Dave Portnoy, July 24, 2018;
https://x.com/stoolpresidente/status/1021934234951475200?s=20

Pg. 242, "Hey @laurawags I mean it…" —tweet from Dave Portnoy, May 9. 2018;
https://x.com/stoolpresidente/status/994252690854203392?s=20

Pg. 242, "I Need Laura Wagner to be…" —blog post, barstool-
sports.com, February 13, 2018; https://www.barstoolsports.com/
blog/935488/i-need-laura-wagner-to-be-my-valentine

Pg. 243, "Total wildcat in the sack…"; "I want to stick my tongue.…" —Robert
Silverman, "Inside Barstool Sports' Culture of Online Hate: 'They Treat Sexual
Harassment and Cyberbullying as a Game,'" *The Daily Beast*, September 24, 2018;
https://www.thedailybeast.com/inside-barstool-sports-culture-of-online-hate-they-
treat-sexual-harassment-and-cyberbullying-as-a-game

Pg. 243, "I couldn't love her any…" —tweet from Barstool Radio, September 13, 2018; https://x.com/BarstoolRadio/status/1040356158974902281?s=20

Pg. 243, "Since I was writing about…" —Robert Silverman, "Inside Barstool Sports' Culture of Online Hate: 'They Treat Sexual Harassment and Cyberbullying as a Game,'" *The Daily Beast*, September 24, 2018; https://www.thedailybeast.com/inside-barstool-sports-culture-of-online-hate-they-treat-sexual-harassment-and-cyberbullying-as-a-game

Pg. 243, "We're a comedy site…"; "After a string…" —Lucia Moses, "'It's just not fair': Barstool Sports founder Dave Portnoy defends his site against accusations of toxicity and misogyny," *Business Insider*, December 18, 2018; https://www.businessinsider.com/barstool-sports-dave-portnoy-responds-to-accusations-of-toxicity-and-misogyny-2018-12

Pg. 244, "Right now, I feel…" —"Best of Week 88, Back in the Mud," Barstool Radio podcast, September 2017, 2018; https://www.podchaser.com/podcasts/barstool-radio-12787/episodes/best-of-week-88-back-in-the-mu-31626488

Pg. 244, "Sociopathic Barstool Founder…" —Laura Wagner, "Sociopathic Barstool Founder Dave Portnoy Giddy about 'Suffocating' ESPN Host Sam Ponder in 'Online War,'" *Deadspin*, September 13, 2018; https://deadspin.com/sociopathic-barstool-founder-dave-portnoy-giddy-about-1829033370#:~:text=Portnoy%20understands%20this%20just%20as,an%20%20E2%80%9Cinternet%20online-%20war.%E2%80%9D&text=%E2%80%9CI'm%20excited%2C%20it's,will%20get%20%23samponderlies%20trending.%E2%80%9D

Pg. 244, "Dave responds to Ponder…" —tweet from Barstool Radio, September 13, 2018; https://x.com/BarstoolRadio/status/1040341685006479361?s=20

Pg. 245, "Reached via text…" —Robert Silverman, "Inside Barstool Sports' Culture of Online Hate: 'They Treat Sexual Harassment and Cyberbullying as a Game,'" *The Daily Beast*, September 24, 2018; https://www.thedailybeast.com/inside-barstool-sports-culture-of-online-hate-they-treat-sexual-harassment-and-cyberbullying-as-a-game

Pg. 245, "Dave always says he goes…" —blog post, barstoolsports.com, December 28, 2018; https://www.barstoolsports.com/blog/1099840/an-overdue-note-from-our-new-ombudsman-eric-sollenberger-eric-sollenbergers-other-twin-brother

Pg. 246, "I don't want to get…" —"Best of Week 88, Back in the Mud," Barstool Radio podcast, September 2017, 2018; https://www.podchaser.com/podcasts/barstool-radio-12787/episodes/best-of-week-88-back-in-the-mu-31626488

Pg. 246, "You don't think she's playing like…" —"Best of Week 88, Back in the Mud," Barstool Radio podcast, September 2017, 2018; https://www.podchaser.com/podcasts/barstool-radio-12787/episodes/best-of-week-88-back-in-the-mu-31626488

Pg. 247, "Would I have liked…" —"Dave Portnoy Breaks Down the Chernin Group Deal that Changed Barstool History," *The Dave Portnoy Show*, Barstool Sports; https://www.youtube.com/watch?v=tMjt5jmpkek

Pg. 247, "There are people who…" —Kristen Fleming, "Hate Erika Nardini? You're not alone, and she couldn't care less," *The New York Post*, October 20, 2018; https://nypost.com/2018/10/20/barstools-female-ceo-claps-back-at-critics-of-100m-brand/

Pg. 247, "Every time anyone mentions…" —Jay Caspian Kang, "Spurned by ESPN, Barstool Sports Is Staying on Offense," *The New York Times*, November 14, 2017; https://www.nytimes.com/2017/11/14/magazine/spurned-by-espn-barstool-sports-is-staying-on-offense.html

Pg. 248, "[Barstool] isn't for everyone…" —tweet thread from Erika Nardini, October 17, 2017; https://x.com/erika_/status/920330164017516544?s=20

Pg. 248, "We have a zero…" —tweet from Erika Nardini, October 11, 2017; https://x.com/erika_/status/918273438812393472?s=20

Pg. 248, "A Blog from the Token…" —blog post, barstoolsports.com, September 27, 2018; https://www.barstoolsports.com/blog/1101145/a-blog-from-the-token-female-ceo-of-barstool-sports

Pg. 249, "There's a very strong…"; "My job as CEO isn't to…" —Kristen Fleming, "Hate Erika Nardini? You're not alone, and she couldn't care less," *The New York Post*, October 20, 2018; https://nypost.com/2018/10/20/barstools-female-ceo-claps-back-at-critics-of-100m-brand/

Pg. 249, "At the heart of it…"; "I liked Dave instantly…" —blog post, barstoolsports.com, January 16, 2024; https://www.barstoolsports.com/blog/3500230/i-am-stepping-down-as-ceo-of-barstool-sports

Pg. 249, "And I am protective…" —Emily Jane Fox, "Dave Portnoy Bought Barstool Back. Can Erika Ayers Badan Keep His Pirate Ship on Course?" *Vanity Fair*, August 14, 2023; https://www.vanityfair.com/news/2023/08/after-the-espn-penn-deal-barstool-just-wants-to-be-itself-which-was-the-problem

Pg. 249, "In these press hits, Nardini…" —Megan Greenwell, "Oh God, Even Our Parent Company Is Airing the Barstool Sports CEO's Evasive, Charming Bullshit," *Deadspin*, April 6, 2018; https://deadspin.com/oh-god-even-our-parent-company-is-airing-the-barstool-1825053242

Pg. 251, "This Is How Things Work Now…" —Laura Wagner, "This Is How Things Work Now at G/O Media," *Deadspin*, August 2, 2019; https://archive.fo/Cko5O

Pg. 252, "I have been repeatedly…" —Maxwell Tani, "*Deadspin* Editor Quits, Rages Against Bosses: 'I've Been Repeatedly Lied to and Gaslit,'" *The Daily Beast*, August 16, 2019; https://www.thedailybeast.com/deadspin-editor-quits-rails-against-bosses-ive-been-repeatedly-lied-to-and-gaslit

Pg. 252, "Oh No!!! Hearing…" —blog post, barstoolsports.com, August 16, 2019; https://www.barstoolsports.com/blog/1392318/oh-no-hearing-megan-greenwell-is-out-at-deadspin-the-horror

Pg. 253, "On Monday, the journalists…" —Marc Tracy, "Stick to Sports? No way. *Deadspin* Journalists Quit En Masse," *The New York Times*, October 30, 2019; https://www.nytimes.com/2019/10/30/business/media/deadspin-sports-staff.html

Pg. 253, "Dear All *Deadspin*…" —www.barstoolsports.com, October 28, 2019; https://www.barstoolsports.com/blog/1467563/dear-all-deadspin-employees-i-will-post-any-blogs-that-your-boss-keeps-deleting-without-your-permission-if-you-ask-me-nicely

Pg. 253, "Oh No. Laura Wags…" —www.barstoolsports.com, October 30, 2019; https://www.barstoolsports.com/blog/1472359/oh-no-laura-wags-out-at-deadspin

Pg. 254, "So by now everybody…" —blog post, barstoolsports.com, October 30, 2019; https://www.barstoolsports.com/blog/1472707/are-samir-paloof-and-drew-magary-the-two-biggest-cowards-on-the-planet

Pg. 254, "Dave Portnoy is the kind…" —"Real Sports with Bryant Gumbel 267," HBO; https://www.hbo.com/real-sports-with-bryant-gumbel

CHAPTER 27

Pg. 255, "Put in some effort…" —"Best of Barstool Radio Week 128, Dressing for the Dunkin' Awards X Chef Battle Royale," *Barstool Radio* podcast; https://www.podchaser.com/podcasts/best-of-barstool-radio-12787/episodes/best-of-week-128-dressing-for-41454199

Pg. 255, "Alright, welcome ladies…" —"Dave Portnoy Roasts His Employees at the 2019 Dunkin' Awards," Barstool Sports; https://www.youtube.com/watch?v=KdQz7gfsUlM

Pg. 256, "It is surreal going from…" —"Barstool Sports Founder Dave Portnoy Reviews the New Office," Barstool Sports; https://www.youtube.com/watch?v=hA6RZtyIY10&t=500s

Pg. 258, "Cancellations made it…"; "The Jersey Transit…"; "He was clearly…" —"Commuters, Mets Fans Face Travel Nightmare after NJ Transit Derailment Wreaks Havoc at Penn Station," adb buli; https://www.youtube.com/watch?v=gpvGZy-kM-c

Pg. 258, "I worked as a court-clerk…" —Dave Portnoy TikTok post; https://www.tiktok.com/@stoolpresidente/video/7270710654888185130?lang=en

Pg. 259, "The problem with our…" —tweet from Dave Portnoy, October 14, 2019; https://x.com/stoolpresidente/status/1183739294718070784?s=20

Pg. 259, "I love when employees complain…" —tweet from Dave Portnoy, November 24, 2021; https://x.com/stoolpresidente/status/1463547418012790792?s=20

Pg. 260, "There's so many…" —"Dave Portnoy Fires Francis after Crazy Week at Barstool Sports, Barstool Sports: Stool Scenes 217"; https://www.youtube.com/watch?v=KiMJjfJCjds

Pg. 260, "By the way…" —tweet from Dave Portnoy, August 26, 2016; https://x.com/stoolpresidente/status/769251639861608448?s=20

Pg. 260, "Mantis [another Barstool employee]…" —tweet from Dave Portnoy, July 29, 2021; https://x.com/stoolpresidente/status/1420912993651642370?s=20

Pg. 260, "Apparently, they are now…" —tweet from Dave Portnoy, September 1, 2023; https://x.com/stoolpresidente/status/1697628812580622506?s=20

Pg. 261, "The follow-up from…" —Milton Tough video on YouTube, Barstool Sports; https://www.youtube.com/watch?v=ODV7lvxVh3Q&t=116s

Pg. 261, "BAHAHA! I hope and…"; "If you work for…" —Eriq Gardner, "National Labor Relations Board to Investigate Barstool Sports Founder's Tweets," *The Hollywood Reporter*, August 16, 2019; https://www.hollywoodreporter.com/business/business-news/national-labor-relations-board-investigate-barstool-sports-founders-tweets-1232632/

Pg. 261, "If you're a boss…" —tweet from AOC, August 13, 2019; https://x.com/AOC/status/1161327815490330624?s=20

Pg. 262, "Welcome to the…" —tweet from Dave Portnoy, August 13, 2019; https://x.com/stoolpresidente/status/1161330937931677696?s=20

Pg. 262, "Well, well, well…" —tweet from AOC, January 21, 2020; https://x.com/AOC/status/1219760658289479682?s=20

Pg. 263, "We have a long history…" —Dave Portnoy Rips apart Employee Live on Air, Dave Portnoy; https://www.youtube.com/shorts/zgKETAjAG8k

Pg. 264, "Barstool Sports Slut-Shames…" —Robert Silverman, "Barstool Sports Slut-Shames Mackenzie Lueck, Murdered 23-Year-Old Female College Student," *The Daily Beast*, June 29, 2019; https://www.thedailybeast.com/barstool-sports-slut-shames-mackenzie-lueck-murdered-23-year-old-female-college-student

Pg. 264, "There're certain things I can't'…" —"Dave Portnoy Fires Francis after Crazy Week at Barstool Sports: Stool Scenes 217"; https://www.youtube.com/watch?v=KiMJjfJCjds

Pg. 264, "If it had been…"; "It's a fine line…" —"Francis Returns to Barstool HQ to Talk with Dave Portnoy: DPS #91," *The Dave Portnoy Show*, Barstool Sports; https://www.youtube.com/watch?v=Fr9vpgjlLQw&t=2004s

Pg. 264, "That's just not true…" —"Francis Ellis Returns to Barstool HQ, Son of a Boy Dad: Ep. 70"; https://www.youtube.com/watch?v=DbnsORKaD50

Pg. 265, "I loved working with…" —tweet from Erika Nardini, June 28, 2019; https://x.com/erika_/status/1144784962929008640?s=20

Pg. 265, "I should just fuck…"; "There's been several times…" —"Dave Portnoy Breaks Down the Chernin Group Deal that Changed Barstool History," *The Dave Portnoy Show*, Barstool Sports; https://www.youtube.com/watch?v=tMjt5jmpkek

Pg. 266, "Essentially, I [wondered at that time]…" —"Dave Portnoy on Barstool, Betting and Bitcoin," *Pomp Podcast* #392; https://www.youtube.com/watch?v=CoTtXaP4F-I and "Dave Portnoy Breaks Down the Chernin Group Deal that Changed Barstool History," *The Dave Portnoy Show*, Barstool Sports; https://www.youtube.com/watch?v=tMjt5jmpkek

Pg. 267, "Barstool Engaged in…" —Ryan Glasspiegel, "Barstool Reportedly in Advanced Talks to Sell to Penn National Gaming," *The Big Lead*, January 10, 2010; https://www.thebiglead.com/posts/barstool-chernin-penn-national-gaming-01dy-8qjjx1p6 (note I changed the "Reportedly" to "Engaged" to fit the tense of the paragraph)

CHAPTER 28

Pg. 268, "We met with everybody..."; "They were scared of..." —"Dave Portnoy on Barstool, Betting and Bitcoin," *Pomp Podcast* #392; https://www.youtube.com/watch?v=CoTtXaP4F-I

Pg. 268, "Hey, Pres, remember..." —blog post, barstoolsports.com, March 17, 2015; https://www.barstoolsports.com/blog/238225/draftkings-is-valued-at-1-billion-dollars

Pg. 269, "I really like the..."; "We had worked with them..." —"Dave Portnoy on Barstool, Betting and Bitcoin," *Pomp Podcast* #392; https://www.youtube.com/watch?v=CoTtXaP4F-I

Pg. 269, "We had a great casino..."; "I was like, wow..." —Jay Snowden, *The Corp Podcast*; https://www.youtube.com/watch?v=SlIepXSrzlg

Pg. 270, "This is what I always ..." —Emily Steel, "Desperate for Growth, Aging Casino Company Embraced 'Degenerate Gambler,'" *The New York Times*, November 20, 2022; https://www.nytimes.com/2022/11/20/business/barstool-sports-betting-david-portnoy.html

Pg. 271, "That had Dave..." —Jay Snowden, *The Corp Podcast*; https://www.youtube.com/watch?v=SlIepXSrzlg

Pg. 271, "A huge part of"; "the last big thing..." —Jay Snowden, *The Corp Podcast*; https://www.youtube.com/watch?v=SlIepXSrzlg

Pg. 271, "Much of the media..." —"Penn Entertainment Boss Defends Barstool Brand Before Massachusetts Regulators," Vixio, December 21, 2022; https://www.vixio.com/insights/gc-penn-entertainment-boss-defends-barstool-brand-massachusetts-regulators

Pg. 272, "Erika, let me ask you..." —Jim Cramer on Barstool and Penn National's $163M sports-betting partnership, CNBC Television; https://www.youtube.com/watch?v=cR5a904jsaU

Pg. 273, "It didn't take us four or five..." —Liana Baker, "How a Poker Dealer's Son Made His Big Barstool Bet," *Bloomberg*, October 22, 2021; https://www.bloomberg.com/news/newsletters/2021-10-22/how-a-poker-dealer-s-son-made-his-big-barstool-bet?embedded-checkout=true

Pg. 273, "We named our price..." —"Dave Portnoy on Barstool, Betting and Bitcoin," *Pomp Podcast* #392; https://www.youtube.com/watch?v=CoTtXaP4F-I

Pg. 274, "If I'm telling the whole story..." —"Bonus Episode: Dave Discusses Massive Investment from Penn National," *Barstool Radio* podcast; https://podcasts.apple.com/ie/podcast/bonus-episode-dave-discusses-massive-investment-from/id1085919903?i=1000464021432

CHAPTER 29

Pg. 275, "Dave was calling me..."; "I was not fighting..."; "I remember I was..."; "I don't remember it being..."; "We got past it..." —"Dave Portnoy Breaks Down the Chernin Group Deal that Changed Barstool History," *The Dave Portnoy Show*, Barstool Sports; https://www.youtube.com/watch?v=tMjt5jmpkek

Pg. 276, "Chernin bought Barstool…" —Dave Portnoy, "Why the Barstool & Penn Partnership Didn't Work out," https://www.youtube.com/watch?v=N_Dn17COzPY

Pg. 276, "Dave hasn't made…" —"Dave Portnoy Breaks Down the Chernin Group Deal that Changed Barstool History," *The Dave Portnoy Show*, Barstool Sports; https://www.youtube.com/watch?v=tMjt5jmpkek

Pg. 276, "I don't know that Chernin's…" —"Dave Portnoy on Barstool, Betting and Bitcoin," *Pomp Podcast* #392; https://www.youtube.com/watch?v=CoTtXaP4F-I

Pg. 277, "There were times…" —"Dave Portnoy Predicts the Future of Barstool Sports after the Full Penn Acquisition," KFC Radio; https://www.youtube.com/watch?v=lwUQtsmfsW0 and "Talking the history of Barstool with KFC," *The Dave Portnoy Show*; https://www.youtube.com/watch?v=d1yuzhNe9hg&t=2833s

Pg. 277, "[Clancy is] going to be…"; "I was doing this…"; "I would literally go…" —"Talking the history of Barstool with KFC," *The Dave Portnoy Show*, Barstool Sports; https://www.youtube.com/watch?v=d1yuzhNe9hg&t=2833s

Pg. 277, "I didn't have to be…" —"KFC Breaks Down Relationship with Dave Portnoy and Discusses Inside Barstool," KFC Radio; https://www.youtube.com/watch?v=b4EicGoLYd4

Pg. 277, "If I had the choice…" —"Talking the history of Barstool with KFC," *The Dave Portnoy Show*, Barstool Sports; https://www.youtube.com/watch?v=d1yuzhNe9hg&t=2833s

Pg. 278, "Emergency Press Conference…"; "Music! 17 years ago…" —"Emergency Press Conference —All Aboard the Barstool Sports Rocket Ship, Barstool Sports"; https://www.youtube.com/watch?v=Tvuux7fg5io

Pg. 279, "I've got unlimited money…" —"Bonus Episode: Dave Discusses Massive Investment from Penn National," *Barstool Radio* podcast; https://podcasts.apple.com/ie/podcast/bonus-episode-dave-discusses-massive-investment-from/id1085919903?i=1000464021432

CHAPTER 30

Pg. 280, "Ok, Emergency Press Conference…" —tweet from Dave Portnoy, June 29, 2020; https://twitter.com/stoolpresidente/status/1277660929908445191?lang=en

Pg. 280, "Rate this piece…" —tweet from Dave Portnoy, December 28, 2022; https://x.com/stoolpresidente/status/1608220742205771777?s=20

Pg. 280, "I'm in Miami house…" —tweet from Dave Portnoy, September 6 2023; https://x.com/stoolpresidente/status/1699464624125444290

Pg. 281, "I may need to throw…" —tweet from Dave Portnoy, January 17, 2023; https://x.com/stoolpresidente/status/1615472288710950912?s=20

Pg. 281, "Happy that my son…" —tweet from Mike Portnoy, July 7, 2021; https://x.com/TheCousinMike/status/1412818624734281728?s=20

Pg. 281, "It's surreal. I can't think…"; "It's really hard to fathom…"; "Dan and I talked about it…"; "Longtime stoolie here…"; "Hey Pres, congrats…"; "Hey, Dave, congrats…"; "Nobody should be worried about…" —"Bonus Episode: Dave Discusses Massive Investment from Penn National," *Barstool Radio* podcast; https://podcasts.apple.com/ie/podcast/bonus-episode-dave-discusses-massive-investment-from/id1085919903?i=1000464021432

Pg. 283, "I wonder if Penn…" —tweet from Pete Overmyer, January 29, 2020; https://x.com/allbusinesspete/status/1222504862941958145?s=20

Pg. 283, "Fuck you, Bryant…"; "This is my dad 101…"; "I knew you'd get that in there…" "We had a long talk about…" —"Bonus Episode: Dave Discusses Massive Investment from Penn National," *Barstool Radio* podcast; https://podcasts.apple.com/ie/podcast/bonus-episode-dave-discusses-massive-investment-from/id1085919903?i=1000464021432

Pg. 285, "'Cancel culture' seems to have…" —Christopher Brito, "'Cancel culture seems to have started as an internet joke. Now it's anything but," *CBS News*, April 5, 2021; https://www.cbsnews.com/news/cancel-culture-internet-joke-anything-but/

Pg. 285, "Americans tune into 'cancel culture'…" —Ryan Lizza, "Americans tune into 'Cancel Culture' —and they don't like what they see," *Politico*, July 22, 2020; https://www.politico.com/news/2020/07/22/americans-cancel-culture-377412#:~:text=A%20majority%20(55%25)%20of,a%20social%20media%20pile%2Don.

Pg. 285, "Why brands need to…" —Kian Bakhtiari, "Why Brands Need to Pay Attention to Cancel Culture," *Forbes*, September 29, 2020; https://www.forbes.com/sites/kianbakhtiari/2020/09/29/why-brands-need-to-pay-attention-to-cancel-culture/?sh=2103f454645e

Pg. 285, "So, I'm going to say something…" —tweet from @RzstProgramming, November 4, 2021; https://x.com/RzstProgramming/status/1456360877779791877?s=20

Pg. 285, "Anybody who disagrees with…" —tweet from @RzstProgramming, June 30, 2020; https://x.com/RzstProgramming/status/1277951253415411712?s=20

Pg. 286, "This is terrible. But then again…" —tweet from Jemele Hill, June 28, 2020; https://x.com/jemelehill/status/1277382360594440192?s=20

Pg. 286, "I'm uncancelable. You don't cancel me…" —Todd Spangler, "Barstool Sports Founder Unapologetic about Using Racist Language in 'Comedy' Videos: 'I'm Uncancelable,'" *Variety*, June 29, 2020; https://variety.com/2020/digital/news/barstool-sports-dave-portnoy-racist-language-videos-1234693013/

Pg. 286, "My FB friends…" —Darrelle Lincoln, "Jemele Hill Apologizes for 2009 Tweet that Called Ex-MLB Star Manny Ramirez a Tranny (TWEETS)," *Total Pro Sports*, June 29, 2020; https://www.totalprosports.com/mlb/jemele-hill-apologizes-for-2009-tweet-that-called-ex-mlb-star-manny-ramirez-a-tranny-tweets/

Pg. 286, "This you?" —tweet from @RzstProgramming, June 25, 2020; https://x.com/RzstProgramming/status/1276200920003592199?s=20

Pg. 286, "I'm not gonna…" —tweet from Dave Portnoy, June 29, 2020; https://twitter.com/stoolpresidente/status/1277660929908445191?lang=en

Pg. 288, "In hindsight, I wish…" —blog post, barstoolsports.com, December 12, 2018; https://www.barstoolsports.com/blog/1171000/in-hindsight-i-wish-i-didnt-dress-in-blackface-to-be-kevin-garnett-a-decade-ago-for-halloween-with-my-2-best-friends-who-are-african-american

Pg. 288, "Hey black people…" —tweet from @RzstProgramming, March 30, 2021; https://x.com/RzstProgramming/status/1376907832965140484?s=20

Pg. 288, "He stands by what…"; "We had a lot…"; "When [Dave] says I know…"; "If it looks like a duck…"; "Forgive me for thinking…"; "I had a long conversation with Dave…"; "I was there actually when Dave…" —"Now It's Gonna Get Extremely Real," *2Biggs* podcast; https://www.podchaser.com/podcasts/2biggs-1142674/episodes/barstool-nigger-now-its-gonna-66744063

CHAPTER 31

Pg. 291 "Barstool Sports Uses…" —Ben Cost, "Barstool Sports uses N-Word in 'Extremely Real' podcast title," *The New York Post*, July 2, 2020; https://nypost.com/2020/07/02/barstool-sports-debuts-podcast-episode-with-n-word-in-title/

Pg. 291, "It's Insanely Unfair…" —blog post, barstoolsports.com, July 2, 2020; https://www.barstoolsports.com/blog/2624745/its-insanely-unfair-that-weve-put-our-black-employees-in-this-situation

Pg. 292, "Ok, Emergency Press Conference…" —tweet from Dave Portnoy, July 2, 2020; https://x.com/stoolpresidente/status/1278785535255941120?s=20

Pg. 293, "I want Barstool to…"; "Going forward, I think…"; "It goes back to the point…" —"Now It's Gonna Get Extremely Real," *2Biggs* podcast; https://www.podchaser.com/podcasts/2biggs-1142674/episodes/barstool-nigger-now-its-gonna-66744063

Pg. 294, "Most of my writing…"; "I did get called…"; "I'm forever grateful…" —"Ask the Original BLK Blogger (feat. Mo) Ep. 5," *2Biggs* podcast; https://www.podchaser.com/podcasts/2biggs-1142674/episodes/recent

Pg. 295, "I am no longer affiliated"; "what has happened…" —tweet from Muj Fricke, July 3, 2020; https://x.com/mujfricke/status/1279176104452947968?s=20

Pg. 296, "Muj is irreplaceable…" tweet from Brandon Newman, July 3, 2020; https://x.com/brandonjnewman_/status/1279192017264926723?s=20

Pg. 296, "Finally, Brandon made me…" —tweet from Dave Portnoy, July 4, 2020; https://x.com/stoolpresidente/status/1279408018535350273?s=20

Pg. 296, "Aye!!! I made Dave…" —tweet from Brandon Newman, July 4, 2020; https://x.com/brandonjnewman_/status/1279411297889726466?s=20

Pg. 296, "The beauty of this…" —tweet from Dave Portnoy, July 4, 2020; https://x.com/stoolpresidente/status/1279423625058230272?s=20

Pg. 297, "If I quit…" —tweet from Brandon Newman, July 4, 2020; https://x.com/brandonjnewman_/status/1279425005034639360?s=20

Pg. 297, "You've been here…" —tweet from Dave Portnoy, July 4, 2020; https://x.com/stoolpresidente/status/1279430486218223616?s=20

Pg. 297, "We're trying to…" —"The Aftermath," *2Biggs* podcast; https://www.pod-chaser.com/podcasts/2biggs-1142674/episodes/the-aftermath-69077879

Pg. 298, "The reason we're hiring…" —tweet from @RzstProgramming, January 26, 2021; https://x.com/RzstProgramming/status/1354127012793876486?s=20

Pg. 298, "Barstool's racism is finally…" —Dennis Young, "Barstool Sports' Racism Finally Catching up with It," *NY Daily News*, July 6, 2020; https://www.nydailynews.com/2020/07/06/barstool-sports-racism-is-finally-catching-up-with-it/

Pg. 298, "It hasn't been a…" —tweet from Samer Kalaf, July 4, 2020; https://x.com/Samer/status/1279446427027025925?s=20

Pg. 299, "Dave's about his…" —"Ask the Original BLK Blogger (feat. Mo) Ep. 5," *2Biggs* podcast; https://www.podchaser.com/podcasts/2biggs-1142674/episodes/recent

Pg. 299, "They've been at it…" —Chris Murph, "Penn's Jay Snowden kicks off SBC Digital Summit North America in style," *SBC Americas*, July 14, 2020; https://sbcamericas.com/2020/07/14/penns-jay-snowden-kicks-off-sbc-digital-summit-north-america-in-style/

CHAPTER 32

Pg. 301, "You have the most…" —"Tucker Carlson Interviews Barstool Sports Owner Dave Portnoy," *TheDC Shorts*; https://www.youtube.com/watch?v=EuexB9UWCds&t=126s

Pg. 302, "I know we used to…" —"KFC on Dave Portnoy's Interview with Donald Trump," KFC Radio; https://www.youtube.com/watch?v=nKf2FbWnd6I

Pg. 302, "I don't really talk…"; "When I go on Fox News…" —"Dave Portnoy Talks His Future with Barstool, Why People Hate Him & How He Got on Joe Rogan's Podcast, Bussin' with the Boys"; https://www.youtube.com/watch?v=vT6Z6heWCO8

Pg. 302, "95% of people…" —tweet from Dave Portnoy, January 6, 2021; https://x.com/stoolpresidente/status/1346920519111610369?s=20

Pg. 302, "White nationalist post-racialism…" —"Researchers explore the racial and gender politics of Barstool Sports," *University of Rhode Island*, November 22, 2022; https://web.uri.edu/artsci/news/researchers-explore-the-racial-and-gender-politics-of-barstool-sports/

Pg. 303, "I don't care if…" —Shawn McCreesh, "Trump White House Meets Its Match with Barstool Sports," *The New York Times*, July 31, 2020; https://www.nytimes.com/2020/07/31/style/trump-twitter-barstool-sports.html

Pg. 303, "Your son is a big…"; "He's a big fan of you…" —"Dave Portnoy Interviews President Trump"; https://www.youtube.com/watch?v=Hois8NpBiw0

Pg. 306, "I did not expect…" —tweet from Dave Portnoy, July 24, 2020; https://x.com/stoolpresidente/status/1286726116594647049?s=20

Pg. 306, "If the sitting president…" —"Dave Portnoy Talks His Future with Barstool, Why People Hate Him & How He Got on Joe Rogan's Podcast, Bussin' with the Boys"; https://www.youtube.com/watch?v=vT6Z6heWCO8

Pg. 306, "This fucking sucks because…" —tweet from Barstool Radio, July 24, 2020; https://x.com/BarstoolRadio/status/1286700009589739521?s=20

Pg. 308, "He [Katz] was upset…"; "I feel differently about…" —"Dave Portnoy Talks His Future with Barstool, Why People Hate Him & How He Got on Joe Rogan's Podcast, Bussin' with the Boys"; https://www.youtube.com/watch?v=vT6Z6heWCO8

Pg. 309, "I feel like we have…" —"KFC on Dave Portnoy's Interview with Donald Trump," KFC Radio; https://www.youtube.com/watch?v=nKf2FbWnd6I

Pg. 310, "Entertainment is Gillie's…" —"Entertainment is Gillie's Top Priority, Million Dollaz Worth of Game"; https://www.youtube.com/watch?v=cKd5zIQ18JY

Pg. 310, "This will be my last…" —tweet from @Barstool_Quotes, October 1, 2020; https://x.com/Barstool_Quotes/status/1311645732634595331?s=20

Pg. 310, "Everything that happened on…" —Scott Logush, "Brandon Newman Explains Why He Left Barstool," *Vendetta Sports Media*, October 1, 2020; https://vendettasportsmedia.com/brandon-newman-explains-leaving-barstool/

CHAPTER 33

Pg. 311, "It's unfortunate that the powers…" —Mara Siegler, "Dave Portnoy slams Nantucket mag as 'spineless' after cover story flap," *Page Six*, May 4, 2021; https://pagesix.com/2021/05/04/dave-portnoy-calls-n-magazine-spineless-over-cover-story-flap/

Pg. 311, "You know what's crazy…" —"Bonus Episode: Dave Discusses Massive Investment from Penn National," *Barstool Radio* podcast; https://podcasts.apple.com/ie/podcast/bonus-episode-dave-discusses-massive-investment-from/id1085919903?i=1000464021432

Pg. 312, "Barstool blew up over…" —www.barstoolsports.com, January 16, 2024; https://www.barstoolsports.com/blog/3500230/i-am-stepping-down-as-ceo-of-barstool-sports

Pg. 313, "I think I just sliced…"; "Am I gonna cry…" —"Dave Portnoy Gives Himself Brutal Unboxing Injury"; https://www.youtube.com/watch?v=7uGq8UQh0TE

Pg. 313, "I don't like the way this whole…" —tweet from Dave Portnoy, July 19, 2021; https://x.com/stoolpresidente/status/1417207993989570566?s=20

Pg. 313, "That's the Suits' entire…" —tweet from Dave Portnoy, September 9, 2020; https://x.com/stoolpresidente/status/1303664124317126656?s=20

Pg. 313, "The blue check marks…" —tweet from Dave Portnoy, May 26, 2020; https://twitter.com/stoolpresidente/status/1265291221922177024

Pg. 314, "The only time CNBC…" —tweet from Dave Portnoy, January 27, 2021; https://x.com/stoolpresidente/status/1354492810733486080?s=20

Pg. 314, "This guy is one of…" —"Dave Portnoy is 100% on point about Sam Bankman-Fried #FTX. SBF just shut up," beNiceMedia; https://www.youtube.com/watch?v=dK5oNsTzZbU

Pg. 315, "I'm proud of the way…" —"Barstool Sports' Dave Portnoy Grills Robinhood CEO Vlad Tenev on GameStop saga," CNBC Television; https://www. youtube.com/watch?v=muio0sMXT4Q

Pg. 315, "I lost one million…" —tweet from Dave Portnoy, September 3, 2020; https://x.com/stoolpresidente/status/1301614191573381125?s=20

Pg. 316, "If you guys…" —Kirsten Fleming, "Barstool Sports' Dave Portnoy speaks out on 'Call Her Daddy' podcast drama," *The New York Post*, May 18, 2020; https://nypost.com/2020/05/18/ barstool-sports-dave-portnoy-talks-call-her-daddy-podcast-drama/

Pg. 317, "I never spoke to her…" —Emily Selleck, "Alex Cooper: 'Toxic' Sofia Franklyn friendship was 'so bad behind the scenes,'" *Page Six*, November 8, 2023; https://pagesix.com/2023/11/08/celebrity-news/ alex-cooper-sofia-franklyn-friendship-was-so-bad-behind-the-scenes/

Pg. 317, "Sofia said no…" —Meg Rotter, "An Official Timeline of All the 'Call Her Daddy' Drama," *Cosmopolitan*, May 21, 2020; https://www.cosmopolitan.com/ lifestyle/a32628219/call-her-daddy-podcast-drama-timeline-explainer/

Pg. 317, "It's almost like Suitman…" —tweet from Dave Portnoy, May 24, 2020; https://x.com/stoolpresidente/status/1264646321170010112?s=20

Pg. 318, "The Bar and Restaurant…" —tweet from Dave Portnoy, December 11, 2020; https://x.com/stoolpresidente/status/1337453710822285316?s=20

Pg. 319, "Hey @stoolpresidente put your…" —tweet from Marcus Lemonis, December 11, 2020; https://x.com/marcuslemonis/ status/1337604798200258566?s=20

Pg. 319, "Introducing the Barstool Fund…Borelli's is the perfect example…" — tweet from Dave Portnoy, December 17, 2020; https://x.com/stoolpresidente/ status/1339674567447556098?s=20

Pg. 320, "Dave Portnoy Launches…" —Jayson Derrick, "Dave Portnoy Launches Barstool Fund to Raise Money for Small Businesses Hurt by Pandemic Shutdown," *Yahoo Finance*, December 18, 2020; https://finance.yahoo.com/news/dave-portnoy-launches-barstool-fund-170148619.html

Pg. 320, "Chicago Restaurant Owner…" —Vi Nguyen, "Chicago Restaurant Owner Gets Helping Hand from Dave Portnoy of Barstool Sports," *NBC Chicago*, December 26, 2020; https://www.nbcchicago.com/news/local/ chicago-restaurant-owner-gets-helping-hand-from-dave-portnoy-of-bar-stool-sports/2402708/#:~:text=Patricia%20Prosen%20is%20a%20single,fund%20 spearheaded%20by%20Barstool%20Sports.

Pg. 320, "Barstool Fund help…" —Angelica Stabile, "Barstool Fund help 'a miracle,' New York restaurant owner says," *Fox Business*, January 3, 2021; https://www.fox-business.com/economy/yonkers-restaurant-barstool-fund-coronavirus-miracle

CHAPTER 34

Pg. 322, "Barstool's Dave Portnoy…"; "A stock is down…" —Noah Manskar, "Barstools Dave Portnoy Shrugs at sex tape as Penn stock slides," *The New York Post*, April 7, 2021; https://nypost.com/2021/04/07/barstools-dave-portnoy-shrugs-at-sex-tape-as-penn-stock-dips/

Pg. 323, "I tell ya, working…" —"Dave Portnoy Leaked Video Shocks Barstool Employees, Stool Scenes 239," Barstool Sports; https://www.youtube.com/watch?v=NMEkC2GzUtU

Pg. 323, "Breaking: Dave Portnoy fucks…" —tweet from Dave Portnoy, December 13, 2019; https://x.com/stoolpresidente/status/1205470582973882368?s=20

Pg. 323, "Hard hitting research…"; "Hi [redacted] Thanks…" —tweet from Dave Portnoy, April 20, 2021; https://x.com/stoolpresidente/status/1384595853910884352?s=20

Pg. 323, "Everybody who likes me didn't comment…" —Collin Lunsford, "Dave Portnoy Calls Upcoming Business Insider Story 'Hit Piece,'" *Barrett Sports Media*, August 23, 2021; https://barrettsportsmedia.com/2021/08/23/business-insider-hit-piece/#google_vignette

Pg. 324, "Elio: Just did a…." —tweet from Dave Portnoy, April 20, 2021; https://x.com/stoolpresidente/status/1384597216933863424?s=20

Pg. 324, "That article's coming…" —Collin Lunsford, "Dave Portnoy Calls Upcoming Business Insider Story 'Hit Piece,'" *Barrett Sports Media*, August 23, 2021; https://barrettsportsmedia.com/2021/08/23/business-insider-hit-piece/#google_vignette

CHAPTER 35

Pg. 325, "I was literally screaming…"; "*Insider* spoke with…"; "After dinner…"; "He leaned in…" —Julia Black, "'I was literally screaming in pain': Young women say they met Barstool Founder Dave Portnoy for sex and it turned violent and humiliating," *Business Insider*, November 4, 2021; https://www.businessinsider.com/barstool-sports-dave-portnoy-sex-choking-violent-stoolies

Pg. 328, "Ok, so *Business Insider*…" —"My Response to the Business Insider Piece that Was 8 Months in the Making"; https://www.facebook.com/watch/?v=210782141133036

Pg. 329, "I don't want to identify…" —"Dave Portnoy Exposes Business Insider Hit Piece"; https://www.youtube.com/watch?v=UW85j-7MAow&t=694s

Pg. 330, "I got to the point…" —"Dave Portnoy Addresses Hit Piece," *The Dave Portnoy Show*, Barstool Sports; https://www.youtube.com/watch?v=tNWn-UW0lKA&t=1085s

Pg. 330, "2 P.M. EST. I WILL…" —tweet from Dave Portnoy, November 11, 2021; https://x.com/stoolpresidente/status/1458766072925020171

Pg. 330, "#portnoy2pm Also this…" —tweet from Dave Portnoy, November 11, 2021; https://x.com/stoolpresidente/status/1458858288615985152?s=20

Pg. 330, "Can we turn one of…"; "I've said this from…"; "I did not film without advanced permission…"; "A bald-faced lie…"; "If this is a baseball…" —"Dave Portnoy Exposes Business Insider Hit Piece," Barstool Sports; https://www.youtube.com/watch?v=UW85j-7MAow&t=694s

Pg. 334, "The reason the establishment…" —tweet from Dave Portnoy, January 29, 2024; https://x.com/stoolpresidente/status/1751978564201660600?s=20

Pg. 334, "I heard the GameStop…"; "There was a wild shorting…" —"Dave Portnoy Addresses Hit Piece," *The Dave Portnoy Show*, Barstool Sports; https://www.youtube.com/watch?v=tNWn-UW0lKA&t=1085s

Pg. 335, "@stoolpresidente —it seems someone…" —tweet from @Unusual_Whales, November 4, 2021; https://x.com/unusual_whales/status/1456308572594196480?s=20

Pg. 335, "@stoolpresidente someone knew about…" —tweet from @MadakatCapital, November 4, 2021; https://x.com/CapitalMadaket/status/1456379801258840074?s=20

CHAPTER 36

Pg. 336, "The only thing that can…" —"Dave Portnoy Addresses Hit Piece," *The Dave Portnoy Show*, Barstool Sports; https://www.youtube.com/watch?v=tNWn-UW0lKA&t=1085s

Pg. 336, "That was the only time I've been *down*…" —"Dave Portnoy Talks His Future with Barstool, Why People Hate Him & How He Got on Joe Rogan's Podcast, Bussin' with the Boys"; https://www.youtube.com/watch?v=vT6Z6heWCO8

Pg. 336, "If you have any additional…" —tweet from Julia Black, November 4, 2021; https://x.com/mjnblack/status/1456282941949202435?s=20

Pg. 336, "I'm walking around…" —"Barstool Gaming Employees Get in Screaming Match," *The Dave Portnoy Show*, Barstool Sports; https://www.youtube.com/watch?v=4pW1xG0KZwY&t=1399s

Pg. 337, "Go through my DMs…"; "After I made that…" —"Dave Portnoy Addresses Hit Piece," *The Dave Portnoy Show*, Barstool Sports; https://www.youtube.com/watch?v=tNWn-UW0lKA&t=1085s

Pg. 337, "Being out in Miami with him…" —"Dave Portnoy Recaps Emergency Press Conference," *The Dave Portnoy Show*, Barstool Sports; https://www.youtube.com/watch?v=6EqlDBCw9oo

Pg. 337, "I'm being heavily pursued…" —"Dave Portnoy Recaps Emergency Press Conference," *The Dave Portnoy Show*, Barstool Sports; https://www.youtube.com/watch?v=6EqlDBCw9oo

Pg. 337, "[But] if you're gonna say it's…" —"Dave Portnoy Addresses Hit Piece," *The Dave Portnoy Show*, Barstool Sports; https://www.youtube.com/watch?v=tNWn-UW0lKA&t=1085s

Pg. 337, "Also, I would call bullshit…and I love our audience, but…." —"Dave Portnoy Addresses Hit Piece," *The Dave Portnoy Show*, Barstool Sports; https://www.youtube.com/watch?v=tNWn-UW0lKA&t=1085s

Pg. 338, "I don't realize —this is gonna sound…" —"Dave Portnoy Addresses Hit Piece," *The Dave Portnoy Show*, Barstool Sports; https://www.youtube.com/watch?v=tNWn-UW0lKA&t=1085s

Pg. 338, "Am I going to be far…" —"Dave Portnoy Recaps Emergency Press Conference," *The Dave Portnoy Show*, Barstool Sports; https://www.youtube.com/watch?v=6EqlDBCw9oo

Pg. 338, "What you're seeing in this…"; "the thing that's most important…" —Erika Nardini, "Barstool CEO Responds to Business Insider Hit Piece"; https://www.youtube.com/watch?v=9qV5-Bjs7Y0

Pg. 339, "Barstool Sports employees…" —tweet from Zachary Petrizzo, November 4, 2021; https://x.com/ZTPetrizzo/status/1456341431409315848?s=20

Pg. 340, "I'm not going to get…" —"Dave Portnoy Gives His Side of the Story after *Business Insider* Hit Piece," *Stool Scenes*, Barstool Sports; https://www.youtube.com/watch?v=vCN13WRtWbg

Pg. 340, "I can speak from going…" —"Kevin Clancy on the Dave Portnoy *Business Insider* Article," *The Kevin Clancy Show*, Barstool Sports; https://www.youtube.com/watch?v=cIEhK05P9No

Pg. 341, "If you read the *BI*…." —tweet from Dan Katz, November 4, 2021; https://x.com/BarstoolBigCat/status/1456352652871229444?s=20

Pg. 341, "People who love Barstool…" —tweet from Mike Portnoy, August 4, 2021; https://x.com/TheCousinMike/status/1428744576056139786?s=20

Pg. 341, "I may have this [tough]…" —"Dave Portnoy Recaps Emergency Press Conference," *The Dave Portnoy Show*, Barstool Sports; https://www.youtube.com/watch?v=6EqlDBCw9oo

Pg. 342, "Imagine not buying…" —tweet from Dave Portnoy, November 5, 2021; https://x.com/stoolpresidente/status/1456612143181275138?s=20

Pg. 342, "The question is…"; "I'm being treated…" —"On Fox News, Tucker Carlson and Dave Portnoy launch attacks on *Business Insider* reporter," *Media Matters*, November 8, 2021; https://www.mediamatters.org/tucker-carlson/fox-news-tucker-carlson-and-dave-portnoy-launch-attacks-business-insider-reporter

Pg. 343, "So, I saw that piece…" —Candice Ortiz, "Dave Portnoy Crashes Talk to Berate Business Insider CEO," *Mediaite*, May 13, 2022; https://www.mediaite.com/entertainment/dave-portnoy-crashes-talk-to-berate-business-insider-ceo-you-fcking-piece-of-sht-coward/

Pg. 343, "I feel like I've won…" —"Dave Portnoy Addresses Hit Piece," *The Dave Portnoy Show*, Barstool Sports; https://www.youtube.com/watch?v=t-NWn-UW0lKA&t=1085s and "Dave Portnoy Recaps Emergency Press

Conference," *The Dave Portnoy Show*, Barstool Sports, https://www.youtube.com/watch?v=6EqlDBCw9oo

Pg. 343, "She arrived at Portnoy's…" —Julia Black, "'I was literally screaming in pain': Young women say they met Barstool Founder Dave Portnoy for sex and it turned violent and humiliating," *Business Insider*, November 4, 2021; https://www.businessinsider.com/barstool-sports-dave-portnoy-sex-choking-violent-stoolies

Pg. 344, "The bigger issue is…" —www.barstoolsports.com, November 1, 2011; https://web.archive.org/web/20111102062711/http://www.barstoolsports.com/boston/super-page/does-this-look-like-the-face-of-a-24-year-old-chick-who-sued-her-74-year-old-billionare-boss-for-sticking-his-tongue-down-her-throat/

Pg. 344, "Take a 2017 episode…" —Julia Black, "'I was literally screaming in pain': Young women say they met Barstool Founder Dave Portnoy for sex and it turned violent and humiliating," *Business Insider*, November 4, 2021; https://www.businessinsider.com/barstool-sports-dave-portnoy-sex-choking-violent-stoolies

Pg. 344, "It's such a preposterous…" —"Barstool Gaming Employees Get in Screaming Match," *The Dave Portnoy Show*, Barstool Sports; https://www.youtube.com/watch?v=4pW1xG0KZwY&t=1399s

Pg. 345, "So if you're interested in…" —*Random Thoughts*, barstoolsports.com, April 7, 2008; https://web.archive.org/web/20080413072410/http://www.barstoolsports.com/randomthoughts/2008/04/07/

Pg. 345, "Blah, blah, blah. Listen, I know a thing…" —*Random Thoughts*, barstoolsports.com, January 29, 2009; https://web.archive.org/web/20090201070618/http://barstoolsports.com/randomthoughts/2009/01/29/

Pg. 346, "If another hit piece…"; "Do you think in a world…" —"Dave Portnoy Recaps Emergency Press Conference," *The Dave Portnoy Show*, Barstool Sports; https://www.youtube.com/watch?v=6EqlDBCw9oo

CHAPTER 37

Pg. 347, "The day after Portnoy's…" —Reeves Wiedeman, "The Dave Portnoy Playbook: Staring down the sports-gambling gold rush—and amid sexual misconduct allegations—Barstool's founder bets on the culture war," *New York Magazine*, November 23, 2021; https://nymag.com/intelligencer/article/dave-portnoy-barstool-sports.html

Pg. 348, "We wanted to reach out…" —Emily Steel, "Desperate for Growth, Aging Casino Company Embraced 'Degenerate Gambler,'" *The New York Times*, November 20, 2022; https://www.nytimes.com/2022/11/20/business/barstool-sports-betting-david-portnoy.html

Pg. 348, "Barstool has delivered on…" —Olafimihan Oshin, "Gambling regulators looking into allegations against Barstool Sports founder," *The Hill*, March 17, 2022; https://thehill.com/regulation/business/598621-gambling-regulators-looking-into-allegations-against-barstool-sports/

Pg. 348, "I'm hearing rumors…" —"Dave Portnoy Recaps Emergency Press Conference," *The Dave Portnoy Show*, Barstool Sports; https://www.youtube.com/watch?v=6EqlDBCw9oo

Pg. 348, "Julia Black and *Business*…" —tweet from Dave Portnoy, January 20, 2022; https://x.com/stoolpresidente/status/1484194008444375042?s=20

Pg. 348, "We had a mole…" —Candice Ortiz, "Dave Portnoy Reveals Barstool Sports Had "Mole at Business Insider," *Mediaite*, April 1, 2022; https://www.mediaite.com/podcasts/dave-portnoy-reveals-barstool-sports-had-mole-at-business-insider-they-were-going-to-publish-so-much-trash/

Pg. 349, "She fucking has…" —tweet from Dave Portnoy, January 20, 2022; https://x.com/stoolpresidente/status/1484194008444375042?s=20

Pg. 350, "3 more women…" —Julia Black and Melkorka Licea, "3 more women say Barstool Sports founder Dave Portnoy filmed them without asking during sex," *Business Insider*, February 2, 2022; https://www.businessinsider.com/dave-portnoy-new-women-sexual-misconduct-allegations-filming-sex-without-permission

Pg. 351, "I remember her joking about…"; "I've never filmed anyone…"; "one of the main themes…" —blog post, barstoolsports.com, February 2, 2022; https://www.barstoolsports.com/blog/3402665/i-am-officially-suing-julia-black-and-business-insider

Pg. 352, "A total of four women…" —Julia Black and Melkorka Licea, "3 more women say Barstool Sports founder Dave Portnoy filmed them without asking during sex," *Business Insider*, February 2, 2022; https://www.businessinsider.com/dave-portnoy-new-women-sexual-misconduct-allegations-filming-sex-without-permission

Pg. 353, "I would never just…" —blog post, barstoolsports.com, February 2, 2022; https://www.barstoolsports.com/blog/3402665/i-am-officially-suing-julia-black-and-business-insider

Pg. 353, "Brettler, [Portnoy's lawyer] wrote…" —Julia Black and Melkorka Licea, "3 more women say Barstool Sports founder Dave Portnoy filmed them without asking during sex," *Business Insider*, February 2, 2022; https://www.businessinsider.com/dave-portnoy-new-women-sexual-misconduct-allegations-filming-sex-without-permission

Pg. 353, "We published our stories…" —Nicholas Carlson, "Editor's note on Insider's Dave Portnoy articles," *Business Insider*, February 2, 2022; https://www.businessinsider.com/why-insider-published-its-dave-portnoy-articles-2022-2

Pg. 354, "The allegations are…"; "From the same paywall," —Thomas Barrabi, "Penn National CEO gripes that new Dave Portnoy allegations came out right before earnings," *The New York Post*, February 3, 2022; https://nypost.com/2022/02/03/penn-nationals-jay-snowden-gripes-that-dave-portnoy-allegations-came-out-before-earnings/

Pg. 355, "Of course, we did not…" —Thomas Barrabi, "Penn National CEO gripes that new Dave Portnoy allegations came out right before earnings," *The New*

York Post, February 3, 2022; https://nypost.com/2022/02/03/penn-nationals-jay-snowden-gripes-that-dave-portnoy-allegations-came-out-before-earnings/

Pg. 355, "Significant and irreparable…" —Luis Fieldman, "Barstool Sports founder Dave Portnoy's defamation suit against *Insider* dismissed by federal judge," *Masslive.com*, November 7, 2022; https://www.masslive.com/news/2022/11/bar-stool-sports-founder-dave-portnoys-defamation-suit-against-insider-dismissed-by-federal-judge.html#:~:text=Portnoy%20claimed%20that%20the%20Insider,was%20published%20in%20November%202021.

Pg. 355, "Clear [the] high bar…" —Marisa Sarnoff, "Federal Judge Dismisses Barstool Sports Founder Dave Portnoy's Defamation Lawsuit over Reports of Sexual Misconduct, Violence," *Law & Crime*, November 7, 2022; https://lawandcrime.com/high-profile/federal-judge-dismisses-barstool-sports-found-er-dave-portnoys-defamation-lawsuit-over-reports-of-sexual-misconduct-violence/

CHAPTER 38

Pg. 356, "I've made some money…" —"The Future of Barstool Sports with Big Cat," *The Dave Portnoy Show*, Barstool Sports; https://www.youtube.com/watch?v=vypABGJ-mVc

Pg. 357, "Yes, I think I would have…" —"Live with Dave Portnoy," *The Kirk Minihane Show*; https://www.youtube.com/watch?v=NJqooSc8Q3Q

Pg. 357, "They [Chicago] are the…" —"Big Cat Gives Us Advice and Speaks on the Unnecessary New York and Chicago Rivalry," Barstool Sports; https://www.youtube.com/watch?v=RN8-CQEvA5U

Pg. 357, "The [NY] office is just…" —"Talking the History of Barstool with KFC," *The Dave Portnoy Show*, Barstool Sports; https://www.youtube.com/watch?v=d1yuzhNe9hg

Pg. 357, "I think there is a…" —"Big Cat Gives Us Advice and Speaks on the Unnecessary New York and Chicago Rivalry," Barstool Sports; https://www.you-tube.com/watch?v=RN8-CQEvA5U

Pg. 358, "I remember when…"; "Barstool is my life…" —"Big Cat Gives Us Advice and Speaks on the Unnecessary New York and Chicago Rivalry," Barstool Sports; https://www.youtube.com/watch?v=RN8-CQEvA5U

Pg. 358, "It's Dave we're missing…" —"Big Cat Gives Us Advice and Speaks on the Unnecessary New York and Chicago Rivalry," Barstool Sports; https://www.youtube.com/watch?v=RN8-CQEvA5U

Pg. 358, "A famous person can't…" —Bobby Burack, "Dave Portnoy Challenges Business Insider's Role in Rough Sex Allegations," *Outkick*, November 13, 2021; https://www.outkick.com/media-analysis/dave-portnoy-challenges-business-insiders-role-in-rough-sex-allegations

Pg. 358, "The reason *Business Insider*…" —blog post, barstool-sports.com, February 2, 2022; https://www.barstoolsports.com/blog/3402665/i-am-officially-suing-julia-black-and-business-insider

Pg. 359, "The guy who tried to…" —Dave Portnoy, "Emergency Press Conference —Henry Blodget Got Fired"; https://www.youtube.com/watch?v=zEoqFZgheU4

Pg. 359, "Wayne Gretzky came up…" —"Never forget Wayne Gretzky the GOAT came up to Dave Portnoy and asked him for a picture," *Spittin' Chiclets*; https://www.youtube.com/watch?v=BRw1SmtSc_o

Pg. 360, "As I've been working remote…" —"Dave is Moving to Miami, Episode #25," *The Dave Portnoy Show*, Barstool Sports; https://www.youtube.com/watch?v=a50d9TpeeuE

Pg. 360, "With Dave, it was never…" —"Talking the history of Barstool with KFC," *The Dave Portnoy Show*, Barstool Sports; https://www.youtube.com/watch?v=d1yuzhNe9hg&t=2833s

Pg. 360, "It is what it is…" —"Talking the history of Barstool with KFC," *The Dave Portnoy Show*, Barstool Sports; https://www.youtube.com/watch?v=d1yuzhNe9hg&t=2833s

Pg. 361, "We are extremely pleased…" —"Penn Entertainment Completes Acquisition of Barstool Sports," *Penn Entertainment*, February 17, 2023 ; https://investors.pennentertainment.com/news-releases/news-release-details/penn-entertainment-completes-acquisition-barstool-sports

Pg. 361, "Barstool and Mr. Portnoy…" —Emily Steel, "Desperate for Growth, Aging Casino Company Embraced 'Degenerate Gambler,'" *The New York Times*, November 20, 2022; https://www.nytimes.com/2022/11/20/business/barstool-sports-betting-david-portnoy.html

CHAPTER 39

Pg. 362, "In a statement, the board…," —Katherine Sayre, "Dave Portnoy Accusations Prompt Scrutiny of Barstool as Penn National Pursues Acquisition," *The Wall Street Journal*, March 17, 2022; https://www.wsj.com/articles/dave-portnoy-accusations-prompt-scrutiny-of-barstool-as-penn-national-pursues-acquisition-11647511200#:~:text=In%0a%20statement%2C%20the%20board,he%20was%20concerned%20about%20Barstool.

Pg. 362, "Very serious, requiring prompt…"; "A creep who has…" —Emily Steel, "Desperate for Growth, Aging Casino Company Embraced 'Degenerate Gambler,'" *The New York Times*, November 20, 2022; https://www.nytimes.com/2022/11/20/business/barstool-sports-betting-david-portnoy.html

Pg. 363, "I'm concerned about some of…" —Esteban Bustillos, "Mass. Gaming Commission red flags over Barstool Sports' ties to sports betting applicant," *GBH*, December 2022; https://www.wgbh.org/news/local/2022-12-06/mass-gaming-commission-raises-red-flags-over-barstool-sports-ties-to-sports-betting-applicant

Pg. 364, "For a year, I'm waiting…" —"Dave Portnoy Talks His Future with Barstool, Why People Hate Him & How He Got on Joe Rogan's Podcast, Bussin' with the Boys"; https://www.youtube.com/watch?v=vT6Z6heWCO8

Pg. 364, "Portnoy is normalizing…" —Emily Steel, "Desperate for Growth, Aging Casino Company Embraced 'Degenerate Gambler,'" *The New York Times*,

November 20, 2022; https://www.nytimes.com/2022/11/20/business/bar-stool-sports-betting-david-portnoy.html

Pg. 365, "I'm worried about the…"; "You can't say 'free…'"; "There's no buf-falo…" —tweet thread from Bill Speros, June 7, 2023; https://x.com/billsperos/status/1666495602861957123?s=20

Pg. 365, "This is a fascinating…" —tweet from Dave Portnoy, June 7, 2023; https://x.com/stoolpresidente/status/1666497659983519762?s=20

Pg. 367, "Bad news: this sucks…" —tweet from Dave Portnoy, May 3, 2023; https://x.com/stoolpresidente/status/1653876074529292289?s=20

Pg. 368, "By the way, for everybody…" —tweet from Dave Portnoy, May 3, 2023; https://x.com/stoolpresidente/status/1653894936977108992?s=20

Pg. 368, "So, I got every…" —tweet from Dave Portnoy, May 3, 2023; https://x.com/stoolpresidente/status/1653901096169996289?s=20

Pg. 369, "Everything I've stood…" —Jenna Lemoncelli, "Dave Portnoy worries firing Ben Mintz will be 'death blow' for Barstool Sports," *The New York Post*, May 4, 2023; https://nypost.com/2023/05/04/dave-portnoy-worries-firing-ben-mintz-will-be-death-blow-for-barstool/

Pg. 369, "Penn got denied licenses because…" —Kristen Fleming, "Traitors beware, says Barstool's Dave Portnoy: I've got my voice back, I'm naming names," *The New York Post*, May 4, 2023; https://nypost.com/2023/08/19/barstools-dave-portnoy-ive-got-my-voice-back-im-naming-names/

Pg. 369, "Anybody who has followed…" —Jessica Welman, "Dave Portnoy blames gambling regulators for firing of Barstool Sports personality," *SBC Americas*, May 4, 2023,; https://sbcamericas.com/2023/05/04/penn-barstool-portnoy-regulators/

Pg. 369, "It was painful on a human…" —Kristen Fleming, "Traitors beware, says Barstool's Dave Portnoy: I've got my voice back, I'm naming names," *The New York Post*, May 4, 2023; https://nypost.com/2023/08/19/barstools-dave-portnoy-ive-got-my-voice-back-im-naming-names/

CHAPTER 40

Pg. 370, "It became clear we…" —Jessica Welman, "Penn believes ESPN will get them to 20% sportsbook market share," *SBC Americas*, August 9, 2023; https://sbcamericas.com/2023/08/09/penn-snowden-espn-bet-launch-november/

Pg. 370, "Barstool is not a company…" —Julie Coleman, "After divesting Barstool Sports, Penn Entertainment CEO says Dave Portnoy is the only 'natural owner' for the company long term," CNBC, August 9, 2023; https://www.cnbc.com/2023/08/09/penn-entertainment-ceo-says-portnoy-is-barstools-only-natural-owner-.html

Pg. 370, "There's probably long-term…" —Jessica Welman, "Penn believes ESPN will get them to 20% sportsbook market share," *SBC Americas*, August 9, 2023; https://sbcamericas.com/2023/08/09/penn-snowden-espn-bet-launch-november/

Pg. 370, "It all happened very…" —"Inside Dave Portnoy Buying Back Barstool Sports," *Stool Scenes*, Barstool Sports; https://www.youtube.com/watch?v=UC94xsIMf1E

Pg. 370, "I was shocked…" —Kristen Fleming, "Traitors beware, says Barstool's Dave Portnoy: I've got my voice back, I'm naming names," *The New York Post*, May 4, 2023; https://nypost.com/2023/08/19/barstools-dave-portnoy-ive-got-my-voice-back-im-naming-names/

Pg. 371, "I care about…" —Kristen Fleming, "Traitors beware, says Barstool's Dave Portnoy: I've got my voice back, I'm naming names," *The New York Post*, May 4, 2023; https://nypost.com/2023/08/19/barstools-dave-portnoy-ive-got-my-voice-back-im-naming-names/

Pg. 371, "When I owned it…" —Kristen Fleming, "Traitors beware, says Barstool's Dave Portnoy: I've got my voice back, I'm naming names," *The New York Post*, May 4, 2023; https://nypost.com/2023/08/19/barstools-dave-portnoy-ive-got-my-voice-back-im-naming-names/

Pg. 371, "Holy shit, I'm floating…" —"Inside Dave Portnoy Buying Back Barstool Sports," *Stool Scenes*, Barstool Sports; https://www.youtube.com/watch?v=UC94xsIMf1E

Pg. 371, "Ok, announcement time…" —"Inside Dave Portnoy Buying Back Barstool Sports," *Stool Scenes*, Barstool Sports; https://www.youtube.com/watch?v=UC94xsIMf1E

Pg. 372, "Just when I think I'm out…" —tweet from Dave Portnoy, August 8, 2023; https://x.com/stoolpresidente/status/1689010643729321985?s=20

Pg. 372, "We helped set this…"; "No, definitely not…"; I'd still take the money…"; "You couldn't restart Barstool now…"; "I don't think…."; "When we started…"; "Do you think…"; "I don't…"; "If you could snap…"; "If all the…."; "I'd still take the money…" —"Talking the history of Barstool with KFC," *The Dave Portnoy Show*, Barstool Sports; https://www.youtube.com/watch?v=d1yuzhNe9hg&t=2833s

Pg. 374, "Penn had an opportunity…" —"Inside Dave Portnoy Buying Back Barstool Sports," *Stool Scenes*, Barstool Sports; https://www.youtube.com/watch?v=UC94xsIMf1E

Pg. 374, "I've got my voice…" —Kristen Fleming, "Traitors beware, says Barstool's Dave Portnoy: I've got my voice back, I'm naming names," *The New York Post*, May 4, 2023; https://nypost.com/2023/08/19/barstools-dave-portnoy-ive-got-my-voice-back-im-naming-names/

Pg. 374, "I'm not going anywhere…" —tweet from Dave Portnoy, August 8, 2023; https://x.com/stoolpresidente/status/1689010643729321985?s=20

ABOUT THE AUTHOR

Charlie Stanton currently resides in New York City. Stanton graduated from Wake Forest University with honors in economics in 2012. In his free time, the author enjoys playing padel, pickleball, paddle, tennis, running, skiing, and hanging out with his three younger brothers.